TOURISM

The Business of Travel

ROY A. COOK
Fort Lewis College

LAURA J. YALE
Fort Lewis College

JOSEPH J. MARQUA
Fort Lewis College

Prentice Hall
Upper Saddle River, New Jersey 07458

D1299573

Library of Congress Cataloging-in-Publication Data

Cook, Roy A.
    Tourism : the business of travel / Roy A. Cook, Laura J. Yale,
  Joseph J. Marqua.
        p.   cm.
  Includes index.
  ISBN 0-13-271032-3
    1. Tourist trade.   I. Yale, Laura J.   II. Marqua, Joseph J.
  II. Title.
  G155.A1C674   1999
   338.4′791—dc21   98-8160
                                         CIP

Acquisitions Editor: *Neil Marquardt*
Editorial Assistant: *Jean Auman*
Production Editor: *York Production Services*
Managing Editor: *Mary Carnis*
Creative Director: *Marianne Frasco*
Director of Manufacturing & Production: *Bruce Johnson*
Manufacturing Buyer: *Ed O'Dougherty*
Interior Designer: *Rosemarie Votta*
Cover Designer: *Bruce Kenselaar*
Cover Art: *Nick Gaetano*
Marketing Manager: *Frank Mortimer, Jr.*

©1999 by Prentice-Hall, Inc.
Upper Saddle River, New Jersey 07458

Printed in the United States of America

10 9 8 7 6 5 4 3 2

ISBN 0-13-271032-3

Prentice-Hall International (UK) Limited, *London*
Prentice-Hall of Australia Pty. Limited, *Sydney*
Prentice-Hall Canada Inc., *Toronto*
Prentice-Hall Hispanoamericana, S.A., *Mexico*
Prentice-Hall of India Private Limited, *New Delhi*
Prentice-Hall of Japan, Inc., *Tokyo*
Prentice-Hall Asia Pte. Ltd., *Singapore*
Editora Prentice-Hall do Brasil, Ltda., *Rio de Janeiro*

Contents

CHAPTER 6: FOOD AND BEVERAGE   124

PART THREE — The Service and Hospitality Environment   201

CHAPTER 9: PUTTING QUALITY INTO HOSPITALITY   202

CHAPTER 10: ECONOMIC AND POLITICAL IMPACTS OF TOURISM   220

CHAPTER 11: ENVIRONMENTAL AND SOCIAL/CULTURAL IMPACTS OF TOURISM   242

Preface

The tourism industry is both dynamic and diverse. Most students come to the study of tourism full of enthusiasm and questions. Yet, the textbooks available have been dry and/or overly focused on travel agencies and transportation modes. Often they are full of facts with little theoretical or macro-issue discussion. As a result, students' enthusiasm soon wanes and their interest in a career in "tourism" diminishes. We decided to write a book that would be as interesting and multifaceted as the field itself.

We have written our book in a conversational style so that it is fun to read and provides a thorough overview of the tourism industry, giving balanced coverage to each component part. The role of the travel agent and the importance of transportation modes are included, but not to the omission of significant coverage of other industry members, such as accommodations, destinations, attractions, and food and beverage operations.

As our title suggests, we look at the tourism industry through the lens of business, specifically by considering the management, marketing, and finance issues most important to industry members. In addition, the book starts with a comprehensive model of tourism and unfolds by considering each piece of the model in succession. All students should find the book enjoyable and educational, no matter which facet of the industry they find most interesting.

WHO SHOULD USE THIS BOOK

We designed our book so that it can be tailored to suit a variety of needs. Its engaging writing style and its hundreds of industry examples make it the perfect textbook for freshman and sophomore students taking their first tourism class. The thoroughness of content also makes it suitable for a similar course introducing students to the hospitality industry. To meet the advanced critical thinking needs of junior and senior students, we have augmented the text's basic content with readings and cases that they can use to apply their knowledge and refine their problem-solving skills.

No matter how experienced the instructor or students, we believe our book is one that professors can teach *with*, not simply *from*. The various text features and teaching supplements allow each instructor to develop the course to fit his or her style and the special needs and learning styles of his or her students.

HOW THE TEXT IS ORGANIZED

The book introduces students to an integrative model of tourism as a dynamic industry and then unfolds, considering each of the model's components in turn. The first section focuses on the traveling public and tourism promoters, explaining the critical linking role that travel agents and tour wholesalers provide. Part 2 familiarizes students with each of the tourism service providers in turn, beginning with transportation and concluding with destinations and resorts. Part 3, The Service and Hospitality Environment, elevates students' attention to macro-issues facing the industry, including service quality and the important impacts that tourism can have on host communities and the world.

Each section of the book is followed by supplementary readings and an appendix selected and developed for the topic of the section. The text concludes with five integrative real-world cases that professors can use during the course as it unfolds or at the end of the course to bring all the pieces together.

SPECIAL FEATURES

We incorporated many features into our textbook to make it engaging for both the instructor and the students.

Feature: Each chapter opens with learning objectives and a detailed outline.

Feature: Each chapter features a real-world vignette that illustrates a major component of the chapter and then is mentioned again within the chapter pages.

Feature: All chapters include ethical/critical thinking dilemmas (termed "You Decide") that are useful in generating class discussion and encouraging students to practice critical-thinking skills. Each You Decide is written to be especially relevant to the chapter in which it appears.

Feature: Each chapter includes many tables and figures that help students understand the more abstract concepts and theories presented.

Feature: FYI (For Your Information) boxed items are sprinkled throughout the chapters. These items serve as examples of chapter concepts and provide helpful travel tips or useful business information.

Feature: Each chapter includes a Tourism in Action topic that provides students with an in-depth industry example of the chapter's content.

Feature: Discussion questions at the end of the chapter are based on the learning objectives.

Feature: The Applying the Concepts section of each chapter offers professors and students a variety of thought-provoking topics to explore or to use as a blueprint for applying newly acquired knowledge.

Feature: A glossary of terms follows each chapter's content, and the index highlights the page on which a term is defined.

Feature: The text is full of concepts and examples of organizations, many of which will be familiar to students to engage their interest, and many are from outside North America.

Feature: The importance of service quality in the increasingly competitive industry is accentuated by giving it full chapter coverage—Chapter 9: Putting Quality into Hospitality.

Feature: In Chapters 10 and 11, students are sensitized to the variety of impacts that tourism can have: economic, political, social, and environmental.

Feature: Three appendixes build student skills in probem-solving, manners, and career/job-seeking.

Feature: Readings follow each of the three text sections, offering the instructor supplemental material and examples for student discussion.

Feature: The text concludes with five integrative cases that have been classroom tested and can be used to give students practice in applying what they have learned and improving their problem-solving/critical-thinking skills.

THE INSTRUCTOR'S TOOLKIT

To fulfill our goal of making the text customizable for individual instructor needs, we have developed a comprehensive instructor's toolkit of resources. The instructor's manual includes the usual elements—detailed chapter outlines and a testbank—but also includes supplemental lecture material and discussion guides to support the use of the readings and cases provided in the text. In addition, discussion suggestions are offered throughout the chapter outlines to generate student debate on several of the textbook features, such as the You Decide chapter dilemmas.

The power of the written word in our text is also supported by a series of videos and a major website that both students and professors will find educational and entertaining. We personally will be updating and adding to the site on a quarterly basis so that it remains current.

ACKNOWLEDGMENTS

The number of friends, colleagues and industry members who helped us in writing this book is far too large to acknowledge individually. To each and every one of them, we offer our heartfelt thanks and appreciation.

We want to recognize our colleagues at Fort Lewis College. So many offered support and special aid in producing our textbook. The following members of the FLC community deserve special mention:

Skip Cave, Dean, School of Business Administration

Leonard Atencio

James Clay

Larry Corman

Thomas Eckenrode

John Hale

Brendan McAlister

Alice McKinney

Rick Mull

O.D. Perry

James Reser

Minna Sellers

Allyn Talg

Chuck Tustin

Deborah Uroda

Several industry members also came to our aid above and beyond their duties:

Lisa Ball, Harrah's Entertainment Corp.

Earl Bebo, The Culinary Institute of America (retired)

Paul Clarke and Treva Ricou, Vancouver Aquarium

Paula Conkling and Jack Musiel, Holland America Cruise Lines

Lee Galati, Aladdin Hotel and Casino

Rick Galligan and his staff at the DoubleTree Hotel, Durango, Colorado

Tom Little, VIA Rail Canada Inc.

R. Michael Thornton, Specialist in Hospitality and Human Resource Management

We are grateful to four photographers who provided the lion's share of the photographs included in the book: Dr. and Mrs. Charles Yale, Dr. Donald Yale, and Ms. Allyn Talg.

Bev Bishop deserves special mention for taking on the herculean task of indexing our book.

Finally, we would like to thank those educators who reviewed our text and made it better through their suggestions and constructive criticism:

Eddie Dry, University of New Mexico

Kathy Dunn, Highline Community College

Joseph Chen, Virginia Polytechnic Institute and State University

Elizabeth Barber, Temple University

Leland Nicholls, University of Wisconsin–Stout

Paula Kerr, Algonquin College

Stephen Hiemstra, Purdue University

Terence McDonough, Erie Community College–City Campus

Michael Sciarini, Michigan State University

Steve Call, Ohio University

Ellen Bailey, Los Angeles Community College

Patricia Bartholomew, New York City Technical College

Ron Bernthal, Sullivan County Community College

Katherine Heiligmann, Salem State College

Sonya Garwood, Cloud County Community College

Donna Morn, Art Institute of Fort Lauderdale

Barbara Steffen, Kingsborough Community College

About the Authors

Roy A. Cook, D.B.A. (Mississippi State University), brings extensive real-world insights to this text. His industry and consulting experiences have spanned over twenty years of service to the hospitality industry. He has held positions ranging from controller and food and beverage manager at the property level to internal auditor and human resource director at the corporate level with organizations such as Hyatt Hotels and Adam's Mark Hotels. He has written and published numerous articles, cases, and papers based on his extensive experience in services industries. Dr. Cook is currently Assistant Dean of the School of Business Administration at Fort Lewis College, Durango, Colorado.

Laura J. (Richardson) Yale, Ph.D., holds B.S. and M.S. degrees in Hotel, Restaurant and Travel Administration from the University of Massachusetts at Amherst. Subsequent to experience in the restaurant, institutional food service, and entertainment industries, Dr. Yale began teaching at Northern Arizona University. While in Arizona, she was instrumental in developing and directing a regional tourism association and served on the Governor's Intrastate Tourism Committee. She received her Ph.D. in Marketing from the University of California – Irvine. Dr. Yale is currently Associate Professor of Marketing at Fort Lewis College, teaching courses and conducting research in Tourism and Resort Management and Services Marketing and Management.

Joseph "Jay" Marqua has degrees from the Culinary Institute of America and Fort Lewis College. His tourism industry experience includes owning and operating inns, resorts, restaurants, and nightclubs. Mr. Marqua developed educational media programs and facilitated educational seminars for The University of New Haven Hotel, Restaurant and Tourism Administration School. He currently serves as president of The Tourism and Hospitality Development Group. The client list for his company has included organizations such as Amtrak, Aramark, the Culinary Institute of America, Ritz Carlton, the Saint James Club in Antiqua, and GWC Gaming. Mr. Marqua remains an active speaker and trainer for tourism organizations.

To my wife, Gwen, who supported me and encouraged me to complete this project, and to our son, Chad, who understood and appreciated the fact that dedication to a goal is important.

–R.A.C.

To Dr. Stevenson W. Fletcher III, whose long years of service at the University of Massachusetts included nudging me down the paths of tourism and education.

–L.J.Y.

To my wife Mary, who is the living expression of Love and Hospitality.

–J.J.M.

The Traveling Public and Tourism Promoters

CHAPTER 1

Introduction to Tourism

Welcome to the world of tourism.
Photo by D.A. Yale.

Travel is fatal to prejudice, bigotry, and narrow-mindedness.

—MARK TWAIN

CHAPTER OUTLINE

Could a Career in Tourism Be in Your Future?

Introduction

Services and Tourism

What Is Tourism?

A Tourism Model

The History of Travel and Tourism
- The Empire Era
- The Middle Ages and the Renaissance Era
- The Grand Tour Era
- The Mobility Era
- The Modern Era

Bringing Tourism into Focus

Geography Provides a Window to the World
- Physical Geography
- Human Geography
- Regional Geography

Tourism in Action

Studying Tourism from Business Perspectives
- Marketing
- Management
- Finance

Tourism's Challenges and Opportunities

Where Do You Fit In?

Topics Covered in Each Chapter

Summary

You Decide

Net Tour

Discussion Questions

Applying the Concepts

Glossary

References

LEARNING OBJECTIVES

After you have read this chapter, you should be able to:

- Understand and explain the basic definition of tourism.

- Identify the major participants and forces shaping the tourism industry.

- Explain historical factors that encouraged the development of tourism activities.

- Explain the impact of physical, human, and regional geography on tourism activities.

- Explain why tourism should be studied from marketing, management, and financial perspectives.

- Identify future challenges and opportunities facing the tourism industry.

- Discuss career prospects in the tourism industry.

Could a Career in Tourism Be in Your Future?

The future that had once appeared to Jackie to be so far away had now arrived. Her first year in college had been fun, but it was time to start thinking about a career and preparing for her future. A combination of travel and part-time work experience had convinced her that a career in travel and tourism would be exciting. Comments she had heard, such as "The future of our economy will be in services"; "Tourism is the largest part of our service economy"; and "Tourism is the world's fastest-growing industry" reassured her that her decision to focus her college studies on tourism was a good one.

Jackie, like many of her friends, had worked in entry-level customer service positions in businesses such as fast-food restaurants, supermarkets, and banks. She considered these jobs temporary stepping stones and sources of extra income; however, tourism seemed to offer a world of career opportunities.

Mike, one of Jackie's friends, described how he started out as a part-time front desk clerk while going to college and had been promoted through several positions to front desk manager. He enthusiastically described the excitement of the business and the satisfaction that came from meeting and serving a wide variety of guests. He encouraged her to consider a career in tourism.

Jackie took Mike's advice and talked with everyone she met who worked in a tourism-related business. She was amazed by their willingness to talk candidly about the opportunities and challenges that existed in their jobs. Carol, the manager of the restaurant where Jackie worked part-time, told her that the food service industry was always looking for well-educated and enthusiastic employees to become managers. She also described internship programs for college students and training programs that were available after graduation.

The enthusiasm that Jackie encountered was contagious and she wanted to know more. She was aware of some of the more visible parts of the tourism industry, like cruise ships, airlines, hotels, resorts, theme parks, travel agencies, and tour operators. From things she had read and heard, there seemed to be a wide variety of career opportunities in tourism, but which one would be right for her? Was there more to tourism than she knew? If she could learn more about the tourism industry, she could decide where she wanted to begin her own career. To begin this search, Jackie, like you, enrolled in a tourism course.

Jackie soon learned that she was similar to many other people who worked in a customer service position. An interest sparked by a part-time job or fanned by a desire to travel eventually turned into a career focused on meeting the needs of the traveling public. That first tourism course answered many of Jackie's questions and provided her the foundation for acquiring the knowledge, skills, and abilities to launch a successful tourism career.

Introduction

Welcome to the study of a dynamic group of industries that have developed to serve the needs of travelers worldwide—tourism! Tourism is the business of travel. Whether we are travelers or we are serving travelers' needs, this exciting and demanding group of visitor services industries touches all of our lives. In this book, you will explore the many and varied segments of this multifaceted industry. As you learn more about tourism, begin thinking about the future challenges and opportunities that lie ahead for all of these industries and how they may influence your life.

Services and Tourism

Services and tourism go hand in hand. You will learn more about services in Chapter 9. However, as we begin our study of tourism, it is important to know that these activities make a significant economic impact on almost every nation in the world! Services are growing at a faster rate than all agricultural and manufacturing business combined. In fact, tourism-related businesses are the leading producers of new jobs worldwide.

Tourism has developed into a truly worldwide activity that knows no political, ideological, geographical, or cultural boundaries. For a long time tourism was disparate and fragmented, but with maturity has come a sense of professional identity. It has formed lobby groups such as the World Travel and Tourism Council, which includes airlines, hotel chains, and travel agents among its members and concentrates on making the case for tourism's economic value to the host countries.[1] The future prospects for tourism are brighter than ever. In fact, tourism-related activities are projected to continue growing and will account for 10% of all international trade by the year 2000.[2] As we will see later, the growth and popularity of tourism activities has not been accidental.

Tourism has become more than just another industry; it has developed into an important part of the economic foundation of many countries. The positive benefits of tourism activities in periods of economic stagnation or decline has not gone unnoticed. Tourism activities have demonstrated a general upward trend in numbers of participants and revenues over the past 50 years. As one leading tourism scholar noted, "While other industries show declines, tourism slows down and may go flat, but it seldom falls into recession."[3]

WHAT IS TOURISM?

As tourism-related activities have grown and changed, many different definitions and ways of classifying the industry have emerged. Use of the term *tourism* has evolved as attempts have been made to place a title on a difficult-to-define group of naturally related service activities and participants. As we embark on our study of **tourism,** it is helpful to begin with a common definition: "the temporary movement of people to destinations outside their normal places of work and residence, the activities undertaken during their stay in those destinations, and the facilities created to cater to their needs."[4]

As our definition shows, tourism includes a wide array of people, activities, and facilities. Although tourism is not a distinctly identified industry, most people would agree that it is a unique grouping of industries that are tied together by a common denominator—the traveling public.

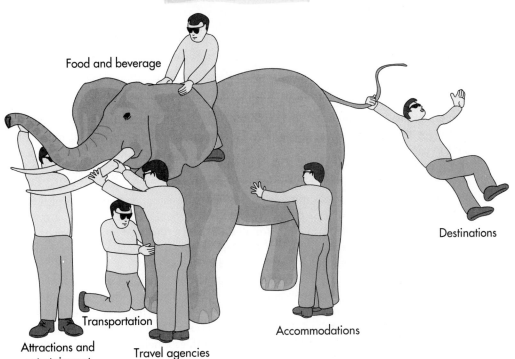

Food and beverage

Destinations

Attractions and entertainment

Transportation

Travel agencies

Accommodations

FIGURE 1.1
The Blind Men and Tourism. Unless we can view tourism as a whole, we may never understand the rich tapestry of this phenomenon and forever see it only in its many pieces.
Based on the poem "The Blind Men and the Elephant" by John Godfrey Saxe. Original design by John Hale.

TABLE 1.1
Standard Industrial Classification Codes

Code	Industry
Major group 40	Railroad transportation
Major group 41	Local and suburban transit and interurban highway passenger transportation
Major group 44	Water transportation
Major group 45	Air transportation
Major group 47	Transportation services
Major group 58	Eating and drinking places
Major group 59	Miscellaneous retail
Major group 70	Hotels, rooming houses, camps, and other lodging places
Major group 79	Amusement and recreation services
Major group 84	Museums, art galleries, and botanical and zoological gardens

Can you describe tourism in your own words? Take a moment to think about this question. You might find it easy to answer this question in general terms, but more difficult to answer if you were asked to provide specific details. In fact, you might find yourself facing a task similar to the one depicted in Figure 1.1. Tourism is much like the elephant: diverse and sometimes hard to describe, but, just like the elephant, too big to be ignored.

As shown in Table 1.1, specific segments of tourism, such as air transportation, theme parks, eating and drinking establishments, accommodations, and museums, have their own standard industrial classification codes (**SIC codes**). However, tourism does not have its own SIC code. Even though tourism cannot be classified as a distinct industry, it is generally agreed that "'[t]ourism' appears to be becoming an acceptable term to singularly describe the activity of people taking trips away from home and the industry which has developed in response to this activity."[5]

Some critics have suggested using a term other than *tourism* to describe the industry because it conjures up many different meanings. One of these suggestions has been to use a more inclusive and descriptive term such as *visitor-service industry*.[3] For convenience and ease of understanding, however, we will refer to tourism as an industry in this book.

A TOURISM MODEL

In an attempt to overcome some of the problems encountered in describing tourism, the model presented in Figure 1.2 was developed to highlight important participants and forces that shape the tourism industry. The model, like a photograph, provides a picture that begins to capture the dynamic and interrelated nature of tourism activities. Although many of the terms in our tourism model may not be familiar at this time, you will be learning more about each one and its importance in later chapters.

As you study our tourism **model,** notice its open nature and how each of the segments is related to the others. Let's begin our study of tourism by looking at travelers (tourists) who serve as the focal point for all tourism activities and form the center of our model. Radiating from this focal point are three large bands containing several interdependent groups of tourism participants and organizations.

Individual tourists may deal directly with any of these tourism service suppliers, but they customarily rely on the professional services provided by tourism promoters shown in the first band of our model. Tourism promoters, such as travel agencies and tourist boards, provide information and other marketing services. Moving to the next band of our model, we see key tourism suppliers who provide transportation, accommodations, and other services required by travelers.

FIGURE 1.2
An Integrated Model of Tourism

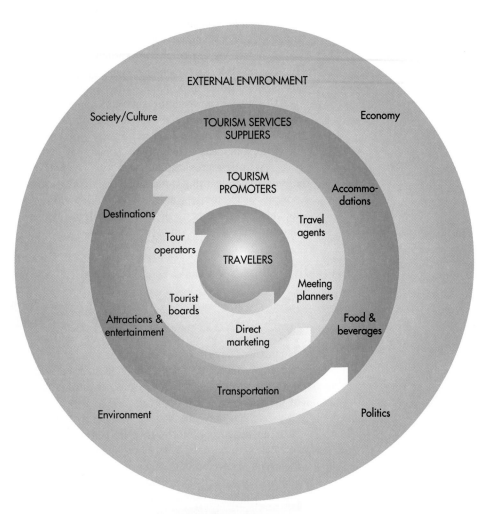

Tourism suppliers may provide these services independently, they may compete with each other, and, at times, they may work together. For example, airline, bus, railroad, cruise ship, and car rental companies may compete individually for a traveler's business. However, they may also team up to provide cooperative packages such as fly–ride, fly–cruise, and fly–drive alternatives. Hotels and resorts may also compete against each other for the same traveler's patronage, yet cooperate with transportation providers to attract tourists to a specific location. Service providers representing all segments of the tourism industry may often work together to develop promotional packages designed to attract tourists to destinations.

How closely these individuals and organizations work together is ultimately influenced by the forces shaping the face of tourism activities. As our model shows, the tourism industry does not operate in a vacuum. All of the participants, either individually or as a group, are constantly responding to a variety of social/cultural, political, environmental, and economic forces. These forces may range from subtle changes, which are noticeable only after many years, to more dramatic changes, which have immediate and visible impacts. Examples of these forces can be found all around us. Gradual changes may be noticed in destinations that were once fashionable but eventually faded in popularity, such as Niagara Falls on the Canadian/U.S. border and Brighton in England. Similar shifts can also be seen in transportation. Steamship passage across the North Atlantic was eclipsed by the faster and more efficient airplane, which opened new horizons for travelers. Immediate impacts can be seen in sudden shifts brought about by currency devaluations, wars, fuel shortages, and natural disasters. A country that was once avoided may suddenly become a popular tourism destination because it is more affordable or accessible. Conversely, a once popular destination may be avoided because of a recent natural disaster or political upheaval.

Let's look at how our model might work. Suppose you (a tourist) want to visit a sunny beach or a snow-covered mountain. You might begin planning your trip by calling different airlines, condominiums, hotels, and/or resorts (tourism service suppliers) searching for possible flight schedules and accommodation options. You could simply call a travel agent (tourism promoter) who would search out the best alternatives to meet your needs, rather than spending time and money contacting each supplier. Another option would be taking a "virtual trip" to your desired destination by surfing the growing number of offerings on the Internet. Finally, you could contact local chambers of commerce or visitors' bureaus to learn more about your preferred destinations.

As you progress through this book, we will focus your attention on specific features of our model, learning more about each component and how it interacts with other components of the tourism industry. We will begin our journey into the study of tourism by looking back in time to discover the origins of these activities and the foundations they laid for tourism as we know it today.

THE HISTORY OF TRAVEL AND TOURISM

Long before the invention of the wheel, travel occurred for a variety of reasons. In the beginning, it was simple. As seasons changed and animals migrated, people traveled to survive. Since these early travelers moved on foot, they were confined to fairly small geographical areas. Travel may have remained a localized experience, but people by nature are curious. It is easy to imagine these early travelers climbing a mountain or crossing a river to satisfy their own sense of adventure and curiosity as they sought a glimpse of the unknown.

We can only guess at the wonder and amazement of early travelers as they made each new discovery. However, there is a rich history of people and cultures that form the foundation of tourism. History provides important insights into the reasons for travel and the eventual development of tourism. Based on early records, we know that many cultures and nations moved great armies and navies to conquer and control resources and trade routes. Although military forces often traveled great distances, it was probably not until the emergence of the Egyptian, Eastern Mediterranean, and Roman Empires that travel began to evolve into tourism as we know it today.

Tourism—Past and Present: Roman theater at Ephesus (Turkey).
Photo by C.E. Yale.

Early recorded history provides a glimpse into ancient tourism activities. The Phoenicians, like many travelers, were interested in travel because of a sense of curiosity and discovery as well as a means of establishing trade routes. Although written records are scarce, other peoples such as the Mayans on the Gulf Coast of what is now Mexico and the Shang Dynasty in what is now present-day China probably traveled for many of the same reasons as the Phoenicians. Evidence of their travels can be found in the artifacts they collected during their journeys to far-away places. One thing we know for sure is that as civilizations became established and spread geographically travel became a necessity.

The Empire Era

The point at which simple travel evolved into the more complex activities of tourism is hard to identify. However, tourism probably began to develop during the Empire Era, which stretched from the time of the Egyptians to the Greeks and finally came to an end with the fall of the Roman Empire. During this time, people began traveling in large numbers for governmental, commercial, educational, and religious purposes out of both necessity and pleasure. The Egyptian Kingdoms (4850–715 B.C.) were the first known civilization to have consolidated governmental functions at centralized locations. Travel to these locations by boat was particularly easy because they could use the Nile River, which flowed northward but was constantly brushed by southward breezes. Since oars were not needed, travel in either direction was relatively effortless. Boats could go north with the current or south with sails.

As travel became commonplace, basic necessities such as food and lodging had to be provided. Several factors combined to encourage travel during the height of the Egyptian, Greek, and Roman empires. Large numbers of travelers began to seek out enjoyable experiences in new locations. The most notable group of these travelers, because of their numbers, was the Greeks.

The Greek Empire (900–200 B.C.) promoted the use of a common language throughout much of the Mediterranean region and the money of some Greek city-states became accepted as a common currency of exchange. As centers of governmental activities, these city-states became attractions in themselves. They offered visitors a wide variety of opportunities to enjoy themselves while away from home. Shopping, eating, drinking, and watching spectator sports and theatrical performances are just a few of the many activities that grew out of travel and evolved into the more encompassing aspects of tourism.

The growth of the Roman Empire (500 B.C.–A.D. 300) fostered expanded tourism opportunities for both middle class and wealthy citizens. Good roads (many of which were built to connect the city of Rome to outlying areas in case of revolt) and water routes made travel easy. As these roads were developed, so were inns, which were located approximately 30 miles apart, making for an easy day's journey. Fresh horses could be hired at the inns and at more frequent relay stations. People could easily travel 125 miles a day on horseback, knowing they would have a place to eat and sleep at the end of the day. These roads, which connected Rome with such places as Gaul, Britain, Spain, and Greece, eventually extended into a 50,000-mile system. The most famous of these roads was the Appian Way joining Rome with the "heel" of Italy.

Many of the hassles of travel to distant places were removed because Roman currency was universally accepted and Greek and Latin were common languages. In addition, a common legal system provided protection and peace of mind, allowing people to travel further away from home for commerce, adventure, and pleasure. Just like the Greek city-states, cities in the Roman Empire became destination attractions or wayside stops along the way to a traveler's final destination.

Has this brief glimpse into ancient history taught us anything of use today? The answer is yes. Even today, tourism activities continue to flourish where individuals have free time, travel is safe, there are exchangeable currencies, common languages are spoken, and established legal systems create a perception of personal safety. The absence of any of these factors can dampen peoples desire to travel and enjoy tourism-related activities, as can be seen in the demise of travel during the Middle Ages.

The Middle Ages and the Renaissance Era

Travel almost disappeared during the Middle Ages (5th–14th centuries). As the dominance of the Roman Empire crumbled, travel became dangerous and sporadic. The **feudal system** that eventually replaced Roman rule resulted in many different autonomous domains. This breakdown in a previously organized and controlled society resulted in the fragmentation of transportation systems, currencies, and languages, making travel a difficult and sometimes dangerous experience.

As the Roman Catholic Church gained power and influence, people began to talk of crusades to retake the Holy Land. There were nine of these crusades (A.D. 1096–1291), but each failed. In 1291, Acre, the last Christian stronghold, was retaken by the Muslims, bringing the Crusades to an end. Although conquest and war were the driving forces behind the Crusades, the eventual result was the desire of people to venture away from their homes to see new places and experience different civilizations.

After the Crusades, merchants like Marco Polo traveled to places well beyond the territories visited by the Crusaders (see Fig. 1.3). Reports of Polo's travels and adventures (1275–1295) across the Middle East and into China continued to heighten interest in travel and trade. The rebirth in travel emerged slowly during the Renaissance (14th–16th centuries). Merchants began to venture farther from their villages as the church and kings and queens brought larger geographical areas under their control. Trade routes slowly began to reopen as commercial activities grew and merchants ventured into new territories. The desire to learn and experience from other cultures heightened the awareness of educational benefits to be gained from travel and led to the Grand Tour Era.

The Grand Tour Era

The Grand Tour Era (1613–1785), which marked the height of luxurious travel and tourism activities, originated with the wealthy English and soon spread and became fashionable among other individuals who had time and money. Travel and the knowledge provided by these travels became a status symbol representing the ultimate in social and educational experiences. Grand Tour participants traveled throughout Europe seeking to experience the cultures of the "civilized world" and acquire knowledge through the arts and sciences

FIGURE 1.3
Marco Polo's Travel Route from His Home in Venice, Italy, to China during the 13th Century.

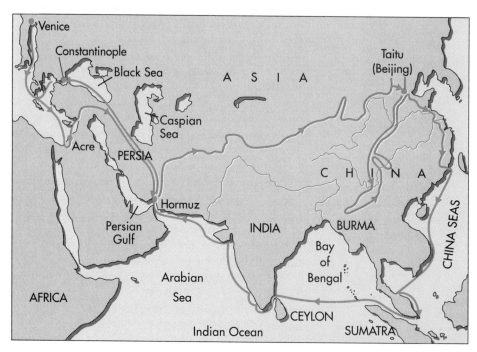

of the countries they visited. Their travels took them to a variety of locations in France, Switzerland, Italy, and Germany for extended periods of time, often stretching over many years.[6]

Although the desire to participate in the Grand Tour continued, the Industrial Revolution (c. 1750) forever changed economic and social structures. Whole nations moved from an agricultural and commercial focus to modern industrialism. People became tied to the regimented structures and demands of factory life and the management of business enterprises. Economic growth and technological advances led to more efficient forms of transportation, the integration of markets across geographic and international boundaries, and higher personal incomes for larger numbers of people. Travel became a business necessity as well as a leisure activity, and tourism suppliers rapidly developed to serve the growing needs of travelers. The days of leisurely travel over extended periods of time to gain cultural experiences faded away as fewer and fewer people were able to take advantage of these time-consuming opportunities.

The Mobility Era

Growing economic prosperity and the advent of leisure time as well as the availability of affordable travel ushered in a new era in the history of tourism. People who were no longer tied to the daily chores of farm life began to search for new ways to spend the precious leisure time they earned away from their jobs in offices, stores, and factories.

The Mobility Era (1800–1944) ushered in travel to new and familiar locations, both near and far. Tourism industry activities began to increase as new roads, stagecoaches, passenger trains, and sailing ships became common sights in the early 1800s. Britain and France developed extensive road and railroad systems well before Canada and the United States. Growth and development of roads and railroads helped to increase the availability of transportation alternatives and reduced their costs, attracting more and more people to the idea of travel.

Thomas Cook (1808–1892) can be credited with finally bringing travel to the general public by introducing the tour package. In 1841, he organized the first tour for a group of 570 to attend a temperance rally in Leicester, England. For the price of a shilling (12 pence), his customers boarded a chartered train for the trip from Loughborough, complete with a picnic lunch and brass band. The immediate success of his first venture and the demand for more assistance in making travel arrangements led Cook into the full-time business of providing travel services.

The next major steps in the Mobility Era were the introductions of automobiles and air travel. Although automobile technology was pioneered in Britain, France, and Germany, it was Henry Ford's mass production of the Model T in 1914 that brought individual freedom to travel, opening new horizons for millions of people. Winged travel was not far behind, and the time required to reach far-away places began to shrink. Orville and Wilbur Wright ushered in the era of flight with their successful test of the airplane in Kitty Hawk, N.C., in 1903.

This has been just a brief journey through some of the changes that began during the era of mobility. In later chapters we will explore more of the historical details and importance of each of these changes as well as some of the more modern changes that have shaped the tourism industry.

The Modern Era

Mass tourism is a recent phenomenon that evolved after World War II (1945–present). During this war, millions of people throughout the world, including over 17 million Canadian and U.S. citizens, were exposed to many new, different, and even exotic locations as they served in a variety of military assignments. Military service forced many people who had never before traveled to do so, and they were eager to share their positive experiences with family and friends when they returned home.

Following the end of World War II, several additional factors helped to encourage the growth of tourism. Cars were again being produced in large numbers, gas was no longer rationed, and prosperity began to return to industrialized countries. The introduction of jet travel in the 1950s and its growing popularity in the 1960s further accelerated growth in both domestic and international travel. Time, money, safety, and the desire to travel combined to usher in an unparalleled period of tourism growth that continues today.

Mass tourism is comprised of two different groups of travelers.[7] These groups are classified as organization mass tourists who buy packaged tours and follow an itinerary prepared and organized by tour operators. The second group is classified as individual mass tourists. These travelers visit popular attractions and use tourism services that are promoted through the mass media.

BRINGING TOURISM INTO FOCUS

The continued growth in tourism and, more specifically, international travel may well make tourism the world's peace industry. "As we travel and communicate in ever-increasing numbers, we are discovering that most people, regardless of their political or religious orientation, race, or socioeconomic status, want a peaceful world in which all are fed, sheltered, productive, and fulfilled."[2]

Our methods of transportation have definitely improved, and the distances we can cover in relatively short periods have greatly expanded, but the sense of curiosity and adventure found in those early travelers is still with us today. However, travel today is more than just adventure, and it has spawned an entire group of service industries to meet the needs of tourists all over the world.

Where people travel, why they choose a particular location, and what they do once they arrive is of interest to everyone in the tourism industry. These data are now collected and recorded based on the reasons given for taking trips. The primary reasons for travel can be broken into three broad categories: vacation and leisure trips, visits to friends and relatives, and business and professional trips (see Figure 1.4). Travel in all of these categories creates demands for other tourism activities.

Travel and tourism have now become so commonplace in industrialized countries that we may fail to think about what has made these activities possible. If you think about it, tourism affects all of our lives and is intertwined throughout the entire fabric of a **host community,** region, or country. Tourism can be viewed and studied from a variety of perspectives.[8] In addition to geography and the commonly studied business disciplines of marketing, management, and finance, other disciplines often included in the study of tourism are

- anthropology,
- sociology,
- economics, and
- psychology.[9]

FIGURE 1.4
Typical Reasons for Travel. The percentage of trips in each category may vary from year-to-year, but is relatively constant over time.
Source: U.S. Travel Data Center, 1995.

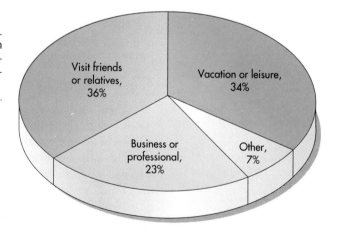

Visit friends or relatives, 36%

Vacation or leisure, 34%

Business or professional, 23%

Other, 7%

Each of these perspectives provides important insights into tourism activities and raises a variety of questions. Some of the more commonly asked questions include:

- Who are these visitors?
- Why do they travel?
- Where do they travel?
- What are their concerns when they travel?
- What are their needs when they travel?
- What forms of transportation do they use?
- Where do they stay?
- What do they do when they travel?
- Who provides the services they need?
- What impact do they have on the locations they visit?
- What types of career opportunities are available in this industry?

These and many other questions point to the need to study tourism.

Casual or common-sense approaches to answering these questions will not prepare us to meet the needs of tomorrow's visitors. Rather than studying tourism from only one perspective, throughout this book you will have the opportunity to learn more about tourism in general, the segments of the tourism industry, and the key issues facing tourism.

GEOGRAPHY PROVIDES A WINDOW TO THE WORLD

Travel is a key component in all tourism activities; therefore, a basic understanding of geography can enrich our understanding of the tourism industry. Information provided through three broad categories of geography—physical, human (cultural), and regional—will enable you to learn more about locations around the world and to provide others with that information without ever having to visit a particular location. Let's look at how you might use some of these basic geographical concepts in a variety of settings. See color insert for maps of these concepts. Figure 1.5 is a world religion map. Figure 1.6 shows a world climate map and Figure 1.7 is a world language map.

Physical Geography

Knowledge of **physical geography** provides the means to identify and describe natural features of the earth, including landforms, water, vegetation, and climate. When these natural features are combined, they create an environment that can either encourage or discourage tourism activities. For example, during winter months in the Northern Hemisphere, visitors might be attracted to snow-covered mountains for skiing or to warm sun and sandy beaches for a break from the harsh realities of winter. As the seasons change, these same physical attributes could deter tourism. As the snow melts and mud appears, the mountains may lose their appeal. The same can be said for the once sunny beaches as the rainy season arrives.

Many different types of maps have been developed to highlight significant physical geographic features. An example of one specific type of map highlighting climatic regions around the world can be seen in Figure 1.6. Could a map like this help you or someone else plan travel and other tourism activities?

Locating and describing destinations requires a knowledge of how to read and interpret maps. Unlocking the information contained in maps requires some basic skills. These skills include an understanding of basic **cartography** notations, i.e., geographic grids (longitude and latitude), legends (symbols and colors), and indexes (locational guides). In addition to the natural features, location and accessibility are also key factors that will influence the level of tourism activity. But geography is more than just landforms, water, vegetation, and climate. It also includes people.

Human Geography

The exhilaration of experiencing other cultures is enjoyed by many through unique languages, foods, beverages, products, arts, and crafts that are typical to particular locations. Simply being in a different location and participating in daily activities can be an adventure in itself. An understanding of **human (cultural) geography** provides the specific types of information that can enhance any tourism experience.

Human geography, which includes people and economic activities, creates the rest of the picture that can be captured and explained through maps. Culture as expressed through language, religion, dress, foods and beverages, and other customs play critical roles in the popularity of many tourism destinations. Other factors such as politics and economic conditions can also play an important role in the ease of travel, especially across international boundaries. Governments can encourage or discourage tourism through passport and visa requirements as well as through policies relating to taxation or the ease of currency exchange.

For example, English is the most commonly spoken language in the industrialized world, but it may not be spoken in some locations. In other locations, Chinese, French, Spanish, Russian, Japanese, or a host of other languages may be common. While this might create a language barrier for some, it can create opportunities for others who provide interpretation or tour services.

Human geography allows travelers to become aware of cultural norms and religious expectations so they do not commit social blunders. In some countries, it is common practice for businesses to close on certain days and times because of accepted cultural norms or for religious reasons. For example, most shops and stores in Germany close at 2:00 P.M. on Saturday and do not reopen until Monday morning. All commercial ac-

Exploring other cultures attracts large numbers of tourists: Thai dancers in Bangkok.
Photo by C.E. Yale.

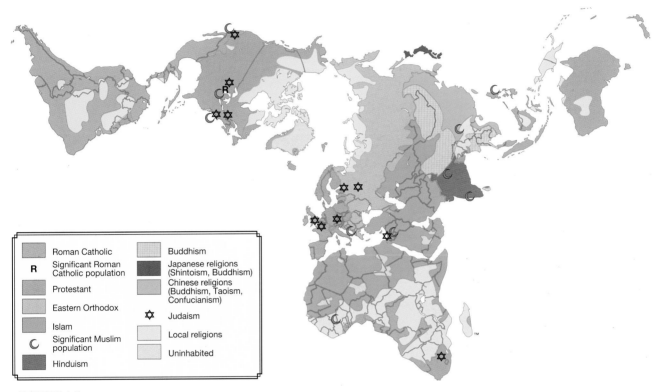

FIGURE 1.5
World Religion Map

(Sources: *Places and Regions in Global Context, Human Geography*, by Paul L. Knox and Sallie A. Marston, © 1998. Reprinted by permission of Prentice-Hall, Upper Saddle River, NJ. Map projection, Buckminster Fuller Institute and Dymaxion Map Design, Santa Barbara, CA. The word Dymaxion and the Fuller Projection Dymaxion™ Map design are trademarks of the Buckminster Fuller Institute, 2040 Alameda Padre Serra, Suite 224, (805-962-0022), Santa Barbara, California, © 1938, 1967 and 1992. All rights reserved.)

Legend:
- Roman Catholic
- **R** Significant Roman Catholic population
- Protestant
- Eastern Orthodox
- Islam
- ☾ Significant Muslim population
- Hinduism
- Buddhism
- Japanese religions (Shintoism, Buddhism)
- Chinese religions (Buddhism, Taoism, Confucianism)
- ✡ Judaism
- Local religions
- Uninhabited

FIGURE 1.6
World Climate Map
(Source: *Geosystems: 3/E, An Introduction to Physical Geography* by Robert W. Christopherson, © 1997. Reprinted by permission of Prentice-Hall, Inc., Upper Saddle River, NJ.)

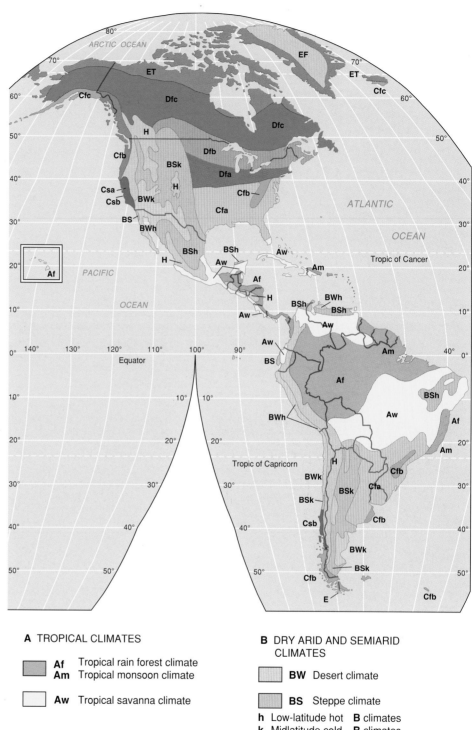

A TROPICAL CLIMATES

	Af	Tropical rain forest climate
	Am	Tropical monsoon climate
	Aw	Tropical savanna climate

B DRY ARID AND SEMIARID CLIMATES

	BW	Desert climate
	BS	Steppe climate

h Low-latitude hot **B** climates
k Midlatitude cold **B** climates

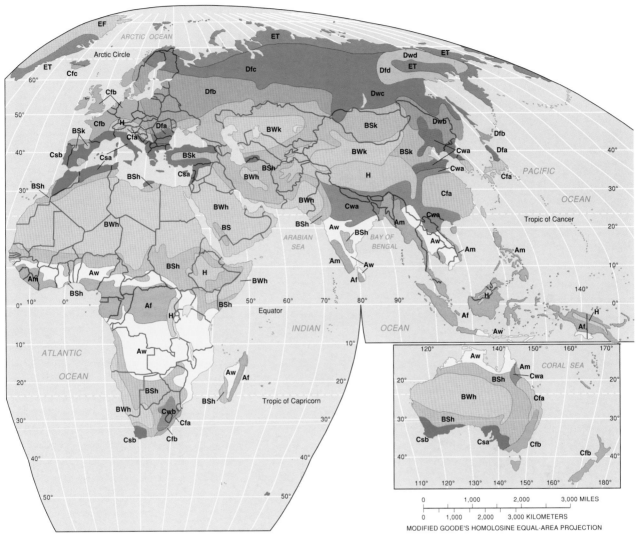

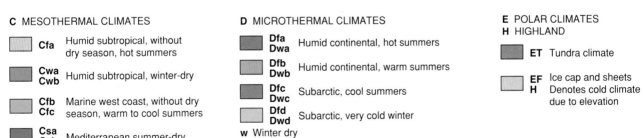

C MESOTHERMAL CLIMATES

Cfa — Humid subtropical, without dry season, hot summers

Cwa
Cwb — Humid subtropical, winter-dry

Cfb
Cfc — Marine west coast, without dry season, warm to cool summers

Csa
Csb — Mediterranean summer-dry

D MICROTHERMAL CLIMATES

Dfa
Dwa — Humid continental, hot summers

Dfb
Dwb — Humid continental, warm summers

Dfc
Dwc — Subarctic, cool summers

Dfd
Dwd — Subarctic, very cold winter

w Winter dry
f Without a dry season

E POLAR CLIMATES
H HIGHLAND

ET — Tundra climate

EF — Ice cap and sheets
H — Denotes cold climate due to elevation

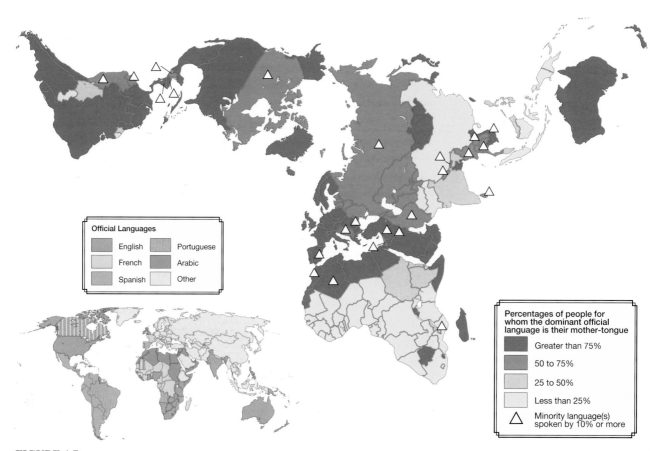

FIGURE 1.7
World Language Map

(Sources: Reprinted with permission of Simon & Schuster from *The New State of the World Atlas, 4th Ed.*, by M. Kidron and R. Segal. Copyright © 1991 by Michael Kidron and Ronald Segal. Maps and Graphics copyright © 1991 by Swanston Publishing Limited. Reprinted by permission of TOUCHSTONE/Simon & Schuster, Inc. Map projection, Buckminster Fuller Institute and Dymaxion Map design, Santa Barbara, CA. The word Dymaxion and the Fuller Projection Dymaxion™ Map design are trademarks of the Buckminster Fuller Institute, 2040 Alameda Padre Serra, Suite 224, Santa Barbara, CA 93103, (805) 962-0022, © 1938, 1967 and 1992. All rights reserved.)

tivity ceases in many Middle Eastern countries during designated prayer times. Figures 1.5 and 1.7 provide examples of maps that identify the specific locations of predominant languages and religions around the world.

Regional Geography

The level of tourism interest and activity in a specific area often depends on a combination of both physical and human geography that come together, making certain locations more attractive than others. It may be curiosity or a combination of natural as well as developed features and attractions that meet visitor wants, needs, and expectations. **Regional geography** is a useful framework for studying the physical and human geography of a specific area or location, providing a convenient way to organize a wide variety of facts.

For example, locations near large population centers combined with access to well-developed transportation systems generally create high levels of tourism activity. Climate also influences the level and type of tourism activity. Factors such as time of year, geographic location, and proximity to major bodies of water all contribute to demand. This may explain why the most popular tourist destinations in Europe can be found along the Mediterranean Sea. We can see a similar pattern in the United States, as six of the top 10 locations for domestic travelers are located near major bodies of water: Arizona, Arkansas, California, Colorado, Florida, Hawaii, Nevada, New York, Texas, and Washington, D.C.[10]

Regions also play an important role in the development and promotion of tourism activities. The Appalachian, Ozark, and Rocky Mountains form natural regions of tourism activities that cross state and, in some cases, national boundaries. Smaller regions such as the wine-growing regions of California, Washington, New York, France, Germany, Italy, and Spain also attract a great deal of tourism activity and have become popular destinations. Other regions may be much smaller and defined by specific boundaries such as Canada's Capital Region, Chicagoland, the San Francisco Bay Area, and the French Riviera.[10]

Geography provides a foundation to help us understand why people visit or fail to visit certain areas, but we also need to learn how to meet their needs efficiently and effectively as they travel. The three primary interrelated business functions—marketing, management, and finance—add the structure to our foundation, providing many of the

 TOURISM IN ACTION

An enormous challenge to any business in the tourism industry is managing information. Who are the many different guests of the business? Where do they come from? What do they have in common and how do their needs differ? What time of year do they come and how long do they stay? What qualities and services do we have or need to develop to fit visitor lifestyles? The questions are endless and so is the amount of data generated by the answers. As introduced in this chapter, the ability to segment markets and serve them profitably are critical components to competing successfully in the global tourism industry. So how do you put all the data into clear, easy-to-use information and put it into the hands of people to use it? One answer is to use a geographic information system (GIS) for presentation and spatial data analysis (information linked to geographic location).

A geographic information system is a set of computerized tools, including both hardware and software. GIS systems are used for collecting, storing, retrieving, transforming, and displaying spatial data. An easier way to think of GIS is as a marriage between computerized mapping and database management systems. In other words, anything that can appear on a map can be fed into a computer and then compared to anything on any other map, and everything on any map can have layers of data and information attached. GIS is a powerful technology and its potential uses are endless.

Tourism companies are now beginning to harness the power of GIS to improve their services. For example, Hertz Corporation is using the technologies of geographic information systems, Global Positioning Satellites (GPS) and electronic route guidance software in its Hertz NeverLost^sm system. When a traveler picks up a Hertz NeverLost^sm equipped rental car, he or she can punch in the address of a hotel and receive computer-generated voice instructions and video display of the directions.

Sources: Creating a profitable customer relationship using segmentation data. *Strategic Planning*, November/December 1995, 16–22; and A cheaper map for success. *InformationWeek*, October 30, 1995, 68.

tools necessary to plan and meet current and future needs of travelers. Let's look at how these business functions work together in the tourism industry.

STUDYING TOURISM FROM BUSINESS PERSPECTIVES

First, marketing concepts provide insights into why people travel as well as possible approaches to meeting their needs as they travel. Second, management concepts provide insights into the processes needed to meet societies' and visitors' current and future demands. Third, financial concepts provide the tools needed to understand, design, and supply profitable levels of visitor services. By combining knowledge from each of these perspectives, a basic understanding of tourism fundamentals can be developed.

Marketing

Studying tourism from the marketing approach provides valuable insight into the process by which tourism organizations create and individual visitors obtain desired goods and services. Everyone who has either worked in or used tourism-related services knows that customers (visitors and guests) can be very demanding. The more you know about these travelers and how to meet their needs, the more successful you will be as a tourism professional. In fact, individuals and organizations who attempt to understand and successfully meet the needs of these visitors are practicing what is called the **marketing concept,** an organizational philosophy centered around understanding and meeting the needs of customers.

Meeting visitor needs relies on a complex set of tools and techniques that are referred to as the **marketing mix.** The marketing mix consists of four variables, which are often called the four Ps of marketing: product, price, place, and promotion. Product refers to the good or service that is being offered. Price is the value of the good or service. This value is the amount of money that will be paid as well as the time "given up" to obtain the good or service. Place includes the location and the activities that are required to make the good or service available to the visitor. Finally, promotion refers to all of the activities that are undertaken to communicate the availability and benefits of a particular good or service. Just think about yourself or someone else who is traveling to another city to attend a concert. How can each of the variables in the marketing mix come together to make that trip a memorable experience?

Although tourists, as a whole, are a very diverse group, they can be divided into subgroups or market segments. Market segmentation allows an organization to develop the most appropriate marketing mix to meet the needs of specifically targeted visitor segments effectively and efficiently. For example, would a young college student want the same types of experiences at Disney World as a family?

Each market segment contains individuals who share many of the same characteristics and common needs. For example, business people may need to get to their destinations as quickly as possible while the summer vacationer may want to take the most leisurely and scenic route. Young college students may need to locate inexpensive accommodations at their destinations while a conventioneer may need to stay at the hotel that is hosting the convention regardless of price. Some visitors may be seeking a variety of entertaining outdoor activities while other visitors are interested in shows and shopping. This list of examples could go on, but the point should be clear: As organizations plan to meet these differing needs, they can no longer afford to try to serve the needs of all visitors. They simply do not have the resources to reach everyone and successfully meet their diverse needs.

You will learn more about the importance of marketing and its role in meeting tourists' needs in the following chapters. As we explore the many facets of the tourism industry, think about yourself as well as other specific groups of visitors who are being served and how these targeted individuals shape marketing as well as management decisions.

Management

Management furnishes additional tools and techniques to serve visitor needs successfully. Management, just like marketing, is essential to the continued success of all organizations, both public and private. The study of **management** provides a unified approach to planning, organizing, directing, and controlling present and future actions for accomplishing organization goals. As our model depicts, economic, political, cultural, environmental, and technological forces effect all tourism organizations. Managers need to understand each of these forces and how they will impact decisions as they plan for the future.

Basically, management is the common thread that holds any organization or activity together and keeps everyone moving in the same direction. For example, managers working for the Forest Service must decide how many people can comfortably use a campsite and when and where new campsites should be built. Government planners and administrators must make decisions about the desirability and necessity of new or expanded highways, airports, and shopping facilities. Restaurant managers must decide how many employees are needed to provide high-quality service and, at the same time, make a fair profit. Resort managers must decide whether or not to expand and what level of service to offer. Think back to that trip you were asked to plan earlier in the chapter and you will begin to see how all of the management functions must fit together to have a successful experience.

The process might go something like this. After you mentioned the possibility of renting a cottage at the beach to enjoy some sun, surf, and sand, several of your friends asked if they could go with you. The first management function used in putting this trip together is planning: where to go, how to get there, and how many will go. Once these decisions are made, the next function used is organizing. You are using the organizing function when you decide who will make reservations, who will buy food and refreshments, and who will call everyone to make sure they show up on time on the day of departure.

The next logical step you would use in putting together your trip would be the directing function. You are directing as you answer questions and coordinate all of your planned activities. Finally, you will use the controlling function. You are controlling as you check maps, directions, itineraries, and reservations to ensure the success of your trip. Although the activities may be more complex, managers in all tourism-related activities are constantly going through the same types of processes.

Finance

Studying tourism from a financial approach provides a basic understanding of how organizations manage revenues and expenses. To continue operating and providing services, tourism organizations must strive to generate revenues in excess of expenses or effectively and efficiently use the financial resources they have been allocated. Even nonprofit and government organizations are being called on to generate more of their own funding and to gain better control of their expenses.

By definition, a **business** is an organization operated with the objective of making a profit from the sale of goods and services. **Profits** are revenues in excess of expenses. They are used as a common yardstick to represent financial performance and are the ultimate measure of financial success. However, some tourism organizations such as governmental agencies, museums, and visitors' and convention bureaus may be classified as nonprofit. Even though they may not technically operate with a profit motive, most still strive to generate revenues in excess of expenses. For simplicity, we will use the generic term *business* in our discussion of financial concepts.

To use and communicate financial information, a common language must be spoken. That language is known as accounting, which is often called the "language of business." **Accounting** is an activity designed to accumulate, measure, and communicate financial information to various decision-makers, such as investors, creditors, managers, and front-line employees. One of the purposes of accounting information is to provide data needed to make informed decisions. Examples of sources of basic financial information for specific segments of the tourism industry are shown in Table 1.2.

To measure and report financial results as accurately as possible, a standard set of procedures are followed, usually referred to as the "accounting cycle." The cycle includes several steps including analyzing, recording, classifying, summarizing, and reporting financial data. The accounting cycle reports data in the form of financial reports. There are two main categories of financial reports: internal and external. Internal financial reports are used by those who direct the day-to-day operations of a business. External financial reports are used by individuals and organizations who have an economic interest in the business but are not part of its management (see Figure 1.8).

Three basic building blocks are used to measure financial success:

1. margin (the amount of each sales dollar remaining after operating expenses have been deducted),

2. turnover (the number of times each dollar of operating assets has been used to produce a dollar of sales), and

3. leverage (the extent to which borrowed funds are being used).

When these three components are multiplied together, they equal **return on investment (ROI),** which measures profit. The ability to operate profitably is critical to tourism organizations since they are typically faced with low margins, high turnover, and the need to use leverage (other people's money). As can be seen in Figure 1.9, managing these three components is a delicate balancing act, and tourism is an industry in which every nickel counts and profits depend on recognizing the importance of pennies.

Let's look at some practical examples of how these building blocks for financial success might work in specific segments of the tourism industry. In its simplest form, margin (25¢) for a food-service operator serving a hamburger would be the sales price ($2.00) minus the cost of preparation, ingredients, and service ($1.75). Airlines would measure

TABLE 1.2
Sources of Financial Information for Tourism Segments

The typical library has many references that can be effectively used to research financial information on the various tourism segments. While it is not practical to list all the possible library reference works that can assist your research, the following are some of the references commonly available at public and university libraries:

The Standard Industrial Classification Manual	*Moody's Industrial Manual*
The Department of Commerce Financial Report	*Compact Disclosure*
Almanac of Business and Industrial Financial Ratios	*The Standard and Poor's Register of Corporations, Directors and Executives*
Industry Norms and Key Business Ratios	*Standard and Poor's Industry Surveys*
Annual Statement Studies	*The Industry Report Service*
America's Corporate Families	*The Standard and Poor's Analyst's Handbook*
The Million Dollar Directory	*The Standard and Poor's Corporation Bond Guide*
The Reference Book of Corporate Management	*The Standard and Poor's Corporation Stock Guide*
The Directory of Corporate Affiliations	*Dunn and Brad Street*
The International Directory of Corporate Affiliations	*Robert Morris and Associate's Standard Industrial Classification Index*
Value Line Investment Survey	*Certified Public Accountant–Industry Audit Guides*
Trade Magazines	

FIGURE 1.8
The Financial Cycle and Reporting

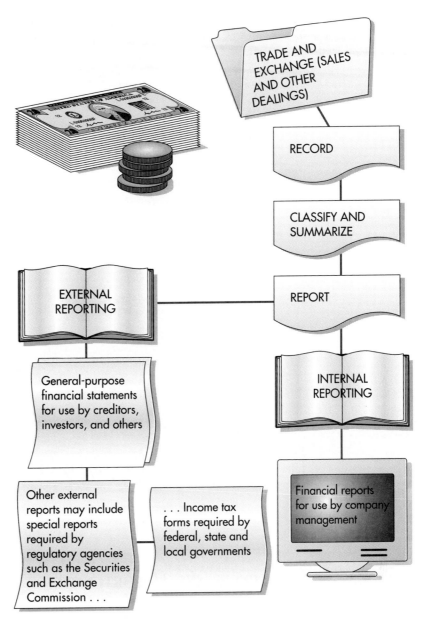

turnover by the number of times a seat was sold during a 24-hour period. Leverage is an indication of how much money has been borrowed or invested in a business. For example, a ski resort wanting to add a new gondola might go to a bank or investor to get the money needed for this expansion. We will explore the importance of finance in later chapters as we examine specific industry segments.

Remember the analogy of the elephant? Financial information is much like the elephant's nervous system. Just as the elephant's nervous system allows it to respond to its environment, an organization's financial information system allows it to read its environment and move in the direction of profitable operations.

Basic knowledge of geography, marketing, management, and finance concepts will provide many of the tools needed for your future success in the tourism industry. However, the importance and practice of hospitality must be added to these basic concepts. To make a profit, managers must use their marketing and management skills to extend hospitality and high-quality service that meet guests' needs. We will explore the importance of providing hospitality and delivering service quality in Chapter 9.

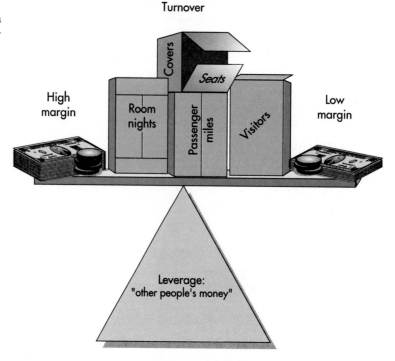

HOSPITALITY

Legend has it that New England sea captains after returning from a voyage speared a pineapple on the iron gates in front of their homes to let it be known that all were welcome. The pineapple has since been known as a symbol of hospitality!

TOURISM'S CHALLENGES AND OPPORTUNITIES

Meeting the needs of travelers by providing tourism-related goods and services has proven to be an attractive form of economic development. Attempts to encourage the development and growth of tourism activities are often desirable because tourism creates jobs and brings money into a community or country. However, unplanned tourism growth can lead to problems.

Although tourism can create greater cultural understanding and enhance economic opportunities, it may also change social structures; may place increasing demands on transportation systems, public services, and utilities; and may lead to environmental degradation. Nowhere do these factors come together in a more visible setting than when countries and cities serve as host sites for Olympic events. Whether we are participants in or beneficiaries of (both positive and negative) tourism activities, we are all in one way or another affected by tourism.

Pause for a moment and consider the following examples of how tourism might affect our lives and communities. For example, tourism could create needed jobs for residents and increase business for local merchants in a small coastal town seeking economic security. However, as that town grows into a more popular destination, it can become overcrowded and the original residents who sought increased tourism expenditures may be driven out because of increased housing costs, higher taxes, and/or changing business demands. Tourism can generate needed funds to improve the lives of an isolated tribe in the rain forests of South America. Yet, it can also forever change the lives of these peoples as they are exposed to the cultures and habits of the tourists who come seeking what they consider to be the ultimate travel experience.

The future of tourism provides many challenges and opportunities as well as many unanswered questions:

- Can tourism growth and development continue without creating environmental problems?
- How will advances in technology change tourism experiences and how tourists and service providers deal with each other?
- As trade barriers are removed and world markets open, will tourism increase?
- As tourism service activities continue to grow, will an adequate workforce with the necessary skills be available?
- Will tourism change the social structure of countries and communities when they experience increased tourism activities?

These are only a few of the questions that may arise as plans are made to respond to the demands of tourism growth. Information presented throughout this book will provide you with the fundamental knowledge necessary to begin forming your own opinions and possible answers to many of the questions and issues that you will face as decision-makers of tomorrow. For a more detailed explanation of problem-solving, decision-making, and ethics, refer to Appendix A.

WHERE DO YOU FIT IN?

The prospects for the future of the tourism industry are bright. In fact, if Jackie were considering a career in tourism today, she would find a wealth of opportunities.

Projections from the World Travel and Tourism Council indicate that tourism will remain the world's largest "industry" and that tourism employment will grow at a rate that is 50% higher than all other industries combined. By the 1990s, 1 in every 15 workers worldwide was working in travel and tourism-related jobs, and the future appears to be promising. Projections indicate that travel and tourism sales will grow at the rate of 4.4% a year, and by the year 2005, worldwide sales will reach $5 trillion.[11] Employment opportunities in the United States appear to be especially positive. As the projections in Table 1.3 show, employment in each of the selected job categories should experience above average growth.

Realizing the significant role tourism plays in everyone's future, we should all attempt to understand how it functions. Only through understanding the participants and forces shaping the tourism industry can we meet the expectations and desires of society. Tourism offers a world of opportunities for you to become involved as either a visitor or service supplier. Like Jackie, you can begin your exploration of tourism through the information presented in this text.

TABLE 1.3
Projected Growth in U.S. Employment by Occupational Category (in thousands)

Categories	1994	2005
Food services and lodging managers	579	771
Chefs, cooks, and other kitchen workers	3237	3739
Food and beverage service occupations	4514	5051
Flight attendants	105	135
Amusement and recreation attendants	267	406
Hotel desk clerks	136	163
Reservation and transportation ticket agents and travel clerks	139	133

Source: Occupational Projections and Training Data, 1996 Edition. U.S. Bureau of Labor Statistics.

Topics Covered in Each Chapter

The text, like our tourism model, is organized around meeting the needs of travelers, who are discussed in detail in Chapter 2. Each of the fundamental participants and forces shaping tourism can be explored through the information presented in the remaining chapters.

Chapter 3 continues our examination of travelers' needs by focusing on tourism promoters who help bring visitors and tourism service suppliers together. Chapters 4, 5, 6, 7, and 8 are devoted to discussing the marketing, management, and financial issues facing primary groups of tourism service suppliers—transportation, accommodations, food and beverage services, attractions and entertainment, and destinations.

Chapter 9 brings us back to the foundations for success in all tourism operations, the support teams, service teams, and hosts who serve travelers' needs. Attracting, selecting, integrating, training, compensating, and building a motivating environment that supports high-quality service are continuous challenges for every tourism operation. In Chapter 9, we will examine successful approaches to managing the most critical resource in any organization—human resources.

Chapters 10 and 11 explore the forces that shape the current and future operating environment for every person and organization that is found in the tourism model. These forces include social/cultural, economic, environmental, and political issues. Chapter 12 explores the future of tourism. Finally, selected readings have been included at the end of the three sections of the book to complement and expand the information provided in the chapters. Integrative cases at the end of the textbook give you an opportunity to apply your knowledge to real world situations.

Questions and exercises at the end of each chapter will allow you to check your knowledge and apply the concepts you have learned. You will also have an opportunity to think about some of the ethical issues facing participants in the tourism industry. Appendix A provides you with the decision-making process and guidelines to ethical behavior to assist you in successfully completing these activities.

Summary

The study of tourism will introduce you to one of the fastest-growing industries in the world. As shown in our model, tourism is a multifaceted service industry that has a rich history and exciting future marked by many challenging opportunities. The career opportunities created from serving the needs of travelers are almost limitless.

Our journey into the study of tourism began with a brief look back in history. History provides many important lessons that help explain the growth and significance of travel in world economies. In fact, the lessons to be learned from history can still be used to help serve the needs of travelers today and in the future. Travel continues to be influenced by factors such as time, money, mobility, and a relative sense of safety.

Tourism industry components, ranging from travel agents to destinations, will be explored in the following chapters. A foundation for examining the development and interdependence of the participants and forces shaping the tourism industry can be gained by considering the importance of geography and the primary functions of all organizations—marketing, management, and finance.

Geography provides a foundation for understanding the development and growth of tourism activities. Marketing, management, and finance concepts will equip you with additional approaches to meet the needs of individuals successfully as they travel. By practicing the art of hospitality, you can use all of your knowledge and skills to meet and exceed visitor expectations. As you explore the world of tourism throughout this book, you will be introduced to the concepts and issues facing tourism today and in the future.

YOU DECIDE

The idea of traveling for education and experience reached its pinnacle in the Grand Tour Era. During that time, travel to locations such as Paris, Rome, and Venice was considered to be the ultimate travel experience. Today's equivalent of the Grand Tour participant, the adventure traveler, may not have the time or money for extended trips, but still seeks the same educational experiences.

Although the adventure traveler may travel to some of the same destinations that were popular on the Grand Tour, these destinations are not new or exotic. Today's adventure traveler seeking new and exotic destinations may be found trekking through Nepal, viewing wildlife on the Galapagos Islands, or braving the elements in Antarctica.

The original Grand Tour participants and today's adventure travelers may have been seeking the same benefits from travel, but their travel impacts were very different. Whereas Grand Tour participants traveled to cities to study, explore, and experience the arts, today's adventure travelers visit remote areas and cultures, seeking new experiences while generating new income sources for the native population. As they popularize these different locations, roads, utilities, buildings, and other environment-altering activities follow.

Think for a moment about the impacts Grand Tour participants had on the areas they visited while traveling throughout Europe. Are the impacts adventure travelers have on today's destinations the same? From an ethical perspective, should tourism activities be encouraged everywhere?

NET TOUR

To learn more about the concepts and organizations presented in this chapter access the home page for *Tourism: The Business of Travel*. Select "Chapter 1: Introduction to Tourism." From this location test your knowledge by taking the chapter quiz, read industry insights, and discover links to other useful sites. You may also want to communicate electronically with other tourism students through the website.

DISCUSSION QUESTIONS

1. Why should we study tourism?

2. History has taught us that people travel and engage in tourism activities in increasing numbers when several basic conditions can be met. Identify and describe these conditions and why they help facilitate travel and tourism activities.

3. What is geography?

4. How do physical, human (cultural), and regional geography influence tourism activities?

5. Why should we study travel and tourism from a marketing approach?

6. Why should we study travel and tourism from a management approach?

7. Why should we study travel and tourism from a financial approach?

8. What are some of the future opportunities and challenges facing the tourism industry?

APPLYING THE CONCEPTS

1. Ask several people of different ages, occupations, and genders to describe tourism to you. Note the differences in their descriptions. List those things which are common in their descriptions as well as some of the distinct differences.

2. Travelers are attracted to countries such as Australia, Canada, England, France, and the United States to participate in tourism activities. However, they have typically avoided countries such as Afghanistan, Cuba, and Iraq. Why are tourists attracted to some countries while they avoid others?

3. Based on your knowledge of the factors and conditions that encourage tourism, find articles in magazines that could explain the popularity of travel and tourism destinations such as Canada, Costa Rica, France, New Zealand, Spain, Thailand, and the United Kingdom. List the things that popular destinations have in common as well as the things that may be missing in less-popular destinations.

4. Go to the reference section at your local library and look at the different types of maps that are available. After selecting or being assigned a nation, state, or

province, make two lists of geographic features: (1) physical and (2) human (cultural). Your lists should provide an overview of significant information that would be of use to someone traveling to the destination you are describing.

5. "Surf" the World Wide Web and find three sources of maps. Prepare a list including Web addresses showing the types of maps available and the information contained on these maps.

GLOSSARY

Accounting A service activity of business designed to accumulate, measure, and communicate financial information to various decision-makers.

Business An organization operated with the objective of making a profit from the sale of goods and services.

Cartography The science or art of making maps and interpreting mapped patterns of physical and human geography.

Feudal system A system of political organization, prevailing in Europe from the ninth to about the fifteenth century, in which ownership of all land was vested in kings or queens.

Host communities Towns or cities that welcome visitors and provide them with desired services.

Human (cultural) geography The human activities that shape the face of a location and shared experiences, including the cultural aspects of language, religion, and political and social structures.

Management The distinct processes of planning, organizing, directing, and controlling people and other resources to achieve organizational objectives efficiently and effectively.

Marketing concept An overall organizational philosophy that is focused on understanding and meeting the needs of customers.

Marketing mix Those things that an organization can do to influence the demand for its goods or services. It consists of four variables, often called the four Ps of marketing: product, price, place, and promotion.

Model A simple representation showing how important features of a system fit together.

Physical geography The natural features of our planet, including such things as climate, land masses, bodies of water, and resources.

Profits Revenues in excess of expenses representing the financial per-

formance and the ultimate measure of the financial success of a business.

Regional geography The components of geography that focus on regional landscapes, cultures, economies, and political and social systems.

Return on investment (ROI) A measure of management's efficiency, showing the return on all of an organization's assets.

Services The performance of actions or efforts on behalf of another.

Standard industrial classification (SIC) code A classification system developed by the Census Bureau to collect and report information from similar establishments in the same industry.

Tourism "The temporary movement of people to destinations outside their normal places of work and residence, the activities undertaken during their stay in those destinations, and the facilities created to cater to their needs."

REFERENCES

1. Travel and tourism: Home and away (1998, January 10). *The Economist*, pp. 4–16.

2. D'Amore, Louis (1988, summer). Tourism—The world's peace industry. *Journal of Travel Research*, pp. 35–40.

3. Waters, Somerset R. (1990, February). The U.S. travel industry: Where we're going. *The Cornell Hotel Restaurant Administration Quarterly*, pp. 26–33.

4. Matheison, Alister, & Wall, Geoffrey (1982). Tourism—Economic, physical, and social impacts. *Annals of Tourism Research, 6*, 390–407.

5. Hunt, J. D., & Layne, D. (1991, spring). Evolution of travel and tourism terminology and definitions. *Journal of Travel Research*, pp. 7–11.

6. Towner, John (1988). Approaches to tourism history. *Annals of Tourism Research, 15*, 47–62.

7. Cohen, Eric (1972). Towards a sociology of international tourism. *Social Research, 39*(1), 164–182.

8. Cook, Roy A., & Yale, Laura J. (1994). In search of a common body of knowledge for introductory tourism courses. *Hospitality & Tourism Educator, 6*(2), 39–41.

9. Jafari, Jafar, & Brent Richie, J. R. (1981). Toward a framework for tourism education. *Annals of Tourism Research, 8*, 13–34.

10. Coming to America (1993, February 22). *Travel Weekly*, p. 43.

11. Jesitus, John (1993, January 11). International report. *Hotel & Motel Management*, pp. 19, 31.

CHAPTER 2

Tourists: The Traveling Public

Outdoor activities attract a wide variety of tourists.
Photo by D.A. Yale.

I have wandered all my life, and I also traveled; the difference between the two being this, that we wander for distraction, but we travel for fulfillment.

—HILAIRE BELLOC

CHAPTER OUTLINE

LEARNING OBJECTIVES

After you have read this chapter, you should be able to:

- Explain the importance of segmenting the tourism market.

- Identify the three major foundations for understanding tourism motivations.

- List and describe the steps involved in segmenting a market.

- Describe the major approaches that are used to segment the tourism market.

- Discuss the importance of business, mature, and international travelers to tourism service suppliers.

- Describe how information gained from segmenting the tourism market can be used to target and meet the wants, needs, and expectations of the traveling public.

A RIDE ON THE WILD SIDE!

"Let's start our own rafting business!" When Jim first mentioned the idea to Andy, they both laughed. Sure, they had been raft guides during summer breaks, but what did they really know about starting and running a business? As they stared through their dorm window at the leaves falling from the trees and thought about their summer adventures, they began to talk about the possibilities.

It had all started on a summer vacation. Like many tourists who visit the Rocky Mountains, they had taken a whitewater rafting trip. During this trip, they struck up a conversation with Casey, the owner of the company. At first, what they learned from Casey seemed almost too good to be true. Was it really possible to spend the summer months guiding people through the rapids on a beautiful mountain river and earn a living at the same time?

The lure of the outdoors, the river, and job offers to work for Casey as raft guides pulled them back to that same small mountain town the following summer. Casey, like most business owners in small tourist towns, was always looking for good potential employees. When he asked Jim and Andy to come back and work for him the next summer, they jumped at the opportunity.

Now, after two summers of experience, Jim wanted Andy to help him start their own whitewater rafting business. Once Andy said yes to the idea, things really started happening. They scanned maps of the Rocky Mountain region to locate premier rafting rivers and thumbed through every outdoor enthusiast magazine they could find. They wrote to government agencies in every location that looked interesting to find out what types of permits and licenses were needed. After months of research, they decided on the perfect location.

On spring break, they visited the town where they wanted to set up their business. It was perfect: no other rafting companies in town and a great place for rent with a barn and an old house right on the river. Everything seemed to fall into place. Jim's grandmother agreed to lend them enough money to purchase their equipment, and two of their college professors helped them to develop a business plan. Casey even offered them some words of encouragement as they prepared to launch their new business.

After graduation, Jim and Andy were ready to put their knowledge and experience to work. They moved in, hung up their sign, opened the doors, and waited for the customers to come to their new business, A Ride on the Wild Side! June was a great month, but July and August were even better! In fact, business was so good and they were so busy, they almost didn't notice a story in the local paper announcing the granting of a permit for another rafting company.

When the rafting season was over, Jim and Andy stored their equipment, counted their profits, discussed their successes and mistakes, and began to think about next year. What would the new competition mean for them? There had been plenty of customers this year, but what about next year? Would there be enough business for two companies? Who were their customers? Where did they come from? How did they find out about A Ride on the Wild Side? Would they return? Would they tell others about their experiences?

To continue their success and prosper with new competition on the horizon, they needed to know more about marketing and customer service. As they thought about the future, they realized many of the lessons they had learned about business in their college courses would be useful.

INTRODUCTION

In the first chapter, we presented a model highlighting the scope and complexity of the tourism industry. Referring back to this model, you will notice that at the center is the focal point and primary reason for all tourism activities: travelers. In this chapter, we will learn more about these travelers (tourists) and how we can plan to meet their wants and needs successfully. Take a minute to look around and notice all the different types of people at your college or university. The diversity of this group may be similar in many ways to the diversity of guests being served in the tourism industry. Since these tourists are at the heart of the industry, we need to know more about who they are, why they travel, and what they expect during their travels.

Any number of activities, including seeking the assistance of a travel agent, flying to another city, or walking through the gates of a theme park, changes a person into an active participant using tourism services. As consumers of these tourism services, we have sometimes similar, as well as different needs. In response to the tasks of understanding consumers, their needs, and the actions they take to satisfy these needs, a whole branch of marketing, **consumer behavior,** has developed.

Consumer behavior is the study of consumer characteristics and the processes involved when individuals or groups select, purchase, and use goods and services to satisfy wants and needs. How we behave as consumers is determined by a variety of interpersonal influences (for example, we learn how to make shopping decisions from our parents) and by our individual characteristics (gender, age, personality, etc.). Consumers will continue to return and use goods and services as long as their needs are met. Consequently, we need to learn more about who these consumers are and what they need and want.

FOUNDATIONS FOR UNDERSTANDING TOURIST MOTIVATIONS

In Chapter 1 you learned that humans have traveled away from their homes throughout history. What has motivated people to leave familiar surroundings and travel to distant places? In this section we will consider what psychological reasons compel individuals to travel. Psychologists have long studied motivations for a variety of human behaviors, including the drive to travel. We will discuss three of the most well accepted theories for tourist motivations: Maslow's hierarchy of needs, Pearce's leisure ladder, and Plog's allocentric–psychocentric continuum.

Maslow's Hierarchy of Needs

Abraham Maslow provided a good general framework for describing human needs in his classic model depicting the hierarchy of needs.[1] This hierarchy, as can be seen in Figure 2.1, begins at the bottom with basic physiological needs and progresses up through safety, belongingness, esteem, and self-actualization needs.

Maslow further grouped these needs into two broader categories: lower-order and higher-order needs. He believed that this hierarchy of needs was shared by everyone. While the hierarchy of needs model was developed to explain human behavior and motivation in general, we will see later in the chapter how these same concepts can be applied specifically to tourists.

To understand an individual's behavior, we begin at the bottom of the hierarchy and move upward. As each level of needs is satisfied, individuals move up to the next higher level of needs. At the lowest levels are basic physiological and safety needs. Basic physiological needs consist of food, water, clothing, shelter, and sleep. Next are safety needs, which consist of protection, security, and the comfort we seek from familiar surroundings. In advanced economies of developed countries like Australia, Canada, Great Britain, Japan, and the United States, most consumers' lower-order physiological and safety needs have been met. Since these needs have been satisfied, they are no longer motivators. Individuals often strive to fulfill their higher-order needs through travel.

These higher-order needs include belongingness, esteem, and self-actualization. Belongingness needs include love, friendship, affiliation, and group acceptance. Esteem needs include the desire for status, self-respect, and success. The highest level in Maslow's hierarchy of needs is self-actualization or the desire for self-fulfillment.

Travelers may be seeking to fulfill more than one need when they participate in a tourism activity. Let's put the ideas in Maslow's hierarchy of needs into practice by looking at specific examples in the tourism industry.

FIGURE 2.1
Maslow's Hierarchy of Needs

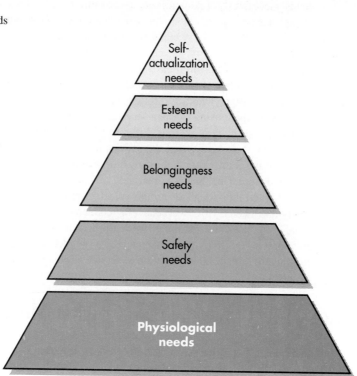

Physiological:

- Tour packages that offer frequent rest stops
- Easily accessible food outlets in theme parks
- Sleeping shelters strategically located along the Appalachian Trail for overnight visitors

Safety:

- Reservation service provided at government-approved agencies or locations
- Cruise ship lines providing medical facilities and doctors as part of their standard services
- Tour guide services provided in exotic or unfamiliar locations.

Belongingness:

- Group tours with people having similar interests and/or backgrounds
- Group recognition gained by belonging to frequent-user programs provided by airlines, hotels, restaurants, and car rental companies
- Trips made to explore one's ancestral roots

Esteem:

- Elite status in frequent-user programs such as gold, silver, or bronze "memberships"
- **Incentive travel** awards for superior company performance
- Flowers, champagne, and other tokens provided to guests in recognition of special occasions

Self-actualization:

- Educational tours and cruises
- Theme parks providing educational opportunities and glimpses of other cultures
- Learning the language and culture before traveling to another country

The hierarchy-of-needs model provides a good foundation as well as a brief glimpse into the fundamentals of motivation. Can you think of other examples?

The Leisure Ladder Model

The leisure ladder model developed by Pearce[2] is similar to Maslow's Hierarchy of Needs, but it goes further by providing more detailed insights into specific tourist behaviors. The leisure ladder model attempts to explain individual behaviors on the basis of stages in a tourist's life cycle. When you think about tourist life cycle stages, it may be helpful to remember that they are very similar to the stages individuals experience in their working careers. Just as a person tentatively enters a career and eventually becomes more proficient and effective based on experience, so do tourists as they venture into leisure activities.

According to Pearce, tourists move through a hierarchy (or series of steps) similar to the one depicted by Maslow. They must first take care of relaxation and bodily needs before they can move up to the successively higher rungs of stimulation, relationship, self-esteem and development, and fulfillment on the leisure ladder. Figure 2.2 shows an example of the various levels in this leisure ladder as applied in a theme park setting. An additional attempt to further understand and broadly describe the differing wants and needs of tourists has resulted in a widely used model developed by Stanley Plog.[3]

The Psychocentric–Allocentric Model

Based on observable and consistent patterns of behavior, it is possible to use personality characteristics to further understand tourists' behavior patterns (see Table 2.1). Plog[3] accomplished this task by classifying tourists along a continuum with **allocentrics** anchoring one end and **psychocentrics** anchoring the other. In general, allocentric travelers are seeking adventure while psychocentric travelers are seeking the comforts of familiar surroundings in their tourism experiences. However, as the model shows, most travelers fall between these two extremes and would be classified as near-allocentrics, midcentrics, and near-psychocentrics.

The allocentric traveler found at one extreme of Plog's continuum (see Figure 2.3) would be referred to by marketers as an "innovator." These innovators seek out new locations and activities before they are discovered by others. As more people become aware of these locations and activities, information about them is communicated or diffused to more and more people. Interest in traveling to these new locations or experiencing these new activities passes from the allocentric to the midcentric and eventually to the psychocentric as these locations or activities become commonplace.

The psychocentric traveler found at the opposite extreme of Plog's continuum would most likely be tradition-bound and tend to be uncomfortable with new and different activities and/or locations. These individuals would be interested only in visiting popular locations and participating in customary activities. They desire predictability and the comforting reassurance that other visitors have enjoyed the same experiences.

Travelers with psychocentric tendencies throughout the world can enter a McDonald's restaurant and find a familiar atmosphere and menu. On the other extreme, travelers with allocentric orientations may be drawn by the allure of seeking out unique travel and tourism experiences that have previously gone unnoticed. Taking a rubber raft down the headwaters of the Amazon River or trekking among the highland villages of Nepal might appeal to the allocentric traveler today, but they will be looking for something new and different tomorrow.

The creators of the Disney mystique may be catering to a broad cross section of visitors. For psychocentric travelers, a Disney theme park assures them of similarity and consistency in operations. However, Disney is continually adding new attractions and entertainment to appeal to a broader market group of visitors. How would you classify yourself along this continuum?

FIGURE 2.2
The Leisure Ladder Model in a Theme Park Setting.
Source: Pearce, Douglas G., & Butler, Richard W. eds. (1993). *Tourism Research Critiques and Challenges*, London: Routledge.

People tend to ascend the ladder as they become older, and more experienced in theme park settings

Higher-level motives include lower-level motives. One motive at a time tends to be dominant. Lower-level motives have to be satisfied or experienced before higher-level steps on the ladder come into play

Fulfillment
People in this group are concerned with feeling peaceful, profoundly happy, magical, transported to another world, spiritual, and totally involved in the setting.

Self-Esteem and Development
People in this group are concerned with developing their skills, knowledge, and abilities. They are concerned with how others see them and want to be competent, in control, respected, and productive.

Relationship
People in this category are seeking to build and extend their personal relationships. They may emphasize tenderness and affection, joint fun, joint activities, altruism – enjoying events through others as well as being directly involved. People here emphasize the creation of a shared history of good times.

Stimulation
People in this group are concerned with the management of their arousal levels. They want to be safe but not bored, excited but not truly terrified. They emphasize the fun and thrill of rides, the experience of unusual, out-of-the-ordinary settings, and different foods and people. The positive side of this level is to heighten or increase one's stimulation and arousal. The negative side is to avoid dangerous or threatening situations.

Relaxation and Bodily Needs
People in this group are involved in restoration, personal maintenance, and repair. They emphasize basic services (food, space, toilets) and enjoy a sense of escape and the lack of demands on them.

SEGMENTING THE TOURISM MARKET

The old saying, "You can't please all the people all the time," certainly holds true for tourism service suppliers. Since you can't please everyone, whom should you please? One common approach to answering this question is to focus marketing efforts by segmenting potential customers into groups with fairly similar wants and needs.

Identifying tourism customers and deciding how to meet their wants and needs is a basic task facing everyone in the tourism industry. In large organizations, this task is often given to marketing professionals. In smaller organizations like Jim and Andy's, A Ride on the Wild Side!, this responsibility might remain with the owner or manager.

As we discussed in Chapter 1, the marketing concept creates a customer-oriented philosophy that is essential to meeting visitors' wants and needs. Let's think about the

TABLE 2.1
Psychocentric–Allocentric Personality Characteristics

Psychocentrics	Allocentrics
Prefer familiar travel destinations	Prefer non-"touristy" destinations
Like commonplace activities at destinations	Enjoy discovering new destinations before others have visited them
Prefer relaxing sun-and-fun spots	Prefer unusual destinations
Prefer low activity levels	Prefer high activity levels
Prefer driving to destinations	Prefer flying to destinations
Prefer heavy tourist accommodations, such as hotel development, family-style restaurants, and souvenir shops	Prefer services such as adequate to good accommodations and food and few developed tourist attractions
Prefer familiar rather than foreign atmospheres	Enjoy interacting with people from different cultures
Prefer purchasing complete tour packages featuring a full schedule of activities	Prefer tour arrangements that include basics (transportation and accommodations) and allow for considerable flexibility

Source: Plog, Stanley C. (1974, February). Why destinations rise and fall in popularity. *The Cornell Hotel & Restaurant Administration Quarterly*, 55–58.

questions raised by Jim and Andy as they considered the future of their rafting business. They both agreed on the importance of knowing more about marketing and customer service, but they weren't sure where to start.

The starting point for any organization planning to implement the marketing concept is to learn more about its customers. But, who are these customers? Although it may sound appealing to think of everyone as a potential customer, marketers have learned that this usually does not lead to a high level of customer satisfaction. A common example with which we can all identify will help explain this statement.

Imagine for a moment you are the president of Ford Motor Company. You decide that it would be profitable to come up with the perfect car—a car everyone would want to drive. Is such a dream possible? If you designed the "average" car—four doors, six cylinders, bright blue, large trunk—do you think every potential car buyer would be equally satisfied with this car? Of course not. Some car buyers want small, two-door, inexpensive, economical cars while others want large, powerful vans. Now, let's put this same mass-marketing idea into a tourism setting. Could you design an "average" vacation pack-

FIGURE 2.3
Psychographic Positions of Destinations

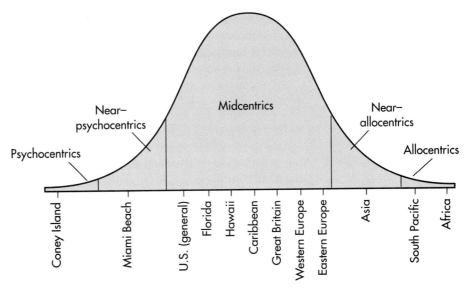

age that would satisfy everyone? Probably not, since trying to meet everyone's needs and wants with the same services would prove to be an impossible task.

The task of meeting diverse needs and wants led to the idea of **market segmentation.** Instead of trying to meet everyone's needs and wants with a single product or service, marketers divide the large, **heterogeneous** market for a good or service into smaller but more **homogeneous** market segments. A heterogeneous market is one composed of people having differing characteristics and needs while a homogeneous market is one with people of similar characteristics and needs.

The task of grouping millions of travelers into groups with similar needs and wants may appear to be a bit complex at first. However, this process can be simplified if we begin to think of the tourism market as a large jigsaw puzzle. Each piece of this puzzle (i.e., each consumer) is unique. Once several pieces are put together, they begin to form similar-looking sections (market segments). Finally, when all of these sections of the puzzle are put together, they form the whole picture (the market).

As you saw in Chapter 1, it is possible to begin segmenting the tourism market by using the broad reasons people give for traveling: vacation and leisure, visiting friends and relatives, and business and professional. Although these broad reasons for travel may provide some initial insight into potential tourism market segments, they do not provide the level of detail needed to understand specific consumer needs. What is needed are segmentation approaches that clearly describe travelers and that can be used as a basis for planning to meet their needs and wants.

Common approaches (called "bases") to segmenting markets can be achieved by grouping customers according to the following variables:

1. geographic characteristics,
2. demographic characteristics,
3. psychographic characteristics, and
4. product-related characteristics.

These segmentation variables provide a good starting point as we begin to fit the pieces of the tourist jigsaw puzzle into a meaningful picture. Each of these segmentation approaches also serves to highlight the breadth, depth, and differences to be found among individuals and groups of tourists. However, as we begin to study groups of travelers, don't lose sight of the importance of meeting individual needs. Remember, Maslow, Pearce, and Plog showed that although we may behave in similar ways, we are all still individuals!

Geographic Segmentation

Geographic segmentation (grouping potential tourism customers based on their location) is the oldest and simplest basis for market segmentation. Even though people in the same geographic location do not usually have similar wants and needs, their location often has an important impact on their selection of tourism goods and services. Commonly used geographic segmentation variables include nations, regions, states/provinces, counties/parishes, cities, and even neighborhoods.

Geographic segmentation has proven especially useful in segmenting the traveling public. Many tourism facilities and attractions market their services regionally, recognizing that the time and money involved in traveling makes them more attractive to consumers within a certain defined geographic area. For example, the Walt Disney Company advertises Disneyland, located in California, heavily in the Western United States and the Pacific Rim countries (such as Japan) while it markets Walt Disney World, located in Florida, more heavily in the Eastern United States and Europe. On a smaller scale, Killington Ski Resort in Vermont is promoted to skiers in Northeastern North America whereas Purgatory Resort outside Durango, Colorado, tries to attract skiers primarily from the Southern and Western United States. Would geographic segmentation provide useful information to Jim and Andy about their potential customers?

Most ski areas have a strong regional appeal.
Photo courtesy of Winter Park Resort.

Demographic Segmentation

While geographic segmentation is the simplest and oldest approach to grouping tourists, **demographic segmentation** is the basis most commonly used for market segmentation. Using this approach, consumers are grouped according to variables that define them in an objective, easily measurable way. These variables include several classifications such as gender, age, ethnicity, occupation, education level, income, household size, and family situation. **Demographics** are frequently used by marketers because information about people's objective characteristics is routinely collected and widely available. A gold mine of segmentation information can be found in data gathered and reported by Statistics Canada and the U.S. Bureau of the Census for marketers who know how to use it.

Examples of tourism organizations using demographic segmentation abound. Club Med is using demographic segmentation when it attempts to serve the needs of two distinct market segments. One segment is composed of young singles and the other of high-income married couples with children. Tour operators and cruise lines are using demographic segmentation when they develop special tours or cruises featuring nostalgic, educational, religious, or ethnic experiences. Can you think of other examples?

Psychographic Segmentation

Geographic and demographic variables provide easy approaches to segmenting travelers, but we all know that people are much more different than these simple pieces of information might suggest. For example, most of us listen to music. And, even though age is an important factor in determining the type of music different people enjoy, you probably know people of similar ages who have different tastes. Some twenty-somethings enjoy rap music while some enjoy old-fashioned rock and roll and still others prefer the sounds of the forties-era swing bands. These differences come from what marketers call "**psychographic** variables."

Psychographic segmentation involves grouping people on how they live, their priorities and their interests. Put all this together and you have a description of a person's lifestyle and personality. Psychographic segmentation has been used by cruise lines and resorts to target individuals with similar hobbies, sports, and musical interests.

A **lifestyle** is broadly defined as a way of living identified by how people spend their time (activities), what they consider important (interests), and what they think of themselves and the world around them (opinions). Some examples of activities, interests, and opinions that might be important to those working in the tourism industry are included in Table 2.2.

The idea of segmenting travelers based on activities, interests, and opinions might seem familiar, since this approach was popularized by Stanley Plog in his psychocentric–allocentric continuum. More recently, three large psychographic segments have been identified in the American travel market. In a proprietary (privately funded) study based on survey information collected from thousands of travelers, a research firm developed segments by associating values expressed by the survey respondents and the type of vacations they preferred.

The largest segment they identified is termed the "family getaway traveler" (38% of American travelers). This segment values family time above all else and seeks activities that all members of the family can enjoy together. The second segment is called the "adventurous/education traveler" (31%). This type of traveler values physical activity and challenge, and enjoys interacting with nature. Segment three is composed of "romantics" (28%). As the name suggests, these travelers value intimate companionship and have a primary desire for comfort and relaxation. Do you see yourself fitting into any of these categories?

Product-Related Segmentation

The previously mentioned bases for segmentation—geographic, demographic, and psychographic—are all used to help marketers move closer to the goal of developing product offerings that better satisfy potential tourism consumers. However, in all these cases, we are indirectly grouping people based on characteristics we *assume* are related to their needs and wants. Since assumptions can sometimes get us into trouble, marketers often try to segment less indirectly and more directly: They attempt to group potential buyers *directly* from what people indicate they need or want in a particular good or service. These product-related variables include:

1. the benefits people seek in the good or service (for example, the ability to guarantee the availability of a room at a hotel);

TABLE 2.2
Psychographic Lifestyle Dimensions

Activities	Interests	Opinions
Work	Family	Themselves
Hobbies	Home	Social issues
Social events	Job	Politics
Vacation	Community	Business
Entertainment	Recreation	Economics
Club membership	Fashion	Education
Community	Food	Products
Shopping	Media	Future
Sports	Achievements	Culture

Source: Wells, William D., & Tigert, Douglas J. (1971). Activities, interests, and opinions. *Journal of Advertising Research, 11,* 27–35.

2. the amount of good or service use (light users such as occasional leisure travelers versus heavy users such as business travelers); and

3. the degree of company loyalty shown by the consumer in relation to the specific good or service (participation in frequent-user programs).

In Chapter 1 we mentioned that travelers are frequently grouped into leisure versus business categories. These groupings serve as good examples of **product-related segmentation.** Tourism suppliers know that travelers seek different benefits based on the purposes of their trips. Think about the benefits a businessperson seeks in accommodations compared to the benefits desired by a person traveling on a holiday or vacation. How would these benefits differ?

Business travelers tend to be the "heavy users" of many tourism services, especially air transportation, hotels, and rental cars. Airlines, hotels, and rental car companies have responded to these needs by developing services and forms of promotion that appeal especially to these busy frequent travelers. Services such as ticketless travel, computer ports in hotel rooms, and the computerized check-in kiosks at many airport rental car locations were all developed to appeal to this special group of travelers. Finally, in a special appeal to this group, frequent-user programs were developed expressly to encourage and reward loyalty and repeat patronage.

Putting Segmentation Knowledge to Work

Now that you know some of the basic approaches to market segmentation, you are faced with yet another challenge: when to segment. It would be nice if we could neatly categorize and slice up all travelers into distinct market segments. However, we can encounter several problems in attempting to segment markets. For example, some markets might be too small to segment. In addition, each of us can be classified as members of many different markets, which tends to complicate the segmentation task.

There are almost as many potential market segments as there are groups of people. In fact, many market segments that were not even considered a few years ago, such as disabled travelers and environmental/ecology travelers, are growing in size and importance.

The task of deciding when to segment can be clarified by answering the following questions:

- Can the market segment be relatively easily identified and measured in both purchasing power and size?
- Is the segment large enough to be potentially profitable?
- Can the segment be reached efficiently and effectively through advertising and other forms of promotion?
- Is the segment interested in the service offered?
- Is the segment expected to be long-term and will it grow or shrink in size?[4]

While this list of questions helps narrow the range of potential segments, the most important reason for segmenting should not be forgotten. Segmenting permits tourism service suppliers to meet specific customer needs and wants better while attempting to increase their satisfaction. Once a segmentation approach has been selected, the next task is to decide which of these segments to target.

Marketers use a five-step approach to accomplish this market segmentation decision process. In Step 1, they choose one or more of the segmentation approaches we have previously described for grouping individuals. Even though we introduced each basis for segmentation separately, most organizations tend to use a combination of these approaches. For example, the Vancouver Aquarium, in British Columbia, might define its market in terms of geographic location and demographic profile. The Aquarium's marketing team might break the potential market for its educational and entertainment services into two geographic segments, such as people within a 200-mile radius of Vancouver and those living more than 200 miles away, and then further group potential visitors by age and family situation.

In Step 2, each segment is profiled in as much detail as is cost effective. This greater amount of detail provides a more accurate understanding of the needs of the segments and is used in developing a basic outline of the **marketing mix** that each segment would require. Continuing with our example, management of the Vancouver Aquarium may decide to conduct a comprehensive consumer research study to gather detailed information about the visitors to the aquarium. The decision-makers can then develop more-thorough profiles of the various segments. In acquiring this consumer information, the research team would need to survey consumers who visit the attraction at different times of the year. Visitors during July may tend to be international travelers from the United States and Japan while visitors in December may tend to be Vancouver locals and other British Columbians.

In Step 3, forecasts are developed for the market potential of each segment being considered. All segments will not be the same in terms of number of potential buyers and amount of purchasing power, nor will they be equally likely to desire the good or service.

In Step 4, an "educated guess" about the share of each segment's business that the organization is likely to be able to achieve is prepared. Some segments are likely to find the organization's offerings more appealing than other segments.

In Step 5, the decision is made as to which segment or segments will be targeted, that is, for which segments a specific marketing mix will be developed. These segments then become the organization's **target markets.** Returning to our example, although school trips to the aquarium are plentiful and acquaint thousands of area youngsters with its marine species, this segment does not bring in large revenues to cover the cost of operations. Other segments with more purchasing power will also need to be attracted to generate the money necessary to keep the aquarium "afloat."

Based on the information gathered in this five-step process, marketers are able to develop sets of "product, place, promotion, and price" that they hope will be attractive to the segments they have chosen to target. As an illustration, the marketing director of the Vancouver Aquarium may decide that the "within 200 mile radius married retiree" segment has great potential during the fall. She may therefore develop a marketing package that offers these consumers special guided tours (including lunch) on Tuesdays during September and October for one all-inclusive price. She may advertise this package on area radio stations that feature swing-era music.

The process of segmenting larger markets and then targeting these specific segments furnishes tourism organizations with the tools to focus their attention on providing appropriate levels of service to their most likely customers. Just like the time and effort it takes to put together an intricate jigsaw puzzle, it may also require time and commitment to identify potential groups of tourism consumers, but the effort will be worth it. When wants and needs are identified and met, tourists will return and often tell others who share similar characteristics about their positive experiences.

SPECIALIZED TOURIST SEGMENTS

There are four large and distinctive segments of tourism consumers that deserve special discussion because of their sizes and importance to the industry. These segments are business and **professional travelers** (product-related segmentation), *incentive travelers* (product-related segmentation), *mature travelers* (demographic segmentation) and *international travelers* (geographic segmentation). Let's take a brief look at the size, importance, and common characteristics of each of these segments.

Business and Professional Travelers

Business travel is considered to be the backbone or "bread and butter" of the tourism industry because businesspeople are often required to travel as a part of their day-to-day activities. Since travel is a part of their jobs, the amount of money they spend on tourism services tends to stay fairly constant, and they are not as price-sensitive as vacation and leisure travelers. Therefore, the demand for business travel services is fairly inelastic. When demand does not significantly change with price fluctuations, it is said to be **inelastic**. In contrast, when demand changes substantially as price fluctuates, it is referred to as **elastic**. The demand for vacation and leisure travel and tourism services is elastic since it can be significantly influenced by changes in prices.

The prices travelers pay for airline tickets provide an excellent example highlighting differences between inelastic and elastic demands. When looking at air fares, you may have noticed the least expensive air fares are the ones booked the furthest in advance of the scheduled departure date. Since businesspeople typically have to travel on short notice, they are willing to pay higher fares to obtain needed services (inelastic demand). However, since leisure travel is elastic and these individuals can plan their trips in advance, they are attracted to lower air fares. How would the concepts of inelastic and elastic demand work for a downtown commercial hotel experiencing heavy demand from business travelers during the weekdays while attempting to fill the rooms with leisure travelers on the weekend?

As companies become more global in their activities, business travel should continue to grow. "Once a small part of corporate travel budgets, international travel has grown sharply since the early 1980s. It now accounts for 10 to 20% of the more than $100 billion U.S. companies spend on travel annually."[5] In fact, travel and the expenses related to travel are the third largest expense for corporations, right after labor and information-processing expenses.[6]

Since business travelers are so important to the profitability and potential success of most tourism service suppliers, it is important for us to know more about these individuals. There are several characteristics that are common to many business travelers, as can be seen in the information provided in Table 2.3.

Professional travelers are similar to business travelers in many ways, although this type of travel is more elastic than business travel. Professional travel is built around the meeting and convention markets. These markets have grown as transportation, especially by air, has become more available and affordable. As professional travel continues to grow, new and expanded meeting and convention facilities have been developed to satisfy this increasing demand. Along with this growth, new management challenges have arisen to serve this specialized market. Some of the key market segments for meeting participants or attendees are associations, businesses, exhibitions and trade shows, religious organizations, political parties, and governments.

For many years, forecasters have predicted the demise of business and professional travel based on the increasing availability and sophistication of electronic communication technology. Although the long-term viability of these segments has been questioned, the

TABLE 2.3
Business Traveler Profile

Total Trips	207,800,000
Average number of household members on trip	1.3
Average number of nights per trip	3.1
Average miles per trip	1022
Traveled by car	63%
Traveled by air	35%
Used a rental car during business trip	22%
Stayed in hotel	66%
Used a travel agent in trip planning	24%
Combined vacationing with business trip	14%
Male	74%
Female	26%

Source: Statistical Abstract of the United States 1997 (117th ed.). Washington, D.C.: U.S. Bureau of the Census. (Based on domestic U.S. travel during 1995.)

future appears to be bright since face-to-face relationships should continue to be an integral part of business and professional activities.[7] The value of face-to-face relations is especially important in international negotiations.

Many futurists have also predicted a decline in business and professional travel with the introduction of **teleconferencing.** However, people continue to have a strong desire to meet each other face-to-face. Although teleconferencing serves to introduce people to each other electronically, they will eventually want to meet in person to interact and network. This need for personal contact and interaction has allowed the business travel market to grow even in the face of advancing technology.

In response to the needs of the business travel segment, tourism service suppliers have offered a wide array of services and benefits. Airlines instituted frequent-flier programs and service upgrades including business class and provided corporate pricing, discounts and rebates; travel lounges; and preferred check-ins. Amtrak developed club service with reserved seating, snack and beverage service, telephones, and conference rooms on some trains. Car rental companies, following the lead of airlines, established frequent-renter programs, which provided corporate pricing, discounts, rebates, upgrades, and special check-in procedures. Hotels and other lodging properties have provided similar benefits to business travelers including corporate pricing, discounts, and rebates; special floors and sections including business centers; frequent stay programs; and **upgrades.**

Business travelers will continue to become more demanding of tourism service suppliers as they come to expect the current level of services and benefits as a standard level of performance. The challenge of retaining and satisfying these individuals will depend on identifying the aspects of the travel and tourism experience that can be modified or improved to truly delight these demanding tourists.

The Marriott Company provides a good example of how to further segment the business and professional travel market successfully. It has designed four types of lodging facilities to serve four distinct segments. The first is the full-service Marriott Hotel that is targeted to the business traveler who wants all the facilities needed while on business trips, such as secretarial support, room service, conference rooms, a variety of restaurants, and other services. The second, Courtyard by Marriott, was designed expressly with the "limited expense account" businessperson in mind. This type of traveler wants the basics of a business hotel but doesn't have the budget to pay for the extras not used. The third concept is Fairfield Inn. It was designed to appeal to the traveler who is simply looking for a clean, comfortable room for the night with none of the extras. Finally, the fourth concept is Residence Inns, which was designed to meet the wants and needs of the business traveler seeking the comforts of home for an extended stay.

Identifying and meeting the needs of various market segments.
Photo courtesy of Marriott Lodging at Miami International Airport.

Until recently, these styles of lodging had been built separately and usually quite a distance from their sister hotels. In an intriguing move, Marriott recently renovated the 782-room Miami Airport Marriott into three hotels: a 365-room, full-service Marriott, a 125-room Courtyard by Marriott, and a 285-room Fairfield Inn. The original hotel had three parts—a main tower and two low-rise buildings in the back. Management realized there was a demand for a Courtyard and a Fairfield Inn, but no available area to build on. Vóila! The two lower buildings were converted to appeal to the unserved segments.[8]

Incentive Travelers

One of the faster-growing segments of the tourism industry is incentive travel, which generates over 11 million trips annually worldwide.[9] Employee productivity and motivation are a concern for all organizations, and incentive travel awards are an attempt to achieve higher levels of both. Incentive programs are designed to create competition, with the winner(s) receiving many different types of awards, including complete holiday get-away packages. The good news for the tourism industry is that, in general, if properly planned, people will work harder to receive an incentive trip than any other type of reward, including cash.

Planning incentive travel awards requires creating a party format for celebrating achievement so the settings for celebrating these successes are spectacular by design. Typical destination locations for recipient awards include Hawaii, Europe, and the Caribbean Islands. Trips to these locations often involve recognition award banquets and many other special activities where the recipients can be honored and pampered.

All aspects of incentive travel are structured so that everything is first class, filled with surprises, and arranged so that participants never have to pay for anything. The incentive travel segment demands the best in service, but, at the same time, is willing to pay **incentive tour operators** top dollar for these services.

Mature Travelers

Another large and growing segment of tourism consumers is mature travelers. The face of the industrialized world's population is changing, as are the profiles of individuals who take advantage of the ever-increasing array of leisure activities. Although it is probably a mistake to lump all mature travelers together into a single market, it is important to understand the immense size of this market. A good idea of the changes taking place in the mature segment of the tourism market can be seen by looking at the changes taking place in the United States. The American population is aging and will continue to increase as a percentage of the total population. By the year 2000, over 76 million Americans will be considered **mature adults** (55 years of age and older).[10] Similar demographic shifts are taking place in many countries throughout the world.

The number of senior citizens in the United States who compose the market segment called "mature travelers" has been growing at double-digit rates. This rapid growth provides many opportunities for firms who recognize and plan to meet the needs of these travelers. The mature traveler market segment is especially important since these individuals spend 30% more than younger travelers and account for 80% of all commercial vacation travel.[11]

Other significant facts about this group of travelers in the United States that may have gone unnoticed or unappreciated are as follows:

* They are the fastest-growing segment of the travel market.
* They control over three-quarters of the United State's disposable wealth.[12]
* They control over 50% of the United State's **disposable income.**[13]

Findings from two recent surveys (see Table 2.4) of travelers over the age of 50 provide useful insights into the needs and expectations of this growing market.

Many mature visitors have the time, money, and energy to travel and enjoy family, friends, new sights, adventures, and active lifestyles. "Most importantly, there must al-

TABLE 2.4
Profile of Mature Travelers

Value excellent food while vacationing more than any other age group
Less interested in bars and nightlife activities than other age groups
Age group most likely to take cruise vacations
Age group most likely to visit casinos
Travel primarily for pleasure: 37% to visit friends and relatives, 32% to seek entertainment
Travel primarily by car, truck, or recreational vehicle: 75%
Take longer trips than travelers overall: 4.8 nights vs. 3.9 nights
Take the longest pleasure trips of all age groups: 903 round-trip miles (ave.)
Age group most likely to purchase package tours

Sources: The 55+ Traveler (1995). Washington, D.C.: Travel Industry Association of America; Morrison, Alastair, Yang, Chung-Hui, O'Leary, Joseph T., & Nadkarni, Nandini (1994). A comparative study of cruise and land-based resort vacation travelers. In Chon, K.S. (Ed.). *New frontiers in tourism research.* Harper Woods, MI: Society of Travel and Tourism Educators; Hsu, Cathy H.C., Cai, Liping A., & Morrison, Alastair (1995). Relationships between sociodemographic variables, travel attitudes, and travel experiences. In Chon, K.S. (Ed.). *New frontiers in tourism research.* Harper Woods, MI: Society of Travel and Tourism Educators.

ways be recognition of the relative vitality, not infirmity, of seniors as a whole."[13] Many marketing and management challenges must be met to serve this demanding and growing segment profitably.

International Travelers

International travelers are a large and growing segment of tourism consumers. Travel to the United States and other destinations by international travelers has been growing at a rapid pace. However, the popularity of the United States as an international travel destination is interesting since less money is spent per capita promoting tourism in the United States than in any other industrialized nation. As might be expected, the largest number of visitors to the United States come from its neighbors to the north, Canada, and the south, Mexico. These countries are followed in numbers of visitors by Japan, Great Britain, Germany, France, and Italy. Projections indicate that the largest growth markets for foreign visitors to the United States will be Germany and South American countries.[14] As can be seen in Table 2.5, Europe is the major international destination region. Even though the United States is a major international destination, citizens of the United States travel

Mature travelers know no limits.
Photo by D.A. Yale.

TABLE 2.5
International Tourist Arrivals by Regions

Region	No. of Visitors
World	592,122,000
Europe	347,437,000
Americas	115,511,000
East Asia/Pacific	90,091,000
Africa	19,454,000
Middle East	15,144,000
South Asia	4,485,000

Source: Travel Industry World Yearbook: The Big Picture, 1996–97. Based on statistics gathered by the World Tourism Organization (WTO).

less internationally than their counterparts in industrialized countries. Table 2.6 shows that Canadians are by far the most active group of international travelers.

As we pointed out in Chapter 1, there are several factors that can influence the level of tourism activity. The current growth and importance of travel into Canada and the United States by foreign visitors, especially the Japanese and Europeans, helps to highlight several of these factors. First, disposable income continues to rise in these industri-

TABLE 2.6
Foreign International Travel from Industrialized Countries

Region	Percentage of Population Traveling Abroad*
Canada	79.1%
United Kingdom	58.5%
Germany	39.4%
France	18.7%
United States	17.2%
Japan	9.5%

*Based on 1992 data as reported in *Japan Almanac* 1995.

TOURISM IN ACTION

Developed in 1974 to fulfill the educational and travel needs of the increasing senior citizen population, Elderhostel has long focused on the mature traveler segment of the tourism market. Pioneered at five New Hampshire colleges and universities, the nonprofit Elderhostel organization developed into a nationwide network on college campuses that used dormitories and classrooms during the summer months. The programs provided inexpensive, residential educational programs for persons 60 years of age and over. In 1995, the eligibility age was lowered to age 55.

Since its humble beginning, the Elderhostel concept has expanded to include programs at over 1900 different locations in 50 countries. Responding to the expanding affluence and sophistication of the retiree population, Elderhostel now offers travel adventures that are far from two weeks on a traditional New England college campus. International Elderhostel programs span the globe from Antarctica to Iceland and can be single-site one- or two-week educational tours to four-week treks through several countries.

For example, Elderhostel has now teamed with the world-renowned auction house of Sotheby's and offers a three-week program in London on "Art at Auction" at a cost of over $4,000 per person! Another intriguing travel program is a two-week expedition of the Cook Islands in the heart of the Pacific Ocean.

Each year Elderhostel serves the educational and travel adventure needs of over a quarter of a million seniors throughout the world. Given the growth in size and financial resources of the mature traveler segment, Elderhostel should continue to expand and thrive in the 21st century. The overriding objective of Elderhostel has always been the self-actualization of older adults, that the "sky is the limit" when it comes to personal potential—at any age!

Source: Elderhostel brochure and catalogs; *Elderhostel*, 75 Federal Street, Boston, MA 02110.

tries. Second, European workers have longer vacation periods than their American counterparts, usually five weeks. Japanese workers are now beginning to have more leisure time. Third, these travelers are seeking new adventures away from their traditional vacation spots. Fourth, international airfares have become very competitive and are enticing increasing numbers of travelers to head to Canada and the United States.[15]

BASIC TRIP-PLANNING ADVICE FOR OVERSEAS TRAVELERS

1. Before you leave the United States, investigate the social customs, tipping practices, and political differences of the countries you intend to visit.
2. Memorize a few key words and phrases of the local language and use them regularly.
3. Buy a map and prominently mark your hotel, the U.S. embassy, and the local police station.
4. Keep a piece of hotel letterhead with you at all times. Show it to your taxi driver to expedite your ride back to the hotel.
5. Carry a pocket calculator to help convert currencies.
6. Leave copies of your passport, credit cards, listing of travelers checks, and itinerary with someone back home.
7. Purchase debit cards for public phones.
8. If you are renting a vehicle, know the phone number for emergency service and the procedure for reporting accidents.
9. If you are visiting several countries, carry a small change purse with compartments for separating the various currencies.
10. Carry an extra set of passport photos in case your passport is stolen.

Source: © AAA reproduced by permission.

A final factor that has made the United States as well as Canada attractive to almost all foreign visitors has been the changing value of the dollar (U.S. and Canadian) in international monetary markets. As both dollars lose value against other currencies, travel into the United States and Canada has become more affordable for citizens of many other countries. This may change in the future as the value of these currencies rises.

These same factors are important for other developed and developing countries and should be considered as plans are made for attracting or maintaining visitors. The level of disposable income, available leisure time, destination attractiveness, relative travel costs, and local exchange rates should be kept in mind as countries seek to attract even more individuals to participate in international travel and tourism activities.

DELIVERING HIGH-QUALITY SERVICE

Simply identifying and attracting targeted customers is not enough. Tourism organizations must then meet customer expectations by satisfying their wants and needs. Every component of the tourism industry is service-oriented. Therefore, providing consistently high quality service is the key to establishing and maintaining a successful operation.

Because the tourism market has become more competitive, service quality has become critical for tourism suppliers. It is no longer good enough simply to provide today's demanding traveler with adequate service. Travelers now expect superior service. Delivery of superior service requires understanding travelers' needs and expectations. We will talk about the specific knowledge and skills needed to deliver service quality in Chapter 9.

SUMMARY

We continue our journey through the dynamic world of tourism by starting at the center of the tourism model, where we focus on the millions of people who travel away from home each day. Because it is impossible to serve all of their wants and needs, we learned more about who these travelers are, their reasons for travel, and how we can meet their needs. As we learned more about these travelers, we could begin segmenting them into groups based on some similar characteristics.

Common approaches to segmenting markets include classifying consumers based on geographic, demographic, psychographic, and product-related characteristics. There are several very large market segments such as business and professional, mature, and international travelers that are particularly important to the future of the tourism industry.

Segmentation and target marketing are used to focus marketing efforts on groups of individuals with common wants and needs. A segment can then be seen as a distinct target that can be served with its own unique mix of services, prices, locations, times, and promotional activities. When customer wants and needs are properly identified and customer expectations are met, they will often tell others about their experiences and return.

Providing service that, at a minimum, results in satisfaction and strives to truly delight customers should be the goal of all tourism organizations. Remember, tourism is a business dependent on human relations and shared experiences. People like to be served and feel that they are welcome, that their business is important, and that service providers care about their experiences. By identifying the specific needs of individuals and groups of guests and visitors, it is possible to meet and exceed their expectations.

YOU DECIDE

Ski resorts in their present form began to appear in the 1950s. As the business evolved, many ski resorts began segmenting the skier travel market to better serve certain ski traveler segments. Beginning in the early 1980s, a new segment emerged, and members of this segment don't even ski! This new segment, the snowboarders, has continued to grow and many ski resorts recognize the revenue potential of this younger segment of snow enthusiasts.

But adding snowboarders to the mix of skiers on the mountain is not without its problems. Traditional skiers, many of whom are aging baby boomers and their parents and young children, complain that the snowboarders are speed demons who throw caution to the wind. In addition, skiers gripe that the snowboarders are noisy, they are sometimes rude and they damage the ski terrain because they scratch the surface and make deep grooves in the slopes.

Although snowboard users have increased in number in the past decade (some ski industry officials predict they will outnumber skiers in the near future), the older skiers still spend more money on their ski trips. A study by Leisure Trends Group, a Colorado-based market research firm, revealed that 35- to 54-year-old resort visitors spend an average of $201 per day while the 16- to 24-year-olds spend $164 on average per day.

Ski resort operators have introduced a variety of policies to try to ease the tension between the two types of visitors. Originally, some resorts such as Park City, Utah, prohibited snowboards, forgoing the revenue potential the segment represented. Some resorts today opt for separation of the groups by designating certain ski runs as skier only and/or snowboarder only. Still other areas have created small snowboard "fun-parks" on parts of ski trails. And some areas simply mix both segments on all slopes. But, as more and more young people take up snowboarding, tensions have escalated. By the 1996–97 season, only four resorts were completely banning snowboards: Deer Valley and Alta in Utah, Aspen in Colorado, and Squaw Valley in California. In fact, signs on the slopes of Vail and Beaver Creek (in the Colorado Rockies) encourage skiers and snowboarders to try to get along with each other.

Managers of ski resorts face a variety of issues when making policies regarding the two segments. They must consider the ethics of denying access to parts of the ski mountain to some patrons when all visitors pay the same price to ski or snowboard there. They must decide whether to target both groups when attracting both virtually guarantees that the satisfaction level of one segment will be reduced by the presence and actions of the other. The solution to this problem situation can best be determined by analyzing the options using the decision-making process. What would you do?

Sources: The battle of the piste. (1993, April 24) *Economist, 327* (7808), p. 96; Keates, Nancy (1996, April 12). Generation gap clouds spring skiing. *Wall Street Journal*, p. B6; Lefton, Terry (1997, January 27) Skiers vs snowboarders: When worlds collide. *Brandweek, 38*(4), p. 28.

NET TOUR

To learn more about the concepts and organizations presented in this chapter access the homepage for *Tourism: The Business of Travel*. Select "Chapter 2: Tourists: The Traveling Public." From this location test your knowledge by taking the chapter quiz, read industry insights and discover links to other useful sites. You may also want to communicate electronically with other tourism students through the website.

DISCUSSION QUESTIONS

1. What do we mean when we refer to segmenting a market?
2. Why do we segment the tourism market?
3. Identify and provide examples of the common approaches to segmenting the tourism market.
4. Why are business travelers so important to the tourism industry?
5. Why are mature travelers so important to the future of the tourism industry?
6. Why are international travelers becoming more important to tourism service suppliers?
7. Why are incentive travelers so important to the future of the tourism industry?
8. Why should the topic of customer service be important to tourism service suppliers?

APPLYING THE CONCEPTS

1. Collect several advertisements for tourism related goods or services. Based on the content of these advertisements, describe the customer segment you believe is being targeted.
2. "Surf" the World Wide Web and find three tourism supplier homepages. Which segments do you think each is targeting based on the information provided on the homepages?
3. Interview the head of a tourism service supplier's marketing or sales department to find out the segments targeted and the relative importance of each of these segments to overall profitability.
4. Interview a member of one of the specialized tourist segments introduced in this chapter. Develop a profile of their travel behaviors. Examples of questions you might ask include: Where do they travel, how frequently do they travel, when do they travel, how do they travel, what do they enjoy doing when they travel, with whom do they travel, etc. What types of service suppliers do they select to meet these needs?
5. Based on what you know about market segmentation, help Jim and Andy by preparing a list describing some of the common characteristics of the people that might be potential customers for their white water rafting business.

GLOSSARY

Allocentrics Travelers who seek adventure.

Business travel Travel-related activities associated with commerce and industry.

Consumer behavior The study of consumer characteristics and the processes involved when individuals or groups select, purchase, and use goods, services, or experiences to satisfy wants and needs.

Demographics Characteristics used to classify consumers on the basis of criteria such as age, education, income, gender, and occupation.

Demographic segmentation Dividing consumer markets based on demographic data such as age, education, income, gender, religion, race, nationality, and occupation.

Disposable income Household income after paying taxes that is available for personal use.

Elastic demand The quantity of goods or services used changes in a proportion that is greater than changes in prices.

Geographic segmentation Dividing consumer markets along different geographical boundaries such as nations, states, and communities.

Heterogeneous Having differing characteristics and needs.

Homogeneous Having similar characteristics and needs.

Incentive tour operators Tour operators who specialize in organizing, promoting, and conducting incentive tours.

Incentive travel Motivational programs designed to create competition, with the winner(s) receiving travel awards.

Inelastic demand The quantity of goods or services used does not change in direct proportion to changes in prices.

Lifestyle A mode of living that is identified by how people spend their time (activities), what they consider important in their environment (interests), and what they think of themselves and the world around them (opinions).

Marketing mix The combination of goods or services, distribution, promotion, and price that are used to accomplish an organization's objectives and satisfy the needs of target markets.

Market segmentation Dividing a broad market into smaller and distinct groups of buyers—each group with similar needs, characteristics, or behaviors.

Mature adults People aged 55 and older; also called "senior citizens."

Product-related segmentation Dividing consumer markets according to characteristics such as the amount of use or benefits consumers expect to derive from the service.

Professional travel Travel by individuals to attend meetings and conventions.

Psychocentrics Travelers who seek the comforts of familiar surroundings.

Psychographics Consumer psychological characteristics that can be quantified, including lifestyle and personality information.

Psychographic segmentation Dividing consumer markets into groups based on lifestyle and personality profiles.

Target market (target segment) A group of people sharing common characteristics that an organization attempts to serve by designing strategies to meet the group's specific needs.

Teleconferencing A meeting that allows people to remain in several locations, but come together and communicate through a combination of television and telephone connections.

Upgrades Receiving a better class of service or facility than was paid for, such as moving from coach to first-class.

REFERENCES

1. Maslow, Abraham (1954). *Motivation and Personality*. New York: Harper & Row.

2. Pearce, P. L. (1991). *Dreamworld. A report on public reactions to Dreamworld and proposed developments at Dreamworld*. Townsville: Department of Tourism, James Cook University.

3. Plog, Stanley G. (1974, November). Why destination areas rise and fall in popularity. *Cornell Hotel and Restaurant Administration Quarterly*, pp. 13–16.

4. Hiam, Alexander, & Schewe, Charles D. (1993, January). Market segmentation: Can it work for your company? *Incentive*, pp. 65–66.

5. Dahl, Jonathan (1993, October 18). Tracking travel. *The Wall Street Journal*, p. B1.

6. Lang, Jeffrey B. (1993). Rx for controlling travel costs. *Management Review*, 82(6), 59–63.

7. Saffo, Paul (1993, autumn). The future of travel. *Fortune (Special Issue)*, pp. 112–119.

8. Richards, Rhonda (1995, August 15). Business travel. *USA Today*, p. 8B.

9. Sheldon, Pauline J. (1995, spring). The demand for incentive travel: An empirical study. *Journal of Travel Research*, pp. 23–28.

10. Spritzer, Dinah A. (1991, May 23). NTA: Mature clients seek adventure. *Travel Weekly*, pp. 32–33.

11. Conaway, Frank (1991, May). Targeting mature markets: Segmenting will unleash mature market potential. *Public Relations Journal*, pp. 18–19.

12. Badinelli, Kimberle, Davis, Nigel & Gustin, Libby (1991, September 9). Special report: Senior traveler study. *Hotel and Motel Management*, pp. 31, 33–34.

13. Conaway, Frank (1991, May). Targeting mature markets: Segmenting will unleash mature market potential. *Public Relations Journal*, pp. 18–19.

14. Doyle, Kevin (1993, April). Incentive travel: U.S. heats up as favored foreign travel spot. *Incentive*, p. 15.

15. Banks, Howard, & Munk, Nuna (1992, August 17). "Der Grand Canyon." *Forbes*, pp. 46–47.

CHAPTER 3

Bringing Travelers and Tourism Service Suppliers Together

Travel agents add the personal touch to travel plans.
Photo by D.A. Yale.

There are no such things as service industries. There are only industries whose service components are greater or less than those of other industries. Everybody is in service.

—THEODORE LEVITT
FORMER EDITOR, HARVARD BUSINESS REVIEW, IN *THE MARKETING IMAGINATION*, THE FREE PRESS, 1986

CHAPTER OUTLINE

LEARNING OBJECTIVES

After you have read this chapter, you should be able to:

- Describe how services are different from goods.

- Explain the importance of intermediaries in the distribution of tourism services.

- Identify and describe the three different types of distribution channels that are used for tourism services.

- Describe the roles of travel agencies in bringing tourists and tourism providers together.

- Describe the roles of tour wholesalers in bringing tourists and tourism service providers together.

- Identify and describe how travelers access information for tourism services.

ONE STOP DOES IT ALL!

Kristin Hatten has just stepped into the office and already the phone is ringing and the message light is blinking. This work day will probably be just like every other work day in her life as a travel agent—always different. The demands of the day will require that she be a true multiprocessor, handling several tasks at once, from answering the phone to entering, retrieving, and verifying data from a sophisticated computer reservation system. At the same time, during all these tasks she must focus her attention on the ultimate goal of providing high-quality customer service. As a travel agent, Kristin serves as an important link between suppliers in the tourism industry and her clients.

As a front-line service employee, Kristin faces a demanding public, who often does not understand the constantly changing industry rules and prices with which she must work. On any given day, she may receive information about changing regulations and prices as well as invitations for seminars and familiarization trips from airlines, hotels, resorts, cruise lines, rental car companies, and a host of other tourism service suppliers. Kristin must sort through this information to learn more about the services that will meet the needs of her clients.

Kristin will spend most of her day answering the phone and serving customers who walk through the door seeking help with their travel plans. She will deal with a wide variety of customers, ranging from her regular business clients who know what they want to first-time customers who have little knowledge about travel and tourism in general. The uncertainties that fill each day can make her job stressful, but the opportunity to learn more about the world and help others meet their travel needs keeps Kristin going.

At the end of a particularly hectic day, she takes a moment to think about her list of appointments and calls to be made the next day. Most of the calls are from her typical leisure customers and require only providing information on basic scheduling options. As she continues reviewing the list, Kristin notices one appointment that she is particularly looking forward to. Mr. and Mrs. Gildea phoned last week to discuss an upcoming trip they were planning from Lethbridge, Canada, to Hawaii. After obtaining some brief information about the Gildeas and their needs, Kristin scheduled an early morning appointment.

Looking at the notes she took during that phone conversation, Kristin begins thinking about the types of information and services the Gildeas might want. A recently retired couple, the Gildeas have always wanted to visit Hawaii and return home with pictures and stories they could share with friends and relatives. They have been reading extensively about the attractions and have some ideas of where they want to go and what they want to see and do, but they are interested in any suggestions Kristin might offer. Before she leaves for the day, Kristin prints out several different itineraries and gathers brochures and other information that she feels will help the Gildeas in making their plans for an unforgettable experience.

INTRODUCTION

When people travel, they need a whole range of tourism services. These services may include airline tickets, car rentals, places to stay, places to eat, places to shop, tickets and admissions to attractions, and information about things to do and see. In this chapter, we will explore the basic concepts of services and how marketing, management, and finance decisions have an impact on the way travelers access the services of tourism suppliers. The success and profitability of tourism service suppliers depends on their ability to reach and meet targeted customers' needs effectively and efficiently.

As you learned in Chapter 2, by dividing the larger tourism market into distinctive groups, we can plan and provide services that are targeted to the needs of a specific segment of the tourism market. Once these target customers and their needs have been identified, the goal of service suppliers becomes reaching, serving and satisfying their needs profitably. This is not an easy task since "competition today demands that service be delivered faster, cheaper, and without defects."[1] By referring to our model of tourism in Figure 1.2, you will see that many different organizations and approaches have been developed to accomplish this task. In this chapter, we will explore the basic concepts of services and discover how travelers obtain information about and access to tourism services.

TOURISM SERVICES

As you learned in Chapter 1, services are the fastest-growing industry in the world, and tourism is the fastest-growing segment in the service industry. Most of us easily recognize and know where to purchase goods such as CDs, textbooks, and toothpaste. However, in the tourism industry, we deal mainly with services, not goods. We may find it difficult at times to describe these services, know where to purchase them, or even make clear distinctions between services and goods. Even these distinctions may at times become blurred since some tourism organizations are involved primarily in the delivery of services while others deliver both services and goods.

These differences can be seen in the services/goods continuum shown in Figure 3.1. At one end of the goods/services continuum, you will find organizations like travel agencies and convention and visitors' bureaus that primarily provide services. In the middle, you will find organizations like restaurants that provide both goods and services. On the opposite end, you will find organizations like retail shops that provide primarily goods and some services.

But wait a minute. Didn't we just say that tourism is a service? Yes, but services are often accompanied by something called a **facilitating good.** Facilitating goods are tangible items that support or accompany the service being provided. For example, if you were to call the Israel Government Tourist Office located in Chicago, IL, and ask questions about the types of documentation needed for travel into Israel, the answers you receive would be a service. If you requested brochures, then you would be receiving both a service and a facilitating good.

Services provided by these and other tourism organizations are called "intangibles" since they cannot be placed in inventories and pulled out of warehouses or off of shelves like a can of beans or a compact disk. Services are not only intangible but they are also highly perishable. Tourism services perish or lose their value with the passage of time just like fresh fruits and vegetables that eventually spoil and must be thrown away. Think about the airplane that has just left the gate, the cruise ship that has just been pushed away from the dock, or the fireworks show that marks the end of a concert. In each of these situations, the opportunity to generate revenue from the seat, cabin, or concert has disappeared forever.

FIGURE 3.1
Goods/Services Continuum

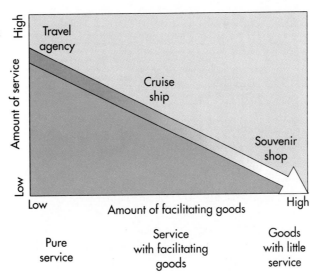

Services are also different from goods because they are actions performed by one person on behalf of another. Sometimes we are merely the recipients of services but, at other times, we become actively involved in the service delivery process. For example, once we have called a travel agency to book a flight, we are through with active participation. The travel agent will find the best route and the best flight and reserve seats for us. However, some tourism organizations may actively involve customers in the service delivery process: airlines may ask passengers to pick up box lunches before boarding; hotels allow guests to check out over the telephone or through the television without ever going to the front desk; and restaurants invite guests to serve themselves at salad bars.

SERVING TRAVELER NEEDS

Remember Thomas Cook, who organized and conducted the first large tour in 1841? He used a variety of marketing, management, and financial skills as he packaged, sold, and escorted that first organized tour. Cook negotiated reduced fares on a train trip between Loughborough and Leicester, England, and arranged for picnic lunches and afternoon tea for almost 600 people. He was serving as an **intermediary.** As an intermediary, he did not work for the railroad company or the bakery, but he sold their services and goods. His clients benefited from his efforts because he took care of their needs while saving them money; the suppliers benefited from his efforts because they received increased revenues without having to spend additional monies on attracting more customers.

Once an organization has developed a service offering, it must be made available for customer use. Consumers are often unable to sample or even see services before purchasing, so they rely primarily on information to make their purchase decisions. Determining how this information will be made available and how travelers will obtain the services they need involves a variety of decisions. For example, should the organization deal with customers directly or should it rely on others to attract and inform cus-

An information source used widely by travel professionals. Photo by D.A. Yale.

tomers about its services? How much money should be spent on attracting customers? Does the organization have the people and talent to distribute information about its services efficiently and effectively, and, at the same time, achieve the desired levels of profit, service quality, and satisfaction?

In answering these questions, managers need to think about two key issues. The first deals with who should be involved in bringing travelers and tourism service suppliers together and the second deals with how to manage these activities. A simple example will help highlight these issues.

Consider for a minute a small coastal resort located in northern Maine. It would probably not have the money or the marketing staff to reach all of its desired target customers effectively. Rather than attempting to accomplish this task alone, the manager of the resort could rely on the help of others. The state tourism office, local visitors bureau, membership in a regional reservations system, cooperative brochures including other local attractions, a posting on the World Wide Web, and a listing in *Hotel and Travel Index* would provide just a few possibilities for informing and attracting potential guests. However, even with all of these efforts, the resort may still not reach enough of its targeted audience to be profitable. To close this information loop, the resort might rely on the professional services of travel agents like Kristin Hatten, whom we met in the chapter opener. As you will see in this chapter, these are just a few of the alternatives a manager should consider when attempting to reach potential customers.

Travelers need access to a wide variety of tourism services. These services may be as simple as having questions answered about the availability of services or as complex as purchasing an all-inclusive prepackaged tour. No matter how simple or how complex the needs are, there are several types of distribution channels that can be used to access tourism services and information about these services. These channels may range all the way from one-level direct access to more-complex three-level arrangements involving several intermediaries. Figure 3.2 shows typical one-, two-, and three-level distribution channels for tourism services.

FIGURE 3.2
Distribution Channels

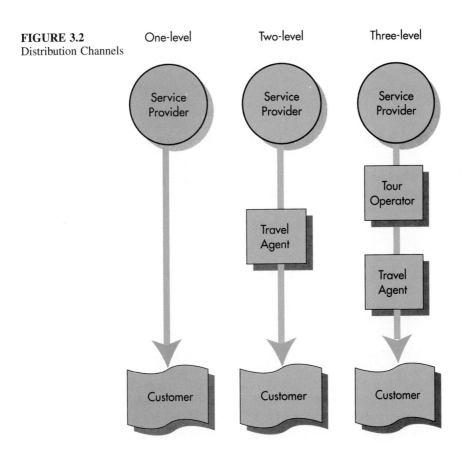

WHY USE INTERMEDIARIES?

Although tourism service suppliers such as airlines, theme parks, and restaurants may reach some of their customers directly, they can also use the distribution services provided by one or more intermediaries. Intermediaries perform a vital function for tourism service suppliers by making the suppliers' services available to large numbers of potential customers in a cost-effective way. These services may be as simple as providing directions for a motorist at a welcome center to more-complex service activities such as packaging, selling, and then escorting tour groups.

Intermediaries in tourism distribution channels perform a variety of value-adding functions. Examples of just a few of these distribution functions are

- providing information about the types and availability of service offerings,
- contacting current and potential customers,
- making reservations and other travel arrangements,
- assembling services to meet customer needs,
- preparing tickets, and
- risk-taking by buying or booking large quantities of services in advance and then reselling them to individuals and groups.

The expenses of selling services through an intermediary typically occur in the form of **commissions** and do not arise until the services have been sold or used. The company providing the final service such as the airline, cruise line, hotel, resort, or car rental company pays the commission on each ticket sold or reservation used. Although the user may pay a small service fee, the cost of obtaining the services are usually paid by the service supplier in the form of a commission and not by the customer.

Why are service suppliers willing to pay intermediaries for their services? The answers to this question can be found in increased sales and efficiencies provided by the intermediaries. For example,

> Prior to the mid-1970s, the airlines booked their flights through their own reservationists. But then, realizing that their overhead for reservationists was much more expensive than the amount they paid in travel agents' commissions on actual ticketed sales, the airlines sold or eliminated many of their ticket offices.[2]

ONE-LEVEL (DIRECT) DISTRIBUTION CHANNELS

One-level distribution channels are the simplest form of distribution, providing travelers with direct access to tourism suppliers. In this type of distribution channel, suppliers deal directly with travelers without the assistance of intermediaries. Airlines, car rental companies, passenger railroads, lodging facilities, resorts, restaurants, theme parks, and attractions all engage in promotions and advertising to encourage people to purchase their products and services directly. These advertising and promotion programs also serve to generate business for other travel intermediaries, such as travel agencies and tour operators.

Information technology offers another promising format for bringing service suppliers and customers together through the touch of a keyboard or the click of a mouse. Personal computers (PCs) in homes and offices provide ready access to domestic and international tourism information. Travelocity, Dr. Memory's Favorite Travel Pages, and Tourism Offices Worldwide Directory provide just a few examples of World Wide Web sites that can be accessed directly by consumers.[3,4] Services such as electronic travel brochures and basic information about airlines, international rail service, passenger bus lines, car rental companies, cruise lines, hotels/motels, and resorts can be accessed through a variety of on-line services and Internet connections.

The future holds many exciting challenges and opportunities for tourism marketers and service suppliers. How we access and use tourism information may not just evolve, but change radically as information technologies develop and improve. Advances in computer technology have made it possible for travelers to visit faraway places without ever leaving their homes or offices. They can connect to reservation systems through their personal computers, search for related travel information, book flights, and make other travel arrangements and reservations. Technology will not only allow travelers to make their own airline reservations via personal computer links, but it will also allow them to move directly from the computer terminal to their airline seat without ever obtaining a piece of paper.

Airlines have encouraged many of these changes because they help reduce operating expenses. First, the airline saves the money that would be paid in commissions to travel agents. Second, they also save on the cost of producing tickets. The cost of producing a paper ticket ranges from $15 to $30. By simply eliminating the tickets and moving to ticketless travel, it has been estimated that the industry could save about $1 billion a year.[5]

TWO-LEVEL DISTRIBUTION CHANNELS

Two-level distribution channels are more complex than one-level direct-access channels. In a two-level channel, travel agents serve as intermediaries bringing suppliers and consumers together. Bringing another person or organization in between tourism service suppliers and the traveler may at first seem a bit more complex than the one-level approach to distribution that we just described. However, it can simplify the travel process for consumers and it is often more efficient and effective for tourism suppliers.

Travel Agencies

In fact, the most popular form of purchasing tourism services is through travel agencies. Travel agencies act as a central focus around which much, if not most, of the sales and reservation activity in the travel industry centers. Although some transactions bypass them, most travel arrangements involve travel agents to a certain degree, usually serving as a link between the client and the companies providing tourism services. Travel agencies have now become the department stores of the tourism industry.

Travel agents offer a wide variety of services, including providing information to travelers, making reservations, ticketing, and securing other services and travel-related documents for them. However, they do not take title to (own) the services they are selling. Figure 3.3 shows the flow of payments, information and delivery of services that are purchased and consumed by travelers.

Travel agencies serve as sales outlets and are compensated on a commission basis by the service suppliers. Commissions are based on the level of sales, which are referred to as "bookings." As you will see later, the commissions that travel agencies can earn are beginning to be reduced. Service suppliers sometimes view them as expenses to be controlled and customers sometimes think it is quicker and cheaper to deal directly with the service supplier. However, since travel agencies continue to play a critical role in facilitating the distribution process, let's take a more detailed look at their operations.

Travel agencies provide an important sales and information link between tourism service suppliers and the traveling public. The beginning of travel agencies goes back to the glory years of railroads and steamship lines, when agents sold tickets for these carriers and received a commission for their efforts. Thomas Cook, whom you met previously, started the concept of the travel agent. By making travel arrangements simple and affordable, he was able to attract growing numbers of people to explore places away from their homes and villages.

By the late 1800s the idea of seeking help for travel arrangements had made its way to the States. A gift shop owner in St. Augustine, Florida, can be credited with starting the idea of a travel agency in the United States. Although he probably never planned to

FIGURE 3.3
Flow of Payments, Information, and Service Delivery

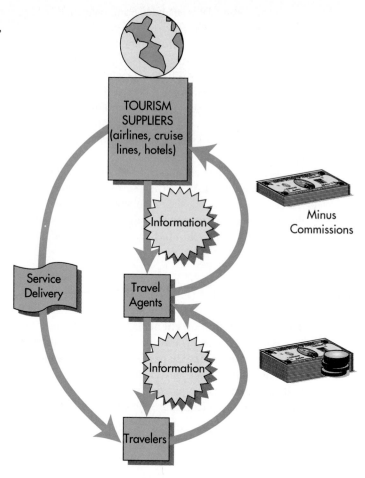

be a travel agent, his knowledge of geography, rail schedules, and hotels soon led him to be the local source for travel information. When anyone had a question about travel, they were sent to "Ask Mr. Foster." In 1888, Ward G. Foster turned his love of geography and his hobby of studying maps, transportation, and destinations into Ask Mr. Foster Travel. Ask Mr. Foster continued to grow and eventually became part of one of the largest travel agencies in the world, Carlson Wagonlit Travel.[6]

From these small service-oriented beginnings, travel agencies have grown to become an integral link in the tourism distribution system. There are now almost 37,000 travel agencies in the United States and Canada, with thousands of agents taking care of travelers' needs on a daily basis. As we saw in the chapter opener, a travel agent's day is still very service-oriented, but it can also be varied and hectic.

> The agent is no longer just an order taker who spends the entire business day making bookings at the client's direction. In fact, only a small portion of an agent's day is spent actually making reservations. Travel agents, as consultants, spend much of their time researching travel products and conferring with clients.[7]

Most travel agencies specialize by focusing their efforts on large target markets such as business or leisure customers, while others serve a general group of customers, or a specific market niche such as cruise-only customers. Even though they may be serving different types of customer needs, they all typically provide a common group of services called a "product mix." These services include: **itinerary** planning; airline, rail, and cruise reservations and ticketing; car rentals, accommodations, and activity reservations; tour packages; travel insurance; theater and event ticketing; and general travel information.

The critical role travel agencies play in generating revenues for different segments of the tourism industry can be seen in the level of reservations they generate. In fact over:

- 95% of all cruise reservations,
- 90% of all packaged tour reservations,
- 85% of all international hotel reservations,
- 85% of all international airline reservations,
- 80% of domestic airline reservations,
- 50% of all car rental reservations,
- 37% of rail reservations, and
- 25% of all domestic hotel reservations

are made through travel agents.[7,8]

Maintaining profitability within the highly competitive travel agency business requires a combined effort focused on generating sales and controlling operating costs. Remember that travel agencies depend on their marketing abilities to generate sales for other tourism suppliers and receive only a portion of these sales in the form of commissions. So, a travel agency that generates $1,000,000 in sales may only receive $100,000 in commissions to cover operating expenses and earn a profit.

As can be seen in Figure 3.4, out of every sales dollar received, approximately 97% is used to cover operating expenses. This leaves only 3% in profit before taxes. Since travel agencies are able to make only a few pennies of profit on each sales dollar, maintaining the financial health of the business by controlling expenses such as salaries and benefits, rent, computer reservation systems, advertising and promotion, utilities, repairs and maintenance, insurance, and other miscellaneous items becomes an important managerial task. The lion's share of these operating expenses can be attributed to salaries and benefits, rent, and computer reservation systems.

As mentioned previously, travel agencies do not take title to the services they sell, so they have little, if any, inventory or cost of goods sold. For example, you may have noticed the racks of brochures and other promotional materials (inventory) when you visited a travel agency; these items are usually provided to the agency at no cost. In addition, "reduced profits in the airline business have forced agents to look elsewhere for income, and clients are asking travel agents to provide additional services."[9] Many travel agencies have been able to take advantage of electronic technology to reduce operating expenses. Through the use of **satellite ticket printers (STPs)** and other electronic ticket-delivery systems, they have improved customer service while reducing operating costs.

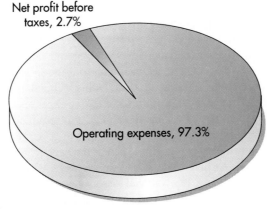

FIGURE 3.4
Travel Agency Profitability
Source: RMA Annual Statement Studies 1997, Philadelphia: Robert Morris Associates. (1997, September).

TABLE 3.1

Do You Recognize the Names of Any of These Travel Agencies?

American Express Travel Services Group

Carlson Wagonlit Travel

Rosenbluth International

Maritz Travel Co.

Liberty Travel

Travel One

Garber Travel

Professional Travel Corporation

Arrington Travel Center

Morris Travel

The travel agency industry can be categorized into two large groupings based on sales. One group contains a small number of large "mega agencies" that generate a substantial portion of revenues and a very large group of smaller agencies that generate a smaller portion of industry revenues. The top 50 agencies in the United States generate almost 30% of all agency sales. You may recognize one or more of the larger, well-known travel agencies listed in Table 3.1.

Airline deregulation has brought about many changes in the operation of travel agencies. Large-volume travel agencies can earn **overrides** and are frequently given "conversion ability." This is the ability to convert a regular full-economy-priced airline reservation to a discounted fare price when all discounted seats are sold out. These two factors have encouraged agency owners and managers to seek affiliation through a **franchise** or a **consortium** to gain the necessary volume of business that can lead to improved profitability.

Although there is a trend toward forming alliances to increase profitability, the travel agencies are still predominantly small businesses that are managed by individuals with an entrepreneurial spirit. In fact, 76% of all travel agencies in the United States have total sales of less than $1 million.[2]

STARTING A TRAVEL AGENCY

Look before you leap! The excitement of travel and tourism and the desire to help others with their travel needs attract many hopeful travel agents and small business owners. Opening your own travel agency can be fairly easy and inexpensive. However, as you have seen in this chapter, it is a highly competitive business with low profit margins. Take the time to gain some experience by working in a successful agency and then, if you still want to strike out on your own, go for it!

Going it alone in this competitive business would probably be attractive to only the most adventuresome of risk-takers. Total start-up costs could range anywhere from $15,000 to $60,000. Some start-up risks can be avoided by purchasing a franchise, which would add another $8,000 to $33,000 to your initial costs. Other than franchise fees, these costs would include renting or leasing office space, furniture, equipment, and initial staffing costs. There may also be other bonding and licensing fees depending on where you decide to locate your agency.

To obtain airline ticket stock that can be used for most airlines and avoid the complications of dealing with individual airlines as well as other tourism service suppliers, a travel agency should seek accreditation by the Airlines Reporting Corporation (ARC) and be accredited or affiliated with other tourism-related organizations. To receive ARC accreditation, an agency must be open for business, accessible to the public, clearly identified as a travel agency, and actively selling airline tickets. The manager must have had at least two years' experience in promoting and selling travel products and services, as well as one year's experience in issuing tickets. In addition, an agency must also meet minimal financial requirements, including a bond or irrevocable letter of credit for $20,000 and an adequate cash reserve to pay expenses during the first year of operation.

If you do decide to take the plunge and set up or purchase your own agency, help is available. In addition to reference books and government small business assistance programs, many other organizations such as the American Society of Travel Agents (ASTA), International Airlines Travel Agent Network (IATAN), Cruise Line International Association (CLIA), the National Association of Cruise Only Agencies (NACOA), the National Tour Association (NTA), and the United States Tour Operators Association (USTOA) can provide useful information and suggestions for success.

Sources: Dondero, John E. (1990, July). Lending to travel agencies. *Journal of Commercial Bank Lending*, pp. 49–56; Off to the right start; with ASTA (1992, May). Alexandria, VA: American Society of Travel Agents; Boyer, Dean (1995). Travel agency. In Suzanne M. Bourgoin (Ed.), *Small Business Profiles*, vol. 1. Detroit: Gale Research Inc.

Improving Service Delivery through Cooperative Systems

The majority of all travel agency business is conducted through **computer reservation systems (CRSs),** which provide access to a wealth of data about tourism service suppliers. CRSs allow travel agents to obtain on-line information on space availability, schedules, rates, and fares. They also provide the means of booking reservations and printing itineraries, tickets and invoices.

Today, travel agencies are linked on-line to one or more of the following four computer airline reservation systems in the United States. Sabre, Apollo, Worldspan, and System One control 37.4%, 28.4%, 19.3%, and 14.9%, respectively, of U.S. travel agency airline reservations.[10] Amadeus, which controls System One, is a worldwide CRS with over 33,000 locations serving North America and "controls approximately 50% of the travel agency market share in Europe and South America."[11] Computerized airline reservation systems have been developed to do more than simply book airline reservations. They now serve as databases for tourism services and travel information as well as reservation systems. Information and reservations for tourism services such as hotels, rental cars, cruises, tours, and more are now standard features on these systems.

Since the majority of travel agency revenues are derived from airline ticket sales, appointment and accreditation by two key agencies are critical to continued success. The **Airlines Reporting Corporation (ARC)** and the International Airline Travel Agency Network (IATAN) operate the financial networks and clearinghouses that allow travel agencies to sell airline tickets and collect commissions. ARC accreditation is the most important since it handles transactions for domestic airlines, many international airlines and Amtrak and Britrail as well. IATAN handles transactions for the international airlines that are not processed through the ARC system.

Membership in the ARC and IATAN not only provides access to blank airline ticket stock, but it also provides a simplified method of remitting funds from ticket sales to the respective airlines. Revenues from both domestic and many international ticket sales that have been collected by travel agencies are deposited in ARC area banks on a weekly basis and then an agency's account is drafted (a request for payment similar to a check) and the appropriate funds are distributed to each airline.

The relationship between the airlines and travel agents has been tumultuous. In the past, airlines actively courted travel agents to serve as their primary channel of distribution and paid generous commissions to reward loyalty and increasing volumes of bookings. However, at times the airlines have also reduced or capped commissions in an attempt to enhance their own profitability. These changes can severely limit travel agency revenues and profitability.

Commissions on these sales may vary widely depending on the type of service being provided and the country where the travel agency is located. For example, commissions in the United States on domestic airline tickets average around 9% with **caps** of $25 on one-way fares and $50 on round-trip fares, while commissions on international airline tickets average around 15%. In the United Kingdom commissions for these same services would be 7.5% and 9%, respectively. However, with overrides, commissions can be increased.

As caps have been placed on many airline commissions, cruise line, tour, and hotel bookings have grown in importance to travel agencies. Organizations such as Hotel Clearing Corporation (HCC) are reporting double-digit growth in commissionable hotel bookings as travel agents seek new sources of revenue.[12]

THREE-LEVEL DISTRIBUTION CHANNELS

Three-level distribution channels involve many of the same activities and characteristics found in the previously described two-level or indirect-access channels. However, they bring in another layer of intermediaries, such as tour operators and convention and visitors bureaus, who market tours and facilitate the process of bringing travelers and tourism sup-

Professional tour escorts are often the most memorable component of a tour.
Photo by D.A. Yale.

pliers together. Many travel agencies are also becoming active participants in these distribution channels as they package and sell tours, especially in the motorcoach market.

Tour operators serve to both create and at the same time anticipate demand by purchasing or reserving large blocks of space and services to be resold in the form of tours at reduced rates in packages. Tour operators do not typically work on a commission basis like travel agents but on a **markup** basis. They buy large blocks of services such as airline seats and hotel rooms at very favorable prices by guaranteeing minimum levels of revenues or by making nonrefundable deposits and then resell these services at a higher price. Tour operators are a particularly significant intermediary in the tourism industry since they supply packages for travel agencies to sell, as well as buying services from airlines, cruise lines, hotels, resorts, car rental companies, and many other tourism suppliers.

Tour Operators

Tour operators are by definition business organizations engaged in planning, preparing, marketing and, at times, operating vacation tours.

> The terms *packager, wholesale tour operator, tour operator, tour wholesaler,* and *wholesaler* often are used interchangeably. In almost every case, the company acting as a wholesaler also operates the tours it creates or packages.[13]

Although there are many different names that can be used to describe this distribution function, for simplicity, we will use the term "tour operator." They may work with all segments of the tourism industry to negotiate rates, block space and coordinate the myriad details found in a **tour package** at an inclusive price. Some of the larger well-known wholesalers and operators are listed in Table 3.2.

Tour packages include at least two of the following elements: transportation, accommodations, meals, entertainment, and sightseeing activities. These packages could range all the way from an **escorted tour,** in which you are accompanied by a professional, to a **hosted tour,** in which you are greeted and have a local contact to assist with any problem or questions, to an **independent tour,** which gets you to your destination and then leaves you on your own.

The tour business holds a certain mystique for many people who like to travel and think that they would like to arrange and package travel and tourism services for others. However, the tour business is extremely risky. Both tour operators and wholesalers are an unregulated segment of the industry since there are no entry requirements for licensing, bonding, or insurance. While every segment of the tourism industry deals with highly perishable services, the problem of perishability is compounded in the tour business. Once a tour has departed, there is no way to sell additional seats on the tour and receive revenues for services that have already been reserved and, in most cases, paid for in advance.

In addition, tour wholesalers and operators often must commit to prices for services far in advance and are therefore faced with the potential problems of inflation and foreign currency fluctuations that may reduce their profit margins. If that weren't enough, there are the additional problems of natural disasters, political unrest, and changing consumer tastes, which are all outside the control of the tour operator.

Realizing all of these potential problems, it becomes critical for successful tour operators to control costs, competitively price the packages they offer and market these packages to the appropriate target market(s). Assembling a package that interests consumers and then pricing it competitively becomes a tricky issue since tour operators must work with a very thin markup, usually 20% or less. Getting out the word on tour packages is also a challenge since most tour operators must develop their marketing campaigns on limited budgets. Therefore, market segmentation and targeting are essential to continued success.

Consolidators and Travel Clubs

Consolidators and **travel clubs** are very special combinations of wholesalers and retailers who perform unique tourism distribution functions. Consolidators buy up excess inventory of unsold airline tickets and then resell these tickets at discounted prices through travel agents or in some cases directly to travelers. Travel clubs also provide an inexpen-

TOURISM IN ACTION

A critical element of many tour packages is the tour director. "Escorted tours," in addition to offering travelers the many services required for a trip (transportation, lodging, meals), provide travelers with a professional who accompanies the tour through its duration. This individual, the tour director, is key to the success of the tour and the satisfaction of the tour group members. During the tour, he or she acts as guide, "troop leader," and problem-solver for the group.

At one time, tour directors were poorly trained and pretty much "on their own" to know how and what to do to serve their tour members. Given the important quality-enhancing (or detracting!) role that today's tour director can have, many tour operators now use specially trained men and women to staff this significant position. A major trainer of tour escorts is the International Tour Management Institute (ITMI). The company's founders, Bill Newton and Ted Bravos, confirm that the demands on tour directors necessitates continuing education and a broader range of skills than in the past.

ITMI was founded in 1976 and over 3500 graduates now work as guides for more than 700 tour companies

throughout the world. Applicants to the tour director school come from all walks of life. "Many have been in professions, in top management, doctors, lawyers, educators, those with tremendous levels of responsibility, and they are applying to us to become tour directors," says Newton. "More than a third of our students are already working, or have been, as tour directors or guides." These students attend ITMI to upgrade their skills.

Approximately two thirds of tour directors are hired as independent contractors by companies that package and/or operate tours. A tour director therefore typically works with a variety of tour companies and is an independent businessperson. What does it take to be a successful tour director in today's competitive travel world? Bravos claims "The tour director who really stands out today is the one who understands what it means to set the mood of the trip, to frame the tour. The tour director must motivate the people individually and as a group." Tour directors also have to have strong management skills so that they can handle the unexpected occurrences and problems that inevitably happen when a group of strangers get together to experience a new world.

Sources: Bill Bowden (1991, July). Tour directors: A changing world. *Courier*, pp. 33–34; International Tour Management Institute information packet.

sive and convenient outlet for members to purchase unused seats at the last minute. Both consolidators and travel clubs perform a win–win function as intermediaries in the distribution channel. They help the airlines sell a highly perishable service and often provide consumers with some real bargains in the process.

Where travel agencies are the department stores of the tourism industry, consolidators and travel clubs are to the airline industry what factory outlet stores are to clothing manufacturers. They are an efficient way to move highly perishable inventories of services to shoppers who have the flexibility to adjust their travel schedules to take advantage of lower prices on scheduled flights for which airlines have not been able to sell all of their available seats. Although there may be restrictions and the frequent fare wars that airlines wage may make the savings differential smaller, bargains can be substantial. Travel clubs also perform the additional function of selling accommodations, car rentals, and other tourism services at reduced rates.

TRIP-CANCELLATION AND TRIP-INTERRUPTION INSURANCE

Trip-cancellation and trip-interruption insurance policies will provide reimbursement for financial losses you might suffer if you can't begin and must cancel a trip or it is interrupted while in progress. This insurance will cover such things as missing a flight due to an automobile accident, a sudden illness, injury, or death, but it doesn't cover changing your mind. Should you buy trip-cancellation insurance? The answer to this question could be yes, no, or maybe. If you are making a large deposit, paying in advance for an expensive tour package or cruise, or if you have purchased any type of expensive non-refundable ticket then the answer is yes. In all other situations, read the fine print and decide for yourself.

Meeting Planners

Meeting planners are another important tourism intermediary. The size and scope of their activities may go unnoticed, but their impact is tremendous. For example:

- Meetings represent $1 out of every $4 spent on air travel.
- In the United States, meetings represent $23 billion of the hotel industry's operating revenue (36% of all hotel room income), and an even higher percentage among the business hotels.
- Almost 4 of every 10 room nights is used in conjunction with a meeting.
- Associations represent 70% of the billions of dollars spent on meetings.
- The number one factor that associations consider when selecting a meeting site is quality of service.

These professionals are employed by corporations, associations, and others who need their specialized services. The main function of a meeting planner is the detailed planning of business meetings, incentive travel, educational meetings, conventions, trade shows, sales meetings, executive retreats, reunions, and association gatherings. Meeting planners, like travel agents, handle many tasks at once. Take a moment to review Table 3.3, which shows just a sample of the decisions that need to be made by meeting planners on a daily basis.

One of the most pressing responsibilities of meeting planners is to control costs for the organizations they serve. As a result of corporate "belt tightening," the need for meeting planners is predicted to expand, and the destinations and number of sites (both domestic and international) they select will continue to grow.

The meetings planned are usually high-profile or of strategic importance to the organization the meeting planner serves, so planning professionals are scrutinized for the level of service, hospitality, and spirit experienced by the meeting participants. This means

TABLE 3.3
A Small Sample of Decisions Made by Meeting Planners

How many people will attend the meeting?
What city of destination will you choose to host the meeting?
What types of transportation services will clients need?
What types of food functions must be planned?
   Meeting catering
   Reception catering
   Event/program catering
   Banquet catering
   Festival catering
   Cocktail receptions
What types of support services will be needed?
   Message and paging service
   Welcome banners
   Registration assistance
   Welcome packets
   Room blueprints
What types of facilities equipment and supplies will be needed?
   High ceilings (for projections)
   Light controls in each space
   Variety in table size
   Overhead projection
   Flip charts
   Portable computer stations
   Teleconferencing
   Simultaneous translation
   Projection screens
   Overhead computer panels
   Video conferencing
What types of activities need to be planned outside of meeting times?
   Tennis
   Horseback riding
   Golf
   Shopping
   Sightseeing
   Tours

the meeting planner must walk a tightrope, balancing cost constraints with the desires of the meeting attendees.

TOURISM INFORMATION SOURCES AND SERVICES

As we have noted, travelers need access to information before and during their trips. Even though professionals such as travel agents use CRSs to make reservations, they still rely heavily on brochures and other printed materials, including directories to obtain detailed information on tourism services.[7] Marketing communications such as advertising, public relations, and personal selling can all be used to provide travelers and tourism intermediaries with information they need about benefits, prices, and availability.

When tourists are seeking general information about travel and locations en route to their destinations, they often rely on the services of tourism offices. These offices may range from national tourism offices (which we will learn more about in Chapter 10) to local chambers of commerce. These information sources help promote tourism activities on both the individual and group level by providing information and other services. In addition, national, state, provincial, and local tourist offices can be accessed to obtain information and updates on currency, transportation, restaurants, and more. Many of these offices also provide toll free telephone access to improve customer service.

Since tourism is an important economic activity, state, provincial and local governments are often actively involved in providing tourist information. In fact, tourist information centers appear to be one of the more important information sources that visitors use in accessing general information about destinations.[14] We will explore more about the roles that governments play in encouraging tourism expenditures in Chapter 10.

The amount of money spent at the local level helps to determine the type of organization that will provide general tourist information. In large metropolitan areas or in cities where tourism is an important economic activity, you will find convention and visitors' bureaus. These offices are often funded by lodging, restaurant, or other tourism-related use taxes. In smaller cities, these same information functions would be provided by the local chambers of commerce. No matter where the operation is located, the primary functions are providing information for visitors and serving as facilitators in bringing together individual tourists and groups of tourists with tourism suppliers.

The best way to gain information and become familiar with a particular location and all it has to offer is to actually visit the location. **Familiarization trips** (also called "fams" or "fam trips") are offered to tourism intermediaries by a variety of tourism-related organizations such as governmental agencies, hotels, resorts, convention and visitors' bureaus, and tour operators at low or no cost. These trips are designed to promote tourism in general and acquaint participants with the specific capabilities of tourism service suppliers.

Most airlines, car rental services, hotel/motel chains, resorts, convention centers, and cruise lines maintain their own sales force and reservations staff. The sales staff may actively solicit business or engage in missionary sales efforts. **Missionary sales** people do not actively solicit business. Their job is to call on travel agencies and other tourism service suppliers, such as tour operators, to answer questions and provide brochures and other information services; in short, to educate others about their company's services so that they may be sold more effectively.

SUMMARY

Tourism is a service-oriented industry that focuses on meeting the needs of the traveling public. The success and profitability of tourism service suppliers depends on their ability to reach and meet the needs of selected target markets effectively and efficiently.

Suppliers in the tourism industry face many unique challenges. The services they provide are highly perishable and cannot be placed in inventory. In addition, some tourism services often involve a great deal of customer involvement and employee contact.

Although providing profitable levels of customer service is important, it is equally important to make sure that these services reach the intended markets. There are several types of distribution channels for providing consumers with access to the suppliers of tourism services, ranging from direct access to more complex multilevel channels involving several intermediaries.

Many individuals purchase services directly from suppliers, but the most popular form of purchasing tourism services is through a travel agent. The majority of all travel agency business is conducted through computer reservation systems, which provide access to a wealth of data about tourism service suppliers. Travel agencies also work closely with tour wholesalers and operators to serve the needs of specifically targeted groups of travelers. By purchasing and packaging transportation, accommodations, and activities, tour operators create service offerings to sell directly to individuals or through travel agents.

Tourists need information to make informed buying decisions. This information may range from general facts about a location to specific details concerning schedules and availability. Organizations such as convention and visitors' bureaus and local chambers of commerce have been developed to provide general tourism information. Tourism service suppliers utilize salespeople and information technologies to supply the specific information needs of the traveling public. As information technologies improve and develop, the ways we access and use tourism information will change radically.

You Decide

Brenda Baumgardner, manager of Discovery Travel, looked at the letter one more time. The offer sounded too good to pass up! Five all-expense-paid days at the Canyon Fire Resort and an opportunity to generate more business for her travel agency. It would be similar to a fam trip only she would be hosted by a client rather than a group of tourism service suppliers.

The letter had come from John Smithers, Corporate Director of Marketing at a local manufacturing company. He had invited Brenda to accompany him on the company's annual incentive award trip. The January date was perfect for Brenda. Business was usually slow at that time of year and the chance to leave the snow behind for the warmth of the desert was appealing. Besides, the enclosed itinerary of activities looked interesting.

John had indicated in the letter that he was considering having his office coordinate some of the travel and meeting planning activities for this annual event. He had typically turned this task over to an incentive travel company, but recent budget cuts might force him to scale back the program or consider other travel awards. John stated that his staff could handle some of the administrative details, but he might need Brenda's agency to help coordinate travel and accommodation needs for future meetings. John had closed the letter by asking Brenda to call him with an answer by the end of next week.

Brenda had visited Canyon Fire on previous occasions and looked forward to a chance to return and enjoy a little fun in the sun. Although she wanted to experience the pampering of an incentive trip firsthand, she was a bit troubled by the invitation. Brenda's agency handled many of the travel arrangements for John's sales managers who had told her that the company was considering establishing an in-house travel agency.

Although Brenda wanted to accept the invitation, she was concerned from both a personal and business perspective. How would her staff and friends view the personal invitation? Would accepting the invitation create a sense of obligation and limit her negotiating abilities in future business dealings with John? Would the sales managers for John's company understand that she was on a business trip and not simply there for pleasure? If you were Brenda, what would you do?

Net Tour

To learn more about the concepts and organizations presented in this chapter access the homepage for *Tourism: The Business of Travel*. Select "Chapter 3: Bringing Travelers and Tourism Service Suppliers Together." From this location test your knowledge by taking the chapter quiz, read industry insights, and discover links to other useful sites. You may also want to visit electronically with other tourism students through the website.

Discussion Questions

1. Describe how services are different from goods.
2. Explain the functions of intermediaries in tourism distribution channels.
3. What are the differences in one-level, two-level, and three-level tourism distribution channels?
4. Why are travel agents so important in the distribution of tourism services?
5. Explain the functions of tour operators and wholesalers.
6. How is information about tourism services made available to the traveling public?

Applying the Concepts

1. Make an appointment with a travel agent at his/her place of business to discuss what they like and dislike about their work and what types of education and training are necessary to be successful in the industry. While you are at the agency, ask for a demonstration of how the CRS is used to make reservations with the major tourism suppliers.

2. Look for the following headings in the Yellow Pages or business section of your phone book: "Tourist Information," "Tours," and "Travel Agencies."

   a. Prepare two lists of organizations that provide tourist information. One list should contain public organizations and the second list should contain private organizations. Explain how you decided in which category to place each organization.

   b. Call or visit one organization from each list. Prepare a brief outline describing the information received from each.

3. Select an article from a magazine or newspaper describing how consumers can use information technology to access tourism information. Prepare a brief (half-page) summary and copy of the article.

4. Using the World Wide Web, perform the necessary steps to make airline and hotel reservations at the destination of your choice. Write down the steps and World Wide Web addresses you visited in completing this task.

5. Find a brochure that describes an all-inclusive tour package. List all of the tourism suppliers that have been linked together to make this tour package possible.

 GLOSSARY

Airlines Reporting Corporation (ARC) The clearinghouse for receiving commission payments for airline ticket sales.

Caps Limits placed on the amount of commission that will be paid to travel agencies on reservations and bookings.

Commissions The percentage paid to a sales agent (travel agent) by tourism suppliers for booking travel arrangements.

Computer reservation systems (CRSs) On-line reservation systems that provide information on space availability, schedules, rates, and fares with capabilities for printing itineraries, tickets, and invoices.

Consolidators Wholesalers who buy excess inventory of unsold airline tickets and then resell these tickets at discounted prices through travel agents or in some cases directly to travelers.

Consortium An affiliation of privately owned companies to improve business operations and gain the necessary volume of business that can lead to improved profitability.

Escorted tour An all-inclusive tour with a structured itinerary and a guide who accompanies the guests.

Facilitating goods Tangible items that support or accompany the service being provided.

Familiarization trips (also called "fams" or "fam trips") Trips offered by governmental tourism agencies, hotels, resorts, and tour operators at low or no cost to acquaint travel salespeople (typically travel agents) with the products and services they offer.

Franchise A license to operate a tourism service business such as a travel agency or hotel with the benefit of trademarks, training, standardized supplies, operating manual, and procedures of the franchiser.

Hosted tour A host is available at each major tour destination to welcome guests, solve problems, and answer questions.

Independent tour A tour that allows the flexibility to travel independently while taking advantage of prearranged services and rates based on volume discounts.

Intermediary Firms that help tourism suppliers locate customers and make sales to them, including tour operators and travel agencies.

Itinerary A detailed schedule of a trip.

Markup Adding a percentage to the cost of a good or service to arrive at a selling price.

Missionary sales Sales calls made by individuals to retail travel agencies and other tourism industry intermediaries to answer questions and educate them about the company's services so that they may be sold more effectively.

One-level distribution channels The simplest form of distribution, in which the supplier deals directly with the consumer without the services of intermediaries.

Overrides Additional bonuses offered to travel agencies beyond their usual commission to encourage the agency to sell more tickets.

Satellite ticket printers (STPs) An airline ticket printer that is installed at an on-site location away from the travel agency for the convenience of business travelers.

Three-level distribution channels Distribution channels in which two or more channel members, such as tour operators or wholesalers, serve as intermediaries between the supplier and the consumer.

Tour package Two or more travel services put together by a tour operator, such as air transportation, accommodations, meals, ground transportation, and attractions.

Tour operator A business entity engaged in the planning, preparing, marketing, making of reservations, and, at times, operating vacation tours.

Travel clubs Membership organizations designed to serve the needs of last-minute leisure travelers at bargain prices.

Two-level distribution channels Distribution channels in which an additional channel member, such as a travel agent, serves as an intermediary between the supplier and the consumer.

REFERENCES

1. Goeldner, C. R. (1995, winter). Conference report: The 1995 travel outlook. *Journal of Travel Research*, pp. 45–48.

2. Dondero, John E. (1990, July). Lending to travel agencies. *Journal of Commercial Bank Lending*, pp. 49–56.

3. Bittle, Scott (1996). Travelocity Internet site debuts, featuring Sabre booking capability. *Travel Weekly*, *55*(21), 1, 57.

4. Denver review (1996). *News & Views* Harper Woods, MI: Society of Travel & Tourism Educators.

5. Dahl, Jonathan (1994, November 30). Airlines try ticketless systems, giving passengers new gripes. *The Wall Street Journal*, pp. B1, B9.

6. *Carlson Wagonlit Travel Background & History* [news release] (1996, May 24). Minneapolis, MN: Carlson Wagonlit Travel.

7. Schultz, Christopher (1994, April). Hotels and travel agents: The new partnership. *The Cornell Hotel and Restaurant Administration Quarterly*, pp. 45–50.

8. Waters, Somerset R. (1996–97). *Travel Industry World Yearbook: The Big Picture*, vol. 40. Rye, NY: Child and Waters, Inc.

9. Reach the agent, reach the customer (1994, October). *Lodging Hospitality*, pp. 22–23.

10. Fairlie, Rik (1993, November). Apollo, Sabre reach a virtual tie for U.S. travel agency installations. *Travel Weekly*, pp. 1ff.

11. Vis, David (1995, May 1). Amadeus, EDS take control of Continental's System One. *Travel Weekly*, 1ff.

12. Bittle, Scott (1996, April 8). Electronic hotel bookings up 25%. *Travel Weekly*, pp. 1, 53.

13. *Dictionary of hospitality, travel and tourism* (3rd ed.) (1990). Albany, NY: Charles J. Metelka, Delmar Publishers.

14. Fesenmaier, Daniel R. (1994, summer). Traveler use of visitor information centers: Implications for development in Illinois. *Journal of Travel Research*, pp. 44–50.

Readings

The Brand Boom

■

BY MEGAN ROWE, SENIOR EDITOR

Riding a wave of prosperity in the lodging business, franchisers are tripping over each other to debut the latest brand concepts. What impact will this flurry of activity have?

Every time you turn around, it seems another franchise company is touting its vision of the future, the new brand concept that savvy travelers crave. This slew of brand introductions is a natural response to half a decade of pent-up creative energy, fettered until recently by lack of development dollars. It's clearly a sign that the lodging business is healthy once again. Less clear is whether it's good for business.

Some observers say the furious pace of brand introduction was a logical outcome of the lack of attention owners paid to their product before the last few prosperous years. "We went through a period where there was no financing available to fix existing properties," says Joseph Strain, senior vice president with Landauer Real Estate. "Now we're in a new market, where it's almost easier to build them than fix an old one."

Others suggest it's a further evolution of the market segmentation that began 10 or 15 years ago. Concepts that were introduced then may have missed the mark by a bit, and new brands have been fine tuned to take over where the existing ones have failed, suggests Bjorn Hanson, industry chairman for hospitality at Coopers & Lybrand. They are also different enough that they stand out in markets that seem to be saturated with other brands, says Thomas McConnell, director of the hospitality consulting group at Arthur Andersen. "It's not just brands for brands' sake; there's a hook to many brands, differentiating factors, and those factors—along with a new sign, a new name, a new distribution system, or at least piggybacking on an old distribution system—work in markets with brand crowding," he says.

Not only are some markets overloaded with brands, many are skirting an overbuilding condition. So what are all these fresh faces going to do to an equation that has only recently achieved equilibrium? Perhaps less than many fear. Some, like the extended-stay properties, take a little more time, money and commitment to erect, and really only make sense in more-popular areas, so it's unlikely they'll overrun the field anytime soon. In addition, all-new-construction chains don't expand as quickly as those that rely on conversions for growth. "It's a slower way of doing it, but over

the long haul, it probably leaves the chain in better standing," says McConnell.

Lenders, still a bit wary of hotel investments, will also likely put the brakes on enthusiasm over the new concepts. "It seems like there's some capital available, but precious little construction financing," says Strain. "There isn't enough construction financing to launch 10 new brands." But some brands, like Wingate Inns, MainStay Suites and Extended Stay America, have deep pockets bolstering their launches.

Stanley Turkel, a hotel industry consultant, disagrees that lenders and developers learned their lesson from the last lodging slump. "We may have more wary or cautious or prudent lenders, but once the cycle has begun, there will be funding and they will make the same mistakes as the last time around," he says. Turkel, a vocal critic of feasibility studies, blames them for the optimism that leads to new construction. "Developers should insist on—and feasibility companies ought to produce—studies that show not everything is rosy and wonderful, that occupancy and rates will not continue to increase and that other factors are involved in whether a new hotel will be successful."

Even if the money were readily available, however, not all these new ideas will fly. "I hate when people use the word 'shakeout' but that's what will happen," Hanson says. Those that perform well and find acceptance by the public will survive, he predicts.

Strain thinks the brands introduced by existing franchisers have two advantages. "The companies that have good reservations systems need to connect the new brand with an old name—like Sheraton/Four Points or Fairfield/Marriott," he says. He also thinks that companies introducing downscale brands can better leverage their position in the market than those trying to move upscale. He uses as examples Fairfield's success compared to the J.W. Marriott line, and Holiday's experience when it debuted Hampton. "I think we have a good history of success going down a notch or two rather than going up a notch," he says.

While the various market segments may mean something to people in the lodging business, what do all these unfamiliar names evoke for the consumer? Nothing says Randy Smith, president of Smith Travel Research. "These segments that we're always constantly dreaming up mean something to us, but to the traveling public, it's just another hotel," he says. He doesn't think that's necessarily bad, though. "It has clearly generated consumer confusion, but outside of that, it hasn't driven anyone off," he says. "Over time, people have managed to sort it out."

Hampton Inns, in fact, may have benefited from confusion by the public. It rode in the shadow of Courtyard by Marriott, which debuted at about the same time, looks very similar, but cost about $15 a night less. To the consumer, Hampton seemed like a bargain.

Other observers give consumers more credit. "The traveling public is a more sophisticated population than it was 20 years ago, when everybody was comfortable staying in a Holiday Inn," says James Anhut, vice president of branding for MainStay Suites. Hanson agrees. "The learning curve is more rapid than consumers are given credit for," he says.

With all this attention on the new products, existing brands stand to get lost in the shuffle. Right now, they're enjoying healthy occupancies and climbing rates, which any

additional supply will likely curtail. The challenge for them will be to maintain quality in the fresh competition.

That is not to suggest, however, that established hotels are at a disadvantage. "The Quality Inns of the world have significant brand equity, and need to continue to leverage that," says Anhut. Meeting customers' expectations and keeping current are key elements in that effort.

In addition, existing hotels already occupy some of the choicest sites, points out McConnell. He thinks they will need to renovate or reposition to survive, a phenomenon that is already under way at several of Choice's brands, at Holiday Inns and at Sheraton (with Four Points Hotels). Those that are unable to adapt are liable to disappear, he predicts.

Change, at any rate, seems inevitable. "Nothing stays the same; we're in a volatile world," says Turkel. "People keep trying to anticipate where the market is going to go next."

From Rowe, Megan (1996, May). The Brand Boom. Lodging Hospitality, *pp. 20–22. Reprinted with permission from LH—Lodging Hospitality, May 1996.*

Even Tested Travelers Can Be "Provincial"

FEW ARE TRULY VENTURESOME; THE MAJORITY LIKE COMFORTS, ESPECIALLY A BATHROOM

BY CATHY LYNN GROSSMAN

Millions of U.S. travelers packing up passports for spring flings abroad are headed for a big surprise.

It's really foreign out there.

We freak out when we hear German—not English—spoken in Germany.

"Americans think if they talk loud and slow, people will understand them. It's incomprehensible that people aren't speaking English," says Elisabeth Olesen of Places International Tours.

We're shaken up to discover "ethnic" isn't Parmesan from a shake-can.

"People think cruising on an Italian ship is like going to the Olive Garden for breadsticks and salad," says Michael London of Cruise Holidays International.

Is this innocence or arrogance abroad? Experts have a world of theories.

"Our view is that Americanism is the world culture," says travel researcher Stanley Plog.

That attitude doesn't fly far in France. Even veteran, independent travelers who like an all-American welcome get rattled there.

"My worst memory is of being in Nice, France, at a cafe on Rue Jean Medicine constantly being insulted by a French waiter," James Rhodes, of Yuma, Ariz., wrote when USA TODAY asked about travel experiences.

Rhodes says "rudeness reached the point where I stood up (I'm 6-foot-1, 220 pounds), seized him by the throat and forced him up against a wall where I informed him that I would choke the life out of him if he did not start treating us like human beings." It worked.

"If we didn't ask about friendliness, Paris would win Best City in our Readers' Choice poll every year," says Irene Schneider, senior editor at Conde Nast Traveler. "Paris really tanks on friendliness."

"Our readers are better traveled than the average but their expectations are surprisingly provincial" says Schneider. In fact the magazine's 30,000 upscale, globetrotting survey respondents ranked four English-speaking cities—Sydney, Australia; Dublin, Ireland; and Auckland and Christchurch in New Zealand—as the world's friendliest.

"English is a huge advantage for a destination. And it helps if you have a culture that is naturally outgoing and friendly. Friendliness is a very high value to Americans, higher than it is to people from many other cultures."

- Debbie Adams of Italian owned Costa Cruise Lines says many travelers are unprepared to cross cultural borders.

She sees this on their ships in the Mediterranean when U.S. passengers often are among just the 10% to 20% English-speaking clients on a sailing.

- Says Adams: "Many people love the idea of meeting people beyond their own countrymen. But the only unhappy client is a surprised client, so we have to be upfront in telling someone, 'You will be a minority in this experience.' "

- London trains his agents to ask questions that go beyond prices and ports. A sampling:

- "What kind of travel have you done in the past? People who prefer escorted tours or all-inclusive resorts may be happiest with 'a floating U.S. city.' "

- "Have you dealt with multiple cultures before?"

- "Would you be offended if the ship we put you on has a nude sun-bathing section or a 'tops optional' deck?"

- "How would you feel about being on a ship with people who may be more aggressive than you are?" Remember, buffet lines are not the norm in many nations.

London tells clients, "Being on an Italian ship can mean a ship with a non-smoking section that's nonexistent; a crew that's much more aggressive with females on board married and unmarried; and entertainment including foreign languages and very little English."

That takes a certain self-assurance we may lack.

Plog says his surveys of U.S. and Canadian travelers show only 4% are "truly venturesome people who want something very unique. They have enough self-confidence that regardless of the setting or situation, they'll get around."

About 16% of travelers, he says, "want a comfortable bed at night and some good restaurants but they still want to experience a foreign culture."

At the opposite extreme, about 20% have little or no interest in international travel.

"The vast majority of people are in the middle," says Plog. Whether they go to Mexico or Moscow, "they want, to a fair degree, the comforts of home, nothing too strange. They want a place that is a little bit different but seems more different than it really is."

Suzanne Hall of Jet Vacations, the tour affiliate of Air France, says "It's intrinsic to the American personality that he is a little insecure traveling. Whereas Europeans, who are so close to so many different countries, find that traveling or being without their language is not such a big deal. "Americans lose their footing" says Hall. "They don't feel like they are in control and know where they are."

Jet Vacations monitors the treatment U.S. travelers get at hotels and restaurants on their tours. It even had a special English-language menu created at the Grand Louvre, a new eatery at the mall museum in Paris.

"Even people eager to experience other things are more comfortable with the familiar," says Schneider.

"Travel is a very stressful thing to do even if you love it. You are translating languages and money all the time. It's a pleasant thing to find an enclave of home abroad. It's a little breather from the struggle." That feeling is universal.

Our Italian passengers complain all the time that we focus too much on the Americans," says Costa's Adams. "No matter what we do on board to make sure all nationalities are pleased, each believes the other is getting more attention."

Olesen's company opens its offices in San Francisco as a sort of informal lounge where their clients touring the USA can find European coffee and newspapers from home.

"Foreign visitors who come here are much more shy and self-conscious than the Americans are abroad," Olesen says. They will likely travel in a group of family or friends and they let the one who speaks English well do all the talking.

"Germans always ask 'Is there a German restaurant here?' There's some pride and there's some connection. They'll go back frequently. It's a little security," she says.

Meanwhile, Olesen notes, Americans are becoming more at ease overseas.

"When we take U.S. travelers to Europe, I see more people who are low-key, more flexible, more interested in learning what a foreign country is about. They are asking more often for smaller, more authentic hotels" she says.

But she adds, "They still want American bathrooms."

Schneider agrees: "Americans love American bathrooms. Let's face it. Our plumbing is the pinnacle and we know it."

Catering to Families

■

Market demographics shift the focus of tour products

BY ERNEST BLUM

Ernest Blum is Chief of Travel Weekly's Southeast bureau.

If you're looking for what's new and trendy in North American tours in 1996, a first glance could disappoint you. Filling the brochure racks are the familiar favorites: Orlando, Las Vegas, Hawaii, the Rockies, the Nation's Capital, the Big Apple, the Big Easy and New England fall foliage tours. The offerings seem as set in stone as Mount Rushmore.

But under the surface, real change is taking root: Destinations like Myrtle Beach are growing fast; new products with air/motorcoach and air/rail transportation are sprouting up, and old itineraries are being spruced up with flair, even a touch of romance.

Shifts in market demographics also are effecting subtle changes in the product. Tours are getting shorter to accommodate younger travelers. Grandparents are being joined by their children and grandchildren to form an incipient family market. And tour companies are offering more service and flexibility in their products.

And all those changes are taking place amid what appears to be a surge in tour bookings for 1996, prompted in good measure by agent disgruntlement with airline commission caps and eagerness to find more profitable fields to conquer.

Perhaps the most interesting new development is the advent of a small but growing family market. In just the last two or three years, for example, the family market has grown to about 8% of the bookings of Presley Tours in Makanda, Ill., company president Thomas Frenkel says.

"Increasingly, family time together is being spent away from home on vacations," he says.

"And an ideal realization of that is touring, where the price is known up front and all family members have the time to interact with each other."

Calling the phenomenon "multigenerational touring," Frenkel says the market is developing from the wish of grandparents to spend more time with their children and grandchildren, particularly on family occasions and during holidays.

"We're seeing families traveling together over great distances," Frenkel says.

"We're also seeing family members traveling separately to join each other at a vacation destination."

Frenkel says that Central Florida offers the classic family tour, consisting of a central destination from where side trips for all members of the family are possible. But he adds that other possibilities abound.

"Wholesome, experience-rich vacations are what families are seeking," he says.

He points to Presley's three-day War Eagle Craft Fair trip in May and October, based in Eureka Springs, Ark., as an example.

Eureka Springs, he notes, is a mountaintop community in the Ozarks which has a rustic setting that interests all members of the family. That interest is sustained, he says, by a short day trip to a semiannual outdoor crafts fair on the War Eagle River.

The family market at Mayflower Tours, Downers Grove, IL, grew by 5% last year, according to co-owner Mary Stachnik.

It's a market we haven't worked on as hard as others," she says, "but it's growing and getting our attention."

Stachnik says she believes the market started as families searched for ways to spend more time together at Christmas and for birthdays. "Choosing a tour takes care of all the planning chores as well as all the hassle of group travel," she says.

Mayflower's eight-day Washington and Williamsburg tour is a favorite of families, she adds. "Spending a week with your daughter, son or grandchildren affords memories that will live on. And the bonding among members of the family is a win-win for everybody."

Another ideal family destination is Nashville, says Amy Goldstein, director of marketing for Kingdom Tours, Plains, Pa. "Opryland Theme Park interests every member of the family." Kingdom Tours just added a three-night Nashville package, including a car rental, with many options to suit different family members.

"Nashville is resurfacing again in a big way," she says. Indeed, she adds, the destination is promoting itself as "the New Nashville."

Carolyn Cardinale, marketing manager for Frontier Tours and Vista Tours in Carson City, Nev., agrees that families are showing more interest in touring.

As a sign of the market growth, the company has changed the name of its family products from "Grandparents Tours" to "Family Tours," Cardinale says.

Noting that even Las Vegas is positioning itself these days as a family destination, she says she would recommend Las Vegas for some families.

But families who want a totally sheltered atmosphere should choose the new country music capital, Branson, she says. "It's a wholesome atmosphere. Even the entertainment has no obscenities; you won't find strip shows in Branson.

"That's one of the reasons we've got people going back," she says. "It's not a flash in the pan."

Cardinale says her company is combining Branson with both Memphis and Nashville in a 10-night Branson and Tennessee Music Tour that explores the roots of American music.

The awakening of the family market also fits in with another trend, the declining age of the tour market, says Mayflower's Stachnik.

She notes, for example, that the average age of Mayflower's clients has decreased from 70 to 60 years over the last decade.

To capture even younger clients, particularly active working clients between 50 and 55, Mayflower is shortening some tours to fit into a weeklong format or less, Cardinale says.

For example, Mayflower's new tour based on Myrtle Beach, S.C., has been formatted to seven days rather than the traditional tour of eight days or longer, according to Stachnik.

Myrtle Beach is one of the year's hottest destinations, owing its success in part to the rise of Branson as a music capital, Stachnik says. "It's 'Son of Branson.' One thing the mature traveler enjoys is good entertainment."

Mayflower, like other wholesalers, is combining the large new entertainment venues of Myrtle Beach with the historic attractions of nearby Charleston and Savannah.

The company's seven-day package for the three destinations is a new product, Stachnik says, running from March through November, including Christmas departures.

Like other wholesaler tours offering the program, Mayflower's gateway city for the tour is Atlanta, offering the company a chance to visit 1996 Summer Olympics sites as part of the tour.

According to Daniel Sullivan, chief executive officer of Collette Travel Service in Pawtucket, R.I., the Atlanta Olympics connection is a fine addition to the Myrtle Beach program this year. Collette also uses the Atlanta gateway for its eight-day Georgia and the Carolinas tour.

"The addition of the Olympics theme to the tour is a nice touch," he says. "The Olympics will get a lot of attention as the year goes on."

Also adding the new program of Atlanta, Myrtle Beach, Charleston and Savannah this year is Brendan Tours of Van Nuys, Calif., says sales manager Graham West.

"The demand for these new programs is based on the popularity of musical entertainment along with the lure of the South's history and stately mansions."

He adds that the new program is also indicative of the increasing demand for air/motorcoach programs.

"When you fly into a touring area, you're not on the motorcoach that long," says Mayflower's Stachnik. "Flying into the destination has the advantage of getting into your vacation that much faster. People love that."

On the other hand, she says, some wish to avoid the hassle of air travel. For them, she advises an all-motorcoach program.

Taking a cue from the air/motorcoach tie-up, Amtrak's three-year-old Great American Vacations tour program, operated in conjunction with United Airlines, is picking up this year, says Bob Pencoast, vice president of MTI Vacations, Oakbrook, Ill.

One reason for the new spurt in the program, which allows air travel in one direction and rail travel in the other from 75 gateways, is the 20% reduction in fares this year, Pancoast says.

He notes that MTI's Trace Miller Division processes reservations for the innovative Amtrak program.

Another new product involves a tie-up between Collette Travel and Air Canada, reports Collette's Sullivan, offering Canadian tours from 40 gateways in conjunction with the Canadian carrier.

The program is spurring bookings to all our Canadian destinations this summer, from Newfoundland to British Columbia," he says. "We're also experiencing record bookings for the Canadian Rockies. Air Canada's promotion for the program is increasing the awareness of Canada."

Also, nature tours, which have grown in popularity because "people want to get away from shopping centers and suburbia," says Cardinale, are being spruced up.

A five-day "California Coastal Tour" offered by Frontier Tours and Vista Tours, she says, goes to more remote spots in Northern California. Starting from San Francisco, clients ride the "Skunk Train" through remote Red Wood forest areas before arriving in Gold Beach, Ore., where they ride a U.S. mail boat delivering the mail on the Rogue River.

MTI Vacations' Pancoast says the increased popularity of his company's Hawaii programs this year is due in part to the continuing strength of nature travel as well as the growth of the family market.

But he says another factor in the success of the program is the added value his company has built into the program: meals at twelve Hawaiian properties. He says that 50,000 room nights sold in Hawaii this year will include breakfast and dinner in the package's price.

Pancoast says the added value fits in with the additional services tour companies are offering their clients.

For example, MTI Vacations offers a $50 credit for sightseeing if clients make a deposit within 48 hours. In addition, the company sells trip cancellation protection for only $40, including a prorated refund if the cancellation is during the actual trip.

Mayflower's Stachnik says her company is also offering the $40 protection plan, which includes transportation from whatever destination—if a client must make an emergency trip home.

Another added-value service offered clients in the Chicago area, she says, is transportation from their homes to points of departure.

Because accommodations in some destinations are extremely scarce, the company's room inventory should be looked at as another service to clients, she says. "We have to compete for the traveler dollar. And since the traveler has many choices, we have to knock our socks off."

From Travel Weekly, *March 28, 1996, pp. 9–10.*

PART 2

Tourism Service Suppliers

CHAPTER 4

Transportation

One of the many forms of transportation used for touring—the Trimaran Ferry from Ireland to Wales.
Photo by C.E. Yale.

Don't tell me how educated you are, tell me how much you have traveled.

—MUHAMMED

CHAPTER OUTLINE

LEARNING OBJECTIVES

After you have read this chapter, you should be able to:

- Explain the importance of transportation to the tourism industry.
- Identify and describe the major components of the tourism transportation system.
- Explain the differences between passenger railroad operations within and outside the United States.
- Explain the importance of automobiles and motorcoaches to the tourism transportation system.
- Describe the role and importance of water transportation in the movement of travelers.
- Describe how airlines operate in a deregulated and competitive environment.
- Describe yield management and how it can be used in various transportation settings.

THE GRADUATION GIFT

When Shawna opened the envelope at her graduation party, it seemed too good to be true. A trip to Europe! Her grandparents had often discussed the benefits of travel and encouraged Shawna to travel to learn more about the world around her. They had taken Shawna with them on some of their travels and she had also traveled with her parents on summer vacations and business trips. These trips had allowed her to see some beautiful and exciting places, but now she was going to faraway places to do things she had only dreamed about.

After the excitement of the graduation party was over, Shawna settled down to carefully read the letter her grandparents had written describing their travel gift. They were going to buy her a round trip airline ticket from her home in Montgomery, Alabama, to her choice of either London or Paris. They also were going to give her the money to buy a Eurail Pass and her choice of a ticket to travel on the Eurostar through the Chunnel between London and Paris or a ticket on one of the ferries that cross the English Channel. In addition, they had included a check for $1,000 to help pay for some of her other expenses.

Shawna knew it was late, but she couldn't wait to call her grandparents and thank them for the gift. When she asked them what airline to call and which one of the channel-crossing options to take, they simply told her that the experiences to be gained from planning her travels were part of the gift. With this in mind, Shawna contacted Derik, her mother's travel agent, for help in designing her itinerary.

On that visit, she learned that she would be using many different types of transportation during her trip. She could begin by driving, riding a bus, or flying on a small commuter airline to Atlanta. Once there, she could fly directly to either London or Paris. After arriving in Europe, Shawna would have several choices of air, rail, and bus transportation. In addition, there was still the question of how she should cross the English Channel between England and France. Derik answered all of Shawna's questions, but his answers only led her to ask more questions. Shawna soon began to realize that there were several ways to meet her travel needs and she wanted to know more. Provided with a whole new understanding of transportation options, she and Derik began to discuss and plan the details of her upcoming trip. Her grandparents were right; planning her trip was a learning experience.

INTRODUCTION

Although we may not think about it, the tourism industry would cease to function without an efficient and effective transportation system; trains, automobiles, and airplanes are just a few of the more obvious parts of this system. However, there are many other modes of transportation from which to choose. The components of this system can be conveniently classified and placed into two broad categories: surface (land and water) and air. As Figure 4.1 shows, transportation is often **intermodal** with travelers often relying on several different modes of transportation to reach their final destinations. How did this system develop and how does it function today?

Modes of transportation evolved slowly until the 19th and 20th centuries; then, as Table 4.1 shows, things really began to happen. By this time, railways crisscrossed the continents of Europe and North America; gasoline-powered cars and the roads to drive them on became common sights; steamships plied the waters across major trade routes; and the possibility of flight became a reality. Transportation has now become so efficient that we often think of travel in terms of time rather than distance.

Even today, the Parthenon in Greece entices visitors from near and far.
Photo by C.E. Yale.

Venice, Italy——a primary stop during the Grand Tour era.
Photo by C.E. Yale.

The beauty and mystery of the Taj Majal in India attracts near-allocentric travelers.   *Photo by C.E. Yale.*

Market segmentation helps the Vancouver Aquarium satisfy differing visitor needs.   *Photo by Skip Young, courtesy of Vancouver Aquarium.*

One stop does it all!
Photo by D.A. Yale.

Anchorage welcomes the world.   *Photo by C.E. Yale.*

Boats called tenders provide ship-to-shore transportation for cruise passengers.   *Photo by D.A. Yale.*

Amtrak offers travelers the experience of rail travel across the United States.   *Photo by D.A. Yale.*

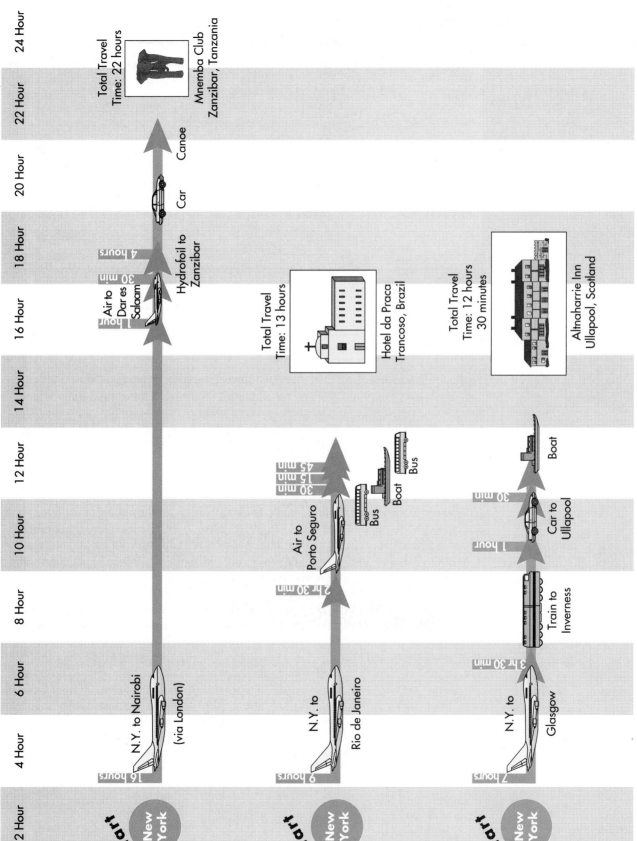

FIGURE 4.1

Intermodal Transportation and Times.

Adapted from *Condé Nast TRAVELER*, (1996, March), pp. 106–107.

TABLE 4.1
Trends in Travel Time

Year	Method	Elapsed Time in Days
Around the World		
1872	Jules Verne—imagination	80.00
1889	Sailing ship—*Nellie Bly*	72.00
1924	U.S. Army aircraft	35.00
1929	*Graf Zeppelin* dirigible	30.00
1947	Pan American Airways Constellation	4.00
1981	Space Shuttle *Columbia*	0.06
Across the Atlantic (New York to London)		
1905	Sailing Ship—*Atlantic*	12.00
1938	Steamship—*Queen Mary*	4.00
1981	Aircraft—*Concorde*	0.15

Source: Owen, Wilfred (1987). *Transportation and World Development.* Baltimore: The Johns Hopkins University Press, 1987.

SURFACE TRANSPORTATION

Just like modern travelers, early travelers probably used both land and water. Modern modes of surface transportation were ushered in with the development of sailing vessels and then passenger railroads and grew with increased personal ownership of automobiles, availability of rental vehicles, and the convenience of motorcoach services. We will briefly examine important historical developments as well as key issues associated with each of these modes of transportation.

Plying the Waves

The power of the wind behind a good sail moved passengers across countless miles of water to many locations for business and pleasure. However, no matter how sleek or fast these ships, they were always subject to the vagaries of the wind. With a favorable wind, it truly was "smooth sailing." But, when the wind died and the sails went slack, there was little for passengers and crew to do other than sit and wait for the wind to return.

With the introduction of steam power, regularly scheduled passenger service on primary water routes became a reality. Like most of the early technological innovations in transportation, steam-powered ships originated in Europe. In 1838, two passenger ships (the *Sirus* and the *Great Western*) crossed the Atlantic from Ireland and Great Britain. By today's standards, and even compared to the speed of clipper ships, their 19- and 15-day crossings were slow. But, they ushered in a new age of dependable scheduled service where travelers had some assurance that they would arrive at their destinations on time.[1]

Transatlantic passenger traffic grew rapidly until 1957 when another technological innovation—the jet engine—heralded the demise of **point-to-point** ocean crossings. Although Cunard Lines still runs scheduled routes between Southampton, England, and New York City and some cruise ships at times carry passengers on point-to-point crossings, ocean-going transportation is now limited. Cruise ship crossings are typically restricted to **repositioning cruises,** in which cruise ships are being moved from one location to another. For example, a cruise line will move ships from the Caribbean to the Mediterranean to take advantage of seasonal changes and passenger demands.

Mention water transportation, and most people think about cruise ships or a brief hop on a ferry when they cross a river, lake, or other short distance on a waterway. However, as you will see in Chapter 8, cruise ships are much more than simply a means of transportation and short ferry rides are often more than just an extension of highway or rail transportation systems.

Water transportation, especially ferry services, are now important links in the total transportation system. Passenger ferries have evolved over time and have become more sophisticated, offering a wide range of services. They are now designed to do more than just carry passengers and vehicles. Some ferries also offer sleeping cabins, restaurants, lounges, gaming, movie theaters, shopping, and child care services.

Passenger ferry routes have been designed to tie in with rail and road systems to facilitate intermodal transportation. These routes create an important link in the transportation systems for many residents and visitors in North American locations such as Alaska, British Columbia, Newfoundland, Nova Scotia, and Washington State. British Columbia, for example, has an extensive system of ferries calling on 42 coastal ports.[2] For the millions of people who travel throughout Asia and the European Community, water transportation is not a luxury, but a necessity.

Riding the Rails

Passenger rail service had its origins in Europe. The first railway service for passengers was inaugurated in Europe on September 17, 1825, when the Stockton and Darlington Railway began offering regularly scheduled service in England. Passenger rail service arrived in North America in 1829, when the South Carolina and Canal Railroad began carrying passengers between Charleston, South Carolina, and Hamburg, Georgia, with steam-powered locomotives. Transcontinental service in the United States began in 1869 and in Canada is 1885.

Long-distance rail travel was given a boost in the United States when George Pullman developed the Pullman coach, with sleeping facilities for overnight travel. The addition of dining cars and legitimate food and lodging facilities pioneered by Fred Harvey heralded the golden age of passenger railroad service in the United States. Dissatisfied with poor food and service, Harvey arranged in 1875 to provide food service for the Atchison, Topeka, and Santa Fe Railroad at its Topeka, Kansas, depot. He became so well known for quality and service that the railroad eventually awarded him all of its dining car services.

Passenger rail service flourished and was an important form of domestic transportation in Canada and the United States until the 1940s. In fact, railroad transportation was so prominent that lodging facilities were developed at major destinations along the rail lines such as Banff, Alberta, Canada, and White Sulphur Springs, West Virginia. However, the forces of change eventually led to the decline of passenger rail service in North America. First, automobile ownership as well as the number of miles traveled by car increased. Then, the Trans-Canada Highway Act of 1949 and the U.S. Federal Aid Highway Act of 1956 enabled provinces and states to begin constructing major highway systems. Both of these factors facilitated long-distance automobile travel. Second, domestic jet passenger service became available. Third, the railroads did not maintain their tracks or customer services. The final blow to U.S. passenger rail service came in 1967 when the post office announced that it would no longer ship mail by train. Without this government subsidy, passenger services became unprofitable and the railroads began to concentrate on moving freight.

AMTRAK AND VIA RAIL CANADA SERVICES

Rail passenger service followed similar tracks of decline in both Canada and the United States until public interest in salvaging long distance passenger train service resulted in government intervention. **Amtrak** was formed in 1971 and **VIA Rail Canada** in 1978 to reduce the number of routes and points served while upgrading the remaining passenger rail systems. Although in different countries, there are many similarities between these two passenger-rail-operating companies.

Amtrak is the marketing name for the National Railroad Passenger Corporation, which is a combination of the passenger rail services of U.S. railroads. Amtrak trains now serve 45 states, with stops in hundreds of communities. (*Note:* The popular Alaska Railroad

Riding the rails in style.
Photo courtesy of VIA Rail Canada Inc.

is not part of the Amtrak system.) VIA Rail Canada is the marketing name for Canada's passenger train network, which links over 400 communities throughout the country. Although they both receive governmental financial support, neither Amtrak nor VIA Rail Canada is a government agency, but corporations structured and managed like other large businesses.

Passenger rail service in Canada and the United States still faces an uncertain future and will probably continue to rely on some form of government subsidies. However, with increased urban growth and new airports being constructed farther and farther from city centers, rail service may grow in importance. Since train terminals were originally built in the center of cities, they now provide a convenient central location and, in many cases, faster and easier transportation in crowded corridors. This is especially true along the eastern seaboard and between major cities in close proximity to each other, such as Montreal and Toronto, New York and Boston, Kansas City and St. Louis, and Los Angeles and San Francisco.

Recent improvements in Amtrak service can be attributed to several factors: introduction of improved service and scheduling in the high-traffic Northeast corridors, aggressive marketing and packaging of vacation trips including rail passes (All Aboard America Fares) and fly/rail packages, membership in the Airline Reporting Corporation (ARC), and listings on airline computer reservation systems. Similar steps such as rail passes **(CANRAILPASS),** fly/drive packages, special tour packages and lodging partnerships have been taken by VIA Rail Canada to increase customer service and rider-ship.

International Passenger Rail Service

Although train travel has declined in Canada and the United States, it has continued to be an important mode of intercity transportation in Europe and Asia. At present, the countries with the largest number of train passengers are Japan, Russia, and India. Heavy population concentrations and attention to roadbeds and tracks have led to the development of high-speed rail service. France, Great Britain, Italy, Japan, Germany, Sweden, Korea, and Spain are just a few of the countries where passengers can travel by train at speeds averaging up to 180 miles per hour. The technology for high-speed rail travel is continually evolving and trains that can travel at speeds of up to 250 miles per hour are in the design and testing stages of development.[3]

Between major population centers within European countries, train travel has become so fast and efficient that it is often more convenient and less expensive than travel by plane when travel to the airport, check-in, and baggage handling times are considered.[4] As you look at the expansiveness and complexity of the European Rail System, which also includes ferry links as shown in Figure 4.2, think back to the limited service provided by Amtrak or VIA Rail Canada. Examples in Table 4.2 indicate how convenient train travel can be between key European cities.

One of the most exciting developments in rail transportation in recent history occurred with the inauguration of high-speed passenger rail service between London, England, and Paris, France. The Eurostar, which travels through the channel tunnel or "Chunnel" allows passengers to make the entire trip in about 3 hours, shortening the trip by 1.5 hours as compared with ferry crossings.

Passenger rail service in Europe has been further enhanced through expansion of the **Eurailpass.** A number of European countries—Austria, Belgium, Denmark, France, West Germany, Italy, Luxembourg, the Netherlands, Norway, Portugal, Spain, Sweden, and Switzerland—introduced the first Eurailpass in 1959. Finland, Greece, and Ireland were added later. Once the Berlin Wall fell, reuniting East and West Germany, the pass became valid throughout the entire German Republic.

The Eurailpass is used as a marketing tool to attract international visitors outside the European community since it is only available to non-European tourists. Pass holders are allowed unlimited travel for varying periods of time throughout Western Europe, with the exception of Great Britain. Recognizing the importance of rail travel to their total tourism package, individual countries such as Great Britain (Britrail pass), Germany (German Railpass), Switzerland (Swiss Pass), Spain (Spain Railpass), and Greece (Greek Railpass) are providing similar services.

In addition to the ready availability of passenger rail service for basic transportation in most developed countries, there are also several specialty trains with particular appeal to tourists. The Orient Express is without a doubt the most famous of all luxurious or scenic trains. With its magnificently restored cars, it runs from London, England, to Istanbul, Turkey. Another classic train, the Blue Train, can be found traveling between Cape Town and Johannesburg, South Africa. With its gold-tinted windows and fine dining, the Blue Train is also renowned for its mystique and romanticism. Other trains such as the Copper Canyon in Mexico, the Palace on Wheels in India, and the Indian-Pacific in Australia are just a few of the many specialty trains that can be found throughout the world.

Most countries consider passenger rail transportation to be of vital national importance and continue to retain government control. Therefore, information on operating results other than ridership and the financial condition of most passenger railroads is not

TABLE 4.2
Comparison of Train and Air Travel between Key European Cities

	By Rail		By Air	
	Time	Fare	Time	Fare
London to Edinburgh	4 hr	$169	1 hr 15 min	$192
Paris to Marseilles	4 hr 15 min	160	1 hr 20 min	123
Madrid to Seville	3 hr 30 min	116	55 min	156
Hamburg to Munich	6 hr	338	1 hr 15 min	332
Rome to Milan	4 hr	84	1 hr 5 min	284

Note: Fares listed are coach class, round-trip for July 1998. Air fares represent those quoted by the country's national air carrier, e.g., Lufthansa for Germany.

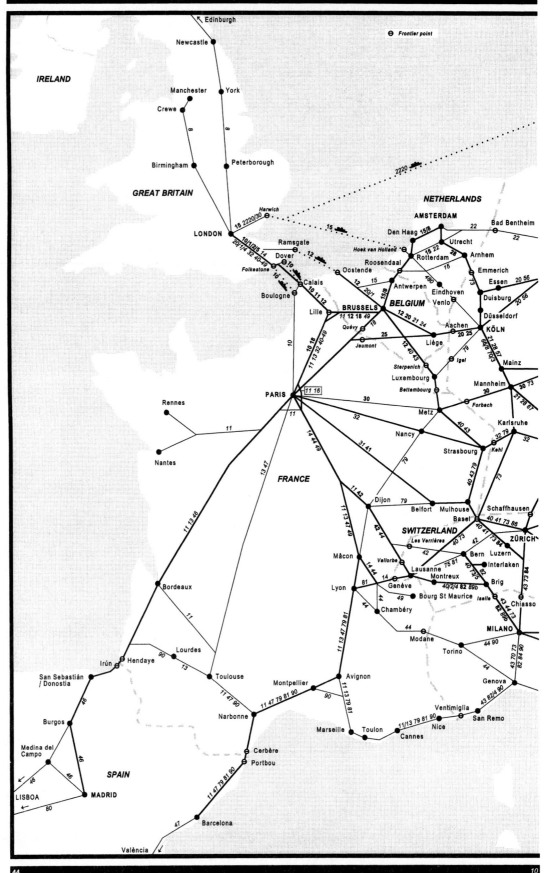

FIGURE 4.2
Example of Rail and Ferry Service in Europe. This is a map of the main *international* rail and ferry services in Europe, representing only a fraction of the full rail network of Europe.

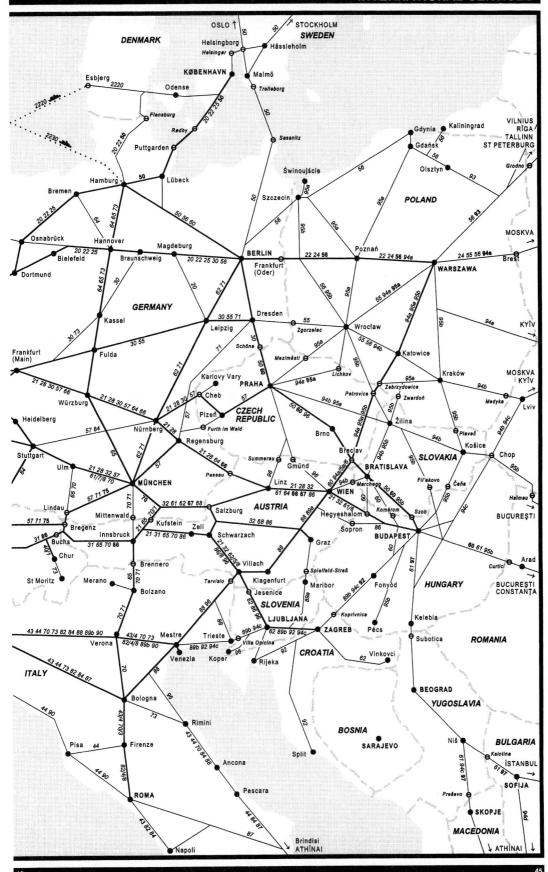

available. This may all change in the future as a trend toward private ownership and reduced subsidies is emerging in European countries, especially Great Britain and Germany. Managers may find themselves venturing into unfamiliar territory, requiring marketing skills to maintain and increase ridership and financial skills to attract the necessary capital to maintain and improve service quality while controlling costs.

CRUISING THE HIGHWAYS AND BYWAYS

The term *highway* came into use as roads were built up from the paths they followed to raise them out of the mud and make them usable on a year-round basis. Innovations in road construction that were pioneered by the French and English soon spread throughout the world.[1] Road construction has continued to progress and now plays a central role in the transportation systems of all developed countries. For example, the first multilane highway, the Autobahn built in Germany during the 1930s, still serves as a vital link in that country's transportation system. These improvements in road systems allowed travelers to move from horses and carts and stagecoaches to automobiles and motorcoaches.

Automobiles

Nowhere in the world is the love affair with the automobile stronger than in North America. Much of the credit for this attraction goes to the pioneering genius of Henry Ford, who ushered in the age of mass automobile travel with his famous Model T. Between 1908 and 1923, 15 million of these affordable cars were produced. The car is now more than simply transportation for most Americans; it is a symbol of freedom and individualized lifestyles. The availability of affordable automobiles and an expansive highway system have made automobile travel the most popular form of transportation in Canada and the United States. In fact, automobiles account for about 76% of all travel away from home and 83% of all intercity miles.

Both Canada and the United States have focused government attention and resources on the development of highway systems rather than rail systems. The Trans-Canada Highway spans 4860 miles between Victoria, Vancouver Island, British Columbia, and St. John's, Newfoundland. The interstate highway system in the United States has resulted in an intricate web of 42,800 miles of divided highways connecting every major city in the country. This system is truly remarkable since it accounts for only 1% of all roads in the United States, but carries over 20% of all highway traffic.

Although automobiles may be the desired form of personal transportation in the United States, less than 20% of the population have ever rented a car. Growth in the rental car business has historically paralleled or exceeded the growth in air travel, with almost two thirds of car rental revenues being derived from airline passengers.[5] In 1985, the number of rental cars available in the United States was approximately 760,000; however, this number had grown to over 1.5 million by the late 1990s.

RENTING A CAR

Although renting cars in the United States is fairly straightforward, except for those under 25 years of age, renting outside the United States can be a more complicated adventure. There can be a variety of charges added to the basic cost of rental, including mileage, insurance, drop-off charges, and airport fees. The list goes on, so it pays to ask questions and shop around as well as to use the services of your travel agent.

Check the restrictions on your credit card coverage before you rent. Most credit cards provide supplemental collision-damage waiver or loss-damage waiver (CDW/LDW) coverage, but only for damages not already covered by your personal automobile or other insurance. If you do decide to rent a car as you travel abroad, take the time to get an international driving permit.

This growth has been led by a few large companies. Enterprise has developed the largest rental car fleet, followed by Hertz, Avis, Alamo, Budget, and National, respectively. At present, the primary users of rental cars are business travelers, who rent over 75% of all vehicles, but car rental companies are beginning to turn some of their attention to leisure travelers. Hertz and Enterprise serve to highlight the differences in marketing strategies among the rental car companies. Hertz controls the largest market share at most major airports while Enterprise has chosen to service a broader range of customers by delivering cars directly to customers from less-expensive off-airport sites.[6]

The range of variables managers must deal with in this industry is staggering. "Picture an industry where costs have more than doubled in just four years, where repeated attempts to raise prices have failed, and where demand is largely determined by demand for a rival product [scheduled airline service]."[5] To deploy fleets of cars across broad geographic areas and achieve maximum **fleet utilization,** managers must anticipate a wide variety of customer demands, including car types, rental periods, insurance, fuel options, and pick-up and return locations.

Logistics also play a key role in successful car rental operations by getting the right cars to the right place at the right time. Recent software developments provide the necessary information for employees and managers to know when to refuse a short-term rental based on the probability that the same vehicle can be rented for a longer term to a different customer.[5] Can operating efficiencies make a difference? The answer is yes, as has been demonstrated by Budget who is able to get almost $2,000 more revenue per car than some of its rivals (see Table 4.3).

In this highly competitive industry, it is often the little things that make a difference. Surveys show that customers want to cut as many hassles out of rental car returns as possible. Car rental companies are responding to these requests by enhancing their services to include valet delivery and parking services to avoid shuttle buses, equipping cars with onboard computerized navigation systems, providing drop boxes for the return of keys and rental forms, and equipping service personnel with hand-held computers to complete rental transactions at the point of return.[7]

Motorcoaches

Motorcoaches have come a long way since their predecessor (stagecoaches) bounced across the countryside. There are now two primary categories of motorcoach (often called bus) transportation—scheduled intercity travel and charter/tour groups. Intercity bus travel, like rail travel, has continued to command less and less of the scheduled travel market in the United States. Just like railroads, the importance of scheduled bus service in the United States peaked in the 1940s, and the decline continues today. In 1980, bus travel accounted for 12% of all interstate travel, but it now accounts for only about 6% of interstate travel. Although the number of passengers utilizing interstate buses has continued a gradual downward trend, this mode of transportation still provides a vital link in domestic and international transportation systems.

TABLE 4.3
Revenue per Car

Company	1997 Revenue (in millions)	1997 Average Fleet	Average Revenue per Car
Hertz	$3,000	250,000	$12,000
Avis	$2,000	200,000	$10,000
National	$1,750	145,000	$12,069
Budget	$1,600	125,000	$12,800
Alamo	$1,300	130,000	$10,000
Dollar	$707	62,000	$11,403
Thrifty	$363	34,000	$10,676

Source: Based on information provided by *Auto Rental News,* Torrance, CA: Bobit Publishing Co.

In the United States, schedules, fares, and routes of intercity buses were closely regulated by the Interstate Commerce Commission (ICC) until passage of the Bus Regulatory Reform Act of 1982, which eliminated most regulations except those pertaining to safety. In this deregulated environment, intercity bus lines in the United States have continued to consolidate and pare their schedules and now focus primarily on trips of less than 250 miles. Several diverse target markets, including lower-income groups and riders under the age of 24 or over the age of 65 are proving to be fertile ground for future growth.

Although intercity bus travel in the United States has declined, motorcoach usage in general has increased due to its popularity among tour and charter operators because of flexibility and economy of operation. In addition, intercity bus travel remains an attractive alternative to rail travel in many countries with high population densities.

Additional growth opportunities for motorcoach travel can be found in the mature-traveler market segment. "During the next two decades, the first wave of baby boomers will begin to enter their senior years, making them a prime target for the domestic motorcoach market."[8] Their primary considerations in selecting motorcoach tours will be service, quality, and comfort. Motorcoach executives predict that health, spa, special event, entertainment, and golf and ski packages will be the primary tours sought by these demanding groups in the future.[8]

As profiles of individuals using motorcoaches have changed, so have the motorcoaches. "Seats are wider. Views are better. There's stereo music and often an integrated video system showing the latest movies, just like the airlines. Increasingly, there's a hot beverage service or even a full galley with a microwave oven."[9] The standard motorcoach has grown from 40 feet to as much as 45 feet in length and passenger capacity has increased from 47 to 55.

Motorcoach operations, whether intercity (bus) or charter (tour operators), have many of the same operational concerns that face every participant in the tourism industry. The financial information presented in Table 4.4 shows the overall expenses and profitability as a percentage of sales for these two groups of motorcoach operators. Competition and government involvement in the intercity bus transportation varies widely outside the United States. In some countries, such as Spain, bus transportation is more important than rail transportation; in other countries, such as Iceland, there is no train service, only bus service; and in Japan, the Japan Rail Pass includes unlimited travel on the bus as well as the train. Therefore, because of the country-specific nature of intercity bus transportation,

TABLE 4.4
Income Data for Motorcoach Operators

	1995	1996	1997
Intercity Bus Service			
Net sales	100.0%	100.0%	100.0%
Operating expenses	93.9	90.7	91.8
Operating profit	6.1	9.3	8.2
All other expenses (net)	1.7	2.3	4.7
Profit before taxes	4.4	7.0	3.5
Charter Bus Service:			
Net sales	100.0%	100.0%	100.0%
Operating expenses	92.5	94.4	92.6
Operating profit	7.5	5.6	7.4
All other expenses (net)	3.0	1.9	1.5
Profit before taxes	4.5	3.8	5.9

Source: Robert Morris & Associates, *Annual Statement Studies,* 1997. Robert Morris Associates (RMA) cautions that the Studies be regarded only as a general guideline and not as an absolute industry norm. This is due to limited samples within categories, the categorization of companies by their primary Standard Industrial Classification (SIC) number only, and different methods of operations by companies within the same industry. For these reasons, RMA recommends that the figures be used only as general guidelines in addition to other methods of financial analysis. (Reprinted with permission, copyright Robert Morris Associates 1997.)

we will leave the investigation of availability and operations in specific geographic locations up to your exploration.

Motorcoaches usually serve many more locations than trains, which are confined to specific routes because of their fixed tracks. They are frequently less expensive to ride and can often take you to places not served by trains, although they are generally slower. However, there are several exceptions to this general rule. In southern European countries, including Portugal, Greece, Spain, and Turkey, bus service may be faster but more expensive than trains.[10] The long-distance bus networks of Britain, Ireland, Portugal, Morocco, Greece, Turkey, and the Czech Republic are more extensive, efficient, and often more comfortable than trains. The new Eurobus programs provide direct competition to train pass programs, with 2 months of unlimited travel on buses accompanied by an English-speaking driver and guide. Destinations in continental Europe include Paris, Amsterdam, Cologne, Prague, Munich, Venice, Rome, and Milan. As with rail passes, passengers get on and off at their leisure.[11]

BUS SERVICE BETWEEN LONDON, PARIS, AND AMSTERDAM

Cityzap, a new express bus service operating between London, Paris, and Amsterdam, has two scheduled departures daily from each city. Air-conditioned buses that seat 50 passengers operate from Victoria Bus Station (London), Galieni Bus Station (Paris) and Central Bus Station (Amsterdam). The trip takes 6 hours between London and Paris, 6 hours between Paris and Amsterdam, and 7 hours between London and Amsterdam. To save time, the London–Paris bus and the London–Amsterdam bus take Le Shuttle train service through the "Chunnel" instead of using ferry service. For the passengers' comfort, each bus has lavatory facilities and TVs as well as a hostess, who serves complimentary beverages and snacks.

Source: Baratta, Amy (1996, February 8). Express bus service to connect London, Paris, Amsterdam. *Travel Weekly*, p. E27.

IMPORTANT TRANSPORTATION LINKS

The final link in the surface transportation system is composed of many modes such as subways, trolleys, intracity busses, and light-rail systems. Although each of these forms of transportation is important to the overall transportation system, we will not examine them in this book because they are used primarily for daily commuting to and from work and do not fall within our definition of tourism. However, they do fill an important transportation need for many individuals who do not want to be burdened with automobiles as they travel.

If short distances are involved and/or individuals do not need a car while at their destination, then they may rely on taxi, limousine, or shuttle services. Taxis fill an important transportation function by efficiently moving large numbers of people within cities, especially in crowded urban areas, as well as to and from airports and railway stations. One of the most significant changes in the tourism industry has been the intermodal tour that combines motorcoach, air travel, railroad, and water travel.[12]

SOARING THROUGH THE SKIES

The first scheduled passenger flight debuted in Europe on August 25, 1919, with a route between London and Paris, and jet passenger service was inaugurated on May 2, 1952, with a flight between London and Johannesburg, South Africa. However, in the United States, passenger service did not begin until April 17, 1926, with an inaugural 6.5-hour flight between Los Angeles and Salt Lake City. Domestic jet passenger service did not appear until 1958, with scheduled service between New York City and Miami.

Talk about intermodal transportation! Look at a large group of tourists who gather in Iowa at the end of July each year and you will find people who have come from all over the world. Who are these intrepid travelers? Bicyclists! Once they arrive via planes, trains, automobiles, tour buses, and recreational vehicles, they quickly revert to an age-old mode of transportation: pedal power. Just imagine thousands of bicycle riders who throng to Iowa each year to participate in the Register's Annual Great Bicycle Ride Across Iowa (RAGBRAI).

These riders soon get a first-hand, up close lesson in Iowa geography. "The RAGBRAI route averages around 467 miles and is not necessarily flat. It begins somewhere along Iowa's western border on the Missouri River and ends along the eastern border on the Mississippi. . . . Eight Iowa Communities along the RAGBRAI route serve as 'host communities' for overnight stays" (RAGBRAI XXIII).

"RAGBRAI began almost accidentally in 1973 when John Karras and Don Kaul, columnists for *The Des Moines Register*, decided to do a 6-day, cross-Iowa bike ride to rediscover the state's roots. Through a story in the paper, they issued an invitation for people to join them. To their astonishment, about 300 did. . . . Today, admission is by lottery with only 7500 riders accepted out of the 10,000 who apply. Even so, organizers estimate that 9000 cyclists participate, since many unregistered riders join in. . . . Thanks in part to RAGBRAI's success, big multi-day tours have boomed. Now cyclists can dip their wheels into an alphabet soup of cross-state trips: BRAN (Nebraska), BRAT (Tennessee), BRAG (Georgia), PALM (Michigan), RAM (Minnesota), RAIN (Indiana), CAM (Maryland), BAMMI (Illinois), NYRATS (New York), and so on" (Bicycle Touring).

And it's not just the cyclists who converge on these events. Their support teams (mostly family and friends) create moving cities of recreational vehicles and tents that creep across the countryside and fill every motel room in sight, eating tens of thousands of meals, and buying everything from necessities to souvenirs. Events like this and bicycle touring throughout the world highlight the economic benefits of recognizing the power of pedalling enthusiasts around the globe.

Sources: RAGBRAI XXIII (1995, July 23–29). *The Des Moines Register*; Martin, Scott (1992). Iowa's rolling party turns 20. *Bicycle Touring*, *10*(2).

With a long and meaningful history, domestic (U.S.) cooperation between airlines has been accomplished through the **Air Transport Association (ATA)** and international cooperation through the **International Air Transport Association (IATA).** Formed in 1936, ATA serves as a united voice for the airline segment of the tourism industry and provides a format for the discussion of safety and service issues and promotion of technological advancements. IATA, which is composed of almost all major international airlines, was formed in 1919 and reorganized in 1945. Its purpose is to facilitate the movement of passengers and freight across a combination of route structures and international boundaries. Through these cooperative agreements, passengers are able to buy a single ticket based on one currency that is valid for travel throughout an air system that may involve many carriers and cross many national boundaries.

Barriers restricting flights across international borders are beginning to fall. The "open-skies" agreement between the United States and Canada opened the world's largest passenger market. Similar agreements with other countries will eventually ease travel for international passengers. Airline passenger traffic experienced strong and steady growth, averaging approximately 5% a year from the late 1950s until the early 1990s. In the United States, it is now estimated that domestic passenger traffic, which accounts for almost 75% of all air passenger traffic worldwide will increase by about 3% a year into the 2000s and international passenger traffic should grow by about 6% a year during this same period.[13]

In an attempt to attract more customers and to develop brand loyalty, American Airlines pioneered a frequent-flier marketing program in 1981. This program was soon copied by other major carriers. These programs have increased customer loyalty, with passengers often going out of their way or taking inconvenient flights to obtain frequent-flier miles, yet few actually cash in their mileage for awards.[14] Airlines are also partnering with a multitude of other organizations both inside and outside the tourism industry by offering miles for purchase to generate additional revenues, increase brand awareness, and heighten customer loyalty.

American Airlines was the first to recognize the marketing power of frequent-flyer programs.
Photo by D.A. Yale.

The number of frequent-flyer miles accumulated is now over 1.5 trillion miles and continues to grow. This accumulated mileage could be a financial liability for some airlines, where revenue-paying passengers could be displaced with non-revenue-paying frequent-flier awardees. Recognizing this potential liability, airlines have increased the number of miles required to obtain frequent-flier awards and restricted the number of seats available for these awards, especially on popular routes.

THE MARKETING POWER OF FREQUENT-FLYER MILES

Frequent flyers are finding some new ways to earn additional miles even when they are not in the air. Airlines are selling frequent-flyer miles to just about any organization from banks and retailers to charities that are willing to buy them. Purchases can be made in minimum blocks of 250 miles at 2¢ per mile. The airlines gain at least $5 from each transaction and the purchasing organizations obtain attractive promotional incentives.

Source: John Naisbitt's Trend Letter, 15(12) 1996.

Airlines, like most other service providers in the tourism industry, operate on very thin profit margins. Therefore, controlling costs and maximizing revenues is a major concern and absolute necessity for survival and profitability. As can be seen in Figure 4.3, the most significant expenses as a percentage of sales in the airline industry are operating costs and equipment. Since costs other than labor are difficult to control, airline companies attempt to maximize revenues. This can be accomplished by obtaining the highest possible **load factor** per revenue passenger mile on each flight.

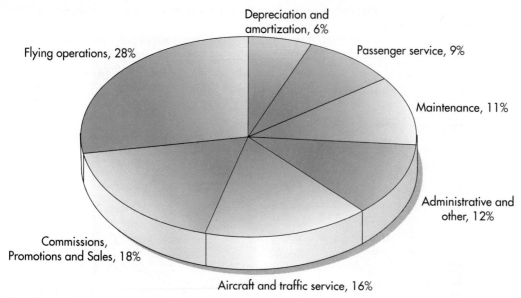

FIGURE 4.3
U.S. Airline Expenses
Source: *The Airline Handbook* (1995). Washington, DC: The Air Transport Association, p. 26.

Operating in a Deregulated Environment

The Airline Deregulation Act of 1978 had profound and lasting effects on domestic (U.S.) airlines. Prior to the passage of the Act,

1. Airlines did not compete on price.

2. Airlines wanting to begin services to new cities had to apply to the Civil Aeronautics Board (CAB).

3. Airlines had to apply to the CAB 90 days in advance and receive formal approval to discontinue service to a city.

4. Airlines were prohibited from entering the tour business.

The crafters of the Deregulation Act envisioned the creation of a freely competitive market that would provide needed air service more efficiently.

To facilitate the move to a competitive market, the CAB and its regulatory capacities were eliminated and the **U.S. Department of Transportation (DOT)** assumed the responsibilities for overseeing operational issues such as the overselling of tickets, smoking on flights, and potentially deceptive advertising practices as well as competitive concerns such as mergers and acquisitions. Air routes were made available to all carriers who could meet safety and service standards, and new carriers were encouraged to provide a variety of low-priced services. The **Federal Aviation Administration (FAA)** has responsibility for the safety of air transportation carriers.

Deregulation removed all the previously listed operating constraints that restricted airline operations. Pricing became very complex. Rather than a simple three-tier structure (economy, coach, and first class), there are multiple prices, and airlines change these prices hundreds of thousands of times each day. Sometimes, very low prices on a particular route may be available for only a few minutes. All these changes are being made as airlines attempt to meet customer needs, maximize load factors, and increase revenues through their yield-management systems. Today, there is little to keep a carrier from entering a new city other than airport safety and capacity constraints.

Airlines may now function as tour operators, providing packaged tours directly to the public. In addition, they may own and operate travel agencies, and they may develop new methods of selling tickets other than directly and through the existing travel agency system. This latter change has resulted in satellite ticketing terminals that operate in a manner similar to automatic teller machines and other forms of electronic access, including ticketless travel.

Deregulation has made the **hub-and-spoke system** the primary route pattern in the United States. Airlines select hubs near major metropolitan areas, where passenger, administrative, and maintenance activities can be concentrated. By designating primary hubs (see Table 4.5), airlines are able to funnel traffic into these centers to feed their **trunk routes** from smaller markets along **spoke routes.** This system allows the airlines to capitalize on **economies of scale** and match the size of the aircraft serving a market to the demand from that market. An example of a hub-and-spoke system is shown on the map in Figure 4.4.

Regional/commuter airlines, which fly about 10% of domestic passenger miles on spoke routes typically operate on a **code share** basis. In a code share agreement, a regional/commuter airline will share the same two-letter identification code of a major airline in the computer reservation system and typically paint its planes the same color.[15]

By utilizing the hub-and-spoke system, airlines are able to increase operating efficiency through scheduling arrivals and departures in **banks of flights.** Banking flights is the process of coordinating flight schedules to maximize the use of ground crews and equipment. In addition, the shorter the period of time that an aircraft remains on the ground, the more time it can spend in the air earning money. Some regional/commuter airlines are able to turn their aircraft around or **push** them in 15 minutes or less, while major carriers may take as long as 45 minutes to do the same tasks.

Deregulation and the growth of passenger air service in general have created several potential problems. The hub-and-spoke system has created bottlenecks at hub airports and increased travel times as many direct flights between pair cities under the old regulated environment have been eliminated. In addition, capacities at hub airports have become strained.

The management teams at airline companies are addressing these problems through the designation of secondary hubs and instituting more direct flights to pair cities. For example, rather than having passengers fly from Indianapolis to Chicago and then on to their final destination in St. Louis, they can fly directly from Indianapolis to St. Louis. Direct flights could increase in the future as aircraft technology advances and smaller, more efficient jets become available. Low-fare airline operations, pioneered by Southwest Airlines, have focused their flight schedules on **point-to-point systems.** These systems fly directly between pair cities, avoiding the transfers involved in hub-and-spoke systems.

TABLE 4.5
Primary Hubs

Carrier	Hub Cities
Air Canada	Montreal, Toronto, Vancouver
American Airlines	Dallas/Fort Worth, Chicago, San Juan, Nashville, Raleigh/Durham, Miami
America West	Phoenix, Las Vegas
British Airways	Heathrow (London), Gatwick
Continental Airlines	Houston, Denver, Newark
Delta Airlines	Atlanta, Dallas/Fort Worth, Salt Lake City, Los Angeles, Cincinnati
KLM	Amsterdam
Lufthansa	Frankfurt
Northwest Airlines	Minneapolis/St. Paul, Detroit, Memphis
SAS	Copenhagen
TWA	St. Louis, New York
United	Chicago, Denver, San Francisco
USAirways	Pittsburgh, Philadelphia, Charlotte, Baltimore

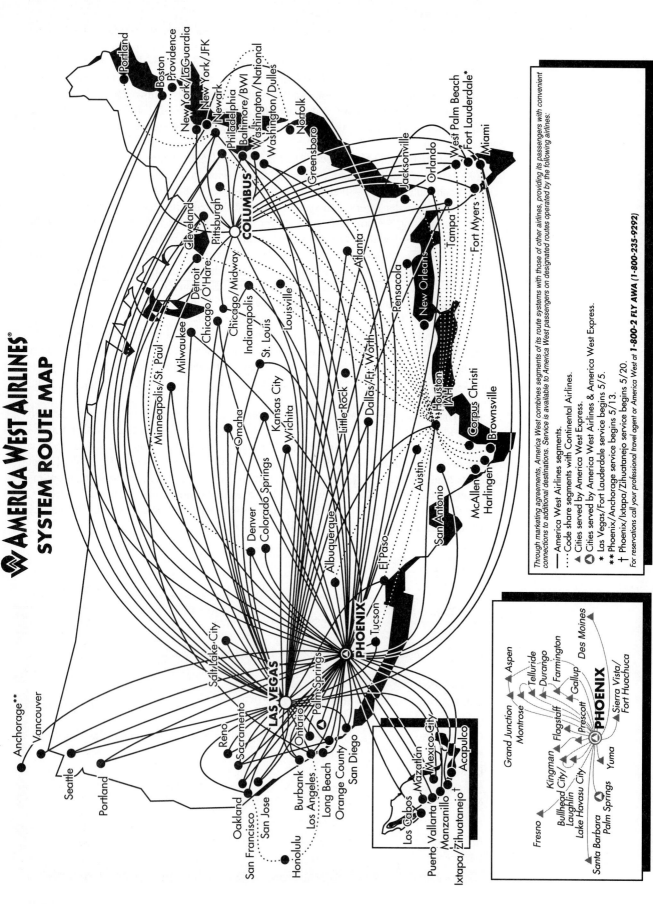

FIGURE 4.4
Hub-and-Spoke System
Airline Route Map courtesy of America West Airlines.

Since it is a common practice for individuals to make airline reservations and not show up for their scheduled flights, airlines overbook in order to fly at capacity. Federal regulations require them to make amends to passengers who are **involuntarily denied boarding (bumped)** because of **overbooking.** It must first ask for volunteers to give up their confirmed reserved space on the flight for some form of compensation.

If there are insufficient volunteers, then the airline will involuntarily deny boarding based on its established policies. Passengers who have been denied boarding are entitled to compensation of up to 200% (or a maximum of $400) of the value of their remaining flight coupons. This amount may be reduced by the airline if comparable transportation can be arranged that will allow passengers to arrive at their scheduled destinations within 2 hours of their originally scheduled arrival time on domestic flights (4 hours on international flights). Other types of benefits offered may include phone calls and/or free or reduced cost lodging and meals if an overnight stay is required.

Decoding the Language of the Airline World

All participants in the tourism industry have their own particular set of terms they use to describe operating issues, but the airline industry has more than most. To understand the airline industry, it is important to be familiar with some of the more common terms.

1. Every airline has its own two-letter identification code. Examples of these codes for the largest airlines in the world are: American Airlines (AA), United Airlines (UA), Delta Air Lines (DL), British Airways (BA), and Lufthansa (LH).

2. Every city with scheduled passenger service has its own three-letter airport code to identify the airport that is served. Examples of these airport codes are: Albuquerque, New Mexico (ABQ); New York/Kennedy International Airport (JFK); Orlando International, Florida (MCO); Omaha, Nebraska (OMA); Orly, Paris, France (ORY); Narita, Tokyo, Japan (NRT); and Toronto, Canada (XYZ).

3. Every airline uses codes to identify class of service. Examples: Supersonic (R), First Class (F), Business Class (C), Coach and Economy Class (Y), Advance Purchase Excursion (APEX).

4. Airline service is also classified as nonstop, direct or through, and connecting. Nonstop flights are from the point-of-origin to a destination with no intermediate stops. Direct or through flights are from the point-of-origin to a destination with one or more intermediate stops. Connecting flights require passengers to change planes to a connecting flight between the point-of-origin and final destination.

5. There are also several types of trips that passengers can book. Examples: one-way— a trip from origin to destination without a return to origin; round-trip—a trip from origin to destination with a return to destination; circle trip—similar to a round trip except that either the outbound or return trip will follow a different route and possibly use a different airline; open-jaw—a round-trip that allows the passenger to utilize different points of origin or departure.

IMPROVING OPERATING EFFICIENCY AND EFFECTIVENESS

Yield management (which is also called "revenue management") was developed by Bell Laboratories in 1988 and initially used as a scheduling tool for the airline industry, but its effectiveness in addressing a host of marketing, management, and financial issues soon expanded its use to other tourism service providers such as hotels/motels, resorts, cruise ships, and car rental companies. Basically, yield management requires allocating capacity to customers at the right price to maximize revenue or yield, enhance customer service, improve operating efficiency, and increase profitability under the following conditions.[16]

- *When capacity is relatively fixed.* For example, when demand increases, airlines cannot simply add more seats; hotels cannot add more rooms; and rental car companies cannot quickly enlarge fleets at specific locations.

- *When demand can be separated into distinct market segments.* For example, tourism service providers can segment demand based on specific customer profiles and needs.

- *When inventory is perishable.* For example, as we have previously mentioned, once a plane has left the gate, there are no more opportunities to fill its seats with revenue-paying passengers on that flight.

- *When services can be sold well in advance.* For example, reservation systems allow leisure travelers to save money by making advance reservations with specific time restrictions.

- *When demand fluctuates substantially.* For example, during periods of high demand, higher rates can be obtained, but during periods of lower demand, lower rates may be necessary to attract customers.

- *When marginal sales costs are low and marginal capacity costs are high.* For example, the cost of selling an additional reservation for an airplane seat or a night's lodging is minimal, but the cost of purchasing a larger airplane or adding rooms to an existing hotel would be very expensive.

Through the effective use of yield management, American Airlines was able to increase its load factor from 64% in 1990 to 70% in 1997.[17] The following example will highlight the importance of yield-management techniques as they are used to enhance revenues in an airline setting. For ease of understanding, we will use a smaller 37-seat aircraft in this example. The principles will remain the same for larger aircraft as well as in other settings where tourism service providers are seeking to enhance revenues.

On a 150-mile flight between cities A and B, we know from past reservation data that we can sell all 37 seats on our flight to leisure travelers. These travelers would be willing to purchase all seats for advance purchase excursion ticket fares of $39.00 each way ($39.00 fare × 37 passengers = $1,443.00). We also know that we could sell 15 full-fare coach tickets to business travelers for $98.00 each way ($98.00 fare × 15 passengers = $1,470.00). If this were an either/or decision, we would choose to sell only full-fare coach tickets since it would result in $27.00 more in revenue ($1470.00 − 1443.00) and we could focus more attention on each passenger with the same required flight crew.

However, neither one of these choices will allow us to maximize revenues for this flight. What we need to do is hold back enough seats in the full-fare ($98.00) category to serve our business customers who need to travel at scheduled times and do not make their travel decisions solely on price. At the same time, we still want to fill the plane to generate as much revenue as possible. We could sell all of the remaining 22 seats at the $39.00 advance purchase excursion fare. However, this choice would still not maximize revenues.

Based on information provided from our yield-management system, we decide to sell 8 seats at $39.00 each if they are reserved more than 30 days in advance, 12 seats at $59.00 if they are reserved more than 14 days in advance, and hold 17 seats at the $98.00 fare that can be sold up to the time of departure. By making these decisions, we have begun the process of maximizing revenues.

Our true yield for this flight will be based on the number of revenue-paying passengers who actually fly on the day of departure. Passengers buying discounted tickets know that these fares are nonrefundable and have restrictions. Therefore, they typically arrive for the flight, claim their reservations, and board the plane. On the other hand, passengers who have paid full fare may not claim their reservations, since they can be canceled and/or changed without penalties. Knowing this, we will overbook the flight, realizing that based on historical information a certain percentage of passengers holding reservations will not show up to claim their seats.

Figure 4.5 shows a seating configuration for a 37-passenger airplane and how these seats might be filled with revenue-paying passengers in our example. By managing our seats to meet the needs of specific target groups, we have generated $2,686 in total revenue even though some passengers failed to honor their reservations. Remember, that for the sake of simplicity in our example, we used a smaller aircraft flying a direct route. As the size of aircraft increases and the number of **legs** multiply, yield-management calculations can become very complex, requiring sophisticated computer hardware and software programs.

There are several other key statistics that can be generated from the data that is gathered to maintain our yield-management system. These data include **available seat miles (ASMs), revenue passenger miles (RPMs),** and **load factor.** In our flight example, we had 5550 ASMs (150 miles × 37 seats). It generated 4500 RPMs (150 miles × 30 revenue passengers), resulting in a load factor of 81% (4500 RPMs ÷ 5550 ASMs).

Although yield management holds the promise of maximizing revenues, it, like most other quantitative management tools, should not be used blindly. Factors such as desired market position, customer satisfaction, employee morale, and demand for related goods

FIGURE 4.5
Yield-Management Example

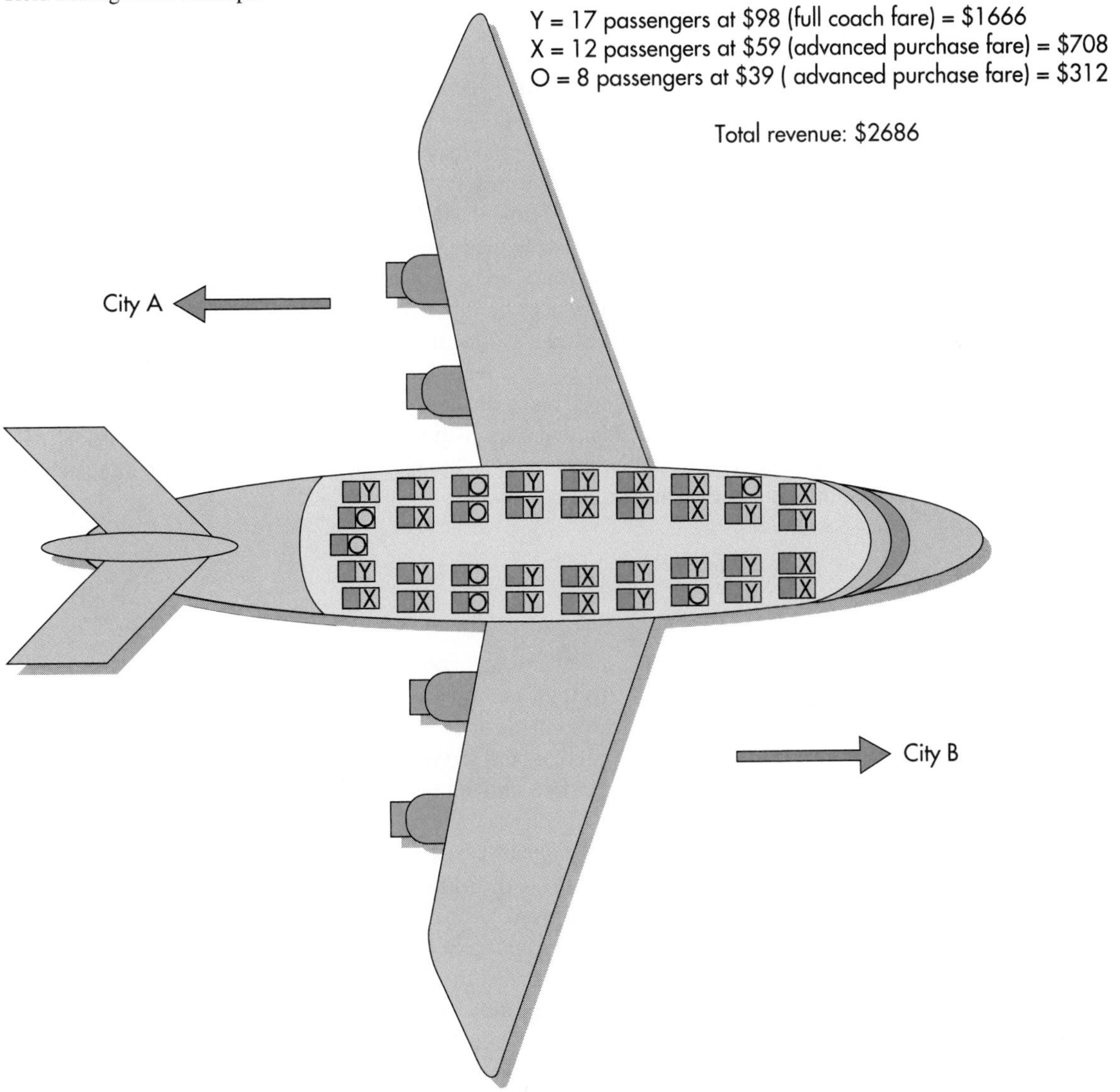

Y = 17 passengers at $98 (full coach fare) = $1666
X = 12 passengers at $59 (advanced purchase fare) = $708
O = 8 passengers at $39 (advanced purchase fare) = $312

Total revenue: $2686

City A

City B

or services must be considered. As competition between transportation service providers increases and more governments privatize or eliminate subsidies to their airlines and passenger rail systems, yield-management techniques will grow in importance.

SUMMARY

Passenger transportation, whether on land, over the water, or in the air is the lifeblood of the tourism industry. Water transportation was the first mode of transportation to move travelers rapidly over long distances, but many other modes have since evolved to meet time and distance requirements. Geography and governmental policies and subsidies combined to create a host of transportation alternatives that vary greatly by country and location.

When it comes to transportation, travelers have the choice of plying the waves, riding the rails, cruising the highways, or soaring through the skies. Which one they choose will depend on where they are going, their budget, and the amount of flexibility they desire.

Ocean-going passenger service, which was once popular across the Atlantic, declined as jet air service increased. However, water transportation alternatives, including ferry services which are designed to carry everything from passengers, to trains, motorcoaches and automobiles are still very important in many parts of the world.

Land transportation revolves around rail service, automobiles, and motorcoaches. Passenger rail service, which originated in the European countries has continued to improve in efficiency and still meets the needs of those travelers, but it is also popular in other countries, especially those in Asia, with high population concentrations and large cities located in close proximity to each other. In other countries, such as Canada and the United States, automobiles account for the majority of all travel away from home. Taxis, shuttles, limousine services, and light-rail systems fill another important transportation need for travelers everywhere. In addition, the flexibility and economy of operations gained from motorcoaches that can serve scheduled routes as well as organized tours continue to meet the needs of travelers worldwide.

Air transportation has proven to be the driving force behind the explosive growth in domestic and international travel. As governmental regulations are removed from air transportation, international barriers fall, and major airlines vie for an increasing number of passengers, competition as well as passenger traffic will continue to increase. Airlines, like most other service providers in the tourism industry, are being forced to rely on more sophisticated marketing and management techniques such as yield management to achieve profitability and deliver high-quality service.

 # YOU DECIDE

Too many calls and not enough time! As Meredith Carpenter, national sales manager for Park Plaza Hotels, reviewed her schedule for the upcoming week, she began to wonder if she had built in enough flexibility. Being pressed for time was nothing new, but five clients in three cities in one week would be pushing it. On top of that, she was hoping to squeeze in a few cold calls as she prospected for new business. Meredith knew it would be hectic, but worth it, if she beat her quota and qualified for her incentive bonus.

Meredith had worked closely with her travel agent to develop an itinerary that would allow her as much time as possible in each city. The itinerary was set up so that she could catch the last scheduled flight as she moved from city to city. This schedule looked good at the time she arranged

it, but she was now beginning to think about how inflexible it might be. What if her appointments ended early or she was unable to connect with decision-makers on her cold calls? Would she be wasting time in one city when she could be more productive in the next one?

Just before leaving, Meredith decided to make some contingency plans in case her business needs changed. Using her Official Airline Guide (OAG), she made reservations on a different airline for an early afternoon flight from each city, arranging to pick up the ticket and pay for it at the airport counter. In addition, she tucked a pocket-sized OAG into her briefcase. Having these schedules with her, she could make last-minute changes and book even more convenient flights if necessary.

It would be hectic, but she was prepared. Armed with two reservations for flights from each city and information at her fingertips for alternative flights, Meredith was prepared for any contingency. If her plans changed and she finished early, she could simply pick up her new ticket at the airport and cancel her reservation for the later flight.

However, if her sales calls went as planned, she would simply "no-show" for the earlier flights and use her original reservations. After all, Meredith thought, airlines always overbooked and no one would be hurt by either a last-minute cancellation or a no-show. Do you think Meredith did the right thing?

 NET TOUR

To learn more about the concepts and organizations presented in this chapter access the homepage for *Tourism: The Business of Travel*. Select "Chapter 4: Transportation." From this location test your knowledge by taking the chapter quiz, read industry insights, and discover links to other useful sites. You may also want to visit electronically with other tourism students through the website.

 DISCUSSION QUESTIONS

1. What are the major modes of transportation, and why are each of these modes important to the current and future success of the tourism industry?

2. How do transportation companies use yield management?

3. Why is passenger rail service more efficient and effective outside Canada and the United States?

4. Describe the changes that have taken place in the types and level of services provided by motorcoach operators.

5. Discuss why many travelers rely on water transportation to meet their transportation needs.

6. Discuss some of the many changes that have occurred since deregulation of the U.S. airline industry.

APPLYING THE CONCEPTS

1. Take on a planning task similar to the one faced by Shawna in our chapter opener. Select three major cities that are serviced by scheduled airlines. One city should serve as your reference point for departure and the other two cities should be two different destinations. One destination city should be in an adjacent province or state and the other city should be located in a different country. Prepare a table showing the following information:
   a. The types of transportation you could use to reach each of your selected destinations.
   b. The distance between each city in air miles and surface miles.
   c. The estimated time it would take to reach each of your selected destinations by both air and surface travel.

   After you have developed the table, explain the pros and cons of each of the available transportation alternatives.

2. Select one mode of transportation that is particularly interesting to you and learn more about it. Either schedule an interview with an employee of a representative company or collect copies of newspaper and magazines articles about the industry and companies in the industry. Based on the information you obtain, write a short report discussing important information you learned from your interview or research containing facts about the industry, the company and the person's job.

3. Using the resources that are available in your local library, develop a list of companies, along with their phone numbers, that are supplying transportation services in your region.

4. Surf the World Wide Web for transportation information. Prepare a list showing each mode of transportation you identified along with at least one company that has listed its services on the web. Describe the information that is available on each site.

5. Choose a long-distance city pair (the origin and destination cities of a flight) and interview a travel agent or access information using the World Wide Web to determine the variety of fares and transportation alternatives available between them.

GLOSSARY

Air Transport Association (ATA) A domestic association that provides a format for discussing safety and service issues and promotes the advancement of technology.

Amtrak The marketing name for the National Railroad Passenger Corporation, which is a combination of the passenger rail service of U.S. railroads.

Available seat miles (ASMs) The distance traveled multiplied by the number of seats available.

Banks of flights The process of co-ordinating flight schedules so that aircraft arrive and depart during similar time periods.

Bumped The process of denying boarding to airline passengers with confirmed reservations due to over-booking (overselling) the flight.

CANRAILPASS Allows 12 days of economy class travel within a 30-day period anywhere VIA Rail goes in Canada.

Code share An agreement allowing a regional/commuter airline to share the same two-digit code of a cooperating primary carrier in the computer reservation system.

Economies of scale Savings in time, money, or other resources organizations enjoy as the result of purchasing and/or selling in large quantities, specialization at a particular job or function, and the use of specialized machinery.

Eurailpass Allows unlimited travel for non-European tourists for varying periods of time throughout Austria, Belgium, Denmark, Finland, France, Germany, Greece, Ireland, Italy, Luxembourg, the Netherlands,

Norway, Portugal, Spain, Sweden, and Switzerland.

Federal Aviation Administration (FAA) Agency within the DOT charged with ensuring air safety and promoting the growth of aviation.

Fleet utilization Percentage of time transportation vehicles are used for revenue-producing purposes.

Hub-and-spoke system The primary airline route pattern in the United States. By designating primary hubs, airlines are able to funnel traffic into these centers to feed their trunk point-to-point routes between major market cities.

Intermodal A trip requiring the use of two or more forms of transportation.

International Air Transport Association (IATA) Association for airlines offering international air service that provides a means of resolving problems for mutual benefit.

Involuntarily denied boarding A situation that occurs when airline passengers with confirmed reservations are denied boarding on scheduled flights due to overbooking. Passengers may either voluntarily give up their reserved space or be involuntarily denied boarding in exchange for compensation.

Leg The segment of a flight between two consecutive stops.

Load factor The number of revenue passengers milers (RPMs) divided by the number of available seat miles (ASMs).

Overbooking Accepting more reservations than there is capacity to serve those customers making the reservations, e.g., accepting reservations for more passengers than there are avail-

able seats on an aircraft or for more rooms than there are in a hotel.

Point-to-point Direct travel between two destinations.

Push The act of pushing an aircraft away from the gate for departure. The term is used to indicate the length of time necessary to unload, fuel, service, and reload on aircraft between time of arrival and departure.

Repositioning cruise The transfer of a ship from one cruising area to another to take advantage of the seasonality of demand.

Revenue passenger mile (RPMs) One seat on an airplane, railroad, or motorcoach traveling one mile with a revenue-producing passenger.

Spoke routes Air service provided from smaller secondary markets to feed passengers into primary hub markets.

Trunk routes Point-to-point air service between primary hub markets.

U.S. Department of Transportation (DOT) Organization within the U.S. government charged with establishing the nation's overall transportation policy, including highway planning, development, and construction; urban mass transit; railroads; aviation; and waterways.

VIA Rail Canada The marketing name for Canada's passenger train network, which is a combination of the passenger rail service of Canadian railroads.

Yield management The process of allocating the right type of capacity to the right kind of customer at the right price so as to maximize revenue or yield.

REFERENCES

1. Ridley, Anthony (1969). *An illustrated history of transportation.* New York: The John Day Company.

2. Sharp, Duane (1994, March). Ferry service promising users a better route with integrated POS solution. *Computing Canada,* p. 20.

3. Reina, Peter, Normile, Dennis & Green, Peter (1994, August). High speed rail ready to boom. *ENR,* pp. 24–28.

4. Lever, Robert (1991, December). Train travel. *Europe,* pp. 15–16.

5. Driven into the ground (1996, January 30). *The Economist,* pp. 64–65.

6. Clipboard (1996, May 6). *Travel Weekly*, p. 43.

7. Carroll, Cathy (1994, October 31). Rental firms singing those low-down, abandoned car blues. *Travel Weekly*, pp. 1, 4.

8. Spritzer, Dinah A. (1992, November 26). Motorcoach firms: Future clients will be a more demanding lot. *Travel Weekly*, pp. 15–16.

9. Field, Mike (1993, March 29). Riding in style. *Travel Weekly*, pp. 8–10.

10. van Itallie, Nancy (Ed.) (1994). *Fodor's 95 Europe*. New York: Fodor's Travel Publications, Inc.

11. Fox, Declan (Ed.) (1995). *Let's Go Europe 1995*. New York: St. Martin's Press.

12. Bowden, Bill (1991, July). Tour directors: A changing role. *Courier*, pp. 33–34.

13. Clipboard (1995, June 22). *Travel Weekly*, p. 21.

14. Blyskal, Jeff (1994, May). The frequent flier fallacy. *Worth*, pp. 60–68.

15. Tourism Works for America Report (1993). Washington, D.C.: National Travel and Tourism Awareness Council.

16. Brotherton, Bob, & Mooney, Sean (1992). Yield management—Progress and prospects. *International Journal of Hospitality Management*, *11*(1), pp. 23–32.

17. Travel and tourism: Home and away (1998, January 10). *The Economist*, pp. 4–16.

CHAPTER 5

Accommodations

The Banff Springs Hotel, Alberta, Canada, continues the grand tradition of hospitality.
Photo by C.E. Yale.

A guest never forgets the host who had treated him kindly.

—HOMER

CHAPTER OUTLINE

Expect the Unexpected

Introduction

Oh So Many Choices!
- No Two are Exactly Alike
- Same Time, Same Place
- Your Attention, Please!
- Enjoying the Great Outdoors

Rooms, Rooms, and More
- Making Sense of Classifications and Rating Systems
- Lodging Lexicon

Organizing for Successful Operations
- Going It Alone
- Franchising
- Management Contracts
- Chain Operations
- Strength in Numbers

It All Begins with Sales
- Providing a Home away from Home
- Meeting Guest's Needs

Tourism in Action
- Achieving Profitable Operations

Summary

You Decide

Net Tour

Discussion Questions

Applying the Concepts

Glossary

References

LEARNING OBJECTIVES

After you have read this chapter, you should be able to:

- Explain the importance of accommodations to the tourism industry.
- Identify and describe the major classifications of accommodations.
- Identify and describe the primary ownership patterns of lodging properties.
- Describe the basic organizational structures in lodging properties.
- Describe the differences between front-of-the-house and back-of-the-house operations.
- Identify and describe key marketing, management, and financial considerations in lodging operations.
- Demonstrate knowledge of basic accommodation terminology.

EXPECT THE UNEXPECTED

The alarm went off at 5:00 A.M., but David knew he couldn't hit the snooze button. It was going to be a busy day and he wanted to be at work by 6:30 A.M. The hotel was full, and a large convention group was checking out with an even bigger group checking in that afternoon. As the assistant general manager of a large downtown hotel, David prided himself on the quality of service his staff delivered to each guest every day. Although his employees were well trained, he liked to be on hand, especially on busy days, to help out where needed.

As he rubbed his eyes and looked out the window, he stared in disbelief and his mind began to race. It was snowing and the parking lot in front of his apartment was covered with snow. If he had been living in the North where snow was common, this would not have been a problem, but he lived in Georgia where snow was a novelty. Could he get to work? Could his employees get to work? Would the airport be open?

The drive to the hotel that morning was a little nerve-racking, but he made it. While he listened to the radio on the way to work, he groaned. The city buses would not be running today and unseasonably cold weather was still in the forecast. Everyone was being encouraged to stay home and several "fender benders" had already been reported.

When he arrived at the hotel, he was relieved to see that some of the kitchen staff had made it. He asked the night auditor and front desk employees if they would stay a few extra hours and help out. Several other employees had arrived after braving the slick streets and sidewalks, but the calls were starting to come in from many more employees who were not able to get to work. By 7:00 A.M., the lobby was beginning to fill with guests and a line had formed in front of the coffee shop.

This may not be a typical day in the life a hotelier, but David had learned to expect the unexpected. The day was still young and there were sure to be many more challenges. Solving problems, meeting needs, training employees and being an active part of the community kept his job from being anything but dull.

INTRODUCTION

"Come in; please be my guest." For years, these words of welcome have greeted weary travelers seeking shelter for the night. Providing travelers with temporary shelter is an age-old profession that can be traced through recorded history to the inns of biblical times. In fact, the term "hostel" (meaning inn) can be traced back to the Middle Ages.

The inns of old, usually no more than simple structures, offered meals and a bed in a room shared with other travelers seeking safety and shelter for the night. By today's standards, these early inns were very crude. They usually had one or maybe two rooms with several beds in each room. The innkeeper would put two, three or perhaps even up to four people in a bed. Although many early innkeepers were not always the most reputable lot, they did provide an important service by meeting travelers' basic needs for shelter and food.

Most early inns looked like any other home along the roadside and could only be recognized by special signs hung by their front doors. As lodging facilities became more sophisticated, they often added taverns, which served as gathering spots for locals. Since these inns and taverns were usually built around courtyards, they became natural entertainment areas for speakers and traveling minstrels and troubadours.

Early "hotels" were usually just overgrown inns. However, it didn't take long for large structures specifically designed for lodging to appear. Most of these hotels were originally built in or around seaports and train depots as well as at major spa resort destinations in Canada, England, France, Germany, and the United States. In fact, development of lodging facilities closely followed improvements in transportation, particularly steamships and railroads. From these modest beginnings, accommodation choices have emerged to meet the needs of today's travelers.

OH, SO MANY CHOICES!

Think for a minute about some of the accommodation options from which you can choose when planning a trip. Where would you spend the night(s) on the way to your destination? Where would you stay once you reach your destination? You can probably think of alternatives ranging all the way from staying with friends and relatives to pampering yourself at a luxury hotel. Over the years, a wide range of facilities have been developed to meet travelers' accommodation needs. Just like inns of old, they have often become a focal point for community gatherings and social activities. In addition, they often attract visitors and create opportunities for these guests to spend more time and money in the area.

Although **accommodations** can be found in many shapes and sizes, these facilities have commonly been grouped under the umbrella term **lodging.** The accommodations segment of the tourism industry consists of many popular alternatives such as bed and breakfasts, condominiums, time-shares, conference centers, hotels and motels as well as recreational vehicle parks and campgrounds.

If you think back to the transportation service providers we studied in Chapter 4, you will also find that many other organizations, which travel over long routes, such as passenger trains (see Figure 5.1), ferries, and even airplanes, often include "accommodations" as part of their total service packages. In addition, resorts provide extensive lodging facilities, and cruise ships are often referred to as floating resorts. We will not discuss resorts or cruise ships in this chapter but, more appropriately, in Chapter 8 as we explore destinations. As you will begin to see, the range of available accommodation alternatives is extensive.

No Two Are Exactly Alike

The bed-and-breakfast (B&B) concept began in small towns and the rural areas of Europe, where a family would open their home to travelers. Known as **pensions,** these original B&Bs were probably a lot like the inns of biblical or medieval times: a room or two with a shared bath down the hall and a homemade breakfast served before departure.

The idea of B&Bs may have started in small towns and rural areas, but this concept has spread across the world and can be found anywhere someone wants to be their own

FIGURE 5.1
VIA Rail Canada Sleeping Car Diagram. Double berths, semiprivate, with wide coach-style seats facing each other. At night converts to upper and lower beds.

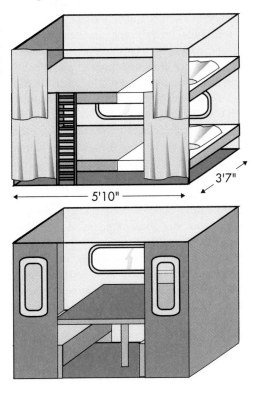

3'7"

5'10"

boss. In fact, after the fall of communism, some of the first businesses to appear in the former Eastern European Bloc countries were B&Bs. However, it should be noted that in the United States, and probably other countries, very small B&B homes are generally operated for supplemental income, tax benefits, and as a means of defraying utility costs rather than as an investment or sole source of income.[1] "[T]he typical American B&B is located in a small town (under 10,000 population), with six or seven rooms, five or six baths and ten parking spaces."[2]

Today, B&Bs come in a wide variety of sizes and service offerings. You can now find Bed and Breakfast Homes (1 to 3 rooms), Bed & Breakfast Inns (4 to 20 rooms), and Bed & Breakfast Hotels (over 20 rooms and sometimes a small restaurant). If you travel to southern Europe or perhaps Quebec, rather than finding B&Bs, you might find pensions, which offer similar accommodations. As B&Bs have grown in numbers, government-sponsored as well as independent reservation and **referral organizations** have evolved to assist owners in marketing their services to travelers seeking the "comforts of home."

Even though they may look different, personal attention and breakfast in the morning are common themes that tie all B&Bs together. Other than the differences in sizes and names, you might also notice that the breakfast foods offered will vary from country to country. For example, a breakfast in England might include stewed tomatoes, beans, and eggs. In Germany, you could be served an assortment of cold meats, hard breads, and cheeses, while, in Canada, you might be served cereals, toast, and fruit.

Same Time, Same Place

Time-shares at condominium properties usually have the same **amenities** found in a typical luxury apartment setting. Condominiums (condos) and other types of accommodations are often marketed as time-shares. The idea of owning time-shares (vacation ownerships), especially in resort locations, is very appealing to individuals who can plan their travel activities in advance and want to be assured of accommodations at set times and in specific locations.

Buying a time-share unit (typically 1/26, or two weeks), on a **fee simple** or **right-to-use** basis assures the purchaser of having specific accommodations for a set time and place each year. Time-share ownership can also provide additional vacation flexibility through the ability to swap occupancy rights with someone who owns equivalent rights at a different location. Through time-share exchange companies such as Resort Condominiums International and Interval International, owners can exchange units and times for accommodations at other units and times at participating locations.

Not surprisingly, the most popular locations for the millions of time-share purchasers in the United States are at popular tourism destinations in California, Colorado, Florida, Georgia, South Carolina, and Texas. Just as there are popular locations, there are also different times of the year that are more popular than others. These time periods are classified by colors indicating the level of demand. Low-demand weeks are classified as "blue," medium-demand "white," and high-demand "red."[3] For example, a week during Christmas in Orlando, Florida, would probably be more desirable than a week during February in Okoboji, Iowa.

The allure of time-share ownership is especially strong in the United States, where purchases are growing at a 9% compounded annual rate.[4] The United States leads the world in the time-share market, with over 3.2 million owners, and Americans are also active buyers of time-shares in other countries. The popularity of time-shares is expected to continue growing as more and more baby boomers enter the prime age for buying second homes (45 to 64) and more hotel companies begin supplying the time-share market. Hotel companies such as Hilton, Hyatt, Intercontinental, and Marriott are being attracted to this industry segment because occupancy rates (about 80%) have been almost 20% higher than at traditional hotel properties.[5] These easily recognized brand names are bringing prestige and increasing acceptability to time-share ownership. Vacationers desiring ownership for longer periods of time turn to condominiums.

In a condominium development, individuals buy units for their own use. When not being used by their owners, the units are frequently made available for rental. These units may be managed under a straight rental agreement or be placed in a **rental pool.** In a straight rental agreement, condo owners receive a portion of the rental revenues based on the rental income received for their units. In a rental pool, all condominium owners share in rental income based on the square footage of their units. In either situation, the owners typically pay for all taxes, utilities, and general maintenance expenses. In return, they receive a percentage of the rental income (usually 49%) while the management company will retain the remainder (usually 51%) as compensation for operating and maintaining the property when owners are not using their allotted times or units.

Your Attention, Please!

Providing accommodations built around a setting specifically designed, equipped, and staffed to host meetings creates the unique environment of a conference center. The first of these facilities was established by former President Dwight D. Eisenhower when, as President of Columbia University in 1950, he opened Arden House, a 30-bedroom house on a country estate outside New York City.[6] Today, there are over 300 conference centers in the United States, including the original Arden House and a host of other locations such as the Scanticon Conference Center in Princeton, New Jersey, the Macklowe Conference Center in downtown New York City, and the Inn and Conference Center at the Biosphere in Oracle, Arizona.

With an employee:guest ratio of from 1:0.5 to 1:2.5, conference center managers can focus their attention on the specific needs of each group and excel at providing the desired experience of living, learning, and leisure. Extra service touches such as rearranging housekeeping schedules to clean guest rooms when attendees are in meetings or adjusting food service schedules based on changing group needs are just a few of the service touches that highlight the flexibility provided in conference centers.

Enjoying the Great Outdoors

Campers have traditionally been viewed as families or individuals wanting to save money or get close to nature and experience the great outdoors. However, with advances in technology, more people are being drawn to camping as they realize that the outdoor experience can be achieved without "roughing it." It is not uncommon to find swimming pools, cable TV hookups, convenience stores, and even restaurants as part of the operations of commercial campgrounds and recreational vehicle (RV) parks. As the levels of convenience have increased, so have the number of people who camp as well as use RVs to take a bit of home along with them.

Campgrounds and RV parks fill a special need in seasonal recreational areas as they can add significantly to the accommodation base. From an economic perspective government-funded as well as privately developed campgrounds have essentially shifted capital investment needs to campers who bring along their tents, camper trailers, trailers, and RVs. Rather than investing in expensive buildings that could remain empty for a large part of the year, limited investments can be made in support facilities when travelers bring along their own accommodations.

In response to the growing popularity of RVs, many lodging facilities are providing parking spaces for these vehicles. Nowhere is the mutually beneficial relationship between traditional lodging facilities and recreational vehicles more evident than at Walt Disney World or in Laughlin, Nevada. Specifically designed campgrounds and parking spaces with full RV hookups are adding to the accommodations base. In addition, whole communities of travelers can be found springing up on a "temporary" basis in Arizona, Florida, and South Texas during the winter months or in the mountains of Alberta, British Columbia, Colorado, New Mexico, Montana, Washington, and Wyoming during the summer months.

Rooms on wheels meet seasonal accommodation needs.
Photo by D.A. Yale.

ROOMS, ROOMS, AND MORE

From some of the more specialized and unique types of accommodations, we now move to hotels and motels that meet the majority of travelers' lodging needs. The construction of the 170-room Tremont House in Boston in 1829 technically marked the beginning of the hotel segment of the tourism industry in the United States. Services and conveniences such as a "rotunda man" (bellhop) to carry guest bags since there was no elevator, a restaurant featuring French cuisine, private rooms with locks, soap and a pitcher of water in each room, and indoor toilets made the Tremont a special place to stay. The opening of the Brown Palace Hotel in Denver, Colorado, in 1892, with its distinctive atrium design marked another significant milestone in lodging history.

The next major change in the development of modern lodging occurred when Ellsworth M. Statler opened the Buffalo (New York) Statler Hotel in 1908. This hotel truly revolutionized the industry since it was designed and operated with guest comfort, convenience, and safety in mind. Each room had an electric light just inside the doorway, a private bath with tub and toilet, and a pitcher of iced water. In addition, free morning newspapers were delivered to each room. The hotel also had fire doors and a host of other standard features.

The Buffalo Statler Hotel ushered in a new era of lodging growth, and the industry continued to flourish into the early 1900s as hotels, designed to be the biggest and best, sprouted up across Canada and the United States. This boom stopped abruptly with the Great Depression (which began in 1929), when nearly 85% of all hotels in the United States went bankrupt as business and leisure travel came to a screeching halt.

Prosperity finally returned with the end of World War II, but the focus shifted to motels rather than hotels. With improvements in road construction and maintenance, increased automobile traffic, and the desire and ability to travel, the motel segment flourished. As families began using automobiles for vacation travel, the old practice of sleeping in cars or camping beside the road no longer met their needs.

In response to changing needs, small wooden structures (the forerunner of the modern motel) were built beside major highways to serve this growing group of automobile travelers. The idea of "tourist courts" for the motoring public caught the eye of another lodging pioneer, Kimmons Wilson. Wilson believed consistent marketing programs and operating procedures could lead to financial success by fulfilling an unmet need: standardized facilities, service, and quality at the end of each day. His answer to meeting this need was Holiday Inns, the first of which was opened on the outskirts of Memphis in 1952.

Based on the promise of providing standardized facilities, Holiday Inns soon grew into a successful chain of motels stretching across the United States. One room looked just like another and travelers always knew there would be free parking, a telephone, air conditioning, a swimming pool, and free ice. In addition, children under the age of 18 could stay free with their parents wherever they found the distinctive Holiday Inn sign.

Hyatt Hotels ushered in the renaissance of downtown hotel properties when they agreed to take over a yet to be completed hotel construction project that other hotel companies had shunned in Atlanta. The hotel's architect John Portman had designed the hotel with an open atrium where conventional wisdom would dictate that another 500 rooms could be built. Hyatt Hotels took on the challenge and successfully opened the first major downtown atrium hotel since The Brown Palace. The atrium concept is now widely accepted and can be found in a wide variety of lodging properties and most of the newer cruise ships.

Making Sense of Classifications and Ratings Systems

A wide variety of lodging **properties** and amenities has been developed to meet the needs of specific market segments. For example, it is now common for business travelers to find computer outlets in their rooms as well as larger desks, better lighting, irons and ironing boards, and hair dryers. As these features and other amenities such as shampoo, lotion, in-room coffee, and free morning newspapers gained in popularity, travelers began to expect these extras at many properties. When they were added and became the norm rather than the unusual, differences between traditional lodging property classifications such as hotels and motels began to blur. To clarify this situation and more clearly communicate the differences in facilities and services among properties, organizations developed standardized classification and reporting systems.

The American Hotel and Motel Association, for example, classifies individual lodging properties into the following six categories based on the distinct market segments served (examples of brand names in each category are shown in parentheses):

1. *Limited-service budget motels.* Simple, basic, clean rooms with no amenities other than clean towels, linens, and soap. (Sleep Inns and Microtel)

2. *Limited-service economy motels.* Upgraded room decor with color television, telephone, vending machines, and generally located close to restaurants. (Motel 6, Super 8, and Red Roof Inns)

3. *Full-service, mid-priced hotels and motels.* 24-hour front desk, upgraded interior and exterior decors, limited food service, extra room amenities, and other services. (Courtyard by Marriott, Four Points Hotels, and Holiday Inns)

4. *Full-service, upscale hotels.* Better quality and more luxurious, upgraded food service and usually **concierge service.** (Canadian Pacific Hotels, Delta Hotels, Hyatt Hotels, Hilton Hotels, and Westin Hotels)

5. *Luxury hotels.* Lavish guest rooms offering the ultimate in room amenities. Noted worldwide for service and surroundings. (Ritz-Carlton and Four Seasons Hotels)

6. *All-suite hotels.* Separate sleeping and living quarters, limited kitchen facilities, and complimentary food and/or beverage service in morning and evening. (Embassy Suites and MainStay Suites)

MOTEL 6

Motel 6 took on its rather distinctive name from its original pricing strategy. When the chain was first developed, each of the motels offered rooms for only $6.00 a night! Several similar motel chains followed suit with names such as Super 8 and National 9.

Other organizations such as Smith Travel Research use classifications such as luxury, upscale, mid-price, economy, and budget to differentiate properties based on room rates.[7] Historic hotels (independently owned properties that are over 50 years old) occupy a special category in the classification system. They not only fulfill all the requirements of a typical full-service hotel, but also have a unique character created through restored architectural structures and collections of antiques and other memorabilia. Each of these classification systems provides managers with reference groups and **benchmarks** against which they can evaluate performance and plan for the future.

DIAMONDS AREN'T FOREVER

DIAMOND RATINGS
A diamond rating is assigned to a property based on the conditions noted *at the time of the inspection*. All physical attributes and the quality of services are considered.

One Diamond
properties provide good but modest accommodations. Establishments are functional, emphasizing clean and comfortable rooms. They must meet the basic needs of comfort and cleanliness.

Two Diamond
properties maintain the attributes offered at the one-diamond level while showing noticeable enhancements in room decor and quality of furnishings. They may be recently constructed or older properties, both targeting the needs of a budget-oriented traveler.

Three Diamond
properties offer a degree of sophistication. Additional amenities, services, and facilities may be offered. There is a marked upgrade in the physical attributes, services, and comfort.

Four Diamond
properties are excellent and display a high level of service and hospitality. These properties offer a variety of amenities and upscale facilities in the guest rooms, on the grounds, and in the public area.

Five Diamond
properties are renowned. They exhibit an exceptionally high degree of service, striking and luxurious facilities, and many extra amenities. Guest services are executed and presented in a flawless manner. The guest is pampered by a professional and attentive staff. The property's facilities and operation help set the standards in hospitality and service for the industry.

Source: *Lodging listing requirements and diamond rating guidelines* (1998). Heathrow, FL: American Automobile Association. © AAA, reproduced by permission.

Lodging Lexicon

Some lodging terminology (see Table 5.1) is very specific and may sound almost like a foreign language the first time you hear it. For example, terms like *occupancy rates, average daily rates, RevPAR* (revenue per available room), and *RevPAC* (revenue per available customer) carry specific meanings and are frequently used to measure financial performance and make comparisons among similar classifications of lodging properties. However, other lodging terminology is more variable and at times causes some confusion. Therefore, it is always advisable to seek clarification when using these terms to ensure effective communications. Figure 5.2 illustrates how some of the more typically used terminology can be applied to a guest room.

ORGANIZING FOR SUCCESSFUL OPERATIONS

Lodging facilities are typically marketed and managed under one of the following ownership patterns: independent properties, franchise properties, management contract properties, or chain properties. With the possible exception of very small **independent properties,** some type of formalized management structure, training programs, and standard operating procedures will be found in most lodging properties.

At first most hotels and motels were operated as independent properties. However, between 1960 and 1990, the trend moved toward **franchise** affiliations and **chain** operations. These affiliations have proven to be profitable because "Three-quarters of business travelers and two-thirds of leisure travelers claim to be brand-conscious."[8] Today, the trend has changed and appears to be moving toward larger properties operated under **management contracts,** although it appears that more and more property managers are once again deciding to go it alone.[9]

Going It Alone

Independent properties are lodging facilities owned and operated as single units with no chain affiliation or common identification. Managers of independent properties have many of the same advantages and disadvantages as the sole proprietors of B&Bs. They are not

TABLE 5.1
Hotel Terminology

Single	Room with one twin bed.
Twin	Room with two twin beds.
Double	Room with one double bed.
Double double	Room with two double beds.
Murphy	Room with a Murphy bed (a bed that folds out of a wall or closet)
Suite	Room with one or more bedrooms and a living area.
Connecting	Rooms that are side by side and have a door connecting the two rooms.
Adjoining	Rooms that are side by side but do not have a connecting door between the rooms.
European plan (EP)	Room only, no meals.
Continental plan (CP)	Continental breakfast (juice, coffee, roll, pastry) included in the room price.
Modified American plan (MAP)	Continental or full breakfast and dinner included in the room price.
American plan (AP)	Continental or full breakfast, lunch, and dinner included in the room price.

FIGURE 5.2
Room Layouts Demonstrating
Lodging Terminology

Connecting rooms
Rooms that are side by side and have a door connecting the two rooms

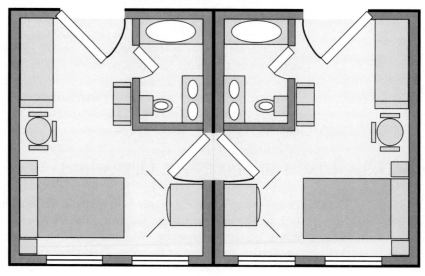

Adjoining rooms
Rooms that are side by side but do not have a connecting door between them

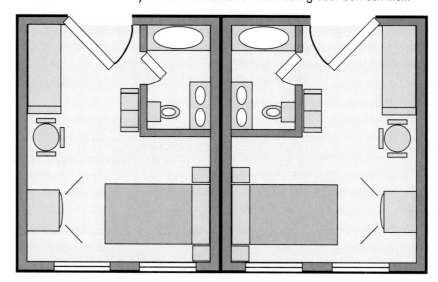

bound by corporate policies, so they are free to be creative and respond quickly to the needs of their guests and communities. The price they pay for this freedom, however, is a lack of marketing, management, and financial support and other resources that are typically provided through larger, multiproperty organizations such as franchises or chains.

Franchising

Franchise agreements provide owners/operators (franchisees) with the use of a recognized brand name, access to central reservation systems, training programs, documented operating procedures, standardized computer software, quantity purchasing discounts, and technical assistance from the parent company (franchiser) in return for **royalties** and fees. Examples of franchise operating fees and requirements are shown in Table 5.2.

In return for the benefits received from the franchiser and in addition to the required franchise fees, franchisees must give up some of their operational flexibility and follow standardized operating procedures and purchasing requirements as outlined in the franchise contract. Although franchising has been favorably received in the United States, it "has not been a great success in Europe and it's been even less successful in Asia, espe-

TABLE 5.2
Franchise Operating Fees and Requirements

Name of Chain	Minimum Rooms	Initial Fee	Royalty Fee	Advertising/ Marketing Fee	Reservation Fee
Budgetel Inns	65	$25,000	5% of gross rooms revenue	1% of gross rooms revenue	1% of gross rooms revenue
Holiday Inns	N/A	$500 per room or $40,000 (min.)	5% of gross rooms revenue	1.5% of gross rooms revenue	1% of gross rooms revenue
Econo Lodge	N/A	$250 per room or $25,000 (min.)	4% of gross rooms revenue	3.5% of gross rooms revenue	Combined with Marketing Fee
Days Inns of America	32	$350 per room or $35,000 (min.)	6.5% of gross rooms revenue	None	2.3% of gross rooms revenue
Marriott Hotels and Resorts	150	$300 per room or $82,500 (min.)	6% of gross rooms revenue, plus 3% of gross F&B sales	1% of gross rooms revenue, plus participation in programs	$5.12 per reservation made plus network charges
Embassy Suites	100	$500 per suite, or $100,000 (min.)	4% of gross suites revenue	3.5% of gross suites revenue	N/A
Radisson Hotels International [United States]	N/A	$30,000	4% of gross rooms sales	3.5% of gross rooms sales	Included in ad/mktg fee
Radisson Hotels International [outside United States]	N/A	$200 per room or $40,000 (min.)	4% of gross rooms sales	2.5% of gross rooms sales	$11 per reservation booked through Radisson system

Adapted from Franchise Fact File (1995, July) *Lodging Hospitality,* pp. 40–43.

cially where there are not enough operations in a single country to establish the brand or to require the services [assistance and support] of the franchisor."[10]

Management Contracts

TABLE 5.3
10 Largest Hotel Management Companies

1. Interstate Hotels
2. Bristol Hotels & Resorts
3. Starwood Lodging Corp.
4. Carnival Hotels & Resorts
5. Prime Hospitality Corp.
6. Tharaldson Enterprises
7. Capstar Hotel Co.
8. Richfield Hospitality
9. Westmont Hospitality Group
10. Remington Hotel Corp.

Source: Top Management Companies (1997, August). *Lodging Hospitality,* p. 47.

The idea of operating hotels under management contract was born in the 1950s with the Caribe Hilton in San Juan, Puerto Rico. "The Puerto Rican government's development agency wanted a modern hotel to encourage tourism and attract industry. [The government] was so anxious to attract a name brand and the management skills needed that it offered to build, furnish and equip the hotel."[10] Hilton was approached and agreed to market and manage the property under a profit-sharing lease agreement.

Management contracts, like franchises, allow lodging chains to expand aggressively into new markets without having to make capital investments in physical facilities. Under a management contract, hotel operating companies (see Table 5.3) act as agents for the owner of the property. The owner of the property "hires" the operating company to fulfill all of the management and marketing functions needed to run the property. The property owner continues to retain all financial obligations for the property while the management company is responsible for all operating issues. For their operating expertise, management companies receive anywhere from slightly under 3% to almost 6% of either total revenues or room revenues.

Chain Operations

Chain operations refer to groups of properties that are affiliated with each other and have common ownership and/or management control and oversight. Chain operations can be created in a variety of different ways. For example, many chains such as Interstate Hotels and Ocean Properties, Ltd. have been developed using franchise agreements or management contracts. In other cases, such as Adam's Mark and Canadian Pacific Hotels, all properties within the chain are owned and managed by a single company.

Parent companies may own, franchise, or contract to manage any or all of the properties they operate. Interstate Hotels, Inc., provides an interesting example of how these combinations can be put together. Interstate operates franchises under the Marriott, Hilton, Westin, and Hampton names as well other properties under management contracts. The use of different brand names allows Interstate to target travelers in a variety of market segments.

Chain operations provide many management, marketing, and financial benefits. These benefits include increased purchasing power, lower costs of operations, common signage and advertising, expanded access to centralized reservation systems, and greater support from professional staff functions such as sales and marketing, finance and accounting, and human resource management.

Strength in Numbers

Can property owners retain operating autonomy and still reap some of the benefits that go along with franchise affiliations or chain ownership? This question may seem like asking for the best of both worlds, but the answer is yes. Membership in referral associations allows property owners to "go it alone" and still share the benefits that come from "strength in numbers."

Referral associations come in all sizes, meeting many different marketing needs. You may already be familiar with the world's largest, Best Western. Claiming more than 3500 properties in over 65 countries, the Best Western logo can be found on all types of properties ranging from airport and convention center hotels to roadside motels and resorts.[11] Others such as the Historic Hotels of America Association and Preferred Hotels and Resorts Worldwide serve the needs of property owners catering to specific market niches.

There is no need for members to meet standardized design specifications or change time-tested operating procedures. In fact membership requirements are straightforward and the benefits can be numerous. After meeting established quality standards and paying an initiation fee, the benefits can begin. The marketing power of instant name recognition, a centralized reservation system and widely distributed membership directories are just the beginning. Additional benefits can come in the form of cooperative purchasing agreements, access to training information, and the ability to share ideas with other managers.

It All Begins with Sales

Lodging properties rely on a steady flow of new and repeat guests to remain financially healthy. Even before a property opens for business, sales and marketing efforts often begin and should never end. These efforts may range from simply operating under a recognized brand name with a toll-free reservation system to a complete in-house staff dedicated to selling and marketing an individual property or an entire chain of properties. No matter how simple or complex the marketing effort, the ultimate goal is to attract future **bookings** of both individual and group business.

Too often, employees fail to recognize that they are an important part of these sales efforts. Just as employees must be trained to deliver high-quality service, they must also be trained to anticipate guest needs and serve as sales ambassadors. For example, when checking in, guests' comments that they are tired and hungry provide opportunities to recommend room service. Or, when checking out, guests who mention that they will be returning in a month provide an opportunity to ask if they would like to make a reservation now for their next visit.

Two important traditions are typically performed when new lodging properties are constructed. First, when the final floor is completed, an evergreen tree is placed on the top of the building. This act signifies that the building will rise no higher. It also symbolically ties the building safely to the ground through the "roots of the tree."

The second important tradition is performed when the ceremonial ribbon is cut on opening day. At that time, the key to the front door is symbolically thrown onto the roof since it will never be used again. This is a symbol signifying that the building is more than just a building. It has become a place that will always be open to those who are seeking a room for the night or more appropriately a "home away from home."

Providing a Home away from Home

Lodging properties are more than just mortar, bricks, and sticks. Once the physical facility has been constructed, a staff must be hired, trained, organized, and motivated to meet guest needs. This task often begins long before reservations are made or guests arrive. Depending on the size of a property, guests may encounter a whole host of service employees.

Basic operating functions that must be performed in all properties include administration (general management), guest contact services (such as front office reception, cashiering, and housekeeping) and guest support services (such as groundskeeping, engineering, and maintenance). In a small motel, inn, or B&B, there may be only one or a few employees performing all of these functions. However, due to the size and complexity of many lodging properties (some with thousands of rooms and employees), additional managers, support staff, and hourly employees performing a variety of specific functions may also be required to ensure an effective and efficient operation.

No matter how large or small, the ultimate responsibility for property management remains with the general manager. General managers hold uniquely important positions

Room inspections ensure guest comfort.
Photo by A. Talg.

as they are the focal point for employees, guests, and the community. As the top manager of a property, they perform many different but interrelated roles. These roles include providing leadership, working with the community, gathering and distributing information, allocating resources, handling problems and coordinating a wide variety of activities and functions.

As properties grow, the primary administrative and senior management duties are typically divided between the Front Office Manager, the Director of Food & Beverage, and the Director of Housekeeping, who report to the General Manager. It is also common in many properties to find the Front Office Manager and the Director of Housekeeping reporting to the Rooms Manager. These duties are further divided between front-of-the-house positions (guest contact services) and back-of-the-house positions (guest support services). For all but the smallest properties, front-of-the-house rooms duties are performed in the front office and by guest service employees such as the bell, conceirge, and valet parking staff. Back-of-the-house rooms duties are typically performed by the housekeeping department. You will learn more about food and beverage operations in Chapter 6.

Larger and more complex properties will require additional functions such as marketing (sales), accounting (controller), human resource management (HR), building maintenance (engineering), purchasing, and security services. An example of a traditional organizational structure for a large lodging property can be seen in Figure 5.3.

Meeting Guests' Needs

The front office serves as the "heart" of all lodging properties as well as the first and last point for guest contact. Front office operations are the nerve center and focal point of all guest activities and many employee contacts. Front office employees are charged with not only meeting and greeting guests, but also fielding their inquiries about other available services and serving as the point of exchange for most financial transactions. Other special assistance that may be provided under the direction of the front office include bell service, concierge service, and valet parking.

A key back-of-the-house guest service support group that is critical to guest satisfaction is housekeeping. In addition to ensuring the cleanliness of all guest facilities, the housekeeping department typically has the largest number of employees in a lodging property. Housekeeping must coordinate its activities very closely with the front office as it maintains the cleanliness and readiness of guest rooms, corridors, and common public areas in addition to managing laundry facilities in many properties.

As can be seen from the information presented in Table 5.4, many items can contribute to guest satisfaction and compliments or lead to dissatisfaction and complaints. Just as David found out in the chapter opener, achieving guest satisfaction is not always an easy task.

Achieving Profitable Operations

The financial fortunes of lodging properties have traditionally gone through boom and bust cycles, reflecting the basic economic principles of supply and demand. When **occupancy rates** and average-daily-rates are high, new construction is typically initiated. As more and more properties are built and opened, both occupancy levels and average-daily-rates eventually decline. Therefore, construction and pricing decisions should be based on the ability to achieve and exceed **break-even** occupancy levels. Pricing and occupancy are doubly important to lodging facilities, which are noted for operating on thin profit margins (see Figure 5.4) due to capital and labor intensity. Building and equipping a lodging facility is very expensive and requires a long-term commitment of financial resources or capital. Once constructed the daily, weekly, and monthly costs of providing adequate staffing continue to be incurred.

The rooms side of hotel/motel operations provides the main source of income and operating profits for lodging properties, typically yielding a departmental margin of approximately 70%. A great deal of management and marketing effort is focused on maxi-

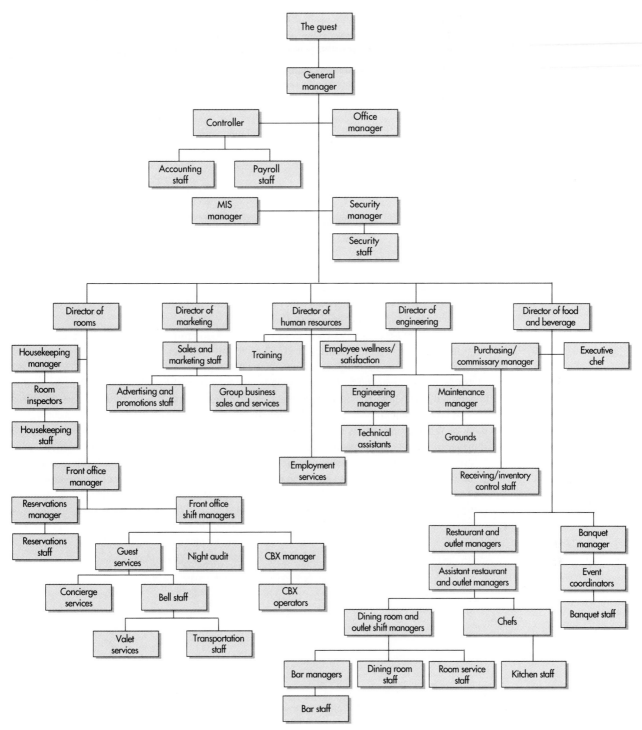

FIGURE 5.3
A Typical Lodging Property Organizational Chart

mizing occupancy levels and room rates by monitoring the rate or pace of future room reservations.

To achieve the maximum occupancy at the best price, hotels and motels have relied on establishing several different rates and borrowed the concept of yield management from the airline industry. Yield-management systems have not been fully accepted in the industry, but they are in use by over 40% of properties connected to some type of central reservation system.[12] These systems help managers achieve the maximum amount of revenue out of a variety of available rates. If you were to walk in off the street, you would

TABLE 5.4
Frequent Complaints and Compliments in Hotels

Complaints	Compliments
1. Price of rooms, meals, and other services	1. Helpful attitude of employees
2. Speed of service	2. Cleanliness of establishment
3. Quality of service	3. Neatness of establishment
4. Availability of parking	4. Quality of service
5. Employee knowledge and service	5. Employee knowledge and service
6. Quietness of surroundings	6. Convenience of location
7. Availability of accommodations requested	7. Management's knowledge of service
8. Checkout time	8. Quantity of service
9. Cleanliness of establishment	9. Spaciousness of establishment
10. Adequacy of credit	10. Quietness of surroundings

Source: Cadotte, Ernest R. & Turgeon, Norman (1988, February). Key factors in guest satisfaction. *Cornell Hotel and Restaurant Administration Quarterly,* p. 48.

probably receive the **rack rate,** the standard and most expensive quoted rate for one night's lodging. Examples of other rates include corporate, government, group and convention, military, weekend, and extended stay.

For yield-management systems to work in lodging properties, "the problems of multiple-night stays, the multiplier effect of rooms on other hotel functions (such as food and beverage), the booking lead time for various types of rooms, the lack of a distinct rate structure and decentralized information systems" must all be addressed.[13] Failing to understand and adjust for these multiple variables can lead to the problem of **overbooking** even when manual systems are used resulting in overbooking.

When a property is overbooked and everyone holding confirmed reservations shows up, some guests must be relocated or "walked" to other accommodations, which costs money and creates guest dissatisfaction. Since a lodging reservation is a binding contract, lodging property managers should be prepared to provide alternative accommodations free of charge plus transportation and a long distance phone call when there is "no room at the inn."

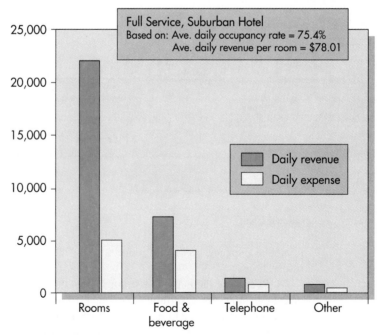

FIGURE 5.4
Lodging Properties—Revenues and Expenses
Adapted from information provided by Smith Travel Research, 1996.

Who says guests want their sheets changed every day? Certainly not the guests, according to an experiment conducted at Disney's Orlando hotels. Guests are informed at check in that the sheets will only be changed every third day unless they request more frequent service. According to a Disney spokesperson, only "a handful a week" choose to have their linens changed on a more frequent basis.

Does this change in operating procedures make a difference? Without a doubt. The annual savings add up rapidly: 6.5 million gallons of water, 5 thousand gallons of cleaning solution, 600 thousand kilowatt hours of electricity, and 37.5 million cubic feet of natural gas.

The experiment is working so well that the idea is even being extended to towels. Guests may keep their towels longer by simply following the directions on the towel racks, which ask them to hang up their towels if they don't want clean ones. Although other lodging properties have tried similar approaches to conservation, Disney's experiment adds credibility and may encourage others in the industry to follow their example.

Actions such as these, which create solutions to operational issues by saving money, meeting guest needs, and protecting the environment are good examples of social responsibility. What's next?

Source: The sheets stay for three days at Disney (1995, August). *Lodging Hospitality*, p. 18.

CHECK-OUT PENALTIES

If you've made a reservation with a major hotel chain such as Hilton, Hyatt, or Westin for 3 days and decide to check out after the second day, don't be surprised to find a $25.00 penalty added to your bill. In an attempt to control room availability and better serve their guests, these and many other hotel chains are adding a check-out penalty when guests fail to honor the full length of their reservations.

Even though properties may grow in size and complexity, the basic business operations remain the same. Providing accommodations to the traveling public continues to be a 24-hour-a-day, 7-day-a-week task that demands dedication to detail and a strong desire to welcome and serve each guest as if that guest were the first and most important person of the day.

SUMMARY

Accommodations create temporary living quarters for guests through a variety of sources, including bed and breakfasts, condominium properties, time-shares, conference centers, hotels, motels, recreational vehicle parks, and campgrounds. Lodging properties, which provide the bulk of overnight accommodations can be traced to biblical times, but did not develop into a significant segment of the tourism industry until rail and ocean-going transportation systems improved and automobile travel became convenient and popular.

Growth in the number of lodging facilities has resulted in the development of several classification schemes that can be used for reporting and comparison purposes. These classification schemes show that lodging facilities come in many sizes and types and, therefore, require varying levels of staffing and managerial expertise for successful operations. Basic functions that must be performed in all lodging properties include administration, front office, housekeeping, and maintenance.

The necessary staffing requirements of properties change as they grow in size and complexity. Additional line functions such as food and beverage and support staff functions such as accounting, engineering, human resource management, security, and purchasing will be added as needed. Since some of the terminology concerning lodging and other accommodation facilities is often loosely used, it is important to seek clarification when talking with guests or other individuals in these establishments.

Providing accommodations to the traveling public requires training, dedication to detail, and a strong desire to welcome and serve each guest. To meet and serve the diverse needs of travelers, a wide variety of accommodations have been developed. Although much of our attention has been devoted to lodging properties, other specialized forms of accommodations such as campgrounds and recreational vehicle parks can significantly increase the number of guests who can be served in any one location.

The statement, "Come in; please by my guest" is more than just words. It is both an invitation and a statement of dedication to provide hospitality to the weary traveler.

YOU DECIDE

"It just doesn't make any sense, Nancy. We've been underbid on four of our last five convention proposals. Worse yet, each time we've been underbid, it's been by the City Center Hotel and they've beat us out by almost 5% on the total value of the contract.

"I want some answers before we submit another bid. It seems to me that we are either totally out of touch with the realities of our marketplace or there are some serious operational problems in your office."

As a downtown hotel that targeted business travelers and convention business, the Forest Park Hotel had traditionally been very successful in following up and capturing its fair share of leads that were developed by the local convention and visitors' bureau. Because of these past successes, Rich Edwards, general manager of the hotel, was particularly disturbed by the failure of Nancy Peak, director of sales, in securing some key convention groups for the hotel.

A heated meeting with Rich was always an uncomfortable situation, but Nancy was particularly troubled by this encounter because she had no immediate answers. After an early morning conference with her sales staff, she was confident they could find the cause of the bidding failures.

Less than 2 weeks had passed when Harvey Zoller sheepishly walked into Nancy's office. He said that he felt

he may have found the source of the bidding problem. He had been tossing draft copies of his estimates and proposals into the trash. Somehow, these papers must have been finding their way into the hands of the City Center Hotel employees since there were suspicious parallels between the contract proposals he had developed and the final bid proposals submitted by the City Center Hotel.

After a thorough investigation, Nancy concluded that, while disposal procedures were normal, they were inadequate in this situation. Further investigation confirmed that the night custodians working for a contract-cleaning firm had been taking discarded worksheets and proposals from the office wastebaskets. Nancy reported her finding to Rich and assured him that adequate control procedures had been implemented to prevent future problems.

However, Nancy failed to tell Rich that she had instructed Harvey to create fictitious worksheets and proposals to be discarded on a current bid proposal. A few weeks later, Nancy was informed that their bid had been accepted and they would serve as the host hotel. She felt that it was poetic justice that the bid proposal submitted by the City Center Hotel had been 5% less than the fictitious work discarded by Harvey, but 2% over the actual bid she had submitted. Did Nancy make the right decision?

NET TOUR

To learn more about the concepts and organizations presented in this chapter access the homepage for *Tourism: The Business of Travel*. Select "Chapter 5: Accommodations." From this location test your knowledge by taking the chap-

ter quiz, read industry insights, and discover links to other useful sites. You may also want to visit electronically with other tourism students through the website.

DISCUSSION QUESTIONS

1. Identify and describe each of the major types of accommodations.

2. Explain how time-shares (vacation ownerships) operate.

3. Describe the differences among independent, franchise, management contract, and chain properties.

4. Explain the importance of this statement: "It all begins with sales."

5. Identify and describe key front-of-the-house and back-of-the-house functions.

6. Identify and describe sources of satisfaction and dissatisfaction for lodging customers. (*Hint:* Review Table 5.4, "Frequent Complaints and Compliments in Hotels.")

APPLYING THE CONCEPTS

1. Although several hotel pioneers were mentioned in this chapter, there are many other individuals who have had a significant influence on the lodging industry. After selecting or being assigned one of these pioneers, briefly describe the contributions that person made to the industry.

2. Arrange to visit a lodging property and schedule an interview with the manager. Your interview should include questions about how the property is marketed, what types of standard operating procedures are followed, and how financial performance is measured.

3. Select one of the hotel management companies listed in this chapter. Using your local library or other sources, list the sizes (number of rooms) and brand names of properties this company manages.

4. Choose four different lodging properties in your area. Based on your knowledge of these properties, assign a classification or rating based on the standardized systems described in this chapter. Provide a brief rationale for why you arrived at each of your decisions.

GLOSSARY

Accommodations Loosely defined as establishments engaged primarily in providing lodging space to the general public.

Amenities Goods and services provided with accommodations that contribute to guest comfort.

Benchmarks Performance measures that are used by similar types of businesses to monitor key operations.

Booking A reservation.

Break-even The level at which total sales equals total costs.

Chain operations Groups of properties that are affiliated with each other and have common ownership and/or management control and oversight.

Concierge services Services provided by employees who specialize in meeting the special requests of guests and provide guest services such as making reservations and supplying information.

Fee simple Right of ownership evidenced by the transfer of a certificate of title. The buyer has the right to sell,

lease, or bequeath the property or interest (as in a time-share).

Franchise A contractual agreement providing for the use of a recognized brand name, access to a central reservation system, training and documented operating procedures, quantity purchasing discounts, and technical assistance in return for royalties and fees.

Independent properties Facilities that are owned and operated as single units with no chain affiliation or common identification.

Lodging Facilities designed and operated for the purpose of providing travelers with a temporary place to stay.

Management contracts Operating agreements with management companies to conduct day-to-day operations for a specific property or properties.

Occupancy rate Ratio comparing the total number of rooms occupied for a given time period to the total number of rooms available for rent.

Overbooking Confirming more reservations for rooms than can be provided during a specified time period.

Pension A small inn or boarding house similar to a bed and breakfast.

Properties Individual accommodations and lodging facilities.

Rack rate The standard quoted rate for one night's lodging.

Referral organizations Associations formed to conduct advertising and marketing programs and generate reservations and referrals for member properties.

Rental pools Groups of condominium units that are released by their owners for rental purposes and are managed by lodging companies.

Right-to-use A type of lease in which legal title does not pass to the buyer. The buyer has the right to occupy and utilize the facilities for a particular time period.

Royalties Payment (usually a percentage of sales) for the use of a franchiser's brand name and operating systems.

Time-share Either ownership or the right to occupy and use a vacation home for a specific period of time.

REFERENCES

1. Poorani, Ali A., & Smith, David R. (1995, October). Financial characteristics of bed-and-breakfast inns. *The Cornell Hotel and Restaurant Administration Quarterly*, pp. 57–63.

2. Emerick, Robert E., & Emerick, Carol A. (1994, spring). Profiling American bed and breakfast accommodations, *Journal of Travel Research*, pp. 20–25.

3. Bouillon, Marvin L., & Wang, Jennifer (1990, spring/summer). Time-share performance: A survey of financial data from developers. *Real Estates Issues*, pp. 44–47.

4. Lodging trends, buying in to timeshare (1997, October). *Lodging* 23(2) p. 13.

5. Bergsman, Steven (1996, June 3). Now that time-shares have come into respectability, they're also coming to town—downtown. *Barron's*, pp. 58–59.

6. Szathmary, Richard (1991, November). The case for conference centers. *Sales and Marketing Management*, pp. 101ff.

7. Smith Travel Research (1997). 105 Music Village Blvd., Hendersonville, TN 37075.

8. Travel and tourism: Home and away (1998, January 10). *The Economist*, p. 7.

9. Gillette, Bill (1996, May 20). Going it alone. *Hotel and Motel Management*, pp. 22–23.

10. Bell, Charles A. (1993, February). Agreements with chain-hotel companies. *The Cornell Hotel and Restaurant Administration Quarterly*, pp. 27–33.

11. Wolff, Carlo (1996). Going golden with Best Western. *Lodging Hospitality*, *52*(9), 34.

12. The time has come for yield management (1997). *Lodging Hospitality 53*(3), 42.

13. Kimes, Sheryl E. (1989, November). The basics of yield management. *The Cornell Hotel and Restaurant Administration Quarterly*, pp. 14–19.

CHAPTER 6

Food and Beverage

A look behind the scenes reveals a beehive of activity.
Photo by A. Talg.

There is no love sincerer than the love of food.

—George Bernard Shaw

CHAPTER OUTLINE

Sometimes It's More Difficult Than It Seems

Introduction

Major Influences on the Development of Food and Beverage Services
- Travel and Discovery
- Science and Technology

Building a Culinary Heritage

Tourism in Action
- The Beginnings of Modern Food-Service Practices
- Planning to Meet Guest Expectations
- It All Comes Down to Rhythm, Timing, and Flow
- Adding Value to Food and Beverage Experiences

Building Profitable Operations
- Balancing Payroll Costs with Productivity
- Food Quality and Food Costs Are the Results of Effective Purchasing

An Ounce of Prevention Is Worth a Pound of Cure

Beverages
- Beverage Operations
- Keeping Spirits Under Control

Summary

You Decide

Net Tour

Discussion Questions

Applying The Concepts

Glossary

References

LEARNING OBJECTIVES

After you have read this chapter, you should be able to:

- Explain how travel and other events in history have influenced the growth and acceptance of different foods and beverages.
- Discuss the impact of science and technology on foods and beverages.
- Explain the importance of rhythm, timing, and flow in food-service operations.
- Discuss the importance of a menu and its impact on production and service delivery.
- Identify the important operational and financial concerns faced by food-service managers.
- Describe how foods and beverages can add value to other tourism services.

Sometimes It's More Difficult Than It Seems

What had begun as an exciting sale soon turned into an important learning experience. It was Carrie's first big sale and she could hardly contain her excitement. As the newest employee on the catering and sales staff at the River Front Hotel, she was anxious to pull her weight and be a productive member of the team.

After dealing with several small groups, Carrie had been assigned to work with Marge Lundstrum of the Women's Resource Society. Marge had already reserved space for the annual luncheon, and the only remaining detail was to select a menu. After a few qualifying questions, she learned that the group would consist of 125 to 150 older women, and they usually had a light lunch just before a short business meeting.

Marge said that they had been served chicken salad in pineapple boats at their last two functions, but this time they wanted something different. She also stated that they didn't want to spend much more than they had in the past. Following a brief discussion, Carrie and Marge decided on bacon, lettuce, and tomato sandwiches (BLTs) with garnish to be accompanied by a fruit salad with poppy seed dressing.

As Carrie reviewed the proposed menu at the weekly staff meeting, the food and beverage director, Martin Yantis, listened in disbelief. The thought of toasting 450 slices of bread would prove to be a logistical nightmare with the other daily activities taking place in the kitchen.

Although Martin thought about having Carrie call Marge to offer her some other alternatives that would be just as appealing and easier to prepare, he decided to turn this potential problem into a learning experience. On the day of the luncheon, Carrie was given the opportunity to work with the preparation staff in the kitchen.

She soon discovered how difficult it was to make so many BLTs. Carrie learned that preparing and serving large meal functions required a team effort and consideration of the physical and human capabilities of the kitchen and staff. Carrie now knew her job was more than just sales and decided to learn more about all of the different aspects of food and beverage marketing, management, and finance.

Introduction

Just think of the lasting memories and friendships that you have developed while sharing your favorite foods and drinks. As we learned in Chapter 2, all of us share some of the same needs. Foods and beverages are instrumental in filling a number of basic human needs. For example, stopping by a quick-service restaurant and grabbing a burger and drink to go may take care of basic physiological needs, but dining out with friends and relatives may fill higher-order social needs. Meeting these needs in locations ranging from airline catering kitchens to destination resorts creates a variety of opportunities for tourism service providers to satisfy their guests and build lasting relationships.

Tourists provide an important source of revenue to many, but not all, food-service operations. Some operations such as Hard Rock Cafe and Planet Hollywood rely on a steady stream of tourist traffic while others cater mainly to local clientele. Location and target segments will determine the relative importance of tourists versus local patronage in an operation's financial success.

Since food and beverage experiences are very personal, the thought of pleasing all these different tastes may seem like a difficult task. What may be pleasing and desirable to you may be completely unappealing to someone else. The good news is that there are fundamentals that can be followed to provide successful food and beverage (F&B) services. In this chapter, you will learn about these principles as well as some of the marketing, management, and financial decisions that combine to create the dynamic and fast-paced working environment of food and beverage operations. You will also discover in Appendix B that manners matter and should be practiced in every professional and social setting.

Major Influences on the Development of Food and Beverage Services

We can trace the most important influences on the development of foods and beverages to travel experiences and innovations in science and technology. Throughout history, travel has introduced visitors to new tastes, and these discoveries continue today. Visiting new locations allows us to enjoy unfamiliar foods. It also allows us to expand understanding and appreciation of new cultures, ceremonies, and traditions. In fact, throughout history, foods and beverages have often been at the center of social gatherings and celebrations.

Travel and Discovery

The quest to explore and conquer new lands that encouraged early travel also led to the spread of different food and beverage offerings. The importance of foods and beverages to the development of travel and tourism can be seen all the way from the expansion and conquests of the Greek and Roman empires to the travels of Marco Polo.

Precious metals and land were not the only treasures sought by these early adventures—so, too, were flavorful spices and herbs. The Greeks brought home food-related "treasures" from their travels in Egypt, Persia, Babylon, and India. These **culinary** treasures were later passed on to the Romans. In fact, at the height of the Roman Empire, the typical Roman cook was a male slave brought from overthrown Greece where cooking skills and **cuisine** were highly developed. The Romans' appetites for pleasurable indulgences placed these cooks in high demand and raised the status of cooking to an art form.[1]

As the world moved into the Dark Ages, travel began to diminish. The art of cooking, however, was preserved during this period because most of the rich cooking styles and the books that discussed foods and beverages were guarded in monasteries. Outside monastery walls, people continued to prepare rough, simple dishes that had been passed down unchanged for generations. The revival of travel during the Grand Tour Era by the wealthy at the end of the Dark Ages had a significant impact on food and beverages. When the noble classes began to expand their travels into new territories, they encountered and brought home many new foods, beverages, and methods of preparation.[2]

As Europeans began to travel to the Americas and West Indies, they returned with many native foods from those regions such as chocolate, chilies, beans, corn, tomatoes, and potatoes. Some of these items were initially avoided and treated with suspicion since they looked different and were often regarded as poisonous. Through the efforts of pioneers such as French agronomist Antoine-August Parmentier and American scientist George Washington Carver, deep-seated fears and misconceptions about different foods were dispelled. Parmentier successfully spearheaded a campaign begun in 1774 that made potatoes a staple on the French dinner table.[2] Research efforts led by Carver resulted in over 300 products including cheese, milk, flour, and coffee made from peanuts.

Once people began emigrating from Europe to the "New Worlds" of North America, they brought along their favorite drinks, breads, desserts, herbs, spices, and fruits. These old favorites were combined with new foods, creating distinctive regional cuisines from New England clam chowder to hominy grits. Now, at the dawn of the 21st century, the majority of people in industrialized countries can afford to travel for pleasure and, through tourism, enjoy new foods and dining experiences. These experiences continue to influence the development of menus and service styles for food and beverage operations as international and regional cuisines are blended together.

In the same way that travel has driven their development, foods and beverages now drive many travel choices. Food and beverage events attract tourists in increasing numbers to resorts, festivals, theme parks, casinos, and many other destinations. For example, travelers come from all over the world to enjoy the sights, sounds, and delights of Oktoberfest celebrations throughout Germany or Fiesta Days in San Antonio, Texas. In fact, pleasant memories of foods and beverages enjoyed as part of a trip often linger and are remembered more often than any other part of the travel experience.[3] Just as travel and the quest for new experiences have awakened our taste buds, science and technology have continued to advance so we can enjoy these new-found treats wherever and whenever we desire.

Science and Technology

Now more than ever before, food and beverage professionals can deliver on the promise "your wish is my command." If a meeting planner wants to arrange a closing celebration banquet for a sales conference in Arizona in January with live lobster and fresh corn-on-the-cob, no problem! Scientific advances and new technologies have made it possible to transport highly perishable foods safely over great distances. Products such as strawberries and asparagus can now be enjoyed anywhere and at any time of the year. Advances in farm technology have increased the quantity, quality, variety, and availability of foods, expanding menu choices all over the world. For example, **aquaculture** now brings high-quality seafoods such as shrimp, salmon, and oysters to the kitchens of the world 365 days a year.

Refrigeration and freezing technologies also allow foods to be stored longer and transported over greater distances without affecting quality. Continuing technological advances have also led to an array of computerized equipment such as internal temperature probes, which can be accurately programmed to regulate oven cooking and holding temperatures. These advances ensure the greatest **yields** and the highest-quality food products. In addition, information and new ideas about food and beverage preparation and presentation are now freely shared. Featured food sections in magazines and newspapers, special television programs, attractive web sites, professional publications, and a cable channel dedicated to food have heightened both awareness and appreciation for this segment of the tourism industry.

BUILDING A CULINARY HERITAGE

Creating the foods we enjoy involves a combination of technology, science, and a great deal of culinary and service talent. This talent can be found in many different types of food and beverage operations. The most common are commercial restaurants serving the general public and travelers who dine for reasons that range from need and convenience to en-

TOURISM IN ACTION

The use of science and technology is further enhanced through the availability of information. This blending of science, technology, and information is especially evident in chain and franchise restaurant operations. For example, Red Lobster depends on sophisticated computer systems to help manage inventory, production, and distribution, along with many other marketing, management, and finance functions to serve over 60 million pounds of seafood a year. Shrimp are purchased in Ecuador and Thailand and shipped to Red Lobster's company processing plant in Saint Petersburg, Florida. Once there, they are peeled, deveined, cooked, quick frozen, packaged, and stored, awaiting distribution to Red Lobster Restaurants throughout the country.

Managers at each restaurant use relational database information systems to forecast demand and schedule kitchen and dining room service staff each day. With this information they are able to determine how many pounds of seafood to purchase, how much time will be needed for kitchen preparation, and the production quantities of each menu item. Schedules can also be prepared showing how many employees will be needed to staff the restaurant adequately.

Finally, no matter which Red Lobster Restaurant guests visit they can be assured of receiving the same quality and quantity for any item listed on the menu. Uniform kitchen preparation standards ensure the same portion sizes, colors, and garnishes of each meal. Food is cooked to precise specifications; swordfish is grilled at 450°F for 4 to 5 minutes per side and 1-lb live Maine lobsters are steamed for 10 minutes. Managers carry thermometers in their pockets and spot check items like clam chowder (no cooler than 150°F) and salads (no warmer than 40°F). Color photographs of each menu item showing such details as how many sprigs of parsley to use are prominently displayed in the kitchen as a final quality check and training tool.

Source: Dinner house technology. (1991, July 8). *Forbes*, pp. 98–99.

tertainment and pleasure. Commercial restaurant operations vary all the way from fast food (quick service) and take-out to elegant, full-service, sit-down operations. While restaurants are the most typical food and beverage (F&B) operation, they represent only one of many types of food and beverage services. Other food and beverage operations can be classified into employee food service, recreational food service, transportation food service, lodging properties, banquet/meeting and catering facilities, and institutional food service establishments. Most of these food service operations touch travel and tourism in some way.

TAPAS

It will always be difficult to categorize every type of food-service operation. Differences arise due to variations in service goals, the number and profiles of people served, menus, atmosphere, seasons, and production techniques. One example of a unique type of food-service operation that originated in Spain is a *Tapas*. The service goal of these operations is to provide guests with a wide variety of foods in appetizer portions. They are most commonly found in the heart of theater districts, restaurant groupings, and other areas of a city where late-night activity thrives. A Tapas's kitchen will often stay open much later than other food-service operations. Tapas also serve as a meeting for guests wanting a drink and an appetizer before going elsewhere to dine. Because of this practice Tapas often thrive when surrounded by restaurants.

The Beginnings of Modern Food-Service Practices

Independent eating and drinking establishments were the first food and beverage operations to evolve and, today, they generate about two thirds of all food and beverage revenues.[4] It all began in Paris, way back in 1765 when Monsieur Boulanger served a typical peasant's dish: sheep's feet (also known as trotters) in a white sauce as a restorative along with ales in his tavern. In fact, the word *restaurant* comes from the French word *restorante*, which means restorative. Tavern keepers in Boulanger's time were limited to serving beers and ales only in accordance with the controls imposed by the medieval guild system. These controls were designed to maintain standards and restrict competition. Since Boulanger was limited by law to serving beers and ales only, he was brought to court to stop the practice of serving food in his tavern. He won the case and the rest is history; the door was opened for restaurants to serve food and drink together.

The French Revolution marked another important milestone in the growth of these new eating establishments. Chefs, who had previously worked for the monarchy of nobility under the constant threat of losing their heads in the guillotine, fled to the countryside and opened their restaurants.[5]

Food-service operations have come a long way from the pioneering days of Monsieur Boulanger. As societal norms, customs, and economies evolved, so, too, did the entire food and beverage industry. The first disciplined approach to the culinary arts was captured through the grande cuisine instituted by Marie-Antoine Carême. His cooking style along, with recipes describing dishes and sauces of the grande cuisine were collected and published in *La Cuisine Classique* (1856) and other books that followed. Although these books were popular in the kitchens of the nobility, they were slow in finding their way to the fledgling restaurants, which offered a simple **table d'hôte.** This type of menu provided little if any choice. Carême's grande cuisine created a new style of service and range of menu choices. Menus expanded through the offering of a "carte" or list of suggestions giving rise to the **à la carte** restaurant.

The next major step in the development of modern food-service operations was marked by the opening of the Savoy Hotel. It opened in London in 1898 under the direction of Caesar Ritz and George Auguste Escoffier. Grande cuisine was still the exception, but it was embraced by these two food-service pioneers who ensured that their à la carte presentations were an event. Diners enjoyed the best of food and service as well as the ambience of elegant surroundings.

Escoffier was the most famous chef of his day and is considered by many to be the father of modern-day chefs. Escoffier revolutionized the methods of food-service and kitchen organization during his years of managing the kitchens at the Savoy and later the Carlton Hotel. He expanded and refined the idea of à la carte service by establishing carefully planned sequences of courses. For example, a typical sequence of courses for today's full-service casual American-style restaurant might start with an appetizer and then be followed by soup, salad, entree, and dessert.

Escoffier also reorganized tasks and activities in the kitchen, eliminating duplication of effort and improving efficiency in operations by creating and defining the work of **stations.** More than anyone else, Escoffier helped to focus food-service providers on the important task of catering to guests' needs and desires by making dining a memorable experience. This was only the beginning, as others contributed to the constantly evolving developments in foods and beverages. Table 6.1 traces the historic evolution of foods and preparation methods from the Egyptian Kingdoms to Ray Kroc's brainchild, McDonald's.

TABLE 6.1
A Food and Beverage Timeline

4850 B.C. to 715 B.C.	Egyptian kingdoms—travel became popular, people sought new foods and experiences.
900 B.C. to 200 B.C.	Greek empire—Greeks traveled to Egypt, India, Persia, and Babylon and brought back knowledge of various cooking methods.
500 B.C. to 300 A.D.	Roman empire—Romans conquered the Greeks, bringing back Greek slaves and their knowledge of food and preparations. The Roman's appetite for indulgence elevated cooking to the status of an art form.
5th to 14th centuries	Dark Ages—travel all but disappeared; the spread of cooking knowledge and skills stopped and even began to diminish.
1275 to 1295 A.D.	Travels of Marco Polo to the Middle East and China brought spicy new "treasures" such as salt and pepper to Europe, renewing interest in travel, trade, and desire to discover new foods.
14th to 16th centuries	Caterina de Medici, an Italian princess who married a French prince, introduced etiquette such as the fork and napkin as well as the Italian Florentine style of cooking.
16th to 17th centuries	• European travel to the Americas and West Indies added new foods such as chocolate, chilies, beans, corn, tomatoes, and potatoes. • Ann of Austria, a member of the Spanish Hapsburg family, married Louis XIII. Her Spanish chefs introduced sauce Espagnol and the use of roux as a thickener for sauces.
1651	Pierre Francois de la Varenne published the first cookbook, *Le Vrai Cuisinier François,* which detailed the cooking practices of the French nobility.
1765	M. Boulanger, a Paris tavern keeper, started the first restaurant.
1789–99	The French Revolution—Chefs who were classically trained and had worked in royal households began to work for wealthy "non-noble" families. The exchange between classically trained chefs and domestic chefs produced a number of culinary innovations and refinements.
1856	Marie-Antoine Carême established the grande cuisine and published *La Cuisine Classique,* systematizing culinary techniques.
1898	The Savoy Hotel opened in London under the direction of Caesar Ritz and George Auguste Escoffier.
19th & 20th centuries	• George Auguste Escoffier introduced the "brigade system." • Soldiers returned from each of the World Wars with appetites for the traditional foods of Italy, Germany, France, and Asia.
1955	Ray Kroc opened the first McDonald's, revolutionizing ideas about franchising and customer service.

Sources: Labensky, Sarah R., & Hause, Alan M. (1995). *On cooking: A textbook of culinary fundamentals.* Englewood Cliffs, NJ: Prentice-Hall; Conway, Linda Glick (Ed.) (1991). *The new professional chef* (5th ed.). New York: Van Nostrand Reinhold.

Planning to Meet Guest Expectations

Food-service operators are not simply in the business of providing food and beverages; they are in the business of creating guest enjoyment. Achieving this goal requires attention to detail and preparation that begins well in advance of welcoming the first guest. The guest experience is determined by a variety of interrelated factors from menu design and place settings to **plate presentation** and style of service. Each of these factors plays a significant role in achieving guest satisfaction and must be made within the physical and human constraints of the operation. Issues such as size of storage areas, production and service areas, types of equipment, and the capabilities of preparation, production, and service personnel must all be considered.

Armed with an understanding of these constraints and capabilities, the first step in preparing to welcome guests is designing the menu. Effective menu design begins with identifying target segments and planning to meet their desires. This requires asking some basic questions. What image should food-service operations support? How many items should be offered on the menu? How diversified should the offerings be and how seasonal should they be? What impact will different menu items have on preparation, production, presentation, and service? The answers to these questions may result in a variety of menu offerings and styles of service ranging from quick-service snacks to full-service formal dining.

The second step involves the design and presentation of the menu itself. Seemingly simple things like deciding what type of menu board should be placed above an ordering station or selecting the paper stock, graphics, color, font, and layout of a menu take on new importance. These decisions communicate an image to guests even before the food is presented.[6] A theme park guest wanting a restful break will have much different expectations than a businessperson on an expense account entertaining clients. The design and presentation of the menu sets the stage for the next important decisions.

The third step involves a variety of decisions that range from selecting service ware to designing place settings. These decisions may be driven by the functional demands of

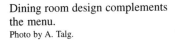

Dining room design complements the menu.
Photo by A. Talg.

serving as many guests as inexpensively as possible or a desire to create an aesthetically pleasing atmosphere. Plastic or paper with self-service areas for condiments may be the best selection for guests in a hurry, but the same choice would not be suitable in a fine-dining situation.

Designing the actual plate presentation is the fourth and possibly most artistic step in the process. Attention to detail in the previous steps comes to life when guests receive their selections. Once the order is delivered, whether hot dogs and fries or Chateau Briand, the eyes always take the first taste. Even with simple dishes, the presentation should be designed to fill our senses through a thoughtful combination of color, texture, shape, aroma, and arrangement. Think for a moment about how many different ways a chicken breast could be prepared and presented. Does your choice encourage the guest to sample and savor or simply eat because it is there and they are hungry?

The fifth and final step in planning to meet guest expectations is accomplished when the type of service is selected for delivering menu items. Service may range from moving down a cafeteria line to formally orchestrated **Russian service.** Whatever the selection, the ultimate goal is meeting guests' needs. Proper planning sets the stage for enjoyable dining experiences.

It All Comes Down To Rhythm, Timing, and Flow

Developing menus and having the right equipment, ingredients, and talent to produce these items is only the beginning of a successful food-service operation. Just like the conductor of an orchestra who brings a musical score to life, food and beverage managers bring menus to life. The **brigade** system, developed by Escoffier, was designed to make this task possible. Under this system, each position has a station (assigned workplace) and clear-cut responsibilities. For example, one station in the kitchen makes all of the **stocks** and **reductions** needed for the bases of soups and sauces instead of everyone making their own. Although the brigade systems (see Tables 6.2 and 6.3) were originally designed for use in fine-dining establishments, they are flexible and can be modified for use in any size or style of food-service operation.

Professionally planned menus, a properly designed and equipped kitchen, well-trained employees, and effective preparation and production systems make up the basic ingredients for delivering high-quality food and service. However, it takes more. A dedicated team constantly striving to balance the rhythm, timing, and flow of production and service delivery add the final ingredients that bring the dining experience to life. To achieve this balance managers must focus on being team leaders or coaches for their employees and move away from the authoritative approach that has been traditionally used by food-service managers.[7]

- *Rhythm* is the coordination of each required task and activity.
- *Timing* is the sequencing of each task and activity to produce desired results.
- *Flow* is the combination of rhythm and timing resulting in a smooth, efficient operation.

To understand the importance of rhythm, timing, and flow, imagine the following setting. You and your friend have just been seated and presented with menus in a full-service American-style restaurant. The typical sequence of courses in this style of restaurant would be appetizer, soup, salad, entree, and dessert.

As you review the menu, you look around and notice that the dining room is full, and there are customers still waiting to be seated. You see a busser (back waiter) moving a highchair toward a table; the captain (host/hostess) reseating guests who did not like their table; a waiter (front waiter) stopping to answer a guest's question; and you just heard the captain take a special request from the guests at the table next to you. While you are watching all of these activities, your water glasses have been filled and your waiter has already taken and served your drink orders.

TABLE 6.2

Typical Stations and Responsibilities in the Classical Kitchen Brigade System

Station	Responsibilities
Executive chef or "Chef de cuisine"	Responsible for all kitchen operations, including ordering, supervision of all stations, and development of menu items.
"Sous (under) chef"	Second in command, answers to the chef, may be responsible for scheduling, fills in for the chef, and assists the station chefs (or line cooks) as necessary.
Station chefs or "chefs de partie"	Line cooks, often with specialized functions such as banquet chef
Sauté station or "saucier"	Responsible for all sautéed items and their sauces.
Fish station or "poissonier"	Responsible for fish items, often including fish butchering, and their sauces.
Roast station or "rotisseur"	Responsible for all roasted foods and related jus or other sauces.
Grill station or "Grillardin"	Responsible for all grilled foods and often broiled foods as well.
Fry station or "friturier"	Responsible for all fried foods. This position is often combined with rotisseur.
Vegetable station or "entremetier"	Responsible for hot appetizers, and often egg dishes. Frequently this station has responsibility for soups and vegetables, starches, and pastas. In the traditional brigade system soups are prepared by the soup station or "potager" and vegetables by the "legumier."
Roundsman or "tournant"	Swing cook; works as needed throughout the kitchen.
Pantry chef or "garde-manger"	Responsible for cold food preparations, including salads, cold appetizers, and pates.
Butcher or "boucher"	Responsible for butchering meats, poultry, and occasionally fish.
Pastry chef or "patisser"	Responsible for baked items, pastries, and desserts.
Expediter or "aboyeur"	Accepts orders from the dining room and relays them to the various station chefs.

Source: Conway, Linda Glick (Ed.) (1991). *The new professional chef* (5th ed.). New York: Van Nostrand Reinhold.

When your waiter takes your orders, you notice that each appetizer and entree will have to be prepared differently. The shrimp cocktail and the mozzarella cheese sticks, just like the grilled salmon and the fettuccini alfredo, will all come from different stations in the kitchen. Your waiter passes through the kitchen doors and you hear a muffled burst of activity before the doors quickly close. When the rhythm, timing, and flow of all of these activities occurs as planned, the dining experience can be as pleasurable as listening to a well-rehearsed symphony. Bon appetit!

Adding Value to Food and Beverage Experiences

Successful food and beverage operators are quick to point out the need for differentiating their operations from their competitors. Operators strive to distinguish themselves by focusing on guest service, adding value through quality or pricing, providing unique atmospheres and dining experiences, or offering innovative foods, beverages, and services. Any of these approaches, when successfully implemented, may attract new guests as well as encourage loyal supporters to come back time and time again and bring their families and friends.

TABLE 6.3
Typical Stations and Responsibilities under the Dining Room Brigade System

Station	Responsibilities
Dining room manager or "maitre d'hôtel"	Trains all service personnel, oversees wine selection, works with the chef to determine the menu, and organizes seating throughout service.
Wine steward or "chef de vin" or "sommelier"	Responsible for all aspects of restaurant wine service, including purchasing wines, preparing a wine list, assisting guests in wine selection, and serving wine properly.
Head waiter or "chef de salle"	Generally in charge of the service for an entire dining room.
Captain or "chef d'étage"	Deals most directly with the guests once they are seated.
Front waiter or "chef de rang"	Ensures that the table is properly set for each course, that the food is properly delivered to the table, and that the needs of the guests are promptly and courteously met.
Back waiter or "busser" or "demi-chef de rang" or "commisde rang"	Clears plates between courses, fills water glasses and bread baskets, replaces ashtrays, and assists the front waiter and/or captain as needed.

Source: Meyer, Sylvia, Schmid, Edy, & Spuhler, Christel (1991). *Professional table service.* New York: Van Nostrand Reinhold.

THE NATIONAL RESTAURANT ASSOCIATION'S ONGOING RESEARCH REVEALS THAT . . .

- 42% of adult females and 31% of adult males have worked in food service at some time.
- Saturday is the most popular day to eat out, followed by Friday and Sunday. Monday is the least popular.
- More than 7 of 10 operators report purchasing products made from recycled materials for their restaurants and roughly three out of four have a recycling program.
- Food-service companies are increasingly entering foreign markets, with operators citing the Pacific Rim and Southeast Asia as offering the best opportunities for foreign expansion.
- Chinese, Italian, and Mexican are the most popular ethnic cuisines.

With many smaller food and beverage operations, managers are usually in close contact with the entire operation, enabling them to gain personal insights into guests' needs. As operations become more complex in settings such as hotels and resorts and the number of outlets increases, the need for formal planning processes and procedures becomes more important. There are two typical designs or approaches to planning and delivering food and beverage services in these large "property" settings. The approach chosen usually depends on factors such as the number of food-service outlets, services provided (for example, room service, event catering, pool-side service, etc.), and the property's overall marketing strategy for attracting and serving guests.

At one location, food and beverage facilities may be designed to provide service to a captive audience of guests while, at another location, facilities may be designed to attract guests. Let's consider a ski area's approach to its food and beverage operations. There may be thousands of skiers on the mountain and many more guests in the base area. Most of the skiers are planning to take a break from skiing between 11:30 A.M. and 1:30 P.M. to have lunch. They expect conveniently located restaurants with a layout that allows traffic to flow smoothly (the skiers want to move about without feeling as if they are stuck in a crowd). They expect to be able to order, receive, and pay for their food without long waits. They expect hot food and beverages to be served hot, and cold items to be served cold. They might expect prices to be a little higher on the mountain because of location and the desire for convenience, but they still expect good food quality. Other guests who have decided not to ski and are staying in the base area or village want the same quality and convenience, but they may desire a larger selection of food and service options.

To run the ski resort's F&B operations successfully, managers must pay close attention to a number of things. For example, organized **commissary** operations will be important to make sure each restaurant has everything it needs. Accurate tracking systems of food and supplies from the commissary to each restaurant will also be needed. By tracking food and supplies accurately, managers know how much it costs to run each food-service outlet. Watching the costs of each of these outlets helps managers to identify and respond to potential problems quickly. Items on the menu for these types of foodservice operations are usually the result of needing to please the "mainstream" desires of guests by providing items quickly and in large quantities.

At another property, such as a destination resort, the typical approach for food and beverage operations might be quite a bit different than the one we just discussed. In this type of situation, foods and beverages may be used to support a property's overall marketing strategy. For example, an oceanside resort in Monterey, California, may use distinctive food and beverage offerings as marketing tools to attract guests and to distinguish itself from competitors. These types of properties tend to use their food and beverage operations for three special reasons:

> *Creating a desired public image and defining their place in the market*. F&B operations can have a significant impact on a property's image in the marketplace by serving as a center for community groups and organizations, causing the property to be perceived as a point of pride in the community.

> *Attracting desired business*. F&B operations can be used to add quality or value to a property's overall image by attracting individuals such as travel agents and meeting planners who influence travel decisions. These operations are often used to attract group business by discounting F&B items, which adds value to the total meeting package and prevents the need to discount sleeping room prices. Actions like this can increase overall profitability since rooms have a greater **contribution margin** than F&B.

> *Creating new business opportunities*. By producing events, a property can use F&B operations to create new business opportunities. Wine tastings, celebrations, theme dinners, balls, brunches, and other combinations of food, beverage, and entertainment often entice people to visit a property. Once there, they may stay longer to enjoy the guest rooms, restaurants, lounges, pools, spas, and golf and tennis facilities. These marketing strategies can be especially effective for generating business during shoulder seasons.

In properties that use food and beverage as part of their overall marketing strategy, the F&B director is expected to run the operations in a way that will best benefit the entire property. In other words, the F&B director should be more concerned with the overall profitability of the property and meeting guests' needs rather than simply the profitability of F&B operations. This approach can be seen in operations in which attention to little details and customer service are the norm. Little things like responding to a guest request for an item not on the menu such as a peanut butter and jelly or grilled cheese sandwich or grander gestures such as hosting a "no charge" cocktail reception as a kick-off to a three-day conference create lasting and positive impressions.

Other tourism suppliers face similar types of decisions. Should foods and beverages simply be provided to fill a basic human need or should they be used as a valuable addition to the marketing mix? To answer that question, think about the approaches taken by two different airlines. Singapore Airlines is noted for its high-quality food-service operations and uses this as a marketing tool, while Southwest Airlines flies only short legs, choosing to avoid the costs and problems associated with food-service operations.

Building Profitable Operations

Competition in the food and beverage industry is fierce, with owners and managers facing the added problem of operating on very thin profit margins. So it is not surprising that the failure rate of food and drinking establishments as reported by Dun & Bradstreet is higher than for all other business groups.[8] Why is this failure rate so high? People seem to become financially involved in food and beverage establishments naively or for many of the wrong reasons. Some are motivated to own or invest in a restaurant because they crave social recognition while others like to dine out and think they know how to deliver the dining experience. Still others venture into this line of business because they have gained status as accomplished cooks from dinner parties put on for friends. Such experiences lead many to believe falsely that they have necessary skills to be good food and beverage operators.

Even if they do have the necessary talent, they may often fail to realize that food-service operators are faced with working long hours and then dealing with many complex problems in today's competitive environment.[8] Profit margins are shrinking, and controllable costs, such as payroll, employee benefits, food costs and taxes, are being forced up by inflation and governmental regulations while food-service patrons are unwilling to accept higher menu prices. In fact, F&B operations require a great deal of attention to detail and they are a business in which every nickel counts and profits are often measured in pennies.

Table 6.4 highlights some of the more common performance measures that are used to evaluate performance in food-service operations. These performance measures include sales per seat, sales per employee, and the number of times a seat turns over in one day. Table 6.5 shows how revenues are generated and where this money is spent. Benchmarks such as sales per seat show how effective marketing efforts have been. Ratios showing how much of every sales dollar is being spent on food, supplies, and labor focuses management attention on key operating expenses. It is important to note that these benchmarks and ratios will vary depending on the type of restaurant. As you think about these benchmarks, refer back to Figure 1.8 (The Art of Finance) and remember the importance of leverage, turnover, and margin in achieving profitability.

Rather than face the complexities of food-service operations alone, tourism service suppliers (especially small lodging properties) are turning in increasing numbers to the expertise provided through branded concepts. Guest needs can be met, kitchen labor costs can be substantially reduced and marketing efforts can be minimized by putting together well-known brands such as Taco John's, Blimpies, Pizza Hut, and Nathan's Famous in a food court setting. Assembling a branded bundle of food-service concepts can also reduce front-line service staffing needs.[9]

Balancing Payroll Costs with Productivity

As Carrie learned in the chapter opener, producing some menu items can be very complicated as well as labor-intensive and costly. Labor is the largest controllable expense for

TABLE 6.4
Food and Beverage Operating Ratios

	Full-Service (average check) under $10	Full-Service (average check) $10 and over	Limited-Service (fast food)
Median* food sales per seat	$4,729	$4,734	$8,451
Alcoholic beverage sales per seat	$410	$1360	N/A
Average daily seat turnover	2.2	1.0	4.8
Median sales per full-time employee	$35,706	$41,345	$43,197

*Median—the middle value; half of items are larger and half of the items are lower.
Source: 1997 Restaurant Industry Operations Report, The National Restaurant Association.

TABLE 6.5
Restaurant Industry Revenues and Expenses*

	Average Check under $10	Average Check $10 and Over	Limited-Service (fast food)
Where it came from			
Food sales	89.6%	76.0%	95.7%
Beverage sales	10.4%	24.0%	4.3%
	100.0%	100.0%	100.0%
Where it went			
Cost of food sold	32.2%	30.0%	28.4%
Cost of beverage sold	3.2%	7.8%	1.2%
Salaries, wages, benefits	31.9%	31.1%	27.9%
Operating expense	29.1%	27.6%	33.0%
Income before income tax	3.6%	3.5%	9.5%
	100%	100%	100%

*All figures are weighted averages.
Source: National Restaurant Association, Restaurant Industry Operations Report—1997.

F&B operations, and it is one of the greatest managerial challenges. High **employee turnover,** the availability and quality of new employees, and the constant need for training all combine to create significant operating costs. Consequently, F&B managers must constantly focus their efforts on making employees more productive through education, training, and technology enhancements.

SOUS VIDE

Since labor in food-service operations may be more than 50% of total operating costs, there is a trend to utilize technology to reduce these costs without sacrificing the quality and variety of menu offerings. One unique response to these concerns involves the use of precooked Sous Vide products. What is Sous Vide? The French phrase literally means "under emptiness" or "under vacuum." Sous Vide refers to a method in which fresh ingredients are combined into various dishes, vacuum packed into individual portion pouches, cooked under vacuum, and then chilled and stored until needed. These products then can be prepared in a matter of minutes to meet individual guest requests.

Increasing employee productivity typically involves investing for future profitability. Keep in mind that recruiting, training, and retaining skilled employees, as well as equipping them with the best tools and technology, will be costly decisions. These decisions are often difficult since the paybacks in efficiencies may be more long term than immediate.

Food Quality and Food Costs Are the Results of Effective Purchasing

Another critical expense in F&B operations is the cost of food. Therefore, just as much attention should be paid to purchasing, receiving, and storing these products as is paid to controlling labor costs. Purchasing is much more than simply ordering and receiving food and beverage products. The greater the food knowledge and skills of the purchasing agent, the more effective the purchasing processes will be. For example, the purchaser must understand the impact that the menu, preparation methods, ingredients, shelf-life, storage facilities, equipment, skill level of the staff, and guest expectations have on production and service delivery. Without this knowledge, problems are sure to occur. In addition, no matter how good the purchasing processes are, they can be made totally ineffective by poor receiving and storage procedures. Simple mistakes such as failing to verify amounts and weights or not checking product specifications against the **purchase order** as well as using newer items before older items can have an adverse impact on profitability and quality.

As it is in many competitive industries, food-service operators are finding it beneficial to create partnership relationships with their suppliers. These suppliers are called "purveyors" in the food-service industry and the relationships they are creating are called "prime vendor agreements." In a prime vendor agreement, food-service operators agree to direct a large portion (typically up to 80%) of their orders to a specific purveyor. In return, the purveyor agrees to categorize purchases into broad groupings, such as, meats, poultry, shellfish, and canned goods and then negotiate prices for items in each category based on a set percentage **markup** above cost. Other incentives such as providing training or lending specialized equipment may also be offered by the purveyor to obtain additional business.

An Ounce of Prevention Is Worth a Pound of Cure

Food-service operators also invest a great deal of time and money in training and technology for reasons other than improving service and profitability. In the same way an airline captain is charged with the safety of crew and passengers, so too, are food-service managers with their employees and guests. They must ensure that safe and proper sanitation practices and procedures are always given priority in daily operations. As you consider the following information, think about the potential dangers that could be created if sanitation were not maintained as a high priority. According to the Food and Drug Administration (FDA), as many as 81 million people become ill every year from microorganisms in food, and foodborne illness results in roughly 10,000 deaths and costs as much as $23 billion dollars annually.[10]

Scientific developments may have increased our understanding of food processing, improved our methods of preparation, and allowed us to improve sanitation and food storage techniques, but common sense is still needed. In the past, traditional safety and sanitation practices focused mainly on the external cleanliness of food production areas and equipment, leaving invisible contaminants free to grow into illness-causing hazards. Most bacteria grow or multiply rapidly when products are held at temperatures between 40 and 140°F, which is known as "The Bacterial Red Zone" (see Figure 6.1). Knowledge of how and when bacteria

FIGURE 6.1
The Bacterial Red Zone. Time and temperature are two very important variables that must be carefully monitored. Food properly maintained at specific temperatures for certain lengths of time can enhance food quality, or, if improper time and temperatures are used can breed disease- causing microorganisms in food.

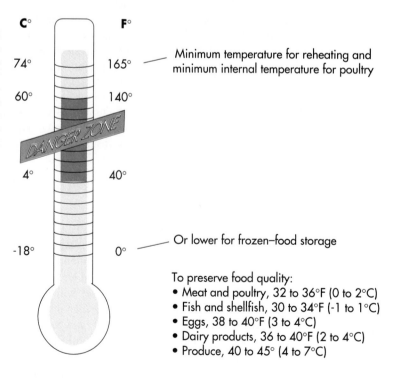

Minimum temperature for reheating and minimum internal temperature for poultry

Or lower for frozen–food storage

To preserve food quality:
- Meat and poultry, 32 to 36°F (0 to 2°C)
- Fish and shellfish, 30 to 34°F (-1 to 1°C)
- Eggs, 38 to 40°F (3 to 4°C)
- Dairy products, 36 to 40°F (2 to 4°C)
- Produce, 40 to 45° (4 to 7°C)

can grow and cause foodborne illnesses as well as the practice of basic sanitation techniques provides the foundations for protecting guest and employee safety and health.

Frequent hand washing, frequent sterilization of food-service equipment, and careful use of cutting boards can go a long way toward preventing future problems. For example, cutting boards can be color coded and dedicated for use with a specific product. One color would be used only for cutting raw poultry, another only for fresh vegetables, and another for breads. This helps to prevent the danger of cross-contamination when handling different types of foods.

BEVERAGES

The distillation, fermentation, and compounding of spirits is surrounded by a history as long and rich as the history of food. No one really knows who the alchemist was who invented the distillation process, so it is no wonder that many people through the centuries have referred to it as a gift from the gods. It was the Arabs or Saracens who gave us the words *alcohol* and *alembic*, the latter word meaning a still. In fact, the word *alembic* is used in all but the English-speaking countries even today.[11]

CATEGORIES OF ALCOHOLIC BEVERAGES

1. Fermented beverages, made from agricultural products such as grains and fruits.
2. Distilled or spirit beverages, made from a pure distillation of fermented beverages.
3. Compounded beverages, made from combinations of either a fermented beverage or a spirit with a flavoring substance(s).

Beers, wines and spirits can enhance foods and add to the overall dining experience. However, a lively bar will seldom complement a candle-lit dining experience just as a great selection of wines does little to enhance a hot dog stand on the beach. Beers, wines, and spirits not only make a good companion for a dining experience, but they are often the predominant flavor in a sauce, entree, or dessert. They can also be used in food preparations to season and tenderize foods.

When alcoholic beverages are used in hot food dishes, the alcohol quickly evaporates leaving only the flavor. In recipes, often desserts, where an alcoholic beverage is not heated and cooked off, the practice is referred to as perfuming. In short, the relationship between foods and beverages is a marriage made in heaven and there are many cultures who take the relationship for granted. For example, in Germany, you can order a beer with your Big Mac and, on a trip to Japan, you can find vending machines offering not only food, but also cold beer or hot sake as well.

Beverage Operations

Successful beverage operations depend on many of the same fundamental business principles that we previously discussed in developing efficient, profitable, and safe food-service organizations. In addition, beverage operations also require a great deal of attention to details since they represent a substantial investment in equipment, furniture, décor, and inventory.

Books, television and movies have all painted a picture of the bartender full of character, serving the guest whose stress is lifted away with a warm greeting. At the guest's request, the bartender reaches for a bottle or pulls the tap. That practice is called "free-pouring," and it is fading away to be recalled as a thing of the past. Today, it is common to see the increasing use of technology in bar operations in response to dramatic drops in profit margins. The cause for the drop is due to heavy taxes on alcoholic beverages and

a change in consumption behaviors as people are drinking less but ordering more premium products. These changes along with guests' intolerance for higher prices are leading to narrower profit margins.

Today, instead of allowing the bartender to free-pour, automated systems strictly control the amount of alcohol poured and electronically transmit information to the computerized cash register system that rings up the sale and updates the bar's **perpetual inventory**. Although these systems are practical, many guests find them to be impersonal and many professional bartenders dislike their inflexibility. Some guests and bartenders perceive the bar as a place for relaxed, social exchanges where technology should be forgotten and handshakes remembered.

Keeping Spirits under Control

Establishments serving alcoholic beverages face a unique set of legal and social challenges. "Many states have Dram Shop or Civil Liability Acts which impose liability on the seller of intoxicating liquors (which may or may not include beer), when a third party is injured as a result of the intoxication of the buyer where the sale has caused or contributed to such intoxication."[12] In addition, society's demand for more responsible drinking and stricter drinking-and-driving laws are creating additional demands on operators who serve alcoholic beverages.

These legal and social concerns are being met with strong industry support for responsible serving practices. Training programs that focus on recognition and service support for customers who have enjoyed too much of a good time are now the industry standard. Simple tactics for bartenders and wait staff that include slowing down the speed of service, keeping "munchies" on the table, and offering appetizer menus and water are just a few approaches to responsible alcohol service. More drastic measures such as denying service, having a guest escorted to their room, or calling a taxicab may also be required.

The laws defining legal levels of blood alcohol before driving impairment occurs vary (typically .08 to .10). So, can a person drink and still drive? The answer is yes, but not much. A good rule of thumb to follow is that a person can drink one ounce of distilled spirits, one beer, or one glass of wine an hour and still be capable of driving legally. Paying attention to customers' needs and enjoyment can go a long way toward protecting the customer, the establishment, and the general public.

SUMMARY

Travel has expanded our awareness and desire for foods and beverages from all over the world. Advances in science and technology have also increased the ways that foods and beverages are produced and prepared.

There are many types of food and beverage operations designed to serve the public. The most common are commercial restaurants, but dozens of other styles of food service exist. No matter the size or type of operation, all food-service organizations are driven by the menus they offer. In delivering their menus, they must integrate the concepts of rhythm, timing, and flow to best serve their guests.

Food-service operations range from free-standing roadside restaurants that rely on drop-in customers to on-site amusement park snack bars that serve a captive audience. No matter where they are located or whom they serve, these operations can achieve a competitive advantage by focusing on guest service, adding value, providing unique dining experiences, or offering innovative foods and beverages.

The food and beverage sector of the tourism industry is exceptionally competitive and profit margins are small, making controlling labor and food costs an everyday challenge. Successful food-service operators must train and retrain their employees as well as carefully monitor purchasing and inventory control procedures. In addition, food and beverage providers must guard the safety and health of their guests and employees by using wise food-handling practices. Managers of beverage operations are also faced with many of the same challenges and opportunities that are found in food-service operations. By paying attention to details and keeping customer service in mind, we can create pleasurable memories and lasting relationships.

YOU DECIDE

Jim Barnes always made it a point to go to the Bull & Bear Restaurant whenever his business trips took him to the Saskatoon area. After a busy day, he enjoyed the ambience and the service for which the Bull & Bear had become famous. Everything was the same this time except for a new computerized cash register system that had been installed since his last visit.

As Jim scanned his guest check at the end of another enjoyable meal, he noticed something else that was different. In the past with the handwritten checks, the waiter had given Jim a receipt showing his total bill only. However, this time, the guest check showed bar, food, and tax.

Jim's company reimbursed meal expenses only, not bar expenses. Since his previous guest checks had always been handwritten, he asked his waiter if he could have a handwritten guest check showing the total amount rather than the computer-generated guest check.

His waiter apologized for any inconvenience, but said they were no longer allowed to hand write guest checks. Undaunted, Jim decided to ask the cashier for a receipt showing the total bill only. When the cashier hesitated, Jim told her that, if she would not give him the receipt, he would have to find another restaurant that appreciated his business. Would you honor Jim's request?

NET TOUR

To learn more about the concepts and organizations presented in this chapter access the homepage for *Tourism: The Business of Travel*. Select "Chapter 6: Food and Beverage." From this location test your knowledge by taking the chapter quiz, read industry insights, and discover links to other useful sites. You may also want to visit electronically with other tourism students through the website.

DISCUSSION QUESTIONS

1. How has travel expanded our acceptance of different foods and beverages?

2. How have scientific and technological advances increased the availability and variety of foods and beverages?

3. Why are the concepts of rhythm, timing, and flow important in food-service operations?

4. How can food and beverage operations be used as a marketing tool?

5. Why must food-service operators pay attention to detail and watch every penny?

6. Why is sanitation such an important issue in food-service operations?

APPLYING THE CONCEPTS

1. Look up restaurants in the yellow pages of your local telephone directory. What categories are used to group the restaurants? Select one category and identify the chapter issues that are particularly related to that category of restaurants.

2. Visit two different food-service operations in your area and compare their decor, hours of operation, staffing, menu offerings, and prices. What are the key differences and what are the similarities in these operations?

3. Make an appointment with a manager/supervisor at a local restaurant, airport caterer, hotel, motel, resort, amusement or theme park, or other location that serves food to tourists. Discuss with them what they like and dislike about their work as well as what types of education and training are necessary to be successful in the industry.

4. Select an article from a travel magazine or the travel section of the newspaper describing foods and/or beverages. Make a copy of the article and prepare a brief summary of the key points.

GLOSSARY

à la carte   A menu in which each item is priced and prepared separately.

Aquaculture   The farming and cultivation of water plants, fish, and crustaceans in large quantities for human consumption such as kelp, salmon, catfish, oysters, and shrimp.

Brigade   A team of food-service employees, for example, the service brigade (all service personnel) or the kitchen brigade (all kitchen personnel), in which each member is assigned a set of specific tasks.

Contribution margin   What is left of the sales price after deducting operating costs.

Commissary   Central storage area where food and supplies are received and kept until requisitioned.

Cuisine   A French term pertaining to a specific style of cooking (such as Asian cuisine), or a country's food in general (such as Mexican cuisine).

Culinary   The creative arts and crafts of preparing foods.

Employee turnover   The number of employees who leave their jobs because they intentionally miss work, quit, or are terminated.

Markup   Difference between the cost of an item and its selling price.

Perpetual inventory   A system of tracking inventory on a continual basis so that current information on the level of stock is always available.

Plate presentation   The process of arranging menu offerings in a visually appealing fashion.

Purchase order   Specifies the item(s) wanted, including a brief description of quality and grade, the number desired, and the price.

Reduction   The result of boiling a liquid (usually, stock, wine, or a sauce mixture) rapidly until the volume is reduced by evaporation, thereby thickening the consistency and intensifying the flavor.

Russian service   A style of service in which the entree, vegetables, and starches are served by the wait staff directly from a platter to a guest's plate.

Shoulder season   The period of time between high and low or closed seasons when demand for services decreases.

Station   A designated work area or department in a kitchen.

Stock   The strained liquid that is the result of cooking vegetables, meat, or fish and other seasonings and ingredients in water.

Table d'hôte   French term referring to a menu offering a complete meal at a fixed price (prix fixe).

Yields   The amount or quantity produced or returned after the preparation, processing, or cooking of a product or recipe.

Atriums, now common in lodging properties, are appearing in cruise lines' megaships.
Photo by D.A. Yale.

Harrah's welcomes visitors with rooms, rooms, and more!
Photo courtesy of Harrah's Entertainment, Inc.

Fine food enhances the travel experience.
Photo courtesy of VIA Rail Canada.

A quiet lounge warms the spirit.
Photo by D.A. Yale.

Butchart Gardens (Victoria, British Columbia) offers guests a bountiful bouquet of color.   *Photo by C.E. Yale.*

Enjoying the excitement of
live entertainment.
Photo courtesty of Harrah's Reno.

Epcot Center——only one reason why Walt Disney World is the world's most visited destination resort.   *Photo by D.A. Yale.*

Plying the waves throughout the ages.
Photo by D.A. Yale.

REFERENCES

1. Mizer, David A., Porter, Mary, & Sonnier, Beth (1987). *Food Preparation for the Professional*. New York: John Wiley & Sons.

2. Conway, Linda Glick (Ed.) (1991). *The New Professional Chef* (5th ed.) New York: Van Nostrand Reinhold.

3. Outlook for Travel and Tourism (1997). Washington, DC: Travel Industry Association of America.

4. *Restaurant Industry Operations Report* (1996). Washington, DC: National Restaurant Association and Deloitte & Touche LLP.

5. Labensky, Sarah R., & Hause, Alan M. (1995). *On cooking: A textbook of culinary fundamentals*. Englewood Cliffs, NJ: Prentice-Hall.

6. Kelson, Allen H. (1994). The ten commandments for menu success. *Restaurant Hospitality*, *78*(7) pp. 103–105.

7. Mills, Susan F., & Hudson Riehle (1993). Foodservice Manager 2000. *Hospitality Research Journal: The Future Issue*, *17*(1), pp. 147–159.

8. Ranti, David (1996, March 10). Out of business as usual. *News and Observer* (Raleigh, NC) pp. 1 & 2F.

9. Luckman, Michael (1997, November). Branding for beginners. *Lodging*, pp. 112–118.

10. Safeguarding against foodborne illness (1994). *Food safety the HACCP way*. East Lansing, MI: Educational Institute of the American Hotel and Motel Association.

11. Grossman, Harold J. (1983). *Grossman's guide to wines, beers and spirits* (7th ed., revised by Harriet Lembeck). New York: Charles Scribner's Sons.

12. Black, Henry Campbell (1979). *Black's law dictionary with pronunciations* (5th ed.). St. Paul, MN: West Publishing Company.

CHAPTER 7

Attractions and Entertainment

One of the many selections on the leisure-time smorgasbord.
Photo by A. Talg.

There are no passengers on Spaceship Earth. Everybody's crew.

—MARSHALL MCLUHAN

CHAPTER OUTLINE

So Many Things to Do and So Little Time

Introduction

A World of Opportunities

Foundations for Understanding Attractions and Entertainment

Heritage Attractions
- Museums and Historical Sites
- Zoos and Aquariums
- Parks and Preserves
- Fairs and Festivals

Commercial Attractions
- Amusement Parks
- Theme Parks

Gaming
- Emerging Gaming Segments
- Place Your Bets

Shopping

Tourism in Action

Live Entertainment
- Sporting Activities
- The Performing Arts

Summary

You Decide

Net Tour

Discussion Questions

Applying The Concepts

Glossary

References

LEARNING OBJECTIVES

After you have read this chapter, you should be able to:

- Describe the major classifications of attractions and entertainment in the tourism industry.
- Understand the differences among heritage attractions, commercial attractions, and live entertainment.
- Identify key marketing, management, and financial issues facing attractions and entertainment operations.
- Describe major types of heritage attractions.
- Describe major types of commercial attractions.
- Describe major types of live entertainment alternatives.

So Many Things to Do and So Little Time

One week was just not enough, but Marie had packed in an exciting agenda of attractions and entertainment during her brief stay in London. When she and her friends first planned to visit London, one week seemed long enough for this tourism Mecca. However, once they arrived, everything was so much better than the guide books had described that their itinerary quickly expanded. Sure, it had rained, but the rain just added to the atmosphere.

The adventure began as they boarded a flight from Toronto for Heathrow Airport. After getting their bags, clearing customs, and taking an express train to Victoria Station, they were in the heart of London. They had agreed to find a bed and breakfast (B&B) to use as a "home base" and meet there each night to discuss the different activities of the day and plan for the next. Finding a B&B was easy compared to fighting the urge to sleep.

For her first day, Marie decided to take a nonstop tour aboard one of London's famous double-decker tour busses to get a feel for the city. A side benefit of the tour was being able to stay awake by riding on the top in the open air. The tour gave Marie an overall view of London and some ideas for scheduling her time. After a fish and chips dinner, she returned to her B&B for a good night's sleep.

Day two began with a typical English breakfast: eggs, sausage, bacon, juice, toast, butter, jelly and coffee. Marie decided to spend this day learning more about the history of London. The Tower of London, Westminster Abbey, Parliament, Buckingham Palace, and Cleopatra's Needle were just a few of the stops on this busy day. Day three was filled with shopping: Covent Garden, Oxford Street and, finally, Knightsbridge, and Harrods. Day four was supposed to be museum day, but, when the sun finally came out that morning, plans changed. A boat ride on the Thames and a visit to Hyde Park and Kensington Gardens seemed like better choices. She also visited Madame Tussaud's Wax Museum and ended the day with a visit to one of London's many theaters.

The weather on her last day was a bit gray and drizzly, so museums were back on the itinerary. There was no shortage of choices, but she finally decided to visit the Natural History Museum and the British Museum. As there were still a few empty spots in her luggage, quick trips to local shops for some last-minute souvenirs for friends and family back home topped off the day.

The plays, the shopping, the museums, the historical sights, Big Ben, the Tower of London, Westminster Abby, Buckingham Palace, Harrods, and that chance visit to the National Gallery! The days had flowed into one another as she enjoyed the delights of one of the world's premier tourism destinations. A rich history combined with a wide array of attractions and entertainment options made London the perfect tourist playground. There had been so many things to see and do that Marie had not had time to record any of her whirlwind week in her diary. Settling back in her seat for the flight home, she pulled out her diary to record the highlights of her trip.

Introduction

People have always been attracted to new, unusual, or awe-inspiring attractions and events in every corner of the world. In the days before recorded history, travelers may have journeyed for miles just to experience the beauty of the setting sun across a mountain valley or to participate in a religious festival in honor of bountiful harvests. Today, we may expect more, but we are still inspired to travel by the appeal of special attractions and events. No matter whether it is the chance to attend a rock concert, to witness Shakespeare being performed in the rebuilt Globe Theater, to climb to the top of the Eiffel Tower, or to view the solitude and majesty of Ayers Rock, tourists are constantly seeking new sights, sounds, and experiences as well as the opportunity to participate in a variety of **leisure activities.**

Whether traveling or staying close to home, just how do people spend their leisure time? The types and varieties of activities in which we choose to participate are as var-

FIGURE 7.1
Entertainment Activities Enjoyed by North Americans.

Sources of attendance figures: Harrah's survey of casino entertainment. Memphis: Harrah's Casinos, 1997. The Wall Street Journal Almanac 1998. New York: Ballantine Books, 1997. US Bureau of the Census, Statistical Abstract of the United States 1997 (117th edition). Washington, DC.

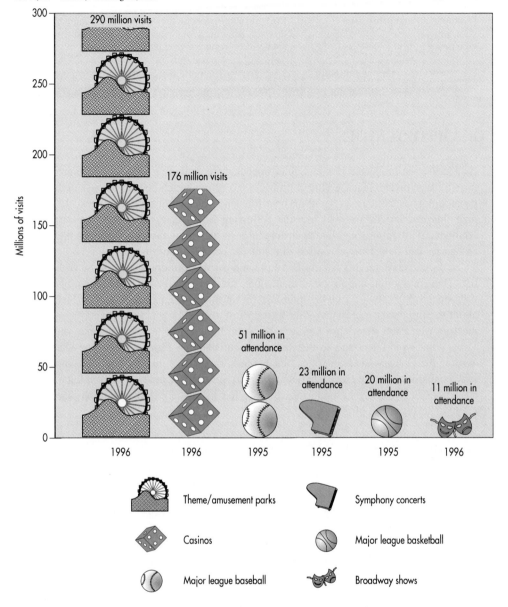

ied as the seasons and the locations to which we travel. Natural attractions such as volcanoes, mountains, caves, seashores, and waterfalls and festivals, such as planting and harvesting celebrations, served as attractions for early visitors and are still popular today. However, times have changed and, although these natural attractions and festivals are still popular, even wider varieties of alternatives have evolved to fill our leisure time. Figure 7.1 provides a brief glimpse at some of the attraction and entertainment alternatives North Americans find most attractive.

Tourists, whether visiting friends and relatives, traveling for pleasure, conducting business, or attending a professional meeting, tend to seek out a variety of attractions and entertainment alternatives to fill their leisure time. When traveling, we may continue to participate in many of our favorite leisure and **recreational activities,** but we also seek to see, do, and experience new things.

TABLE 7.1
An Attractions and Entertainment Sampler

Commercial Attractions	Heritage Attractions	Live Entertainment
Amusement and theme parks	Museums and historical sites	Sporting activities
Gaming	Zoos and aquariums	The performing arts
Shopping	Parks and preserves	
	Fairs, festivals, and events	
Can you think of other attraction or entertainment alternatives?		

A World of Opportunities

As Marie soon found out in the chapter opener, the menu of attractions and entertainment possibilities travelers face is almost limitless. Selecting which ones to discuss in this chapter is almost as difficult as deciding how to spend our leisure time as we travel. To organize this discussion, we will use the following broad categories: heritage attractions, commercial attractions and live entertainment. As shown in Table 7.1, each of these broad categories can be further classified into more specific subgroups.

As you can see, this is only a sample and many more options could be added to the list. These attraction and entertainment opportunities may be selected as simply a sidelight on a trip or they may be the main reason for travel. In Chapter 8, you will learn more about the important role many other leisure-time recreational activities such as golf, tennis, and water and snow sports play in the overall appeal of tourism destinations.

What would you add to this list? The Philadelphia Flower Show, the Carnival of Venice, the Calgary Stampede, . . .? Remember, things that interest you and your friends may be totally different from what others might seek to experience or enjoy. Each of these attractions or live entertainment opportunities has its own special appeal and place on the menu of leisure-time offerings.

Foundations for Understanding Attractions and Entertainment

Attractions are similar in some ways to live entertainment alternatives. Visiting attractions or enjoying entertainment opportunities requires travelers to make choices about how travelers will use their leisure time. Some attractions are planned around historic sites and natural settings while others are designed and constructed around planned activities, themes, and events. Depending on the purpose or setting, they may be controlled and operated by not-for-profit organizations that are dedicated to preservation and interpretation or commercial organizations dedicated to meeting guests' needs while making a profit. Live entertainment opportunities may also be found in these same settings and be operated on a not-for-profit or a for-profit basis. However, there are some key differences between attractions and live entertainment **venues.**

Attractions are natural locations, objects, or constructed facilities that have a special appeal to both tourists and local visitors. In addition to these attractions, tourists and other visitors are also drawn to see and be part of a variety of live entertainment opportunities. While most attractions are permanent, entertainment alternatives are often temporary. In contrast, **events** such as fairs and festivals are temporary attractions that include a variety of activities, sights, and live entertainment venues. In addition, visitor attendance as well as the financial fortunes of almost all attractions are influenced by seasonal changes, while entertainment venues can be planned to take advantage of seasons and tourism flows. As can be seen in Figure 7.2, even at a popular location such as Disney World, there are definite highs and lows in attendance patterns.

FIGURE 7.2
Annual Attendance at Disney
World. Attendance figures repre-
sent weekly averages.
Source: Sehlinger, Bob (1998). *The unoffi-
cial guide to Walt Disney World*. New York:
Macmillan Travel.

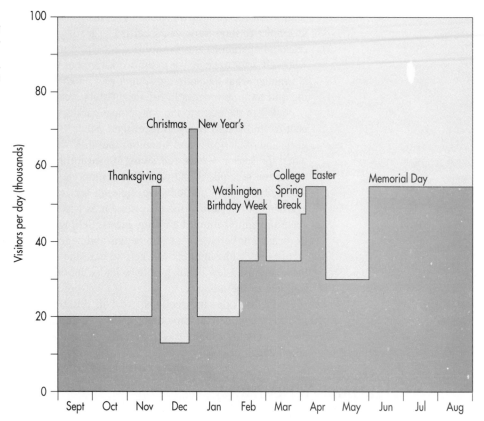

While many heritage attractions as well as amusement and theme parks are heavily
used during the summer months, they may experience much less traffic in the winter
months and so they close down. Even commercial attractions that were originally intended
to be open year-round, such as Sea World in San Antonio, Texas, have seen their visitation numbers drop so much during the colder months that it is no longer profitable to operate on a year-round basis. Yet, these attractions may still have very appealing shoulder
seasons, which can meet the needs of many visitors and still generate sufficient revenues
to cover operating expenses and/or generate a profit.

This seasonality of demand raises some key operating concerns for attractions. First,
from a marketing perspective, how can more visitors be attracted during less-popular shoulder seasons and how can they be encouraged to spend more time and money during their
visits? Second, from a management perspective, how can large numbers of employees be
recruited and trained to deliver high-quality customer service? Finally, from a financial
perspective, how can cash flow be managed so that enough money is available to meet
payroll and other operating expenses during the busy periods while retaining enough funds
to meet maintenance and administrative expenses that occur on a year-round basis?
Attraction operators address these concerns through a variety of activities.

To generate shoulder season attendance, marketing efforts have been altered to target groups of potential visitors with flexible schedules such as mature travelers and families with students on year-round education calendars. In addition, activities have been
added to match the seasons. For example, ski resorts have added mountain biking and
alpine slides to attract summer visitors, and amusement and theme parks are hosting large
groups at special promotional prices during traditionally slow shoulder seasons. Attractions
are also cooperating in their marketing efforts. "To help boost attendance, the Toronto
Metro Zoo has entered into cross-promotions with Paramount's Canada's Wonderland, a
large amusement park located about 30 minutes from the zoo."[1]

Attracting and retaining the traditional pool of high-school- and college-aged employees through the entire busy season has been accomplished through implementing wage

scales that increase as the season progresses and the payment of completion bonuses if an employee stays through a specified target date. In response to fluctuating demand, many seasonal operations are also finding it helpful to recruit older workers, especially retirees who still want to be active in the work force or simply want to supplement their incomes. No matter what the source of employees, managers must maintain a continuous recruiting and training process to fill vacant slots created by employee turnover.

When the gates to the amusement park open or the ski lifts start running, guests expect to find a staff ready to meet their needs. They also expect the same array of foods, gifts, and other goods and amenities that they would find if they had arrived a month later when the season was in full swing. Since most attractions operate on a cash basis from admission receipts, initial payroll and supply expenses must be paid before revenues are received. Planning and creative thinking are required to ensure that adequate funds are available at the start of the busy season as new employees are hired and supplies are received in anticipation of arriving guests. Selling season passes at a discount at the end of the season or before the season begins and negotiating a **line of credit** and extended payment terms with suppliers can help to ease the cash flow squeeze. As you will soon see, these are just a few of the problems and solutions facing tourism service suppliers in this segment of the industry.

In the following sections, we will describe and explore many of the heritage attractions, commercial attractions, and live entertainment alternatives that are available for people to enjoy as they travel. You may be amazed by the variety of opportunities available in each of these categories.

HERITAGE ATTRACTIONS

Heritage attractions can be found in a variety of shapes, sizes, and locations throughout the world. These attractions may range from a small community museum dedicated to preserving memories and experiences to incredible feats of human ingenuity and determination like the Great Wall of China. But heritage attractions are more than just museums, monuments, and archaeological treasures. They also include show places for natural wonders such as **botanical gardens** and aquariums as well as parks and preserves that are dedicated to public enjoyment and the protection of natural resources. In addition, fairs and festivals create special venues for celebrating and sharing a variety of accomplishments and cultural activities.

Museums and Historical Sites

Archeological evidence shows that once people began to live in communities, they began collecting, preserving, and displaying various items of interest from a cultural and historical perspective. These collections have provided a means of displaying history and passing on important information to future generations as well as "outsiders." Our continuing fascination with the past has created a growing demand for museums and cultural heritage sites. Although the majority of these sites are operated on a nonprofit basis, they serve as major tourist attractions, generating important cultural and economic benefits.

Today people are attracted by the diverse cultures of other people and the past that are displayed in **museums.** The number, types, and locations of museums can be counted in the hundreds of thousands, and the list of people who visit these museums each year can be measured in the millions. The number of available museums throughout the world continues to grow. For example, in Europe, for every museum that existed in 1950, there are now more than four. The list of museum types is extensive but the following list provides some examples of the more common options from which visitors can choose: general, art, history, science and technology, military, and natural history. Whether there are too few or too many museums is the subject of much debate. However, as societies grow and change, museums provide a valuable foundation for studying the past and thinking about what the future may hold.

THE MUSEUMS OF OTTAWA, ONTARIO

Canadian Museum of Civilization
Canadian Museum of Contemporary Photography
Canadian Museum of Nature
Canadian War Museum
Central Experimental Farm
Currency Museum
Fort Henry
Laurier House
Mackenzie King Estate
National Archives of Canada
National Aviation Museum
National Library of Canada
National Museum of Science and Technology
Royal Canadian Mint
Upper Canada Village

Source: Ottawa, Canada's Capital Region, *Destination Planners' Guide*.

You may have heard of or even visited Colonial Williamsburg, Virginia, or Old Quebec and recognize that they are major historical attractions. These are just two examples of historic sites, yet there are many other places beckoning tourists and dependent on tourism revenues to continue preservation activities. Figure 7.3 shows the brochure map provided to visitors to Historic Deerfield (in western Massachusetts), one of the oldest communities in North America.

Sites like Historic Deerfield and others throughout the world are attracting record numbers of visitors, especially international tourists. More and more communities and countries are taking steps to preserve historical treasures and attract visitors through active restoration and interpretive programs. "In heritage tourism, sites and structures of genuine historical significance are made available to the public who visit as individuals, with friends and family or as participants in group tours [p. 3]."[2]

Zoos and Aquariums

Large collections of animals, which were originally called menageries, have served as magnets for visitors since the times of the ancient Chinese, Egyptians, Babylonians, and Aztecs. Modern zoos (sometimes referred to as zoological parks) now come in many sizes and can be found throughout the world. The Philadelphia Zoo was the first (1859) location in the United States dedicated to the large-scale collection and display of animals. While this facility is still of great importance, it has been eclipsed by more spectacular zoos such as the Bronx Zoo and the San Diego Zoo. Other notable zoos around the world can be found in Montreal, Vancouver, Frankfurt, London, Paris, Moscow, New Delhi, Tokyo, and Sydney. Historically, most zoos were established as not-for-profit organizations, but that form of operation is changing. Today over half of all the zoos in the United States operate as for-profit organizations or only partially depend on government funding.[1]

Some of these zoos are very large, creating a great deal of public interest and publicity as well as generating significant international tourism traffic. This interest and traffic is based on unusual exhibits, collections of animal species, and efforts to recreate the natural setting found in the wild. Even the Walt Disney Company is banking on the continued draw of zoos. In the summer of 1998, Disney unveiled its Animal Kingdom theme park, which features a blend of live displays of existing animal species and animatronic displays of species from the past, such as dinosaurs. Figure 7.4 shows just how popular animal attractions have become.

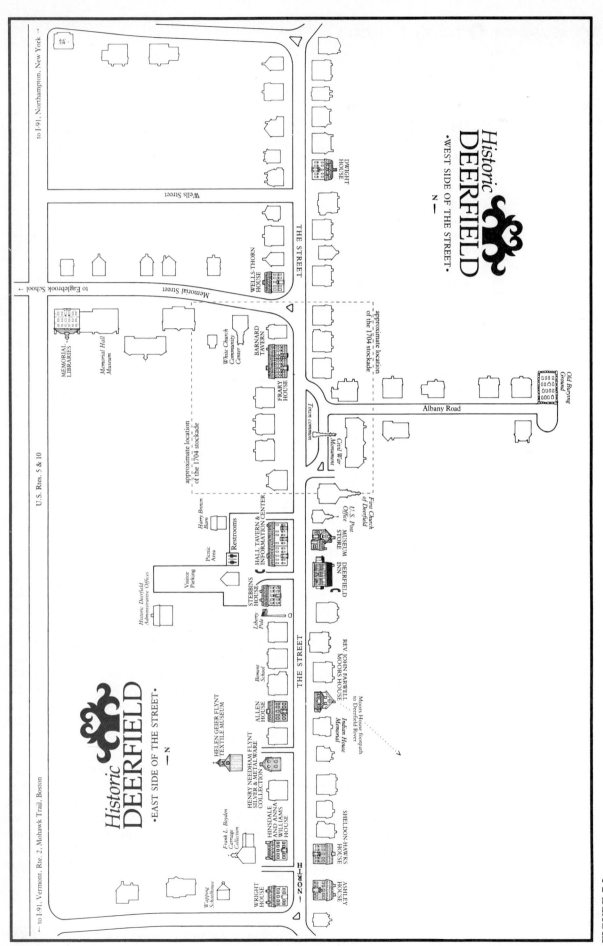

FIGURE 7.3

Historic Deerfield Map

Map by Bill Gill, courtesy of Historic Deerfield.

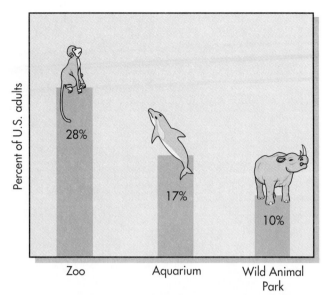

FIGURE 7.4

Attendance at Animal Attractions[*]

[*]Approximately 40% of adults visited animal attractions in the past year. In the 18-to-24 age group the percent was even higher—53%.

Source: Sloan, Gene (1996, April 24). Wave of new aquariums may face rough waters. *USA Today*, p. 4D.

28%

17%

10%

Zoo   Aquarium   Wild Animal
Park

Although aquariums are only about half as popular as zoos and wild animal parks combined, they are increasing in number, size, and attendance. The huge Oceanarium in Lisbon, Portugal, opened as the flagship attraction of Expo '98, represents the newest and possibly the most spectacular of the world's hundreds of aquariums. The first public aquarium was established in London at Regents Park in 1853. Although it eventually failed because of poor design and management, the idea of a preservation attraction devoted to water life proved to be a success. Annual attendance at U.S. aquariums alone has reached the 40 million mark![3]

Many aquariums are supported and managed as not-for-profit foundations, such as Canada's largest, the Vancouver Aquarium. Others have been developed as for-profit enterprises, such as the chain of Sea World Parks. Recently, many cities, such as Camden, New Jersey, and Long Beach, California, have funded aquariums to help revitalize waterfront areas by attracting tourists and residents to oceanside regions of these cities. One of the most successful aquariums, Baltimore's National Aquarium, helped ensure the success of that city's redeveloped Inner Harbor.

VANCOUVER AQUARIUM MISSION STATEMENT

"The Vancouver Aquarium, Canada's Pacific National Aquarium, is a self-supporting, non-profit association dedicated to effecting the conservation of aquatic life through display and interpretation, education, research and direct action."

Reprinted with permission of Vancouver Aquarium.

Each new generation of aquariums seems to strive to wow audiences with bigger and better exhibits. In 1996, Monterey Bay Aquarium, near San Francisco, unveiled a $57 million wing that is devoted to life in the open seas, including a million-gallon indoor ocean! The Tennessee Aquarium, on the Chattanooga riverfront, offers visitors a unique all-fresh-water aquarium experience.

Parks and Preserves

Every park and preserve is a little bit different. They may range from famous urban parks like Central Park in New York City or Hyde Park in London to forests and preserves such as Prince Albert National Park in Canada and Nairobi National Park in Kenya. Although they may be different in appearance and purpose, they are dedicated to protecting the natural beauty of landscapes, plants, and animals for future generations as well as providing

Bringing natural wonders up close.
Photo by Al Harvey, courtesy of Vancouver Aquarium.

visitors with open spaces for rest, relaxation, and recreation. Achieving this balance requires meeting the needs of visitors while maintaining the resources contained within the lands that have been set aside for public use. To serve all these needs, the potential impacts of all activities must be monitored and managed. For example, day-use areas and camp sites that are accessible by motorized vehicles and have full sanitary facilities require more upkeep and labor than wilderness areas that are accessible by foot or on horseback only.

The importance of parks as major tourist attractions was ushered in with the dedication of Yellowstone National Park in 1872. The idea of national parks soon spread north to Canada, where in 1887, the first national park was established with the opening of Banff National Park. National parks can now be found throughout the world as countries strive to preserve and protect their more pristine natural treasures. The grandeur and importance of some of these national parks, such as Jasper National Park in Canada and Grand Canyon National Park in the United States have become legendary and draw millions of visitors each year to enjoy their breath-taking beauty.

Some attractions such as Nairobi and Tsavo National Parks in Kenya and Serengeti National Park in Tanzania have gained such international acclaim that they serve as some of these country's primary tourist attractions. Although people from around the world are drawn to these well-known national parks, there are also millions of acres of land that have been set aside for public enjoyment on the state, provincial, and local levels. From these giant parks to the small pocket parks tucked away in the corner of a city, not a day goes by that visitors and locals alike are not relaxing or taking in a little bit of nature.

The U.S. park system is a large operation in itself, employing over 360,000 people and spending over $1.4 billion to serve almost 270 million visitors a year.[4,5] As a not-for-profit government agency, the national park service depends on **appropriations** as well as other sources of revenues. These other sources include admission (user) fees as well as revenues generated from over 650 **concessionaires,** who supply a wide range of goods and services from food and lodging to transportation and souvenirs. However, the majority of operating funds (65% in 1994) still come from appropriations. Figure 7.5 shows how these funds are spent.

Botanical gardens are another important part of the tourism attraction mix for many communities. Some botanical gardens are renowned for their magnificent displays, and they draw visitors from all over the world. The oldest botanical garden was established at the University of Pisa in Italy in 1544. The Royal Botanical Gardens in Edinburgh, the Munich Botanical Gardens, the Montreal Botanical Gardens, and the Missouri Botanical Gardens in St. Louis are just a few examples of some of the more popular and frequently visited botanical gardens.

Fairs and Festivals

Fairs and **festivals** hold unique positions in the attractions and entertainment segment of the tourism industry because they are a little bit of everything—heritage attractions, commercial attractions, and live entertainment. A fair was originally a temporary marketplace set up with the idea of stimulating commerce by creating an event that would bring together buyers and sellers. You might recognize the modern-day version of the original fair as a flea market. Festivals, on the other hand, were gatherings devoted to times of celebration.

Up through the middle ages, there were fairly distinct differences between fairs and festivals. However, over time, many of the same types of activities such as food, shows, and musical entertainment could be found at both fairs and festivals. The idea of having fun at these events is probably not surprising since the word "fair" comes from the Latin word *feria*, which means holiday.

As commerce grew, so did the idea of fairs that were designed to be large and last for longer periods of time, maybe as long as several months. Many major exhibitions highlighting achievements and industries were held before the first "World's Fair." Two of these were the Paris Exhibition of 1889 and the 1904 Louisiana Purchase Exhibition in St. Louis, Missouri.

The idea of these very large fairs that bring together exhibitors and visitors from all over the world proved to be so popular that international leaders decided to bring some uniformity to the concept. With the signing of a diplomatic convention in Paris in 1928, 43 countries agreed to the frequency and basic operational goals of events that would be officially recognized as World's Fairs. This agreement created the International Bureau of Exhibitions (BIE), which divided the world into three zones: Europe, North and South America, and the rest of the globe. It also stipulated that fairs would not be held in consecutive years in any one country and that no fees would be charged for the exhibits of

FIGURE 7.5
U.S. National Parks Expenditures.
Source: Statistical Abstract of the United States 1996, Washington, DC: Government Printing Office, p. 250.

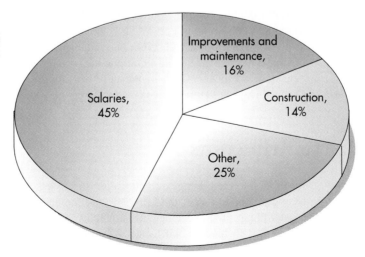

foreign governments. Since its formation, there have been a number of notable World's Fairs including the New York World's Fairs (1934 and 1964), Brussels Universal and International Exhibition (1958). Expo '67 in Montreal, Canada (1967), Expo '70 in Osaka, Japan (1970), Expo '86 in Vancouver, Canada (1986), World Expo '88 in Brisbane, Australia (1988), and Expo '92 in Seville, Spain.

Another very popular visitor attraction is the regional, state, or county fair. Most of these have evolved around the display of agricultural and livestock exhibits, but they often include industrial exhibits and many other entertainment activities. The Eastern States Exhibition, or "The Big E" as it is called, is an annual, regional 10-day fair held each summer in West Springfield, Massachusetts; it celebrates the crafts, industries, and agricultural products of the northeastern states of the United States. Some of these fairs, such as the Canadian National Exhibition in Toronto and the National Western Livestock Show in Denver, draw tens of millions of visitors. However, whether it is a World's Fair, State Fair, or County Fair, people still travel from all over to exhibit and participate in the festivities.

Festivals celebrate a variety of special occasions and holidays. Some are derived from religious observances, such as New Orleans' or Rio de Janeiro's huge Mardi Gras festivals. Other festivals focus on activities as peaceful as ballooning (the Albuquerque Balloon Festival) or as terrifying as the running of the bulls in Pamplona, Spain. Often, festivals center on the cultural heritage of an area, such as the clan festivals that are prominent in the North Atlantic province of Nova Scotia. Seasons are also reasons for festivals such as the Winter Carnival held in Quebec City or Milwaukee's Summerfest. More recently, food has become the center of attention at locations such as the National Cherry Festival in Traverse City, Michigan, or the Garlic Festival in Gilroy, California.

EXPERIMENTAL AIRCRAFT ASSOCIATION'S (EAA) INTERNATIONAL FLY-IN AND SPORT AVIATION EXHIBITION

One week each summer, hundreds of thousands of aviation enthusiasts from all over the world converge on Oshkosh, Wisconsin, for the biggest air show this side of Paris, France. The location of this event is special. In addition to being the busiest airport in the world for one week, Wittman Air Field is also home to a historic airport hangar filled with antique planes and is a short hop away from the EAA Aviation Center and Air Museum. The EAA festivities come complete with an opening parade, exhibits, acrobatic demonstrations, fly-bys, and shopping booths. So many people attend that every available form of accommodations from campgrounds and dormitory rooms at nearby University of Wisconsin, Oshkosh, to hotels is used every year.

Anytime people visit a fair or a festival, it is a time of celebration, and what celebration would be complete without fun and food? From the Oktoberfest in Munich to the Three Rivers Festival in Fort Wayne, Indiana, festivalgoers can expect to find a tempting array of music, foods, and drinks. Community leaders have discovered that tourists can be drawn to even the smallest communities for fun-filled events. The National Cluck-off held during Chicken Days in Wayne, Nebraska, or the Oatmeal Cook-off held at the Oatmeal Days in Oatmeal, Texas, attest to people's desires to attend and be a part of festivals.

COMMERCIAL ATTRACTIONS

In addition to the heritage attractions just discussed, a host of commercial attractions has been developed to meet travelers' leisure-time needs. Whether it's the thrill of the roller coaster plunge, the excitement of gaming or the joy of an armload of boxes after a day at the mall, both tourists and locals welcome the opportunity to visit and enjoy these attractions.

Amusement Parks

The first amusement parks, which were called pleasure gardens, were built in England and France. As the name *pleasure garden* implies, these attractions began as manicured gardens designed to provide a temporary escape for city dwellers from the every day drudgeries of life. Rides such as carousels, games, and food and drink stands were added to these pleasure gardens to meet guest needs. The idea of parks with rides and other entertainment activities soon found its way to the United States. Interest in amusements in the United States heightened when the Ferris wheel was introduced at the 1893 Chicago World's Fair. The name for this new amusement that became the centerpiece of most early amusement parks was taken from its inventor George Washington Gales Ferris.

Lights, sounds, rides, games of chance, food, and a flurry of activities proved to be natural draws for those early thrill-seeking visitors to such places as Coney Island in Brooklyn or the Steel Pier in Atlantic City. Many smaller amusement parks in the United States were originally located at the edge of town, where the trolley lines stopped. These amusement parks, called "trolley parks," were established as marketing tools to encourage ridership during the slow weekend periods. As automobiles and busses replaced trolleys, these and other amusement parks faded in popularity as their captive audiences disappeared. However, the concept of family fun and amusement was kept alive during the first half of the 20th century with traveling carnivals that moved across the country as a source of entertainment at many fairs and festivals until a landmark event that occurred in 1955. That year marked the opening of Disneyland in Anaheim, California.

Disneyland was much more than an amusement park. Although it drew on some of the basic attributes of an amusement park, Disneyland was the first theme park, and its opening served to rekindle respectability and interest in amusement parks.[5] Since that time, the operations of amusement parks have become more sophisticated, with technology playing a far more important role. However, the basics of fun, excitement, and fantasy remain the keys to amusement park successes.

Amusement parks, family entertainment centers, and water parks serve as important recreational outlets for their host communities and also attract considerable tourism interest from the region. Some of the larger amusement parks that may be recognizable to you include Elitch's Garden in Denver, Kentucky Kingdom in Louisville, Kennywood Park (one of the original trolley parks) in West Miffin, Pennsylvania, and Grand Slam Canyon in Las Vegas.

ROLLER COASTERS

From 6 to 60 mph, the roller coaster has always found itself at the center of attention. Thanks to Russian ingenuity and some early daredevils, the first ice slides were built in the 15th century. The thrill of rocketing down steep ice slides in cars built of ice with straw seats created the desire for a year-round alternative. The answer to this demand, the roller coaster, was introduced in St. Petersburgh, Russia, in 1784.

Some of these early roller coasters allowed riders to sit sideways and traveled at a leisurely speed of 6 mph. But riders wanted more speed and thrills, and the engineers went to work. By 1817, speeds of 40 mph were reached in Paris and loops, twists, turns and breath-taking drops weren't far behind. Now speeds of 60 mph are common, and with a little more help from the engineers, opportunities for adventuresome fun seekers to experience speeds of over 100 mph are on the horizon.

Source: A History of Roller Coasters (1996, May). *Funworld*, pp. 20–28.

Theme Parks

The distinction between amusement and theme parks is beginning to blur, but there are several unique characteristics that set them apart. Theme parks create a destination in themselves. By combining entertainment, food, and beverages and an environment different from that found outside the gates, visitors are allowed to escape reality as they enter. Through the magic of technology and elaborate staging, theme parks can replicate almost any location in the world. As visitors are transported into this simulated environment, they are afforded the luxury of being in another location without the expense or any of the potential problems of faraway travel.

> Together, one Disney World and two Disneylands form a nation whose total acreage would make it one of the smallest countries on earth. Yet combined attendance figures make these fantasy lands earth's number one attraction destination. . . . In let's pretend lands, no passports are needed. There is no foreign currency to deal with, no customs, no sweat (p. 54).[6]

In addition to providing a theme around which a park operates, such as the Dark Continent (Africa) at Busch Gardens in Tampa, Florida, or Ocean Park in Hong Kong, successful parks also meet several other basic requirements. These requirements include:

- A sufficient target market of day-trippers who have the necessary disposable income to visit and enjoy park attractions.

- A site of at least 100 acres or more of rolling or well-drained land for the park, parking, buffer areas, room for future expansion, and easy highway access.

- Access to a large pool of prospective part-time employees.

- A minimum of 140 rain-free days between April 1 and November 1.

- Access to large quantities of water since most theme parks usually contain popular water attractions.[7]

There may be a tendency on the part of North Americans to think that they are the center of amusement park attractions. However, remember that the idea was imported from Europe and a trip to that continent will show that it has not lost its place in the theme park spotlight. Blackpool Pleasure Park in Blackpool, England; Parc Asterix and Disneyland Paris just outside Paris; Port Aventura on Spain's Costa Dorado; Efteling Leisure Park in Kaatsheuvel, Netherlands; LEGOLAND in Billund, Denmark; and Phantasialand between Cologne and Bonn, Germany, are just a few of Europe's premier parks. Other park locations around the world such as Tokyo Disneyland in Japan; Dreamworld at Coomera on Australia's Gold Coast; Lotte World in Seoul, Korea; La Ronde in Montreal, Quebec; and Burlington Amusement Park on Prince Edward Island, Canada, serve to highlight the international appeal of these attractions.

"The contemporary American typically associates theme parks with concepts of permanence, gardened park-like settings and single price admission" (p. 51).[8] Theme parks meeting these criteria range from elaborate parks such as Disney World in Florida and Canada's Wonderland in Toronto to local and specialty theme parks such as Worlds of Fun in Kansas City, Missouri, and Six Flags over Georgia, in Atlanta, providing a wide range of choices for the consumer. To differentiate product offerings and successfully compete, theme park operators must become more aware of consumer perceptions and concerns. There are several core conditions that must be met by theme park operators to retain repeat patronage and attract new patrons.

From an operating point of view, the parks must create a family atmosphere and be clean and visually pleasing. Park designers must provide a wide variety of rides, especially roller coasters and water rides, while reducing the perception of crowding. Patrons are also interested in being able to enjoy a wide variety of shows as well as being able to enjoy some activities with an educational orientation.[8] In addition, new rides and features must be added on a periodic basis to maintain guest interest and ensure repeat patronage. All of this costs money, and as Figure 7.6 shows; after general operating expenses, maintenance and marketing are the two largest expense categories.

FIGURE 7.6
Theme Park Attendance and Revenue Breakdowns.
Source: IAAPA 1996 Amusement Industry Abstract.

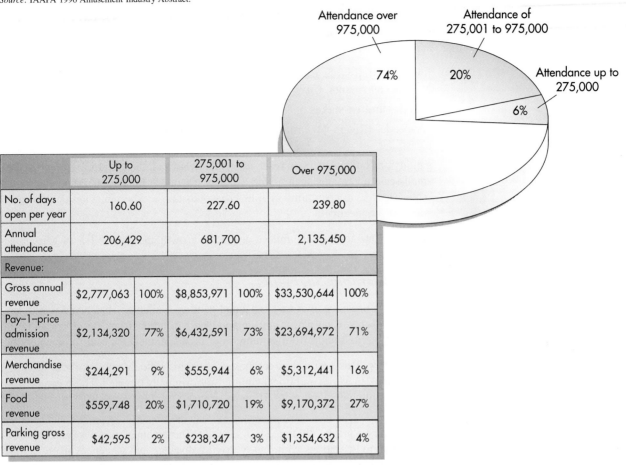

	Up to 275,000		275,001 to 975,000		Over 975,000	
No. of days open per year	160.60		227.60		239.80	
Annual attendance	206,429		681,700		2,135,450	
Revenue:						
Gross annual revenue	$2,777,063	100%	$8,853,971	100%	$33,530,644	100%
Pay-1-price admission revenue	$2,134,320	77%	$6,432,591	73%	$23,694,972	71%
Merchandise revenue	$244,291	9%	$555,944	6%	$5,312,441	16%
Food revenue	$559,748	20%	$1,710,720	19%	$9,170,372	27%
Parking gross revenue	$42,595	2%	$238,347	3%	$1,354,632	4%

GAMING

Casino gaming has experienced an explosive growth in popularity and availability across the United States and Canada during the past few years. When gaming was legalized in Nevada in 1931 to attract tourists during the depression, few would have envisioned that over 50% of the adult U.S. population and 25% of the adult Canadian population would be spending some of their entertainment dollars inside casinos.[9,10] Some type of gaming operation can now be found in 26 U.S. states and in nearly all Canadian provinces. In fact, the increasing availability and ease of access to gaming locations has resulted in more Americans visiting casinos than attending major league and collegiate football games, arena concerts, symphony concerts, and Broadway shows combined.[10]

Five basic factors combine to explain the current success and future prospects of the gaming industry. First, voters have been increasingly willing to approve new gaming alternatives because these activities have come to be viewed as a "voluntary tax"[11] or form of economic development while politicians have been unwilling or unable to pursue new taxes.[12] Second, more people than ever before are choosing casino gaming as an acceptable leisure activity. Four out of five adults now report that they consider casino gaming to be a "fun night out."[13] Third, retirees comprise the single largest segment of the casino market,[14] and their numbers continue to grow. Fourth, casinos have devised marketing programs to attract the previously ignored "low roller,"[15] and fifth, expanded availability of gaming opportunities is attracting many individuals who have never before visited casinos for entertainment.[16]

Prior to the 1990s, traditional casino gaming was not adopted by a majority of Americans because they needed to travel to Atlantic City or Nevada to participate in legal gaming. This made gaming relatively unattractive as a leisure-time activity as compared with closer tourism attractions and activities. Now, with more locations and new technologies, the characteristics of gaming as a leisure-time activity have changed. Currently, there are four broad categories of gaming alternatives:

* traditional full-scale casino gaming, including the well-established locations in Nevada and Atlantic City;
* historic, **limited stakes** operations such as those in Colorado's mining towns;
* "dockside" (Riverboat) casinos, such as those operating on the Mississippi and Gulf Coast; and
* gaming on Native American reservations that varies all the way from limited stakes, small-scale operations such as the Sky Ute Casino in Ignacio, Colorado, to large-scale Vegas style operations such as Foxwoods on the Mashantucket Pequot reservation in Connecticut.

Table 7.2 highlights some of the milestones in the growth and availability of gaming activities.

Emerging Gaming Segments

The development of new games and expanded gaming availability has given rise to several gaming segments, each with a profile somewhat different from the others and each with different benefits sought from gaming. Four broad segments appear to be emerging:

1. *High rollers.* This segment is composed of sophisticated gamblers (both domestic and foreign), to whom traditional gaming was originally targeted. These gamers tend to be wealthy, older, and male. High rollers tend to play games of skill rather than luck.

2. *Day-trippers.* Retirees dominate this segment. These gamers make several short-duration trips to operations within easy driving distance and wager relatively significant amounts per trip, but tend to play slots and other video gaming options.

3. *Low-stakes/new adopters.* Gamers in this segment have only recently discovered and accepted gaming as an interesting day or evening diversion when it is close to home

TABLE 7.2
Milestones in Gaming's History and Growth

Year	Event
1931	Gambling legalized in Nevada
1964	State lottery begun in New Hampshire
1978	Gambling legalized in Atlantic City
1988	Indian Gaming Regulatory Act
1989	Limited-stakes gaming in Deadwood, South Dakota Limited-stakes gaming in three mountain communities in Colorado (Central City, Cripple Creek, and Black Hawk) Limited-stakes riverboat gaming legalized in Iowa
1990	Riverboat gaming legalized in Illinois
1991	Riverboat and dockside gaming legalized in Mississippi
1993	Gaming legalized in New Orleans Riverboat gaming legalized in Louisiana
1994	Limits removed from gaming in Iowa

Source: Cook, Roy A., & Yale, Laura J. (1994). Changes in gaming and gaming participants in the United States. *Gaming Research and Review Journal, 1*(2), 17.

Playing the odds.
Photo courtesy of Harrah's Casinos.

or when traveling. Members of this segment are mainly part of the growing cadre of aging baby boomers and their retiree parents, with the time and money to enjoy the entertainment associated with gaming. Many gamers in this group are younger women who tend to play video gaming alternatives and Generation X young adults.

4. *Family vacationers.* Due in part to the development of complementary tourism attractions such as theme parks, this segment tends to gamble as an off-shoot of a family vacation.

Place Your Bets

The availability of new and expanded gaming opportunities for tourists to try their hands at "Lady Luck" are likely to continue to grow. Although many present and future gaming locations do not have the marketing advantages of destinations such as Monaco or Las Vegas, they do have one factor in common with already well-established and successful operations in places like Hull, Ontario; Atlantic City; and Laughlin, Nevada: a location within easy driving distance of a large population base. This ease of access combined with the social acceptance and novelty of gaming as recreation has attracted many first-time gamers and should continue to generate repeat visits.[17]

Serving this growing market for locals and tourists who are seeking the excitement and entertainment of gaming is creating attractive investment and employment opportunities. In contrast to other segments of the tourism industry that operate on very thin profit margins, gaming generates margins of up to 35%. Gaming opportunities continue to grow as visitors can choose from a variety of venues including riverboats, Indian reservations, destination resort casinos, and the traditional casino meccas of Las Vegas and Atlantic City. International destinations such as Macao, Isla De Margarita off the Venezuelan coast and Bermuda tempt tourists to gaming tables from around the world. Figure 7.7 shows

FIGURE 7.7
National Casino Gaming Win by State, not including Indian casino gaming.
Source: Individual State's Gaming Commissions.

State	1995 Gaming revenue (win)	% of total U.S. gaming win
Nevada	$7,368,580,000	45.5%
New Jersey	$3,748,155,643	23.1%
Mississippi	$1,724,400,000	10.6%
Illinois	$1,177,400,000	7.3%
Louisiana	$1,050,000,000	6.5%
Missouri	$466,400,000	2.9%
Colorado	$384,343,000	2.4%
Iowa	$239,000,000	1.5%
South Dakota	$45,931,670	0.3%
Total:	$16,210,410,313	100.0%

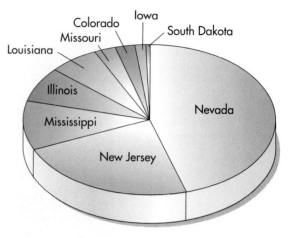

that as many new venues have opened, gaming revenues are no longer restricted to traditional gaming locations.

SHOPPING

Shopping may be part of the travel experience or it may be the primary focus of travel. Shopping is an activity that crosses all market segments. "As long as cities have existed, the pattern of 'going into town' has included a leisure experience, and visiting towns is an essential part of the tourist market."[18] While some visitors simply pick up necessities or a souvenir as a reminder of their travels, others may travel to specific locations for the primary purpose of shopping. "Shopping will continue to represent a sizable portion of the travel budget. For example, international visitors to Texas spend 25.7% of their travel budget on shopping. In Mississippi, shopping comprises 24% of travel expenses among all travelers (p. 31)."[19]

"Shop till you drop." This statement applies to more than just local shoppers as more and more malls are turning to tourists in search of new customers and growth. For some travelers, a visit to a mega shopping mall has become reason enough to take a trip, especially as these malls are transforming themselves into tourist destinations by adding amusement parks and other cultural attractions and entertainment activities.[19] The success of Canada's West Edmonton Mall in attracting tourists to the shopping experience with over 800 stores and a variety of attractions has not gone unnoticed south of the border.

In fact, the number one tourist attraction in Minnesota is a shopping mall. The Mall of the Americas in Bloomington, Minnesota, attracts over 40 million visitors a year. The experiences and successes of mall operators offer valuable insights into the importance of shopping as a tourism attraction.

What brings visitors from far and wide to these shopping meccas? It's more than just the wide array of retail shopping alternatives. For example, the Mall of the Americas comes complete with an 18-hole miniature golf course, a 14-screen theater, and nine nightclubs. But even as successful as the retailing and attraction mix is at the Mall of the Americas, management is not counting on its past decisions for future success. They know customers can become jaded, so they are planning new attractions to keep visitors returning. The recent addition of Underwater World, a 1.2-million gallon walk-through aquarium, will provide one more reason for shoppers to plan a trip to experience a unique mall environment.

Other malls such as Woodfield Mall in Schaumburg, Illinois, and Gurnee Mills Mall in Gurnee, Illinois, do not rely on added attractions to draw in visitors, just good solid shopping opportunities. And does this work? The answer is a definite yes as these two

A mall is a mall is a mall. Not so! Imagine a shopping and entertainment paradise that covers over 110 acres and attracts over 20 million visitors a year. Now, imagine this attraction sitting on the plains of Canada in the city of Edmonton, Alberta. If you have not visited this "shopping center," then you have missed seeing and experiencing the biggest mall on Earth—West Edmonton Mall. This mammoth package of tourist services attracts people from all over the world in record numbers.

The West Edmonton Mall is not like most other malls: It is massive in size and excites the imagination. Sure, it has shops, shops and more shops. In fact, it has more than 800 stores. But the mall has more than shops and shopping to attract visitors. Almost 40% of the mall's space is dedicated to attractions as well as a hotel and more than 100 food outlets, and it is all under one roof. It takes over 15,000 employees to accomplish all of the administrative and operating duties to keep this giant enterprise ticking.

The Fantasyland Hotel has 355 guest rooms, but 127 of these rooms have been specially "themed" and decorated to fulfill guests' desires for travel adventures. When it's time to take a break from shopping there are a number of things to do and see including Galaxyland Amusement Park, World Waterpark, Ice Palace, Europa (miniature) golf course, Deep Sea Submarine Adventure, Dolphin Lagoon and Sea Life Caverns, a full-scale casino, a bowling emporium, three cinema complexes, and a replica of one of the ships of Christopher Columbus.

Deciding what to do can be as difficult as deciding what to buy. Viewing the many animal attractions exhibiting more than two hundred species of animals such as dolphins, fish, exotic birds, and a colony of breeding penguins takes you back to nature. A ride on the Mindbender roller coaster will find you dropping 14 floors at over 70 mph, while the tranquility of the submarine ride will transport you to exotic coral reefs. Or, you could splash down into the water park that covers an area the size of five NFL football fields.

Source: http://westedmall.com; and Carlisle, Tamsin (1997, March 7). Gamble by the world's biggest mall pays off. *The Wall Street Journal*, pp. B1, B18.

malls are Illinois' number one and two tourist attractions, drawing in over 28 million visitors a year. Marketing efforts that provide incentives to tour operators and support from tourist bureaus keep the shoppers coming back in record numbers. As previously stated, the shopping experience knows no geographical or cultural boundaries.[18]

Shopping opportunities can also add another dimension to heritage attractions. For example, Wall Drug in Wall, South Dakota, has a quaint advertising slogan, "free ice water." Maybe it is the inducement of free ice water that beckons in travelers as they pass through the Badlands of South Dakota. Or it could be the mall-like atmosphere of the 25 shops featuring everything from cowboy curios to designer western wear that attracts passing motorists. Whatever it is, Wall Drug draws in over 1.5 million visitors a year.

LIVE ENTERTAINMENT

Visiting heritage and commercial attractions and participating in activities at these locations could easily be classified as entertainment. However, live entertainment opportunities fill a special need for travelers and others seeking additional leisure-time activities. The choices of live entertainment venues can run from the deafening crowds at hallmark sporting events such as the World Cup or the Super Bowl to the serene pleasures of the ballet.

Sporting Activities

For thousands of years, sporting activities have drawn visitors to scheduled events from near and far. Over 3500 years ago the Greeks initiated the idea of staging athletic competitions. The most famous of these competitions were the Olympic Games held in Olympia. These competitions began as part of their religious festivals and were staged in towns throughout Greece and Italy. The original competitions in Greece were organized as contests, but the Romans expanded the idea of these competitions and staged them as games for public entertainment. Although the grand athletic competitions and festivals such as the classical Olympic Games faded and disappeared under Roman rule, the idea did not go away. With the formation of the International Olympic Committee (IOC), the modern-day Olympic Games were reborn and a new athletic tradition began in Athens, Greece, in 1896. This first modern Olympic competition was held in the summer and drew less than 500 athletes from 13 nations. In contrast the 26th Olympiad held in the summer of 1996 in Atlanta, drew over 10,000 athletes from 197 nations and territories. In addition, spending by out-of-state visitors injected an estimated $2.5 billion into the local economy.[20] The winter Olympic games were not added until 1924 with the competition first staged in Chamonix, France.

Modern-day professional and intercollegiate sporting events such as football, soccer, baseball, basketball, and hockey draw millions of visitors each year to regularly scheduled games and playoffs. Special sporting events such as the Superbowl, the Stanley Cup Championship, The World Cup, the Pro Rodeo Championship, the Indianapolis 500, and the College World Series, to name just a few, attract international attention and vast numbers of spectators to host communities each year. These same sports are often played on local and regional levels and, although they may not draw as many spectators, they are still just as important to the participants and spectators who are attracted to the excitement of the event. In addition to team sports, there is also a wide array of sporting activities such as golf, tennis, swimming, hiking, biking, fishing, rock climbing, and snowboarding/skiing that round out the list of alternatives from which travelers can choose.

The Performing Arts

The performing arts have been a popular form of entertainment for thousands of years. For some areas, such as Branson, Missouri, they serve as primary tourism revenue generators; for other areas, such as Las Vegas, they serve as one more ingredient in the menu of attractions and entertainment that the area can boast of to interest visitors and encourage them to extend their stay. Live entertainment has always been a draw for travelers. For some it may be the opportunity to select from a wide variety of plays in London's theater district; for others, a chance to attend a concert featuring the newest entertainment idol. For still others, it could be the opportunity to attend a country jam or an opera performance.

The classical performing arts include theater (live stage plays, not the movies), ballet, opera, concerts, and the symphony. When combined they become "big business," generating over $8 billion a year in revenues in the United States alone.[4] Contemporary performing arts include all these and more, such as stand-up and improvisational comedy, rock concerts, and even the band that is playing in your favorite local "hotspot." Performing arts entertainment, especially the classical forms, are frequently offered in locations such as concert halls developed for the express purpose of showcasing the art form. If you have seen the Oscar-winning movie *Moonstruck*, then you are familiar with one of the world's most famous performing arts centers, the Lincoln Center in New York City. The Kennedy Center in Washington, DC, is another well-known arts venue.

Theaters, concert halls, and other large-seating-capacity facilities exist in almost all cities throughout the world and each, no matter how plain or impressive, serves as a draw for visitors. Some, such as the Sydney Opera House, are even renowned as landmarks. Many performing arts companies, whether a repertory acting group or symphony orchestra, have a season (a few months each year) when they stage productions and perform for the public. For example, the Desert Chorale is a classical choir that performs each summer in Santa Fe, adding to the entertainment options offered in that renowned arts city.

Think for a moment of all the performing arts productions you enjoyed in the past year. Which were of the classical form and which would be considered contemporary? Maybe you even have experience as a participant in the performing arts? Band? Chorus? Local theater? We will discuss other cultural aspects of tourism in Chapter 11.

SUMMARY

So many things to do and so little time sums up the delightful dilemma travelers face when selecting from the menu of attractions and entertainment options. How we choose to spend our leisure time while traveling can find us seeing and doing things ranging from the simple to the exotic. Sometimes we look for the comfort and convenience of the familiar, while at other times we seek new or unusual sights, sounds, and activities.

The list of leisure-time alternatives from which visitors can choose can be conveniently classified into three broad categories: heritage attractions, commercial attractions, and live entertainment. Each of these categories contains even more choices, ranging from museums and zoos to gaming and shopping, and the list goes on. Attraction and entertainment alternatives are limited only by our curiosity, imagination, ingenuity, and resources.

Heritage attractions provide a unique two-way window that allows us to peer into the past for a fleeting glimpse of what the future may hold. While heritage attractions meet our needs for self-fulfillment and education, commercial attractions can transport us to lands of make-believe for excitement and enjoyment. When live entertainment is added to the mix of other attraction and entertainment opportunities, travelers are faced with a broad menu of choices for filling their leisure time.

Whether our leisure-time choices are simply a sidelight along the way or the main reason for a trip, attractions and entertainment add special spice and memories to our travels. Although the goals of providing visitors with self-fulfillment and enjoyment may be common threads that tie attractions and entertainment together, there are a variety of business decisions that make these operations challenging. They may be operated on either a for-profit or not-for-profit basis, creating the need to look to different funding sources. They are typically affected by dramatic shifts in seasonal demand, creating the need for skillful marketing, management, and financial decisions for continued success.

 YOU DECIDE

The idea of having members sell another case of candy bars or raffle off another color TV just did not appeal to Terry. As this year's fundraising chair, he was determined to do something different, and the board had authorized him to try some new ideas.

"Group Day" at Wonder World seemed to be just the ticket. As a way of saying thank you to local charitable service organizations and to create goodwill in the community, the marketing department at Wonder World had developed a popular promotional program offering group discount admission packages to these organizations. These group packages included a 25% discount off the regular $30 admission price and a special package of coupons for additional discounts on food, beverages, and merchandise inside the park. Purchasing a minimum of 20 tickets was the only requirement to participate in this program. The idea had proven to be very popular, and many of the community's nonprofit service organizations had taken advantage of the program.

Terry decided that purchasing a block of these discounted admission packages as part of the "Group Day" program would be a good fundraising activity and a change from the ordinary. After purchasing 200 tickets for $22.50 each in the club name, members were asked to sell the packages for $25 each. Demand for the admission packages was better than expected, although only eight club members actually purchased a package. When Terry reported that the Wonder World campaign had raised $500, a motion was made to make this an annual and even bigger event in the future.

The motion was seconded and the discussion that followed was lively. Some members thought that it was a good idea, but others began to question the ethics of this approach to fundraising since most of the ticket purchasers were not members of their organization. Was it right to take advantage of a marketing program that was designed as a thank you to the local nonprofit charitable service organizations that are helping the community?

NET TOUR

To learn more about the concepts and organizations presented in this chapter access the homepage for *Tourism: The Business of Travel*. Select "Chapter 7: Attractions and Entertainment." From this location test your knowledge by taking the chapter quiz, read industry insights, and discover links to other useful sites. You may also want to visit electronically with other tourism students through the website.

DISCUSSION QUESTIONS

1. Why are attractions and entertainment important components of the tourism industry?

2. How does seasonality create marketing, management and financial challenges for attraction and entertainment operators?

3. Explain the similarities and differences between heritage attractions and commercial attractions.

4. Why has gaming experienced a surge in growth and participation?

5. How have shopping malls been turned into tourism attractions?

APPLYING THE CONCEPTS

1. Ask several people of different ages, occupations, and genders to describe their favorite leisure-time activities while traveling. Make a list of these activities and note the similarities and differences depending on whether they are traveling on business, for pleasure, or to visit friends and relatives.

2. Prepare a list and a basic description of attraction and entertainment alternatives that are available in your area. Limit yourself to 10 entries, but be sure to include at least one location or event from each of the major categories: heritage attractions, commercial attractions, and live entertainment venues. After you have prepared your list, fill in the hours of operation, admission or entry fees if any, services offered and whether operations are for-profit or not-for-profit.

3. Arrange to visit an attraction or entertainment location in your area and schedule an interview with the manager or local administrator. Your interview should include questions about the typical marketing, management, and financial issues they face in completing their job duties.

4. Surf the World Wide Web for locations or organizations mentioned under the headings of heritage attractions, commercial attractions and live entertainment venues in this chapter (limit your search to one per heading). Describe the information that is available on each site.

GLOSSARY

Appropriations Funding provided through governmental entities.

Attractions Natural locations, objects or constructed facilities that have a special appeal to both tourists and local visitors.

Botanical gardens Gardens dedicated to the preservation, display, and study of growing plants.

Concessionaires Individuals or companies who have been granted the right to provide a particular service, such as food service, guide service, sanitation service, or gift shop.

Events Special occasions and scheduled activities.

Fairs Temporary gathering places for the exhibition of products and services, often accompanied by entertainment and food and beverage services.

Festival A time of celebration, with scheduled activities.

Heritage attractions Places, structures, and activities with historical and cultural significance.

Leisure activities Activities performed during one's free time away from work.

Limited Stakes Legislative limits placed on the dollar amount that can be wagered on any single bet (typically $5).

Line of credit An agreement with a bank in which loans are automatically made up to an established limit.

Museum The International Council of Museums uses the following definition: A non-profit-making, permanent institution, in the service of society and its development, and open to the public, which acquires, conserves, researches, communicates and exhibits, for the purposes of study, education, and enjoyment, material evidence of humans and their environment.

Recreational activities Activities and experiences people pursue for personal enjoyment.

Venue The location of an event or attraction.

REFERENCES

1. Roberts, Russell (1996, November). Zoos off the endangered species list. *Funworld*, pp. 60–65.

2. National Trust for Historic Preservation (1995). *Touring Historic Places*. Lexington, KY: National Tour Association, Inc.

3. Sloan, Gene (1996, April 24). Wave of new aquariums may face rough waters. *USA Today*, p. 4D.

4. Department of Commerce, Economics and Statistics Administration (1996). *Statistical Abstract of the United States 1995: The National Data Book*. Washington, DC: Bureau of the Census.

5. *The World Almanac* (1997). Mahwah, NJ: Funk & Wagnalls Corporation.

6. Caproni, Joanna S. (1992, winter). Travel as theater: A new challenge to the credibility of tourism. *Journal of Travel Research*, pp. 54–55.

7. Foden, Harry G. (1992, fall). Destination attractions as an economic development generator. *Economic Development Review*, pp. 69–72.

8. Thach, Sharon V., & Axinn, Catherine N. (1994, winter). Patron assessments of amusement park attributes. *Journal of Travel Research*, pp. 51–60.

9. Clines, Francis X. (1993, December 5). Gambling, pariah no more, is booming across America. *New York Times*, p. S1.

10. *Harrah's survey of U.S. casino entertainment* (1995). Memphis, TN: Harrah's Brand Communications.

11. Worsnop, Richard L. (1990, November 9). Lucrative lure of lotteries and gambling. *Editorial Research Reports*, pp. 634–646.

12. Kleinfield, N. R. (1993, August 29). Legal gambling faces higher odds. *New York Times*, p. E3.

13. *Harrah's Survey of U.S. Casino Entertainment* (1997). Memphis, TN: Harrah's Brand Communications.

14. Withiam, Glen (1988, November). Doing well, thank you. *Cornell Hotel and Restaurant Administration Quarterly*, p. 93.

15. Kristof, Nicholas D. (1985, November 28). Strategy part of comeback. *New York Times*, p. D1.

16. Troy, Timothy N. (1994, February 1). Getting in while the gaming's good. *Hotel and Motel Management*, p. 24.

17. Cook, Roy A., & Yale, Laura J. (1994). Changes in gaming and gaming participants in the United States. *Gaming Research and Review Journal*, *1*(2), 15–24.

18. Jansen-Verbeke, Myriam (1991, March). Leisure shopping: A magic concept for the tourism industry? *Tourism Management*, pp. 9–14.

19. Tarlow, Peter E., & Muehsam, Mitchell J. (1992, September-October). Wide horizons: Travel and tourism in the coming decades. *The Futurist*, pp. 28–32.

20. Glesson, Patrick C., & Arbes, Tina P. (1996, June). Economic impact on the state of Georgia of hosting 1996 Olympic Games. *Government Finance Review*, pp. 19–21.

CHAPTER 8

Destinations

Providing a change of pace in a hectic world.
Photo by C.E. Yale.

To many people holidays are not voyages of discovery, but a ritual of reassurance.

—PHILIP ANDREW ADAMS

CHAPTER OUTLINE

LEARNING OBJECTIVES

After you have read this chapter, you should be able to:

- Explain how destinations combine many of the suppliers in the tourism industry.

- Describe the similarities and differences among destination resorts, resort areas/communities, and urban tourist destinations.

- Identify the major classifications of destination resorts.

- Identify the types of services and facilities that may be included in resort operations.

- Identify the recreational amenities that guests may encounter at resort locations.

- Explain why cruise ships are considered floating destination resorts.

Dreams Can Come True

The brochures answered most of their questions, but it was Richard and Connie's first time and they were still a bit nervous. Had they forgotten anything? Had they picked the right time and place? Would they really have as much fun as their friends had said? Would it be anything like the Love Boat?

With a little encouragement from their friends and a lot of help from their travel agent Vanessa, Richard and Connie were set to take their first cruise! Still, there were many questions and uncertainties as they prepared to board the plane to Miami.

Connie had always wanted to take a cruise because she thought it would be relaxing and romantic: No meals to prepare, no dishes to wash, being waited on hand and foot, sitting by the pool and reading, moonlight walks on deck, and dancing the night away! However, Richard was easily bored and he had dreaded the thought of being "stuck" on a ship in the middle of nowhere with nothing to do.

When Connie met with Vanessa to book her dream vacation cruise, she shared some of Richard's concerns. As Vanessa described the different cruise ships, ports of call, and on-board activities that would meet their needs, Connie knew it would be everything she had imagined. And there would be more than enough opportunities for Richard to be entertained for four days.

Their cabin was smaller than a hotel room, but it didn't matter because they were seldom there. With gourmet meals served five times a day, shows, games, dancing, gambling, shopping, and shore excursions, there just weren't enough hours in a day. It seemed as if the staff had thought of everything! There was even an afternoon on the ship's own private island, complete with beachcombing and snorkeling lessons. The activities were endless.

As Richard and Connie prepared to disembark, the only thing they knew for sure was that four days just had not been long enough. They were ready for another cruise; but, the next time, Richard said the cruise would be for a full seven days! There had been too many things to do and not enough time!

Introduction

Up to this point, our journey through the tourism industry has introduced you to a variety of tourism suppliers. Each of these suppliers, from those providing transportation to those providing entertainment, plays an important role in meeting specific needs. However, as you will learn in this chapter, when the services of these suppliers are brought together in one location, we have arrived at another important stop on our journey—tourist destinations. These destinations can be found in locations ranging from rural retreats to bustling cities.

Destinations could be popular tourist cities and communities like Paris, France; Vienna, Austria; San Diego, California; and Branson, Missouri. They could be attractive geographic regions like the Napa Valley in Southern California or the Costa del Sol in Spain. Or they could be the final stop on a trip to visit friends and relatives. In fact, the final stopping place on any trip can technically be considered a destination, but, in this chapter, we are interested in the locations, communities, and properties that have evolved or been developed primarily to serve the needs of vacationers.

In a hectic world, filled with time pressures and a multitude of demands, people often want to "escape" daily routines. Destination locations provide the perfect setting for a brief change of pace or a more extended stay accompanied by a variety of activities. Destination locations can come in all sizes and shapes and are found almost everywhere, from mountaintop resorts to cruise ships sailing the high seas.

As we learned in Chapter 1, geography plays an important role in the development of tourism activity. People are naturally attracted to areas with pleasing natural beauty such as the snow white sands of Destin, Florida, or the majesty of the Canadian Rocky

Mountains at Banff, Alberta. They are also attracted to areas that have developed as entertainment magnets such as Las Vegas, Nevada, and Orlando, Florida. And areas with mild climates such as the Canary Islands off the coast of Africa have been consistently popular with tourists.

As destinations grow in popularity, so do the services needed to meet visitors' needs. Airport services are enhanced; accommodations are improved and/or expanded; restaurants, retail shops, and visitor information services are added to deal with growing popularity. At some destinations, such as the islands of Hawaii, these services and facilities have often been added with little planning or consideration for the scenic beauty of the location. At other destinations, such as Cancun, Mexico, the national government has developed underutilized natural resources, beautiful beaches, and a near-perfect climate into a tourist destination.

All of the examples just mentioned have another important destination component in common: ease of access. Even locations that may not be pristinely beautiful can develop into popular destinations if they are easily accessible and close to heavily populated areas. For example, the gravel beaches on the cold English Channel at Brighton have become a popular summertime destination. With over nine million potential visitors living in London, only a short train or car ride away, it is no wonder that Brighton has become a vacation playground.

FROM RESORTS TO URBAN DESTINATIONS

The Romans were the first to enjoy the pleasures of **resorts,** which were built around public baths located at natural mineral springs like those found in Bath, England. Visiting these baths and enjoying the relaxing atmosphere of the destination became the primary reason for travel. However, with the fall of the Roman Empire, travel for pleasure and leisure pursuits disappeared. When travel once again became safe and practical during the Industrial Revolution, the popularity of visiting resorts for enjoyment and pampering spread once again throughout Europe. With new-found wealth and leisure time, members of the upper classes sought pleasurable places outside of the industrialized cities to enjoy the sun, sea, sand, snow, and more.

The first resorts in America, like their European counterparts (especially those found in the Czech Republic), were built around spas and focused on health and escape from the daily rigors of life. Many of these early spas, such as The Greenbrier at White Sulphur Springs, West Virginia, The Homestead at Hot Springs, Virginia, and Karlsbad in the Czech Republic have since grown into world-class destinations. Although these early resorts were built around spas and the idea of rest, relaxation and rejuvenation, later resorts began to expand by appealing to a broader cross section of market segments. To these new resort-goers, recreation became more important than simply a restful break, and a wider variety of activities was added to the mix of facilities and services provided, including retail shops, recreational facilities, and casinos.[1]

Resorts are now much more than just health spas or locations with a single purpose, catering to a single target segment. "Through the concentration of facilities, the resort acquires an identity and character, it becomes a specific place to enjoy in its own right in addition to serving as a gateway to other resources" (p. 62).[2] In fact, both **resort destinations** such as Vail, Colorado, and **destination resorts,** such as Disney World, now appeal to very diverse market segments ranging from individuals and families to conventions and corporate meeting groups. As can be seen in Table 8.1, most of these resort locations have certain characteristics in common.

You can find settings that fit the description of resort destinations in communities and small towns such as Jackson Hole, Wyoming, as well as in destination locations such as Mackinac Island, Michigan. Visitors also enjoy self-contained resort properties such as Marriott's Tan-Tar-A Resort, Golf Club and Spa at Lake of the Ozarks, Missouri, and Sheraton's San Marcos Resort near Phoenix. Certain cities around the world have even developed into urban tourist destinations. Paris, Rome, Vienna, San Francisco, San

TABLE 8.1
Common Characteristics of Resort Locations

Attractive natural settings and recreational opportunities
Easy accessibility for visitors
Lack of or only limited manufacturing facilities
Major employment opportunities center around service-oriented tourism-related businesses
Large number of residents employed out of the resort area and commute to nearby cities
Very large proportion of the population (with the possible exception of ski resort) is retired
Typically seasonal employment opportunities and tourism activities, with periods of intense activity followed by periods of little or no activity
Resort towns are typically small.

Source: Robinson, H. (1976). *A geography of tourism.* Estover, Plymouth: MacDonald and Evans.

Antonio, Seattle, and Vancouver can all claim to be great destinations that encourage and promote **urban tourism.** Whatever the location, tourist destinations are special places that meet guests' desires for rest, relaxation, fun, excitement, and entertainment even when visits are combined with the demanding schedules of business and professional meetings.

CLASSIFYING DESTINATIONS

There are several different types of locations and properties that can be classified as destinations. Although each of these locations may share some of the same activities, facilities, and amenities, the operational issues they face such as staffing, meeting varying guest expectations, and managing cash flows will differ depending on geographic location, size, markets served, and primary season of operation.

Operational issues were probably not on the minds of early resort developers, since many resorts and destinations were simply developed in locations with natural beauty, favorable climates, and easy transportation access. In fact, one popular classification system that has been used to describe resorts relies on the historically seasonal operational patterns that defined the markets of many resorts. Using this system, Northern Hemisphere resorts can be classified as summer resorts (beach and mountain locations operating Easter through Labor Day), winter resorts (northern and eastern locations operating November through April), winter vacation resorts (southern and southwestern locations operating January through April) and four-season resorts (mountain location or in mild climates).[1]

For many resort properties and tourist destinations, the luxury of being open for operation during only one season is proving to be financially impractical. In today's highly competitive economic environment, investors, lenders, and governmental agencies are no longer willing to commit to financing large capital expenditures for airports, hotels, conference centers, and other facilities that may be used only for a few months during the year. As resorts and other tourist destinations have responded to these financial demands and broadened their market appeal, other classification approaches appeared. One such approach relies on identifying the type of trip being taken. By using trip types, destinations can be conveniently grouped into categories such as cruise, beach, casino, ski, and summer country.[3] Another approach has relied on broader categories to bring several different types of resorts and destinations under common umbrella classifications. These groupings have resulted in categories such as integrated resorts, town resorts, and retreat resorts. Integrated resorts are self-contained developments planned around natural settings or recreational activities; town resorts are communities that primarily focus on resort activities; and retreat resorts are small-scale operations located in remote areas.[4]

Separating and classifying the final stopping points on trips from true destination locations may seem difficult, but there is help. Figure 8.1 introduces you to many of the different types of popular tourist destinations that include attractions, entertainment, and all of the supporting facilities needed to draw and host visitors. It provides a convenient

FIGURE 8.1
Tourist Destinations

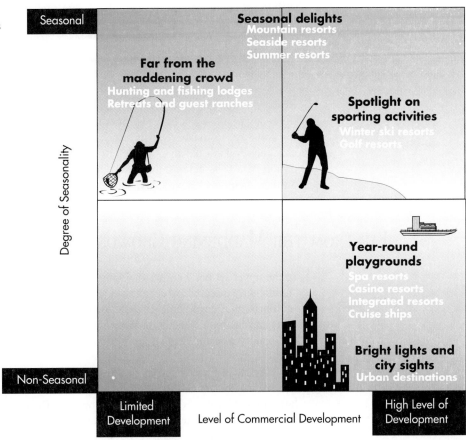

approach to classifying these destinations based on seasonality and level of commercial development.

Using a concept called "strategic grouping," we can categorize these destinations into groups that share similar characteristics. These groupings provide a useful framework for understanding the similarities and differences among types of destinations.

As you look at this figure, notice that, although there may be some overlap and gray areas between the groups, there are five groupings that emerge when the primary influences of seasonal weather patterns and the level of investment in commercial facilities are taken into consideration. We have chosen to label these groups using the following descriptive phrases:

- Far from the Maddening Crowds,
- Seasonal Delights,
- Spotlight on Sporting Activities,
- Year-Round Playgrounds, and
- Bright Lights and City Sights.

As we explore each of these destination groupings, see if you can think of specific examples that would fit in each category.

Before we move on, consider the following two brief examples that show how Figure 8.1 can be used to place different types of destinations into strategic groupings. Winter ski resorts (Spotlight on Sporting Activities) are obviously affected by seasonal changes that bring snow, and these locations also require significant commercial investments in ski lifts and snow-making equipment as well as other mountain operations facilities such as restaurants, retail shops, and base-area accommodations. However, cruise ships (Year-Round Playgrounds) are not significantly influenced by seasons since they can be moved to take advantage of seasonal changes, yet they are very expensive to build and require a significant commercial investment. Now, let us take a more in-depth look at each of these strategic groups.

FAR FROM THE MADDENING CROWDS

In the upper lefthand corner of Figure 8.1, you will see a group of destinations that are significantly affected by changes in seasonal weather patterns, yet have little in the way of commercial development when compared to other destinations. Traveling to destinations and taking advantage of seasonal weather patterns along with the solitude, beauty, and bounty of nature has a long history that can be traced back to the Romans, if not before.

You will find two types of destinations in this classification. One includes hunting and fishing lodges and the other includes retreats and guest ranches. These destinations have limited levels of commercial development. Development is usually a lodge with guest rooms and common areas and a few other support buildings, built and operated to be open only during set time periods each year. For example, dude ranches in Arizona are open primarily in the winter and spring, while fishing lodges in Alaska serve visitors during the summer and fall.

Destinations that are grouped in this category face many of the same challenges as those faced by seasonal attractions, which were discussed in Chapter 7. For example, managers must hire and train a staff in a very short time and then bring all systems into operation by opening day each season. Taking care of the basics such as ordering supplies, manicuring the grounds, and deep-cleaning guest rooms are routine operations that can be easily scheduled. However, other tasks can become more difficult since facilities are often located in out-of-the-way places where there is limited access to potential employees and other services. Just think about how difficult it might be to find on short notice a plumber or an electrician for a remote fishing lodge in Manitoba or a guest retreat in upstate New York.

SEASONAL DELIGHTS

Moving toward the middle of Figure 8.1, you will find destinations that are still affected to some degree by seasonal weather patterns, but that also have a greater degree of commercial development. In this strategic grouping, you will find mountain, seaside, and summer resorts that have served through time as traditional destinations for tourists seeking a place to play in the water or escape the heat of summer. In fact, "[t]he resort hotel in America was traditionally a summer operation which offered, besides a comfortable room and good food, a seaside or mountain location with scenic, historical, recreational, or therapeutic advantages" (p. 23).[1] Today, these resorts have been developed not only to take advantage of the best Mother Nature has to offer during the primary season of operation, but also to attract visitors during other seasons.

Mountain, seaside, and summer resorts may be found in different geographic locations, but they offer one thing in common—escape from summer's sweltering heat and a variety of warm-weather recreational activities. Depending on the location, hiking, swimming, boating, golf, tennis, and just lying in the sun or relaxing in the cool breezes head the wish list of seasonal activities visitors expect to find at these destinations during their primary operating season. Add other activities such as biking and horseback riding and it is easy to see why vacationers are attracted to warm-weather paradises. As the following example shows, in addition to a primary operating season, these destinations are also expanding the number and types of activities and facilities to attract visitors during **secondary seasons.**

The Wisconsin Dells (the "Dells") provide an excellent example of an area that began as a summer holiday refuge and developed into a major resort destination. Visitors still come in large numbers during the summer months to enjoy the natural beauty and warm-weather attractions that have been developed along this stretch of the Wisconsin River. However, they also come at other times of the year because of the commercial development that has taken place in the area.

> Packed in a lush "North woods" geographic area of a bit more than 3 by 5 miles are examples of just about any type of attraction ever established to entertain tourists. More than 700 amusement parks, beaches, family entertainment centers, museums, lodgings, restaurants and other attractions [from golfing and snow skiing to horseback riding and sleigh rides] in the area cater to a mix of visitors ranging from "daytrippers" with children to empty-nest couples spending busy weeks in local resort accommodations (p. 27).[5]

Over three million visitors a year come to this resort area that is located midway between Chicago and Milwaukee. The total area encompasses two towns, Wisconsin Dells and Lake Delton, that have a year-round population of about 3500 people. During peak seasons, this population temporarily swells with nearly 6000 housing units ranging from B&Bs to condos and luxury hotels plus campsites and RV parks.

Through active support of the Dells Visitor and Convention Bureau, businesses in the area reap the benefits of a coordinated marketing campaign and a five-state employee

TOURISM IN ACTION

Looking for a summer place to unwind, rest, relax, and recharge your batteries? To experience the hospitality and delights of a true summer resort destination take a trip back in time to Mackinac Island. Take a look at the World Wide Web (http//www.mackinac.com) home page for Mackinac Island, which contains the following statement, and begin preparing for a unique adventure.

> Welcome to the breathtaking beauty of Mackinac Island, one of Michigan's most photographed and talked about travel destinations. Located between Michigan's upper and lower peninsulas, the Island offers you unforgettable natural and historic treasures surrounded by the sparkling blue waters of The Great Lakes.

There are only two ways to get to this picturesque island destination. One is by airplane and the other is by boat. Scheduled ferry service runs from April through December. For a brief period of time each winter, those hearty souls who can brave the bitter cold and winds travel to the island by snowmobile across the natural ice bridges that form in the strait.

After you have made the journey across the Straits of Mackinac and arrive on the Island, what is there to do? First, don't plan on renting a car because the only forms of personal transportation allowed on the Island are bicycles and horse-drawn carriages. But, don't worry if you want to travel the entire distance around the Island (8.3 miles); it only takes about an hour on bicycle.

You could stay at the historic Grand Hotel (where *Somewhere in Time* was filmed) or at any of the Island's other accommodations ranging from small hotels to B&Bs. After checking in, you can join the bustle of activity surrounding the shopping district by the commercial docks or explore the many natural wonders and historic sites, like Sugar Loaf and Fort Mackinac, that the Island offers.

If exploring is not to your liking, then try out your golf game at either of the Island's two courses. Whatever you decide to do, you must stop at one of the many confectionery shops and indulge yourself. Mackinac Island is famous for its fudge. Thousands of pounds of natural ingredients are mixed together in huge copper kettles, cooled on marble slabs, and cut into delectable rectangles for tourists every summer. The fudge and the tourists are welcomed sites each summer on Mackinac Island.

recruiting effort. Marketing efforts range all the way from responding to requests for information (almost half a million per year) to creating major promotional campaigns. In addition to the recruiting campaign, joint customer-service seminars (area businesses employ about 6000 seasonal workers) are conducted to prepare employees for the seasonal summer surge in visitors. This high level of cooperation continues to pay off, as can be seen by the astounding number of repeat visitors (78%). Increased marketing efforts have also attracted additional visitors during the secondary fall and winter seasons to enjoy the fall colors, hunting, and winter sporting activities.[5]

SPOTLIGHT ON SPORTING ACTIVITIES

In the upper righthand corner of Figure 8.1 are a group of destinations that are not only affected by seasonal weather patterns, but are also highly developed with specific recreational activities. Destinations in this grouping offer recreational activities, primarily participation sports, such as skiing, golf, and tennis.

Destinations that specialize by offering these activities share two things in common. First, they are affected by weather patterns that dictate primary operating seasons. For example, although golf can be played year-round in Arizona, winter and spring are much more attractive than summer, when temperatures soar to well over 100°F for most of the day. Second, these destinations are easily identified by their high levels of commercial development, such as ski lifts, snow-making equipment, golf courses, tennis courts, and other supporting facilities.

Winter Ski Resorts

Wherever they are located, all winter ski resorts need the same natural wonders (steep slopes and snow) to attract winter recreational enthusiasts, and all have the same operational problems that accompany these snowy remote locations. The continued problem of unpredictable weather patterns has required large investments in snow-making and grooming equipment to start, maintain, and extend ski seasons. Snow-making not only costs money, but it also raises environmental concerns. Snow-making draws heavily on available water supplies during typically dry times of the year, and additional grooming requires an increase in exhaust-producing grooming vehicles to be placed on the mountainside. Further, the demographic shifts resulting from an aging population are reducing the potential number of skiers. Efforts to expand existing ski areas are being met with tough opposition from environmental groups, resulting in extensive environmental impact assessments and challenges to the use of government lands for single-season recreational use.[6]

Managers at mountain ski resorts, like managers at other seasonal operations, must cope with seasonal changes to survive and succeed. Table 8.2 provides some examples of

TABLE 8.2
Factors That Have an Impact on the Survival and Success of Winter Ski Resorts

Capital-intensive, yet produce extreme fluctuations in cash flow to pay for these necessary investments.
Labor-intensive and seasonal, resulting in the need to both hire and lay off large groups of service employees.
Weather-dependent, resulting in the need to invest in expensive snow-making equipment and draw heavily on an area's water resources.
Sensitive to economic fluctuations, since they are relatively expensive, yet they must attract consumers with adequate discretionary income.
Located in remote locations, which creates potential transportation problems for both guests and employees.

challenges faced in these types of seasonal destinations. Think about seasonal resorts with which you are familiar. Do they face the same, similar, or different problems?

Winter ski resorts were developed to serve guests who enjoy playing in the snow or relaxing in a "winter wonderland." However, to smooth cash flows, appeal to a broader market, and position themselves as year-round destinations, many traditional warm-weather activities such as golf and tennis have been added to their product offerings. The increasing popularity of mountain-biking has also improved ski resorts' revenue potential. By offering bikers a "lift" up the mountain and providing trails for the way down, many ski resorts have substantially boosted the number of summer visitors.

Golf Resorts

No one is really sure where the game of golf began, but it has been a popular recreational sporting activity throughout the world for years. The origins of the game may have come from the Romans, but St. Andrew's Golf Club in Scotland, which was first used in the 16th century, is the oldest course in the world. The first permanent golf club did not appear in North America until 1873, when the Royal Montreal Club was founded in Canada.

Golf has continued to grow in popularity throughout the world. In the United States alone, there are over 25 million active golfers.[7] With all of these golfers, it should be no surprise that golf is an especially attractive destination amenity, and the development of new golf courses is not keeping up with demand. In fact, at the current growth rate of participation it has been estimated that a minimum of 100 new golf courses must be built each year in the United States to keep up with growing demand.[8]

The only significant sports activity that meeting-planners say influences their decisions in selecting a resort destination is golf. Why is it that meeting-planners and others look to golf when making travel plans? Golf is both a recreational activity and a social event. The majority of the time spent golfing is more than just for sport. It is also social activity and an opportunity to enjoy the natural surroundings. The manicured landscaping and natural settings provide the perfect environment for socialization and relationship-building.

A good golf course does more than present a pretty picture. It is designed and operated with the players and employees in mind for enjoyable play and ease in maintenance. The usual layout is in loops so that the finishing hole is near the beginning one. A

For tourists, golfing is far more than simply sport.
Photo by Christopher Marona, courtesy of Tamarron Hilton Resort.

golf course at a resort location must be designed with the average player in mind but still challenging enough to be interesting. It may be pretty to look at, but, if it is too difficult to play, guests will become frustrated and not return.[9,10]

Designing a course that will meet player and employee needs as well as create the desired image for the resort requires several key ingredients. First, a regulation-length 18-hole course requires 140 to 160 acres of preferably rolling and interesting natural terrain or vegetation. Second, the design requires laying out a functional routing plan with existing topography and player comfort in mind. Third, to ensure player enjoyment, a rotation in pars should be planned so that each hole is "followed by one of a different par, such as 4-5-4-3-" (p. iii).[10]

> Each individual hole should be a complete picture within itself, with each area of the hole being a unified part of the total effect. Tee design, contouring throughout the entire length of the hole; mowing patterns at tee, fairway, and green; tree types and locations; water courses and lakes; and perhaps the most important part of the whole picture, the individual design of each green, together with locations of those seemingly necessary, but oh, so troublesome cart paths; all are part of the picture to be developed (p. iv).[10]

The greens' fees generated by golf courses are an important resort revenue center. In addition, supporting services and facilities such as lessons, cart rentals, restaurants, and retail shops generate additional cash flows that enhance the financial attractiveness of golf course operations. However, golf resorts are more than just golf courses and related services. They must also cater to other guests and golfers when they are not on the links. These needs are being met with the addition of tennis, swimming, fitness centers, meeting rooms, shopping, dining, and more.

YEAR-ROUND PLAYGROUNDS

Located in the middle right-hand side of Figure 8.1, you will find a group of destinations that are highly developed commercially and only slightly affected by changes in seasonal weather patterns. What visitors experience at these types of destinations is a complex blend of facilities and services that you can see listed in Table 8.3. They may be spread across hundreds of acres or confined to the dimensions of a cruise ship. From a management viewpoint, each of these components should be planned with ease of maintenance and guest service, safety, security, and satisfaction in mind. We will explore each of the destinations in this group, but we will focus the majority of our attention on cruise ships.

Spas

Technically, the word *spa* means "a mineral spring," but the use of this term has been expanded in recent years to describe a place where people go to rejuvenate bodies and minds.

TABLE 8.3
Components of Resort Developments

Accommodations
Restaurants and lounges
Entertainment and recreational facilities
Retail shopping facilities
Conference and meeting facilities
Parking and/or transportation services
Storage and maintenance facilities
Public information/administrative facilities

Guests can choose to visit a spa that is part of a total resort package or a **spa resort,** which is designed for the total spa experience (for example, The Oaks at Ojai, California, or Lake Austin Spa Resort, Texas). Although they may differ in their operating focus, the same basic ingredients will be found in either spa type: healthy food, exercise classes, baths, massages, herbal treatments, and educational training programs. The locations chosen will depend on each guest's personal desires. Guests may choose to visit spa resorts to experience the spa itself or they may choose to enjoy the services and other recreational and social activities offered at the resort.[11]

The facilities and services provided through spas are now an important addition to the entertainment, shopping, and recreational activities found at many resorts. Through effective marketing programs and efficient management practices, spas can be an attractive revenue generator or profit center for resort properties. Marketing efforts may be focused on the individual à la carte user or packaged as an incentive along with other resort activities. Just as you learned in Chapter 6 that food and beverages can be used as a marketing tool in resort properties, so, too, can spa services. Building and equipping the spa with customer satisfaction in mind is a must, but it takes more. A staff well trained to pamper guests ensures that the goal of total customer satisfaction will be achieved (see Table 8.4).

Cruise Ships

Cruising is booming. In fact, it is currently the fastest-growing segment of the travel industry, averaging almost 9% in annual growth since 1980.[12] Expanded fleets of ships combined with new amenities and effective marketing efforts have helped to reposition the cruise experience in consumers' minds as destination resorts rather than as transportation. Growth in the number of cruises has led to other changes as cruise line operators continue efforts to improve service and expand their marketing reach.

The number of ports and the quality of facilities where passengers may **embark** and **disembark** has grown and improved. Cruise-line companies have also expanded the number of available cruising options and targeted specific market segments. Because of the flexibility provided in cruise-line operations, each cruise can be designed to meet the tastes and needs of a specific cruising audience, with focused activities such as fitness, big band or rock music, and mystery parties.

Cruise ships have an operational advantage over destinations that are anchored to a specific geographic location and must suffer through changing weather patterns. Sailing itineraries can be changed through repositioning cruises to take advantage of the best seasonal patterns and passenger demand anywhere in the world. In addition, "Cruise ships are an operator's dream. They run at 95% of capacity or higher, when hotels are pressed

TABLE 8.4
Staffing a Spa

Massage therapists who can perform different types of massages and some body treatments
Cosmetologists who can style hair and perform manicures, pedicures, and makeup
Aestheticians who can perform facials, depilatory waxing, and makeup
Fitness employees who can teach classes, do one-on-one personal training, conduct fitness evaluations, and coordinate certain recreational activities
Spa assistants or attendants who can supervise the locker room, maintain cleanliness, and perform some body treatments
Front-desk people who can meet and greet guests, act as concierges, and schedule all guest services

Source: Monteson, Patricia A., & Singer, Judith (1992, June). Turn your spa into a winner. *The Cornell Hotel and Restaurant Administration Quarterly,* p. 42.

to manage 70%. And cruise passengers, unlike hotel guests, cannot wander off to eat their dinner elsewhere."[13]

With the flexibility to meet vacationer and meeting-goer needs, cruise lines are now targeting many of the same people and groups who previously stayed in traditional destination resorts. The primary geographical markets for cruise-line passengers are California, Florida, New York, Illinois, Pennsylvania, and Texas. And, the primary ports for cruise ships serving U.S. and Canadian markets are located in Miami, New York, Port Everglades, Los Angeles, San Francisco, Seattle, and Vancouver. Most cruise ships sailing from these ports go southward to Mexico, the Caribbean, and the Panama Canal or northward to Alaska. Figure 8.2 shows a typical cruise ship itinerary.

Today, cruise-line passengers come from a wide range of income levels and ages. However, the fastest growth in cruisers is in the 25- to 40-year-old and family segments, which has caused the median age of cruisers to drop from 58 to 43. These new and expanding groups of cruisers are not only selecting cruise ships based on sailing itineraries, activities, and length of time at sea, but they are also changing the way in which they incorporate cruise ships into their travel plans. Today, the usual pattern involves a fly–cruise package.

These efforts are proving successful as cruise lines can offer many of the same, if not more, features than a traditional resort (see Figure 8.3) at an **inclusive price.** In fact, there are activities galore. Everything from trap shooting and golf lessons to dancing, dining, and more dining!

> Call them contemporary lifestyle vessels. They come with computerized exercise equipment, health spas, conference centers and small televisions inside cabins. There are movie theaters, Vegas-style shows, financial seminars, shopping arcades and casinos (p. 11).[14]

Even the amount of tips for on-board service personnel is clearly communicated to all guests in information brochures.

Although cruising itineraries can be commonly found in 3-, 4-, 7- and 14-day (or more) lengths, short cruises are proving to be the most popular and fastest-growing segment of this industry group. As was the case with Richard and Connie in our chapter opener, first-time cruisers are especially attracted to shorter cruises to test the waters and sample the cruising experience before committing to a longer itinerary. In addition, there are other factors contributing to the popularity of shorter cruises. Families and two-income households are finding short cruises to be attractive as they try to coordinate busy and often conflicting schedules that interfere with attempts to take extended vacations. Workers in pressure-filled jobs are seeking shorter and more frequent stress-relieving breaks to rest, relax, and recharge.

FIGURE 8.2
Map of Cruise Ship Itinerary for MS Maasdam.
Reprinted by special permission of Holland America Cruise Lines.

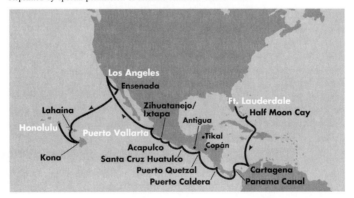

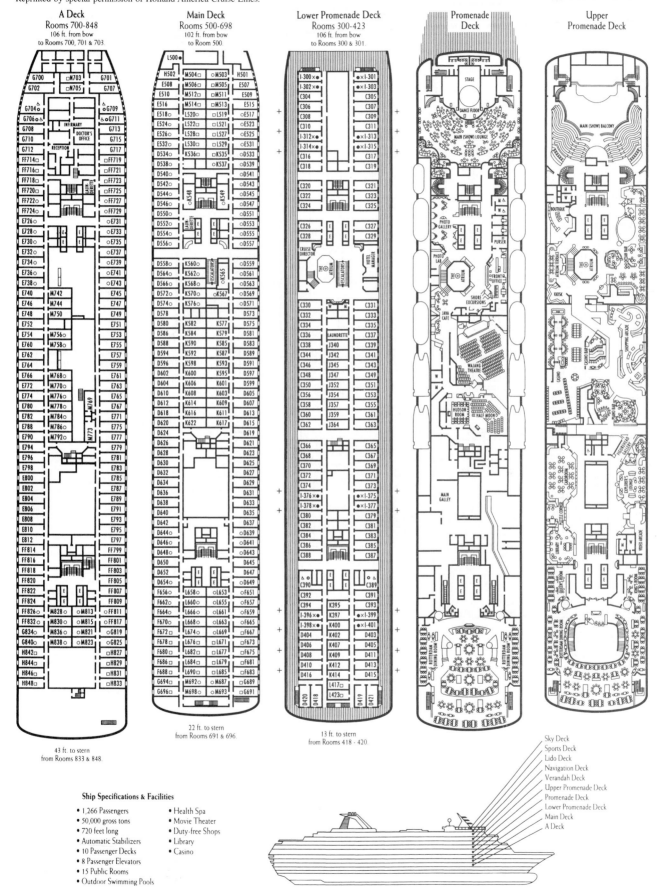

FIGURE 8.3
Exploring Holland America's MS Maasdam.
Reprinted by special permission of Holland America Cruise Lines.

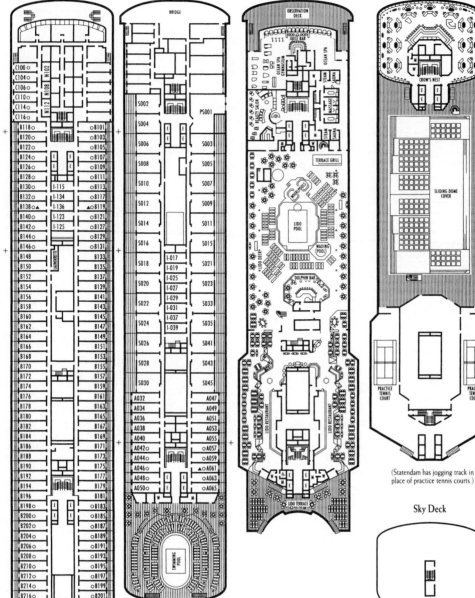

ms STATENDAM
ms MAASDAM
ms RYNDAM
ms VEENDAM

DECK PLANS & STATEROOMS

The deck plans are color-coded by category of stateroom, and the category letter precedes the stateroom number in each room. **Important Note:** Not all staterooms within each category have the same furniture configuration and/or facilities. Appropriate symbols within the rooms on the deck plans describe differences from the stateroom descriptions below. All staterooms are equipped with television, telephone and multi-channel music.

OUTSIDE STATEROOMS

PS Penthouse Suite: Bedroom with 1 king-size bed, oversize whirlpool bath & shower, living room, dining room, dressing room, private verandah, pantry, 1 sofa bed for two persons, VCR, mini-bar, refrigerator, guest toilet, floor-to-ceiling windows.

S Suites: 2 lower beds convertible to 1 king-size bed, whirlpool bath and shower, large sitting area, dressing room, private verandah, 1 sofa bed for two persons, VCR, mini-bar, refrigerator, floor-to-ceiling windows.

A Mini Suites: 2 lower beds convertible to 1 queen-size bed, whirlpool bath and shower, sitting area, private verandah, VCR, mini-bar, refrigerator, floor-to-ceiling windows.

B Mini Suites: 2 lower beds convertible to 1 queen-size bed, whirlpool bath and shower, sitting area, private verandah, VCR, mini-bar, refrigerator, floor-to-ceiling windows.

C Large: 2 lower beds convertible to 1 queen-size bed, bathtub & shower.

D Large: 2 lower beds convertible to 1 queen-size bed, bathtub & shower.

E Large: 2 lower beds convertible to 1 queen-size bed, bathtub & shower.

F Large: 2 lower beds convertible to 1 queen-size bed, bathtub & shower.

FF Large: 2 lower beds convertible to 1 queen-size bed, bathtub & shower.

G Large: 2 lower beds convertible to 1 queen-size bed, bathtub & shower.

H Large: 2 lower beds convertible to 1 queen-size bed, bathtub & shower.

INSIDE STATEROOMS

I Large: 2 lower beds convertible to 1 queen-size bed, shower.

J Large: 2 lower beds convertible to 1 queen-size bed, shower.

K Large: 2 lower beds convertible to 1 queen-size bed, shower.

L Large: 2 lower beds convertible to 1 queen-size bed, shower.

M Large: 2 lower beds convertible to 1 queen-size bed, shower.

N Standard: 2 lower beds convertible to 1 queen-size bed, shower.

Verandah Deck
Rooms 100-220
156 ft. from bow
to Rooms 100 & 102.

30 ft. to stern
from Rooms 205 & 220.

Navigation Deck
Rooms 001-065
205 ft. from bow
to Room 001.

112 ft. to stern
from Rooms 050 & 065.

Lido Deck

Sports Deck

(Statendam has jogging track in place of practice tennis courts.)

Sky Deck

Stateroom Symbol Legend

⊙ Shower only
● Bathtub and shower
○ Triple (2 lower beds, 1 sofa bed)
▲ Two lower beds, no sofa bed. (Veendam only)
▢ Quad (2 lower beds, 1 sofa bed, 1 upper)
X Fully obstructed view
+ Connecting rooms (Maasdam, Ryndam, Veendam only)
♿ Staterooms C389, C390, G704, G706, G709 & G711 are wheelchair accessible, shower only.

Public Room Names

	MAIN (SHOW) LOUNGE	ATRIUM TERRACE	LIBRARY
STATENDAM	Van Gogh Lounge	Fountain Terrace	Erasmus Library
MAASDAM	Rembrandt Lounge	Krystal Terrace	Leyden Library
RYNDAM	Vermeer Lounge	Fountain Terrace	Delft Library
VEENDAM	Rubens Lounge	Krystal Terrace	Hugo De Groot Library

FIGURE 8.3
Continued.

What Is Not Included in Cruise Prices?

- Transportation between the passenger's home and port of embarkation although it is included in some package prices.

- Port taxes and personal expenditures, including medical expenses, gambling chips, some sports activities, use of special services such as beauty salons and spas, alcoholic beverages, and shore excursions.

- Tips (gratuities). The amounts will vary. On some ships there is "no tipping" (tips are built into the package price). On others, the tips are automatically added for services. Still other ships may post guidelines in cruise line brochures and have them explained by **cruise directors.** As a matter of professional respect, it is important to remember to tip only **hotel personnel,** never **ship personnel.**

Note: Purchases for goods and services not included in the cruise price can be charged while on board and then settled with the **purser** at the end of the cruise by using a credit card or personal check.

Whether it is the inclusive pricing policies, one class of service (everyone receives the same service no matter how much they paid for their cabin), close attention to service details or convenient itineraries, people seem to not only enjoy but also praise their cruising experiences. "The satisfaction rating for cruises is the highest in the travel business: over 85% are 'extremely' or 'very satisfied.'"[15] Cruises are able to achieve these high levels of satisfaction because they can deliver high-quality service in addition to effectively combining two important characteristics of a good trip. First, passengers see and experience new activities, sights, and cultures through on-board activities and different ports of call. Second, passengers enjoy these experiences with a feeling of safety, security, and comfort in familiar surroundings, established schedules, and attentive service.

Basics of Planning a Cruise

If you decide to cruise or want to help someone else plan to enjoy this activity, there are several things to consider.

1. *Decide on time of year.* Summer is the perfect time to cruise to Alaska. Late fall or winter are ideally suited for cruising in the Caribbean, South Pacific, or Far East while late spring is the time for cruising the Mediterranean, Greek Islands, Turkish coast, Middle East, and Baltic.

2. *Find out which ships cruise on desired dates.* Consult *Official Steamship Guide International,* which is published monthly and covers the next 12 months of cruise-line schedules.

3. *Select an appropriate ship based on the desired level of services, size, food, entertainment, and ports of call.* These factors will influence who will be cruising with you; swinging singles, families, mature citizens, **affinity groups,** etc.

4. *Select cabin size and location as well as desired meal seatings.* The choices will be many—inside cabins, outside cabins, upper decks, lower decks, portholes, balconies, first seatings (main, 7 A.M. breakfast, lunch at noon, and 6 or 6:30 P.M. dinner), second seatings (late, 8:30 or 9 A.M. breakfast, lunch at 1:30 P.M., and 8 or 8:30 P.M. dinner).

5. *Book the desired cruise.* You can book either directly with the cruise line or through a travel agency. Travel agencies will relieve you of some of the hassles, but if your preferred cabin type is not available, call the cruise line and place yourself on a waiting list. Call weekly to check on cancellations. There are typically many!

It may be necessary to book cruises anywhere from 6 months to a year in advance on some ships during popular cruise dates. The most popular cruising times are New Year's, Easter, Memorial Day, the Fourth of July, Labor Day, and Christmas.

Once on board a cruise ship everyone, no matter how much they paid for the cruise or where their cabin is located, is treated the same. One class of service and variable pricing levels means the cruise lines depend on high occupancy levels. Cruise lines depend on generating additional high-margin revenues to achieve profitability. Some of these profit centers include spas, beauty salons, gaming, alcoholic beverage service, shopping, and shore excursions. None of these goods and services is included in the all-inclusive pricing structure.

Trends in cruise-line operations include the building of new ships of all sizes from yacht-like vessels to superliners, new programs and itineraries, and new on-board facilities. Between 1997 and 2000, 23 new megaships will take to the seas, the largest increase in cruise capacity in history. Yet, even with all of this growth, it is still estimated that less than 7% of the adult population in the United States has cruised, leaving plenty of room for growth.[16] Cruise industry insiders also believe that the industry will experience a "shake out" during which larger cruise lines will take over smaller cruise lines. For example, in 1997, Royal Caribbean purchased Celebrity Cruise Lines. A Carnival Cruise Line executive expressed this opinion, "There are about 26 brands on the market. About 16 are viable now" (p. 127).[16]

GRANDE DAMES OF THE HIGH SEAS

In cruise ships, who is the fairest of them all? P&O Cruise Line's Grand Princess, that's who. The largest of all cruise ships, the Grand Princess began her maiden voyage in the spring of 1998. She weighs 109,000 tons, towers 15 decks above the ocean's waterline and is capable of carrying 2600 passengers. She boasts three showrooms, three dining rooms, five pools—even a virtual reality theater! But her reign as the queen of the high seas will be short. In 1999, the Royal Caribbean Cruise Line will launch the newest grande dame, weighing an incredible 130,000 tons!

Sources: Princess Cruise Line Brochure; Flanagan, William G. (1997, July 7) Thanks for the subsidies. *Forbes*, pp. 120–127.

Casino Resorts

Casino resorts comprise a large and growing segment of the tourism industry. Travelers who participate in gaming activities are demanding more when they visit these resort destinations. They are no longer satisfied with finding gaming and lodging at their destination; they want a total entertainment experience. And their demands have been met, first with a wide array of dining and entertainment alternatives and then with a menu of activities that range all the way from golf to theme and water parks.

As you learned in Chapter 7, gaming locations continue to spread across the United States and Canada. What visitors will find at any one location is limited only by the imaginations and financial resources of the developers. Casino resorts located in Nevada provide some excellent examples of the diversity that can be found in successful casino resorts that have broadened their appeal to attract the family market. At **mega-resort** theme park/casinos such as New York, New York; MGM Grand; and Treasure Island located in Las Vegas (an urban tourism destination itself), complete leisure and entertainment facilities have been created to appeal to our fantasies and provide a little something for everyone. At other more out-of-the-way desert locations, such as Players Island in Mesquite, Nevada (which is on the Utah border), visitors are tempted with spas, golf, tennis, dining, entertainment, gaming, and more to fill their days and nights. Or, high in the Sierra Nevada mountains, visitors can combine water sports, golf, and tennis in the summer or skiing in the winter with gaming, dining, and entertainment.

Integrated Resorts

Integrated resorts (also called "four-season resorts") are similar to other tourism destinations we have been studying. They provide many of the same facilities, activities, and en-

TABLE 8.5
What You Will Find at the Mauna Kea Resort

Accommodations: 660-room resort comprised of two world-class hotels

Dining: 10 restaurants

Golf and recreation: 36 holes of championship golf, including the number-one-rated course in the state, 13 tennis courts, sports shops, 2 freshwater pools, fitness center, sailing, scuba diving, deep-sea fishing, horseback riding, and jogging trails

Meeting facilities: Over 21,000 square feet of indoor meeting and function space, including an 8500-square-foot ballroom and multifunction break-out rooms

Source: Mauna Kea Resort, *Hotel and Travel Index,* winter 1995–1996, p. 805.

tertainment opportunities that you would expect to find at any resort location. However, they are different from other destinations because they are located in settings where they can offer guests the same menu of leisure-time activities on a year-round basis. For example the Mauna Kea Resort on the Big Island of Hawaii has the top-ranked beach in the state and more as can be seen in Table 8.5.

However, even year-round resorts experience operational problems that result from fluctuations and spikes in demand. Integrated resorts are designed to serve a demanding group of vacationers each of whom has his or her own ideas about the meaning of rest and relaxation. While one guest may describe the perfect four-season resort destination as "a haven for peace and quiet, calm, rest and relaxation," another guest might describe it as "a giant country club with rooms." So integrated resorts must create a setting that meets diverse needs.

Travelers are now comparing the services and amenities they receive on cruise ships with what they receive at integrated resorts. Both types of destinations are designed to be self-contained vacation retreats. As you learned in the section on cruise lines, most services on a cruise are provided at an inclusive price. Integrated resorts are responding to this benchmark in hassle-free experiences by instituting strategies such as marketing themselves as non-tipping properties, and inclusive pricing for the use of spa facilities, golf, and other activities.

BRIGHT LIGHTS AND CITY SIGHTS

The final destination grouping we will discuss is located in the lower right-hand corner of Figure 8.1. This group is composed of urban areas that have developed into unique tourist destinations. Most cities will attempt to attract tourists because of the economic benefits these travelers bring to the local economy. However, travelers do not consider all cities to be tourist destinations. What is it that sets some large urban areas apart from others and makes them stand out as special tourist destinations? It is a strong desire on the part of city planners, civic leaders and businesses to attract and serve the needs of visitors.

Using a research technique that is popular among marketers, the Canadian Tourism Commission, through the help of **focus groups,** has identified what tourists consider to be some of the key attributes of a destination city.

> For some people it was a feeling, a flavor, or an image, that made the city a beloved destination. For others it was something more concrete: an ocean or a waterfront setting, beautiful architecture, great food, a sense of history, or friendly people that give a city its appeal. . . . For many people it's the range of interesting things to see and do that makes a city a great destination (p. 8).[17]

What we can learn from this research is that tourist destination cities have their own unique character. Tourists are attracted to these locations because they are special places to visit

Some cities are easily recognizable tourist destinations.
Photo by C.E. Yale.

Some cities are easily recognizable tourist destinations.
Photo by C.E. Yale.

and enjoy, and they offer a wide variety of accommodations, attractions, entertainment, restaurants, lounges, and other activities and amenities tourists desire.

BUILDING ON SUCCESS

As the opportunities for leisure travel for workers in industrialized countries grows and the number of mature travelers continues to increase, travel to resorts and other destinations will continue to grow in popularity. To remain competitive and attract more guests, these destinations may need to focus on attracting more than one market segment as well as increasing or improving their service offerings. Through market segmentation, resorts are meeting this challenge by developing packages that appeal to a variety of specific guest segments. At the same time, destination resorts are focusing efforts on specific segments such as group tour business, incentive travel, meetings, and conferences. Many resorts are also breaking these focused markets into smaller segments. For example, a property might focus first on attracting association meeting business and then target the American Association for Retired Persons. These efforts are generating more year-round business and leveling out the traditional seasonal fluctuations in cash flows.[18]

The complex task of developing, marketing, and managing tourist destinations goes well beyond the physical location itself. Other concerns, such as employee housing and labor availability, capital investment requirements, recreational and attraction development, infrastructure requirements, social and cultural effects, environmental impacts, land use, tax receipts, and other public benefits and problems must be considered by private developers, citizens, and government officials. Tourist destinations thrive on positive relationships between residents and visitors, and these relationships must be sustained for future success. We will be exploring these issues in greater depth in Chapters 10 and 11.

SUMMARY

Bringing together all of the components provided by tourism suppliers into one location creates the potential for a tourist destination. Destinations are the final stopping points of trips where tourists seek to "escape" their daily routines and enjoy rest, relaxation, recreation, and entertainment. These destinations can be found anywhere in the world and range all the way from quiet and secluded guest retreats to those floating resorts we call cruise ships. No matter where they are located or how attractive the destinations might be, tourists will not come unless the facilities and activities they desire are provided.

Spas were the original destination "resorts" built by the Romans, but the types of destinations from which travelers can choose today are numerous. Although each destination has its own unique appeal to tourists, they often share many similarities based on seasonal demand and the level of commercial development needed to meet guests' needs. These shared similarities allow us to classify destinations into the following strategic groups: Far from the Maddening Crowds, Seasonal Delights, Spotlight on Sporting Activities, Year-Round Playgrounds, and Bright Lights and City Sights.

Destinations that are grouped in each of these categories face similar marketing, management and financial opportunities and challenges. Some destinations face dramatic seasonal shifts in demand, but others experience more consistent demand throughout the year. Shifting patterns in demand can impact a variety of decisions, including marketing plans, staffing patterns, cash flow projections, and capital expenditure plans. Steps are therefore being taken at most tourist destinations to attract additional visitors during less-popular time periods.

Tourist destinations continue to grow in popularity and so do the choices travelers face when selecting their perfect destination. It could be a fishing lodge, a winter ski resort, a seaside resort, a golf resort, a spa resort, a cruise ship, an urban tourist mecca or (YOU FILL IN THE BLANK). As the choices grow and the opportunities for leisure travel increase, tourist destinations must focus on meeting a variety of guest needs while continuing to improve service offerings for future success.

 # YOU DECIDE

Cruises are one of the best buys in vacationing today. According to *Forbes* magazine, prices have not increased in over a decade yet the amenities on board have improved year after year. And the service is second to none. Passengers are pampered by employees at every turn; by the pool, in the many dining rooms, in the casino, and in their cabins, with a steward on call 24 hours a day.

How can cruise ships afford to provide so much personal attention and service? One way is by controlling labor costs. Nonprofessional cruise employees work between 16 and 18 hours a day and they are paid about $1.50 for a day's work. The vast majority of their earnings come from tips, which can add from $1,000 to $2,500 per month to their income. Cruise workers not only work long hours, but they are also generally at sea for 10 months a year and receive two days off per month. Employees, of course, receive room and board, in addition to their pay and tips, and benefits are generous by international standards.

Most cruise-line employees come from Third World or former Soviet Union nations. Although many are college-educated, they are unable to find good-paying employment in their home countries. Cruise-line personnel agencies are virtually flooded with applicants from around the globe, from Honduras to Romania. The demand for cruise-ship jobs is high because wages in most nonindustrialized countries are so low. For example, an elementary school teacher in Romania is paid $70 per month, and the annual per-capita income in the Philippines is less than $1,000. By comparison, the Jamaica-born head bartender of Royal Caribbean Cruise Line's *Song of America* earns about $30,000 per year.

Cruise lines can decide how much to pay employees because they are not subject to the employment regulations of industrialized countries, such as minimum wages, maximum working hours, and overtime pay. They are able to avoid these regulations by registering their ships abroad in countries such as Panama and Liberia. Should cruise lines be pressured to comply with employment laws in developed countries?

Sources: Prager, Joshua Harris (1997, July 3). For cruise workers, life is no 'Love Boat,' *Wall Street Journal*, pp. B1; B6; Flanagan, William G. (1997, July 7). Thanks for the subsidies. *Forbes*, pp. 120–127.

NET TOUR

To learn more about the concepts and organizations presented in this chapter access the homepage for *Tourism: The Business of Travel*. Select "Chapter 8: Destinations." From this location test your knowledge by taking the chapter quiz, read industry insights, and discover links to other useful sites. You may also want to visit electronically with other tourism students through the website.

DISCUSSION QUESTIONS

1. Describe the various tourism supply components that must be brought together to create a successful tourist destination.

2. What are the major classifications of tourist destinations and the similarities and differences among these classifications?

3. Why are tourist destinations attempting to attract more visitors outside of their prime seasons?

4. Describe the factors that have an impact on the survival and success of a seasonal tourist destination like a winter ski resort.

5. Why are cruise ships called "floating resorts"?

6. What is it that sets some large urban areas apart from others and makes them stand out as special tourist destinations?

APPLYING THE CONCEPTS

1. Select one type of tourist destination that is particularly interesting to you and learn more about it. Either schedule an interview with an employee or representative of the destination or search for articles in the library about that type of destination. Based on the information you obtain, write a short report discussing important facts you learn from your interview or research.

2. Select an article from a travel magazine or the travel section of the newspaper describing two different cruise ships and itineraries. Make copies of the articles to include with your report describing the similarities and differences between the two vacation options.

3. Surf the World Wide Web for resort information in a location that you may want to visit some day (use search terms such as *Manitoba and resorts* or *Florida and resorts*). Prepare a list showing the type of information that is available for the area along with specific information on one property at the destination.

GLOSSARY

Affinity groups Groups that share common interests.

Cruise Director The person who plans and operates passenger entertainment and activities on board a cruise ship.

Destination resorts Properties that are relatively self-contained and provide a wide range of recreational and other leisure-time activities.

Disembark To go ashore from a ship.

Embark To go on board a ship.

Focus group An in-depth interview about a topic among 8 to 12 people, with a researcher (called a "moderator") leading the discussion.

Hotel personnel All individuals responsible for the care and service of cruise-ship passengers.

Inclusive price Guests are charged one price for a package of services such as accommodations, food, and activities.

Mega-resort A destination resort containing multiple facilities and world-class attractions and entertainment venues. Each revenue center at these destinations could operate as a separate business venture.

Purser A ship official responsible for papers, accounts, and the comfort and welfare of passengers.

Resort destinations Communities or areas that contain attractions, entertainment, and supporting facilities needed to draw and host tourists.

Resorts Destination locations that are distinguished by the combination of attractions and amenities for the ex-

press purpose of attracting and serving large numbers of visitors.

Secondary seasons Periods when tourism activities are either increasing toward peak levels or declining from peak levels, also called "shoulder seasons."

Ship personnel All individuals responsible for the safety and navigation of cruise ships.

Spa resort A resort property dedicated to fitness and the development of healthy lifestyles.

Urban tourism Tourism that takes place in large cities, where hotels and other facilities and services have become an integral part of urban activities.

REFERENCES

1. Gee, Chuck Y. (1988). *Resort development and management* (2nd ed.). East Lansing, MI: Educational Institute of the American Hotel and Motel Association.

2. Baud-Bovy, Manuel, & Lawson, Fred (1977). *Tourism and recreation development*. Boston: CBI Publishing Company.

3. Morrison, Alastair, M., Yang, Chung-Hui, O'Leary, Joseph T., & Nadkarni, Nandini (1994). A comparative study of cruise and land-based resort vacation travelers. In: *New frontiers in tourism research: Proceedings of research and academic papers* (vol. VI) The Society of Travel and Tourism Educators Annual Conference, Lexington, KY. Chon K. S. (Kaye) (Ed.).

4. Inskeep, Edward (1991). *Tourism planning: An integrated and sustainable development approach*. New York: Van Nostrand Reinhold.

5. Whitworth, A. W. (1996, October). Area profile. *Funworld*, pp. 26–35.

6. Smith, Valene L. (1991). Recreation trends and mountain resort development. *Journal of Travel Research*, *30*(2), 53.

7. Bronstein, Barbara (1997, March/April). Fore!cast. *Commercial Real Estate Investment Journal*, pp. 16–19.

8. Bergsman, Steve (1990, November 5). Company sees profit on resort golf greens. *Hotel and Motel Management*, pp. A118–A119.

9. National Golf Foundation (1985). *Golf operations handbook and golf facility development guide*. North Palm Beach, FL: National Golf Foundation.

10. Snyder, Arthur Jack (1989). A good golf course (what is it?). In: Wright, J.C. (Ed.), *Golf courses: The complete guide* (pp. iii–iv). Oakland, CA: Lanier Publisher International.

11. Monteson, Patricia A., & Singer, Judith (1992, June). Turn your spa into a winner. *The Cornell Hotel and Restaurant Administration Quarterly*, pp. 37–44.

12. Apfel, Ira (1996, March). Big business for big boats. *American Demographics, pp. 23–24.*

13. Travel and tourism: Home and away (1998, January 10). *The Economist*, p. 14.

14. Hirsch, James S. (1992, November 27). Cruise firms prosper by transforming stuffy liners into floating fun houses. *Wall Street Journal*, p. 11ff.

15. Booth, Cathy (1992, February 17). Against the tide, *Time*, pp. 54–56.

16. Flanagan, William G. (1997, July 7). Thanks for the subsidies. *Forbes*, pp. 120–127.

17. Reflections on what makes a great city destination (1997, spring). In: *Americas Bulletin* Ottawa, Ont.: Canadian Tourism Commission, pp. 7–9.

18. Macdonald, Julie (1992, November 2). Resorts pursue travelers' needs. *Hotel & Motel Management*, pp. 97, 107–108.

Readings

Hub-and-Spoke Networks and the Evolution of the Airline Industry

■

BY JAN K. BRUECKNER AND PABLO T. SPILLER

JAN K. BRUECKNER IS PROFESSOR OF ECONOMICS AT THE UNIVERSITY OF ILLINOIS. IN ADDITION TO RECENT WORK ON THE AIRLINE INDUSTRY SUPPORTED BY THE NATIONAL SCIENCE FOUNDATION, HE HAS PUBLISHED WIDELY IN THE FIELDS OF URBAN ECONOMICS, PUBLIC ECONOMICS, AND REAL ESTATE FINANCE. HE SERVES ON THE EDITORIAL BOARDS OF SEVERAL JOURNALS, AND IS ALSO EDITOR OF THE JOURNAL OF URBAN ECONOMICS.

PABLO T. SPILLER IS W.B. MCKINLEY PROFESSOR OF ECONOMICS AND PUBLIC UTILITIES AT THE UNIVERSITY OF ILLINOIS. HE HAS PUBLISHED EXTENSIVELY IN THE FIELDS OF INDUSTRIAL ORGANIZATION, REGULATION, AND POLITICAL ECONOMY. HIS AIRLINE RESEARCH, AS WELL AS HIS WORK ON THE POLITICAL ECONOMY OF THE SUPREME COURT, IS SUPPORTED BY THE NATIONAL SCIENCE FOUNDATION. PROFESSOR SPILLER IS CURRENTLY A CONSULTANT TO THE WORLD BANK AND SERVES ON THE EDITORIAL BOARD OF THE JOURNAL OF ECONOMICS AND MANAGEMENT STRATEGY.

Deregulation of the airlines has led to fundamental changes in the industry. While fares were set by the Civil Aeronautics Board prior to deregulation, the carriers are now free to determine ticket prices. Thousands of fares change daily in response to changing competitive conditions, in stark contrast to the fare stability that prevailed prior to deregulation. In addition, deregulation has given the airlines the freedom to fly wherever they wish, abolishing the CAB's control over route assignments. This freedom has spurred the creation of new route structures. The airlines have abandoned point-to-point route systems, where cities are connected by nonstop flights, in favor of hub-and-spoke networks, where passengers change planes at a hub airport on the way to their eventual destinations.

By feeding passengers through a hub airport, the hub-and-spoke network generates high traffic densities on its "spoke" routes. This allows the airline to exploit "economies of traffic density," under which cost per passenger falls as traffic on a route rises. These economies arise because higher traffic density allows the airline to operate larger, more efficient aircraft on a route, to fill these planes more effectively (raising "load factors"), and to operate the aircraft more intensively by increasing flight hours per day. Because of economies of density, the cost of transporting passengers is lower on the dense spokes of a hub network than on the less-travelled routes of the old point-to-point system.

The cost savings from higher traffic densities translate into lower fares. Our research shows that when traffic density on a route increases by 50 percent, the cost of carrying an extra passenger falls by 24 percent, and fares fall by 9 percent. By raising traffic densities on U.S. routes, the growth of hub-and-spoke networks has thus put downward pressure on fares. Along with freer price competition, the hub-and-spoke revolution helps explain the decline of inflation-adjusted airfares in the post-deregulation period.

On the negative side, reliance on the hub-and-spoke network has imposed time costs on passengers that were not present under the point-to-point system. A typical passenger may now spend an extra hour or more travelling because of the need to change planes at a hub. Although passengers complain about this extra travel time, they often overlook the fact that fares are lower due to the efficiencies of hub operations.

In addition to stimulating the growth of hub-and-spoke networks, deregulation has led to structural changes in the industry, some of which are viewed as ominous by public policy makers. Most importantly, after some initial growth in the number of carriers, the industry has become more concentrated at the national level due to a spate of mergers and bankruptcies. In 1991 alone, the industry witnessed the liquidation of three carriers: Eastern, Midway, and Pan Am. It is feared that this development may place excessive market power in the hands of the large carriers, with potentially adverse effects on fares.

The development of monopoly hubs, or hub airports dominated by a single carrier, is another consequence of deregulation. The emergence of these monopoly hubs has raised concerns about the exercise of market power over local traffic at the affected airports. However, while concentration has increased at the industry level and in the monopoly-hub markets, competitive conditions in the average city-pair market have actually improved over the period of deregulation. In particular, the number of competing airlines per market has increased over the period, despite the growing concentration of the industry.

These changes in industry structure are in part a consequence of the growth of hub-and-spoke networks. First, because major carriers operate large, dense networks, they enjoy low costs per passenger and thus have a competitive advantage. This network-related advantage may help explain the demise of smaller carriers and the difficulty of entry by new firms. Second, since the operation of a hub-and-spoke network requires heavy use of a hub airport, such an airport tends to become dominated by the network airline. Thus, acquisition of local market power in the hub city is often concomitant to the development of a network. Finally, the increase in competition in the average market may be due in part to an additional effect of hub-and-spoke operations: the lowering of entry costs into individual city-pair markets. Airlines can now enter a host of new markets by simply adding a new city to the network; service can then be provided between that endpoint and any other city served from the hub. Since the cost of operating the new spoke route to the hub is spread across all the new markets, the cost of adding service to any particular market is low.

Our research suggests that efficiency gains from hub operations and the increase in market competition outweigh the negative effects of the growth of hub-and-spoke networks. As a result, we believe that up to this point, network growth has benefited passengers. Hub-and-spoke networks are also likely to play an important role in the future evolution of the airline industry, and two questions about the future seem especially urgent. What is the likely long-run effect on airfares of the growing concentration of the industry? How will competition evolve in the expanding international airline markets? The answers to these questions are tied to the industry's hub-and-spoke revolution.

The domestic airline industry is likely to be dominated by four or five national carriers by the year 2000, and an important question is whether this extreme concentration will lead to an escalation of fares and a reduction in consumer welfare. Industry concentration may affect fares in two ways. First, as competitors fall by the wayside, traffic densities within the route systems of the surviving airlines can be expected to rise. In effect, the national traffic pie will be divided among fewer carriers. Because of economies of density, this increase in each carrier's traffic translates into lower cost per passenger, which in turn puts *downward* pressure on fares. At the same time, the reduction in the number of carriers might create unfavorable competitive conditions at the individual market level, putting upward pressure on fares. If this latter effect is sufficiently strong, the net effect of industry consolidation would be to increase fares.

Given the ease of entry into new markets under a hub-and-spoke route structure, it appears that concerns about inadequate competition following consolidation of the industry can be discounted. It is likely that some subgroup of the remaining national carriers, each of which will operate multiple hubs, will battle for traffic in any given city-pair market. Will the resulting level of competition be sufficient to prevent fare increases? Our research shows that the benefits of extra competition in a city-pair market are exhausted once three or four carriers serve the market. Since this is the level of competition we would expect in most markets in an industry with five aggressive national carriers, worries about inadequate competition are misplaced. With continuing competitive pressure, part of the benefit of industry consolidation (i.e., the cost reduction arising from higher traffic densities) will be passed on to consumers in the form of lower fares.

Turning to our second question about the future, the recent entry of the large U.S. carriers, American, United, and Delta, into a host of new international markets will have a profound impact on competition and fares in those markets. The reason again relates to hub-and-spoke operations. Unlike TWA and Pan Am, the traditional U.S. overseas carriers, the new entrants operate vast domestic hub-and-spoke networks that can be used to funnel traffic onto their international routes. This will allow the new entrants to achieve higher densities on the international routes than was possible under the old regime. The resulting low cost per passenger is likely to reduce fares and stimulate international air travel.

Foreign carriers will be hard pressed to generate the international traffic densities of their new U.S. rivals. In Europe, for example, cross-border service is restricted by bilateral agreements between countries, and this makes it difficult for a given airline to collect traffic from a large number of endpoints for transfer to its international routes. In effect, international restrictions prevent European carriers from developing U.S.-style hub-and-spoke networks, and this obstacle may limit their ability to match the traffic densities of their new U.S. competitors on the North Atlantic routes. With low traffic densities saddling the European carriers with a cost disadvantage, these airlines may find the profitability of their North Atlantic operations threatened in future years.

This discussion has explored the role of the hub-and-spoke revolution in the recent history of the U.S. airline industry, as well as its implications for the future. We have argued that the efficiencies of the hub system have helped to keep airline fares low, and that hub-and-spoke operations will mitigate the effects of future consolidation in the industry. In addition, we expect that by exploiting traffic feed from their domestic hub-and-spoke networks, U.S. airlines are likely to be formidable international competitors in the years to come.

Foodservice Manager 2000*

■

SUSAN F. MILLS AND HUDSON RLEHLE, NATIONAL RESTAURANT ASSOCIATION

ABSTRACT

As demanding as a foodservice manager's job already is, the future is liable to demand more. To address the changes, the Delphi method was used to address the issues of the future. This article summarizes the findings of the study.

INTRODUCTION

Absorbed by the daily problems of running a restaurant, few foodservice managers find time to ponder the future. From overseeing food quality, to dealing with customers, to making staffing decisions, a typical foodservice manager handles hundreds of varied yet critically important tasks every day. As many restaurateurs know, the manager's capabilities and day-to-day performance often determine the ultimate success or failure of a foodservice operation.

Yet, as demanding as a foodservice manager's job already is, the future likely to demand more. What will be required of the foodservice manager at the turn of the century? How will responsibilities change? Which segments of the industry will experience an increased or decreased demand for managers? How will educational priorities for foodservice managers in 2000 differ?

To address these and a host of additional issues, an unusual futuristic study of the foodservice industry in the year 2000 was undertaken. The research technique used to conduct the project is referred to as the Delphi method. This technique, described in the appendix, allows maximum flexibility to identify issues important to the foodservice manager's future.

Results of the Delphi study "Foodservice Manager 2000" suggest that tomorrow's managers will need to be better administrators and much more adept at dealing with people—both employees and customers.

Managers at the turn of the century will be much more involved in teaching, training, and motivating staff and in handling all manner of human resources issues. They will need to possess superior interpersonal and communication skills, function as effective team leaders, and supervise a more culturally diverse staff. Not surprisingly, Delphi panelists predict that managers will need greater computer proficiency to tap into more advanced management information systems and are expected to play a greater role in foodservice waste management and recycling efforts.

With lower real growth rates projected for the nation's economy until 2005, managers will find service becoming a more competitive point of difference. Delphi panelists predict that managers will empower front-of-the-house employees to render better service and will need to cater to the service demands of a more diverse customer base.

In addition, because managers will be dealing with consumers who are more knowledgeable about nutrition, they will need to be more sensitive to health and dietary issues and will need to have greater knowledge of ingredient and nutritional content.

Delphi panelists predict that managers in 2000 will place more emphasis on their own career development and will be better educated. Consequently, manager compensation is expected to be more closely linked to individual performance, but managers can expect to work long hours. Also, Delphi members predict that managers will be required to have a sanitation certificate.

Hotel, restaurant, and institutional management (HRIM) schools will respond positively to the changing responsibilities and challenges facing tomorrow's foodservice managers. Members of the Delphi panel believe HRIM schools will emphasize more leadership and management skills in their curricula, offer more foodservice industry intern programs, and work more closely with the industry.

Regarding demand for foodservice managers in 2000, Delphi panelists predict that the need for managers will increase most in the casual-dining-table-service and nursing-care segments.

In sum, Delphi panelists believe that the future for foodservice managers at the dawn of the 21st century will be filled with new challenges and opportunities. This research is designed to help guide the efforts of those navigating a successful transition to the new century.

ADMINISTRATION

According to the National Restaurant Association's Delphi panel, the most likely development for managers at the turn of the century is the need for computer proficiency. Among the many changes forecast by the Delphi participants, the need for greater computer proficiency was the most important single issue—the skill, that is, most likely to be needed.

According to comments from Delphi panelists, more foodservice units and organizations will move to comprehensive computer-based information systems. Consequently, managers will be required to access, monitor, update, and use these information data bases on a recurring basis. The Delphi panelists indicated that foodservice managers in 2000 will need better computer skills whether they are using a stand-alone personal computer or accessing a major organizational computer information system.

Delphi participants believed that a manager's need for computer familiarity in 2000 will grow as more routine administrative tasks become automated. According to the comments of survey participants, computer use by managers will range from solving scheduling issues, to forecasting demand for specific menu items, to compiling unit sales over a specific time frame, to monitoring inventories. Since managers in 2000 will have a higher level of involvement with computer-based information systems, they will need to be comfortable using associated computer hardware and software in their daily management tasks.

Reflecting a national trend toward greater cultural diversity in 2000, Delphi study participants indicated a strong likelihood that managers in foodservice, as in other industries, will oversee a much more diverse, multiethnic work force. In fact, the likelihood of this development was ranked second highest among all the changes anticipated by the Delphi panel for the foodservice manager in the year 2000.

One implication of this development, according to panelist comments, was that sensitivity training for managers regarding various cultures and their customs could be helpful in dealing with employees from a wide range of ethnic backgrounds. Consequently, many panelists commented that managers in 2000 would find being multilingual a distinct asset, allowing for better ongoing communication with employees.

Managers in 2000 will be much more involved in teaching and training their staffs, according to the Delphi panelists. With work force training receiving greater emphasis at the turn of the century, managers will need to know

TABLE 1
Highlights of Delphi Panel: Foodservice Manager 2000

Managers

Most Likely Developments Managers Will Face in 2000

Managers are likely to:

- Need greater computer proficiency
- Supervise a more culturally diverse staff
- Find service will become a more competitive point of difference
- Need better teaching and training skills
- Possess greater people management skills
- Need better skills for managing people
- Need excellent interpersonal skills
- Play an increased role in waste management and recycling
- Deal with a customer more educated about nutrition
- Need to cater to the service demands of a more diverse customer base
- Empower front-of-house employees to render better service

Ten Least Likely Developments Managers will Face in 2000

Managers are less likely to:

- Find customers who expect lower service levels
- Be dealing with union issues more
- Be too busy with other responsibilities to deal with marketing
- Find tipping replaced by service charge
- See less committed staffs providing lower levels of service
- Find working conditions will not change
- Work shorter hours
- Discover labor is too expensive for on-the-job training
- Handle more customer grievances due to poorer service
- Find more peers have a master's degree

Industry

Higher Demand for Managers

Top three segments:

- Casual dining
- Nursing care
- Fast food

Lower Demand for Managers

Bottom three segments:

- Military
- Fine dining
- Kiosks

Educational Priorities

Top Five Areas

- Communication
- Leadership
- Customer relations
- Training
- Motivation

how to interact with unit personnel and will need to develop enhanced interpersonal skills to effectively teach their employees.

According to Delphi panelist comments, managers will be required to effectively lead training of groups of employees, and any skills that facilitate this task, such as public speaking, presentation, interpersonal skills, and leadership abilities, will be in demand. Delphi panelists noted that foodservice managers in 2000 will probably spend more time training employees and less time managing paper.

The prediction that managers in 2000 will need better teaching and training skills is just one component of what the panelists believed was a need for increased human resource expertise. This Delphi panel conclusion is discussed in greater detail in the human resources section.

MANAGER'S ROLES

Finance

Because on-line, computer-based financial systems for restaurants will probably become more prevalent, Delphi panelists predict that managers in 2000 will need to be computer proficient. The comments of Delphi panelists indicated that this development will be most likely to occur in chain restaurant operations. Still, panelists noted that point-of-sale systems, as well as other electronic input devices, will most likely make a manager's traditional accounting responsibilities more obsolete at the turn of the century in both independent and chain operations.

Delphi panelists noted that more efficient financial systems will be in place at restaurants in 2000 and that managers who are computer proficient and able to use financial and accounting software, such as spreadsheet analysis, will be better administrators. Panelists noted that as a result of increased computerization of the financial functions, managers will be able to report more effectively on a unit's financial condition. Consequently, the unit should be run more efficiently and profitability.

Delphi survey participants also indicated that as the world of electronic banking continues to grow, managers can expect their establishments to be handling more credit-card and debit-card transactions.

The Delphi panelists predicted that because more financial and accounting information will be available to restaurant managers at the unit level in 2000, the managers will be more likely to have their compensation linked to performance through bonus and incentive systems. Panelists believed that managers in 2000 will assume a greater responsibility for the bottom line of the operation.

Despite the fact that there will be increased pressure on managers regarding bottom-line results, managers will not focus more on optimizing check averages and less on customer counts. Panelist comments indicated that managers at the turn of the century can be expected to assume a greater responsibility for managing costs and expenses, as well as sales and revenues. Delphi participants said that linking compensation to efficiently managed income and expenses will provide the incentive and motivation for managers to optimize the potential of their operations.

Human Resources

At the turn of the century, managers will need better skills for managing people, according to the Delphi panel. Study participants indicated that managers will need to be team leaders, or "coaches," and less authoritarian in nature. In addition, Delphi participants forecast that managers in 2000 will have staffs that are better cross-trained.

The Delphi panel noted that managers will need to be much more adept at dealing with people—employees as well as customers—and should find that human resource issues will become a top priority. Since managers are expected to have more difficulty recruiting employees, the Delphi panel predicted that managers in 2000 will have a greater range of compensation options to offer employees to aid in retaining qualified personnel. The Delphi panelists did not believe managers will be dealing with union issues more or that labor will become too expensive to allow for on-the-job training.

Delphi panelist's comments indicated that managers in 2000 will place more emphasis on reducing labor turnover and retaining employees. Panelists commented that managers will need to become better team leaders who focus on creating an environment where people want to work and achieve common objectives. Panelists noted that a host of factors will come into play to create the proper work environment—compensation tied to performance, enhanced fringe benefits, appropriate work schedules, ongoing training programs, comprehensive appraisal systems, and better retirement benefits.

Panelists commented that ongoing training of staff by managers will become more prevalent in 2000, and, just as a coach does with an athletic team, managers will find themselves encouraging, advising, and motivating their employees. Therefore, according to Delphi panelists, it is likely that employees will sense that managers and foodservice organizations have a higher commitment to their career development, which ultimately should translate into lower turnover and a more productive work force.

Facility Maintenance

Delphi panelists felt that managers at the turn of the century will play an increased role in foodservice waste management and recycling. This development was ranked among the top 10 most likely changes.

Delphi survey participants indicated that since recycling and waste management issues will only continue to grow in importance over the next decade, it is logical that managers will play a more important role in recycling and managing waste in the years ahead. Panelists commented that managers will very likely be charged with ensuring proper sorting of recyclable materials by staff in the back of the house as well as with promoting recycling among consumers in fast-food operations. Panelists also commented that managers in 2000 can be expected to deal with more federal, state, and local environmental regulations and procedures regarding foodservice recycling and waste management.

To reduce potentially higher liability costs, managers in 2000 can be expected to place greater emphasis on unit security and safety issues from both a customer and employee perspective. Delphi panelists predicted that managers will develop more employee-safety committees and programs that will heighten safety concerns among employees.

Panelists commented that foodservice facility design will emphasize security for both the front and back of the house, as well as for exterior areas, including parking lots and drive-thru areas.

In 2000, managers can be expected to place greater emphasis on preventive maintenance programs. Panelists commented that because repairs and maintenance costs are expected to escalate, proper facility maintenance will become more important to ensuring profitability and that there will be less tolerance for equipment downtime. Consequently, managers will place greater emphasis on continuous preventive maintenance and, as some panelists commented, could become more reliant on outside maintenance expertise. Both equipment and building maintenance are expected to be more important to managers to control utility and maintenance costs.

Sanitation and Food Safety

At the turn of the century, foodservice managers will probably be required to have a sanitation certificate, according to the Delphi panel. Panelists expected managers to face mandated sanitation testing by most states, as well as more stringent regulations on food handling.

In addition, according to panelists, managers will most likely be required to undergo continuing education on sanitation issues. Despite the increased emphasis on sanitation and good handling, panelists did not necessarily believe that more food handling would be done off site. The possibility of more off-site food preparation because of greater food safety and sanitation concerns was one of the two least likely developments foreseen by the Delphi panel in the food safety and sanitation arena.

Delphi panelists commented that managers in 2000 will develop greater expertise regarding sanitation and food safety and will more effectively communicate the importance of these issues to staff. In fact, many panelists commented that more and more employees will be required to have some sanitation training.

Of particular note is the Delphi panel prediction that managers will face greater restrictions on the use of pesticides and cleaners. Panelists commented that more natural cleaners are likely to be developed and used by managers in restaurants at the turn of the century.

Service

According to the Delphi panel, managers in 2000 will find that service is a more competitive point of difference. This development was ranked the third most likely to occur. Only the need for greater computer proficiency and the supervision of a more culturally diverse staff were viewed by the Delphi panel as having a greater likelihood of occurrence.

Panelists predicted that managers will need to cater to the service demands of a more diverse customer base and solicit more feedback from customers. Of particular note were the developments that the Delphi panel deemed had the least likelihood of occurring—customers expecting lower levels of service and staffs providing lower levels of service. In addition, panelists did not expect managers in 2000 to be handling more customer complaints about poorer service.

Delphi panelists expected that managers in 2000 will empower employees to render better service. The theme of employee empowerment runs throughout the Delphi survey results.

Panelists' comments indicated that both managers and employees will need to be trained and to more sensitive to customer needs and desires, and, perhaps most important, these employees need to have the flexibility and training to react immediately to satisfy customer requests. Panelists pointed out that allowing managers and their staffs to take action to satisfy customers will result in a greater sense of accomplishment and will help develop unity among the staff.

Accordingly, Delphi panelists indicated that managers in 2000 can expect to spend more time on customer relations and most likely set more standards for employees regarding customer satisfaction and employee service performance. Consequently, managers will become more responsible for providing feedback to their employees regarding service. In addition, comments indicate that many managers in 2000 will show their commitment to service by spending more time talking to customers and personally overseeing the delivery of service on an hour-by-hour, day-by-day basis.

Not surprisingly, Delphi panelists predicted that service will become a more competitive point of difference and that both managers and staff will assume greater responsibility in achieving an excellent service standard. Good service has always been fundamental to winning and retaining restaurant customers.

Of the top 10 most likely developments that Delphi panelists predicted for managers in 2000, 3 are related to service—the greatest number for any topic category covered by the Delphi survey. Consequently, it is easy to see that service training will be one of the most important issues for managers to address as the 21st century approaches.

Marketing

Members of the Delphi panel predicted that managers at the turn of the century will increase their in-store marketing efforts. Consequently, Delphi panelists expected managers will need a better understanding of the demographics of their markets, as well as a better understanding of their competitors and customers.

Delphi panelists commented that a unit's ultimate success at the turn of the century will be intrinsically linked with the manager's ability to market to neighborhood and local consumers and to identify and satisfy the distinct preferences of these individuals. Some panelists noted that managers, even in chain operations, will have greater latitude to adapt both menu items and decor to suit local tastes. In addition, panelists commented that managers in 2000 will most likely become more knowledgeable about how to reach local consumers and will be more responsible for leading the unit's in-house marketing efforts, regardless of whether the manager is associated with an independent or a chain operation.

Delphi panel members noted that for larger foodservice chain operations, the primary marketing functions such as creative development, market research, and media purchasing will remain centralized and be directed by corporate staff. Panelists commented that economies of scale will continue to dictate this centralized arrangement. Still, managers in 2000 can be expected to assume greater responsibility for local store marketing, as well as in-store marketing efforts. Panelists commented that managers will be held more responsible for the execution of in-store marketing programs and can be expected to promote their establishments actively to both customers and the local community as neighborhood restaurants. Consequently, Delphi results suggest that managers will need to know more about advertising and public relations alternatives to reach neighborhood consumers. Delphi panelists emphasized that managers at the turn of the century will not be too busy to deal with marketing issues. In addition, Delphi members noted that suggestive tableside marketing by wait staff will undoubtedly increase in 2000, with managers becoming more responsible for teaching suggestive selling techniques to wait staff.

Food and Beverage

According to the Delphi panel, foodservice managers in 2000 will most likely be dealing with consumers who are more knowledgeable about nutrition. Panelists predict that managers will be more sensitive to health and dietary issues and will be required to have greater knowledge of ingredient and nutritional content. In addition, managers are expected to assume more responsibility for quality control and product consistency.

In line with the Delphi prediction that managers will become more responsible for the bottom line, Delphi participants expect that managers in 2000 will be more aware of the financial impact of their purchasing decisions and will pay closer attention to inventory control. Panelists' comments indicate that managers at the turn of the century will be allowed more flexibility to promote food and beverage items that sell well in their specific market, aiding profitability.

Managers in 2000 are likely to be using more video training to educate employees on food-and-beverage quality

standards, according to Delphi panelists. Panelists' comments confirm that one of the manager's primary responsibilities will be to ensure the highest possible quality of product preparation. The least likely development expected is that managers will assume less responsibility for food-and-beverage decisions due to the growth of off-site commissaries. In addition, managers are not expected to spend more time on menu and recipe development.

WORKING CONDITIONS IN 2000

Delphi participants predicted that foodservice managers in 2000 will require more education to meet the challenges of the new century effectively. Consequently, managers will find career development becoming more important to them and will pay more attention to quality-of-life issues and healthy life-styles.

Delphi members expected that, compared with today, managers in 2000 will receive more competitive salaries and benefits and should enjoy better working conditions. Some panelists commented that as a result of more education and better compensation levels, managers could enjoy higher public and peer esteem, and that this greater emphasis on managerial professionalism could attract additional managerial talent to the foodservice industry.

Although Delphi panelists predicted that managers will find an improvement in quality of life on the job, the number of hours managers will work in 2000 is not expected to decline. In fact, one of the 10 least likely developments forecast by Delphi panelists is that managers will work shorter hours. Delphi members predicted that managers at the turn of the century will continue to work long hours compared with other industries. The comments of Delphi panelists indicated that one reason for managers working longer hours is that units will be open a greater number of hours because of a more competitive operating environment.

Panelists predicted that managers in 2000 will require more education and will deal with greater levels of stress, but that they will earn higher rewards as a result. Comments indicated that stress will still be a major factor for foodservice managers because of the basic nature of the job, but that stress training could make an important contribution to dealing with this issue. Of particular note, Delphi panelists did not think it is likely that managers will experience a higher level of burnout in 2000.

BACKGROUND, EDUCATION, AND HRIM SCHOOLS

Delphi panelists felt strongly that managers in 2000 will need to possess excellent interpersonal skills. The need for managers to have superior interpersonal skills was ranked among the top 10 most likely developments. Panelists also predicted that at the turn of the century managers will need better communication skills.

The importance that the Delphi panelists attached to interpersonal skills complemented their prediction that managers will deal with more human resource issues, ranging from managing cultural diversity and employee motivation to team building and customer relations. Excellent interpersonal skills and communication skills will be important tools for managers to possess in order to deal with human resource issues in the 21st century.

Panel comments indicated that the manager in 2000 will need to be more of a generalist and less of a specialist. Managers will be responsible for creating a positive work environment to achieve their goals, and communication and interpersonal skills are critical to achieving this success. According to panel comments, technical skills are not expected to be as important to the manager at the turn of the century.

Managers in 2000 will have to be more astute in managing people to obtain required results. Delphi panelists noted that tomorrow's manager will need to be more democratic and less autocratic and will be required to have a more flexible personality. Managers will have to be able to handle a variety of tasks simultaneously and, according to panelists' comments, present an image of grace under pressure to both staff and customers.

The least likely development for managers in 2000, according to the Delphi panel, it that more of their peers will have advanced degrees. Also, managers will not be expected to teach English to their employees, despite the greater cultural diversity of the work force at the turn of the century.

How will HRIM schools respond to the changing responsibilities and challenges facing the foodservice manager at the turn of the century? Members of the Delphi panel believed that HRIM schools will emphasize more leadership and management skills in their curricula. Panelists expected that those schools will work closer with the foodservice industry, offer more internship programs, expand their selection of business and computer courses, place more emphasis on managers' continuing education, and require more on-the-job training.

Not surprisingly, Delphi panelists expected HRIM schools will be seeking more qualified instructors to meet these additional educational challenges. According to the panelists, HRIM schools in 2000 will find their role changing, but they are not especially likely to grow in number.

INDUSTRY NEEDS

Compared with today, which sections of the foodservice industry will experience increased or decreased demand for foodservice managers? According to Delphi panelists, demand for managers will increase most in the casual-dining-table-service segment, followed by the nursing-care and fast-food segments.

By predicting a strong demand for managers in 2000 in the casual-dining-table-service segment, the Delphi panelists indicated that the current popularity of casual dining among consumers is likely to continue through the remainder of the decade.

Increased demand at the turn of the century for foodservice managers in the nursing-care segment reflects the aging of the nation's population and subsequent increased need for nursing-care facilities. Delphi members expected that the fast-food segment, driven by the continuing need for convenience, will also experience higher demand for managers at the turn of the century.

Which sectors of the foodservice industry are likely to experience lower demand for managers in 2000 compared with today? According to Delphi panel members, military foodservice should experience the greatest drop-off in demand for managers, most likely reflecting anticipated troop reductions over the coming years. The fine-dining segment was also targeted by Delphi panelists as one segment of the industry where higher demand for managers is not expected at the turn of the century.

EDUCATIONAL PRIORITIES

According to Delphi panelists, developing administrative capabilities should be emphasized in the education of a foodservice manager who is to run a successful operation in 2000. Among the top 10 educational priorities, the two which were ranked highest—communication and leadership—are administrative in nature. Team building, another administrative function, was also included among the top 10 educational priorities for managers at the turn of the century.

In addition to the high educational priority given to administrative duties, Delphi panel members indicated that managers will need to be better educated in a variety of human resources skills. Among the top 10 educational priorities, 4—training, motivation, team building, and supervision—are related to managers' human resources duties.

Consequently, 7 out of the top 10 educational priorities for managers in 2000 are related either to administration or human resources. Other educational priorities, according to the Delphi panel, included customer relations, food handling, and cost control.

Which areas should receive lower educational priority for managers in 2000? Banking, off-premises or delivery, market research, menu design, and policy/procedures were among the ones least favored by Delphi panelists.

APPENDIX

The Delphi Method

Originated during the 1960s by the RAND Corporation, the Delphi approach used a panel of industry experts to identify and analyze issues by subjective judgment. The process has been found to work well when the topic being investigated lends itself to subjective judgments rather than to precise analytical techniques. The Delphi method allowed panel members to identify and analyze issues through an ongoing process with other members of the panel. The basic approach was to collect judgments by questionnaire from the Delphi panelists, summarize the responses, and then feed the summary back to the panelists for reassessment.

Panel Composition

The most important aspect of conducting a Delphi study was selection of a panel of experts. In this case, the panel was charged with developing a better understanding of what will be required of foodservice managers in the year 2000. Nevertheless, finding a highly qualified panel of experts for this study was easy—the Board of Directors of the National Restaurant Association and the Board of Trustees of the Educational Foundation of the National Restaurant Association. With many years of personal experience in foodservice, these board members are well equipped to give an astute forecast for the foodservice manager in 2000.

To complement the participation in the Delphi study by the Association's Board of Directors and the Educational Foundation's Board of Trustees, a variety of other foodservice experts were invited to join the panel. Included were human resources professionals and training directors who belong to the Council on Hotel and Restaurant Trainers (CHART); educators who belong to the Council on Hotel, Restaurant and Institutional Education (CHRIE); state restaurant association executives; operators (both independent and chain); consultants; and other foodservice industry experts.

Methodology

In March 1991, the first phase of the Delphi research project on the foodservice manager in the year 2000 was initiated. Questionnaires were sent to the Association's Board and the Educational Foundation's trustees, as well as to the other selected foodservice industry experts.

The format of the first questionnaire was open-ended, offering panelists a chance to list any and all issues that they believed would be important to the foodservice manager at the turn of the century. Several broad topics were listed on the first-phase Delphi questionnaire to start panel participants thinking about changes occurring in the manager's job, as well as educational priorities at the beginning of the 21st century. Topic headings included:

- administration;
- finance;
- human resources;
- facility maintenance;
- sanitation and food safety;
- service;
- marketing;
- food and beverage;
- working conditions;
- external issues;
- background and education; and
- industry needs.

After completed responses were returned and reviewed, 12 distinct categories were developed: administration, finance, human resources, facility maintenance, sanitation and food safety, service, marketing, food and beverage, working conditions, background and education, industry needs, and educational priorities.

By August 1991, the second phase of the Delphi study was under way. A structured survey based on the responses generated by the first phase was circulated to panel members. This survey was designed to elicit opinions about specific issues, events, and developments that would shape the foodservice manager's job in 2000.

The second-phase questionnaire contained a series of statements and asked respondents to indicate the likelihood of occurrence of each statement on a scale of 1 to 10, on which 1 equated "very unlikely" and 10 equated "very likely." For the industry-needs section of the second-phase questionnaire, 1 equaled "lower demand" for managers in 2000 and 10 equaled "higher demand." For the educational priorities section, 1 equaled "low educational priority" in 2000, and 10 equaled "high educational priority."

A total of 120 panel members returned the detailed Delphi survey upon which this article is based. Survey development, processing, and analysis were carried out by the Research Department of the National Restaurant Association in coordination with Educational Foundation staff.

Editors' Note. The editors of the *Hospitality Research Journal* express their appreciation to the authors, who submitted this article at the request of Guest Editor Thomas F. Powers.

Mills, S.F. and Riehle, H. "Foodservice Manager 2000." Hospitality Research Journal, *vol. 17, No. 1, 1993, pp. 147–159.*

---

*This article has been adapted from the National Restaurant Association's Current Issues Report "Foodservice Manager 2000" (1992).

PillowTalk

■

BY JACK COX

When you check into a room at the Airport Hilton in Phoenix, you'll find a 150-word message printed on a 4-by-5 ½-inch card propped against the pillow.

"To Our Guests," it announces. The format suggests you're about to be advised of a problem with the air conditioning or warned about some high-crime area nearby. But as it turns out, this is not an admonition so much as an invocation.

"In ancient times there was a prayer for 'The Stranger Within Our Gates,'" the pale yellow flyer begins.

NOT YOUR BASIC GREETING

"Because this hotel is a human institution to serve people, and not solely a money-making organization, we hope you will be granted peace and rest while you are under our roof," it goes on.

"May this room and hotel be your 'second' home. May those you love be near you in thoughts and dreams. Even though we may not get to know you, we hope that you will be comfortable and happy as if you were in your own house."

Wait. There's more: "May the business that brought you our way prosper. May every call you make and every message you receive add to your success. When you leave, may your journey be safe."

Furthermore: "We are all travelers. From birth until death we travel between the eternities."

And finally: "May these days be pleasant for you, profitable for society, helpful for those you meet, and a joy for those who know and love you most."

This elaborate "turndown card," as such welcome notes are called in the business, is not exactly your basic "Have a Nice Day" salute. Nor is it particularly original. One just like it has been greeting guests in Denver's Brown Palace Hotel since at least 1960.

BIG SELLING POINT

But in spite of its length and lofty language—or maybe because of it—the prayer has proved to be one the Phoenix hotel's biggest selling points in the three years or so since it was introduced.

"We have a lot of people write on the guest comment cards that they really appreciate it," said Donna Lynsdey, director of sales and marketing for the independently owned franchise.

"They say the average guest decides whether he likes a hotel or not within the first two minutes he's in the room.

This gives you more of a welcome and a warm feeling. And that's important, since traveling is hard even under normal circumstances."

Increasingly, it seems, innkeepers are embracing the notion that it's homey little touches like this, rather than physical amenities like fitness centers or breakfast buffets, that lure the return business to keep a place thriving.

The personalized approach "used to be the domain of luxury hotels alone," said Scott Hannah, a Denver marketing consultant.

"But as the industry gets to be in better shape and recognizes the importance of customer retention, the 3-star and 4-star hotels are paying more attention to it."

Specially prepared turndown cards—named for the practice of turning down the bed covers as the time to turn in approaches—are perhaps the most visible sign of the trend. But hotels are focusing on other niceties as well, such as addressing guests by name, offering candy or fruit or other treats to welcome them back on subsequent visits, and leaving the latest weather forecast on the pillow or lamp table each night so they'll know how to dress the next morning.

"It's part of an effort to build a relationship with the customer so the customer will feel more at home and want to return," Hannah explained.

The Doubletree chain welcomes each new arrival with two big, freshly baked chocolate-chip cookies.

Sheraton hotels have provided little teddy bears so homesick guests would have a friend to cuddle at night.

Another chain once handed out rubber duckies.

Others have strewn flower petals on guests' pillows or left sachets of lavender with little notes explaining that the scent is said to induce sleep.

"AMENITY CREEP"

"I think people want more personal things," notes Kathy Bialke, marketing director for the Salt Lake Doubletree in Utah's capital. "They say, 'Don't try to wow and kazowe me.' They just want to feel that the hotel cares, that they're not just being treated like revenue—business travelers especially."

Not incidentally, hotels also have found that upgrading customer service is generally cheaper than providing new facilities or furnishings. As Hannah point out, "amenity creep"—in which bathrooms are stocked with bottles of mouthwash as well as soap, shampoo and conditioner, for example—"can add thousands and thousands in costs over a year's time."

At many high-end hotels today, guests experience the new approach when they call the desk and find themselves greeted by name. The clerks learn who's calling by scanning digital readouts on their phone consoles.

PHOTO LINEUP

The Marriott City Center in downtown Denver goes one better. On the "Platinum Marquee" floor, which is off limits to the ordinary guest, photos of the premium-level customers are posted in the service kitchen to enable the staff to identify them by face as well as name.

"Our guests are typically flattered by that," said marketing assistant Danny Blessing.

"We try to avoid leaving a generic letter," he commented, "because a lot of our guests are return customers, and to get a letter one week and then the same one a week later can be insulting."

At the Loew's Giorgio Hotel in Glendale, said general manager Matthew Kryjak, "For our guests returning to us, we do a handwritten note to each one, saying something like we hope they had a good holiday or telling them what's new since their last visit."

Sometimes, he added, even the hotel's shoe shiners get into the act. When they finish polishing, they've been known to insert a note in the heel collar saying, "Hope your feet have a nice day."

In addition, the Giorgio keeps track of each regular customer's favorite newspapers, snack food and other items, using a "guest profile" card filled out by the guest after the third or fourth visit and entered into a computer file for future reference.

"We also try to be a little bit special around the holidays, like over Valentine's Day we gave a rose and truffles to each of our guests, and during Christmas we left candy canes at turndown time," Kryjak reported.

MONOGRAMMED ROBES

The list of amenities offered at different hotels also may include sewing kits, in-room irons and ironing boards and the use of monogrammed terrycloth bathrobes.

Denver's venerable Brown Palace, which provides these and other services, is considering yet another attraction—bottled water from its own in-house source, a 720-foot-deep well beneath its property that it shares with the Deep Rock Water Co.

The 104-year-old hotel also provides such high-tech amenities as voice mail, computer ports and video games.

"And soon we'll be doing video checkouts, where you pay your bill using the TV," said Deborah Dix, public relations director for the Brown.

It is the turndown cards, however, that may do most to capture the customer's loyalty.

"I think hotels are seeing the card they put on pillows at night as a great way to communicate, whereas before, they might have just put down a mint," remarked Maryanne Yuthas, director of public relations and advertising for the Hyatt Regency in Denver.

The Westin La Paloma in Tucson, Ariz., for example, has gotten positive response to a series of seven turndown cards created by local schoolchildren who entered a contest to design a special "Sweet Dreams" message for its guests.

"Thanks for choosing us for the night," reads one such message, penned by Sara, age 10. "We hoped you liked our beautiful sights. So put on your jamies (sic), and sleep tight, cause now it's time to say 'Good-night.'"

HYATT PLAYS TO KIDS

The Hyatt in Denver is planning a similar contest for children to create cards reflecting Colorado themes, Yuthas said.

As for the inspirational message laid out nightly at the Phoenix Airport Hilton, its exact origin is obscure, even though it is virtually identical to a turndown card long used by the Brown Palace.

Kathy Bialke, who worked in Phoenix before taking her current job in Salt Lake, acknowledged that the version used at the Arizona hotel was adapted from another source.

However, she asserted, "I can't remember where I found it, I honestly can't. . . . I'm big on reading religious books, so I must have come across it somewhere (in one such volume)."

Kryjak, a veteran hotelier who has been in charge at the Giorgio since 1990, said he had never heard of the "Prayer for the Stranger Within Our Gates." But he wryly observed, "A good idea usually finds its way around."

Cox, Jack (1996, March 2) PillowTalk. The Denver Post, pp. E1–2.

The Service and Hospitality Environment

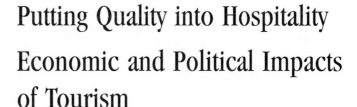

CHAPTER 9

Putting Quality into Hospitality

A warm welcome sets the stage for customer satisfaction.
Photo by A. Talg.

We have 50,000 moments of truth out there every day.

JAN CARLZON, PRESIDENT, SCANDINAVIAN AIRLINES

CHAPTER OUTLINE

LEARNING OBJECTIVES

After you have read this chapter, you should be able to:

- Use the Service Encounter Diagram to explain the different factors that affect a guest's service experience.

- Explain how a person develops expectations of a service and how tourism organizations can meet or exceed these expectations.

- Name and describe the five service-quality dimensions.

- Explain how a comparison of service expectations with the actual service encounter can give rise to three possible satisfaction levels.

- Explain what tourism managers can do to ensure high-quality service.

- Explain how negative "breaks from the script" should be handled in order to "turn a frown upside down" and create guest loyalty.

- List the important aspects of a service guarantee.

ALL'S WELL THAT ENDS WELL?

After a short night's sleep, six hours of air terminal waits and airline flights, and a hectic taxi ride, Jamal and Kayla Johnson were ready for the peace and quiet of their hotel room. However, when they arrived at the Town Center Hotel to begin their vacation in Vancouver, things got off to a bad start. Although they had received a written confirmation of their room reservation two months ago, the Town Center was completely full for that night.

The Johnsons were furious! They showed Mike their reservation confirmation form. Mike apologized sincerely, admitted the mistake, and explained that several guests had stayed over unexpectedly so there were no available rooms. Mike next picked up the phone to find the Johnsons suitable accommodations nearby. Although the city was virtually full due to a major conference in town, Mike was able to obtain a suite for the Johnsons at a hotel nearby and explained that the Town Center Hotel would pay for the suite to compensate the Johnsons for their trouble.

To keep their inconvenience to a minimum, Mike also arranged for a taxi to take the Johnsons to their new hotel. To ensure that friends and relatives could contact them if need be, they would be listed in the Town Center database so any calls could be forwarded to their new hotel.

The next day, a room at the Town Center was available for the Johnsons. Mike welcomed them as they returned the next afternoon and again apologized for the inconvenience. As they were escorted to their room by a bellman, Mike thought, "I'll call the Johnsons in about an hour just to check and make sure they are settled in and satisfied." It was an unfortunate situation, but he was certain the Johnsons would forgive the error and give the Town Center another chance the next time they came to Vancouver.

INTRODUCTION

Quality. Hospitality. In the case of tourism, these two words are inseparable. When thinking about a high-quality experience in any tourism service, whether a restaurant meal, a hotel stay, an airline flight, or a guided tour, most people think of friendly, helpful personnel who treat them with concern and kindness. The concept of quality with its important hospitality component is the focus of this chapter.

As the tourism marketplace becomes more competitive, quality becomes more crucial for continued financial success. Consumers are more critical and demanding today than they have ever been. Simply providing guests average service is not good enough in this competitive environment. In a market full of tourism suppliers, a company needs to offer more and better service because guests can always take their business elsewhere. To be successful, a tourism firm needs to understand what quality means to prospective customers and strive to improve the service quality offered so customers keep coming back again and again.

Take a moment to think back on a memorable tourism service experience that you would label as very high in quality. What were the circumstances? Why is this encounter more memorable than others? What aspects of it make you recall it as high quality?

QUALITY

As we have already suggested, different travelers have different needs and wants. What is "high quality" to one may be perceived as entirely unacceptable to another. Think of Mexican food. Some restaurant patrons believe that high-quality Mexican food must make you perspire and set your tongue on fire. Many other fans of South of the Border fare like their food much less combustible and prefer milder versions of Mexican classics. Those red chili burritos may be delicious to you but, to a friend born and raised in Santa Fe,

New Mexico, they may seem bland and tasteless. So quality is a complex concept, difficult to define in terms on which all can agree.

Defining Quality

As Figure 9.1 shows, quality can have several definitions. Most of us probably think of quality as synonymous with "excellence." Technically, from a management and marketing perspective, quality represents a form of measurement like a thermometer or ruler. Products have some *amount* of quality: we talk of high quality or bad quality, good quality or poor quality. Quality is both objective and subjective in nature. Objectively, we can measure some aspects of quality because they involve objective, or measurable, amounts of certain attributes or ingredients. A spacious hotel room would be rated as higher quality than a smaller one simply based on the measurable dimensions of the two rooms. Likewise, a flight that takes off on time and arrives ahead of schedule would be thought of as higher in quality than a late flight, based on the quantifiable aspect of time as measured in minutes.[1] However, this measurable concept of quality is not the complete picture of quality. Much of quality is subjective—in the "eye of the beholder."

TIPS

One commonly used but often misunderstood measure of service quality is tipping. Although many employees rely on TIPS to supplement their income, they may fail to recognize the origin of the term "TIPS." TIPS is actually an acronym for the phrase: "**T**o **I**nsure **P**rompt **S**ervice." TIPS are not automatic; the amount (if any) a guest leaves is often a pointed comment on the service received.

In addition to these objective versus subjective concepts of quality is the idea of value. The value-based definition of quality incorporates the notion of a trade-off; the trade-off between service attributes and service performance with the price paid for the quality received. Even if you are an infrequent flyer, you no doubt have recognized the objective quality differences between first or business class and coach. In first class, passengers sit in leather-covered, spacious "lounger" style seats with more leg room between the rows. In addition, they receive bountiful amounts of food and beverages served on fine china. But how many of you believe the quality received in first class is worth the difference in price?

FIGURE 9.1
Quality Definitions

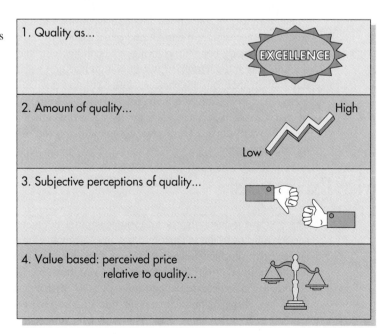

First and business class airfares are often three to five times as expensive as coach class fares, yet everyone takes off and arrives at the exact same time in the exact same place. In the case of air travel, the value-based concept of quality therefore involves a person's perception of the best use of his or her travel and time budget. For example, frequent business travelers value the quiet time and space for relaxing or working that is provided in first-class seating. The values of leisure travelers vary. If you believe that "getting there is half the fun," you may decide to spend the extra money to enjoy the benefits of first class travel. But if you believe that the plane ride is simply transportation to be endured in order to get to where the fun starts, you are more likely to save those travel dollars to spend at your destination.

Why is quality so important? Higher quality can result in three important benefits for companies. First, when consumers perceive a company's product as superior in quality, they are willing to pay higher prices, which can translate into higher profits. Second, superior quality can lead to increased **market share.**[2] Third, superior quality can generate truly brand-loyal customers. These are customers who will accept no substitutes, do not respond to competitors' promotions, and pass along positive word-of-mouth messages enhancing a company's reputation even further. Can you think of a local tourism provider in your area who has a superior quality reputation? Keep this business in mind throughout the rest of this chapter and see if the ideas we present explain why this business is such a success.

Quality Differences

Quality in services, including tourism services, is more difficult to define and measure than in hard goods. When manufacturers design and build hard goods, they engineer in a specified quality level. In some instances, the specification **standards** are very high, as in the case of Rolls Royce automobiles, but in most cases, manufacturers focus on the value component of quality. How much quality is the customer willing to pay for? The GM Saturn is perceived by most consumers as a high-quality car because the value trade-off is positive. For a modest price the car buyer receives a comfortable, stylish, and reliable automobile. Both Rolls Royce and the General Motors Company design a car with certain **specifications** that are then met in virtually every model that rolls off the assembly line.

Unfortunately, we do not manufacture services. Remember, services are actions performed on behalf of a customer. In most cases, human beings perform at least part of the actions, and therefore consistency in actions is much lower than if a machine performed the actions over and over. Machines can be programmed to repeat the same action thousands of times. People are far less consistent than machines. In addition, tourism services frequently necessitate the input and participation of the consumers themselves. When you purchase a teddy bear for your niece's birthday, you had absolutely no input into the production of that toy. However, when you go hiking, you are intimately involved in the "production" of that tourism service. Your skill and decisions about which trails to hike play a large part in determining how much "quality" you perceive during your trip. In the case of many tourism services such as hiking, the weather also has an impact on the enjoyment you will derive. Even your companions on the hike can affect whether your day is terrific or terrible.

SERVICE ENCOUNTERS

The tourism industry is one of close customer contact, and every interaction between a service employee and a customer becomes a **service encounter.**[3] Both tourism customers and tourism supplier personnel bring to each encounter expectations about what will occur during the interaction. As customers and suppliers, we learn what to expect in tourism encounters from past experiences and from the experiences of others that we observe. In a sense, we all perform an important role in a service encounter "play." As customers or suppliers, we both have role expectations of each other which dictate appropriate behavior for each party.

Although we can think of service encounters as little plays that involve **service scripts,** we all realize that they do not involve a rigid prerehearsed set of lines. After all, a stay at Motel 6 is not expected to be as well rehearsed and performed as Shakespeare. Each encounter will be somewhat similar to but also different in some ways from every other encounter, depending on the individual customer and the individual service employee.

These service encounters are frequently called "moments of truth" because it is through these encounters that customers derive their quality impressions about a service. What features of a service encounter are important? The service encounter diagram in Figure 9.2 shows the variety of factors that can affect the service experience that any guest will have during a single interaction with a tourism supplier.[4]

Take a careful look at the figure while thinking about your favorite full-service restaurant. What are the invisible parts of the service facility that guests do not see but that are important in determining the experience any guest will have? What physical areas of the restaurant, from the parking lot to the "powder room," will the guest encounter that

FIGURE 9.2
Service Encounters.
Figure adapted from MANAGING SERVICES MARKETING: TEXT AND READINGS. Third Edition by John G. Bateson, copyright © 1995 by The Dryden Press, reproduced by permission by the publisher.

Physical Elements of Tourism Service

Behind the Scenes

Guest A

• Operations,
• Systems, and
• Employees

Guest B

Employees Having Direct Contact with Guests and Visitors

Invisible to Guests | Visible to Guests

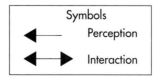

Symbols
Perception
Interaction

TOURISM IN ACTION

Many cities are realizing that visitors begin their journey to satisfaction or dissatisfaction immediately on arrival at the air terminal. Who, then, represents the first "ambassador" of a city? The cab drivers! Singapore has had special educational and licensing programs for cab drivers for many years. The drivers must learn guest relations skills and then pass rigorous tests to become officially licensed cab drivers. These skills include proficiency in English, safety, and knowledge of a wide variety of locations. Drivers in London must exhibit similar strengths.

Over the years, New York City, unfortunately has become renowned for its rude, less than professionally knowledgeable cab drivers. In 1996, New York's Taxi and Limousine Commission began a campaign to better its cabby's manners. Chairman of the Commission, Christopher Lynn stated, "The cab driver is often the first

and last New Yorker that a tourist meets. I think it will be a boost to our image and tourism." The program includes:

- courteous statements to use when dealing with visitors,
- videos of driver-passenger conflicts and the best behaviors to handle each situation, and
- "undercover operations" in which police monitor cabbies by posing as passengers.

The final exam for the course covers courtesy statements and passenger-driver relations, as well as map-reading skills, taxi regulations, and knowledge of the English language. It may take years for New York to rid itself of the rude cab driver image. But by following the examples of Singapore and London, New York may someday be viewed as taxi passenger heaven!

Sources: Kotler, Philip, Haidera, Donald H., & Rein, Irving (1993). *Marketing places*. New York: The Free Press; Filling in cabby's verbal pothole (1996, May 6). *New York Times*, pp. B1, B6.

can affect how she perceives the restaurant? What restaurant employees is she likely to see and/or interact with whose appearances and actions can influence her quality perception? Finally, think about how other patrons can influence the guest's enjoyment of her meal. If she is dining with her fiancé, she is probably hoping for a quiet, intimate dinner experience. If the hostess seats a family with three overtired children at the next table, our guest and her date are likely to have a lower-quality restaurant encounter than they had originally hoped.

This preliminary discussion of service quality and the service encounter diagram should help you realize that quality assurance in tourism services is quite a challenge. Management of all the factors that affect service quality requires skilled planning, organizing, staffing, directing, and juggling. In the following section we will introduce a comprehensive quality model that can be used to show the link between quality and hospitality.

SERVICE QUALITY MODEL

The diagram in Figure 9.3 begins with the factors that lead to quality expectations of a service.[5] When you go to a water park for the first time, do you have some idea of what benefits you will receive from that particular attraction? Of course you do. And how did you develop these **service expectations?** You may have talked with friends who had been to the water park (word-of-mouth communications). You may be going to the water park because you believe it will be fun and provide relief from the heat (personal needs). You may have been to other water parks and therefore, have a general impression of what water parks are like (past experience). And, finally, you may have seen commercials on TV giving you an impression of the park (**marketing communications**). These factors combine and lead to expectations about the type of experience you will have during this tourism service encounter.

Once you enter the park, what elements of the experience will be important in shaping your perception of the quality of this park? People generally consider five dimensions when judging the quality of a service. In Figure 9.3, these dimensions link to the expected and perceived service boxes.

FIGURE 9.3
Service Quality Model
Adapted from Parasuraman, A., Zeithaml, Valarie, & Berry, Leonard. A conceptual model of service quality and its implications for future research. *Journal of Marketing, 49*, 41–50.

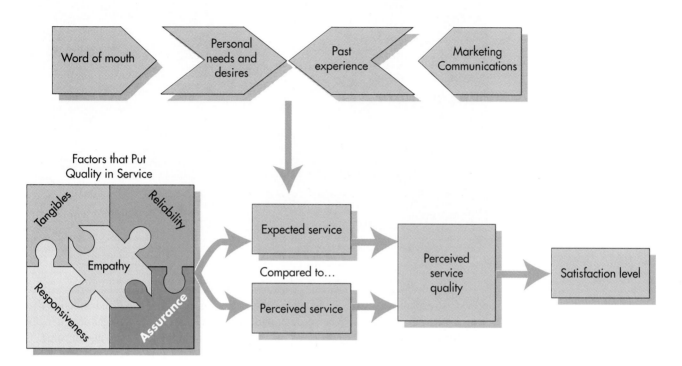

How service expectations are formed...

Factors that Put Quality in Service

How satisfaction is determined . . .

Tangibles are those physical aspects of the service that we can see and with which we interact—the physical appearance of the facilities, the equipment we use or which service employees use for us, the appearance and uniforms of the employees, and any signs or other communications materials that are provided. For instance, in our water park example, you may be provided with a brochure that includes a map and information about support facilities such as lockers and places to buy a snack or soft drink.

Reliability refers to the ability of service personnel to perform the promised service accurately and consistently. For example, if the water park provides you with the opportunity to learn how to snorkel, do the instructors teach you well enough so that you can snorkel without drinking half of the pool?

Responsiveness involves service employees' willingness to help customers and their promptness in providing service. You expect snack bar personnel to wait on you as soon as possible and to provide your food without unnecessary delay.

Assurance is a catch-all quality dimension that involves the faith we have in the service personnel. Do they seem well trained? Are they knowledgeable about the park as a whole? Do they seem trustworthy? After all, the lifeguards at a water park literally have guests' lives in their hands.

Finally, *empathy* is the "warm, fuzzy" piece of service quality, the part of quality that is heartfelt. Empathy is the quality element that shows that service personnel care about you and understand your needs and frustrations. It involves setting operating hours for the convenience of guests, not management or employees. It includes caring about waiting times and fairness in waiting line systems. For example, our hypothetical water park's management realizes that many people will be waiting in lines in their bare feet on hot pavement. For guest comfort, they have located shade trees and shade umbrellas over the line areas so that you can jump from one shady area to the next while waiting your turn.

Imaginative design of tangibles is a Disney hallmark.
Photo by D.A. Yale.

Empathy is also the element of a service that makes us feel special, when service providers recognize that we are individuals. It is the care and individualized attention that is (or is not) provided to us. When a water park "host" suggests that you might need to reapply your sunscreen because your skin is beginning to turn pink, he is showing empathy.

EMPATHY

A great example of the empathy quality dimension is provided at the Old Faithful Lodge in Yellowstone National Park. Fishing is one of the most frequently experienced recreational activities enjoyed by visitors to the park. But what can a hotel guest do with a fish he or she catches? Bring it to dinner! Guests can deliver their personal "catch-of-the-day" to the main dining room at the Lodge and chefs will prepare it for the guests to eat as their entree for dinner. Price for this service? $8.95, including salad, choice of potato, vegetable, and dinner roll.

QUALITY AND CUSTOMER SATISFACTION

How are expectations of the service received and service quality factors linked? Figure 9.3 shows that customers compare their prior expectations of the service to their "during service" judgments of the five service-quality elements—their overall quality perception of "actual quality." The result of this comparison of *expected quality* to perceived **actual quality** is the customer's level of satisfaction. Figure 9.4 shows the three possible satisfaction outcomes customers can have. If a customer perceives that the quality of the service actually received (after-the-fact perceptions) was better than expected, the guest would be pleasantly surprised and highly satisfied. On the other hand, if the guest perceived the service actually delivered to have fallen short of before-the-fact expectations, the guest would be unpleasantly surprised and therefore dissatisfied.[6]

A third quality comparison is also possible. The third possible outcome is that expectations are met exactly. If the service quality actually received is almost identical to expectations, the guest would likely be "just" satisfied. The guest received the service quality expected so is neither pleasantly nor unpleasantly surprised.

FIGURE 9.4
Satisfaction Equations

Actual service > expectations.. 😊 👍

Actual service = expectations.. 😐

Actual service < expectations.. 😞 👎

If meeting a customer's expectations yields satisfaction, organizations should determine exactly what customers expect and then deliver it, right? Not usually. In many services, such as most tourism services, there are major added benefits to delivering more than is expected so that the customers are delighted, not simply satisfied. As some airline companies discovered, simply relying on statements that showed customer satisfaction can lead to trouble. Airline customers indicated they were satisfied with the present level of service but they were eager to switch to carriers that provided improved quality service.[7]

The Value of Highly Satisfied Customers

Studies have found that customers who are highly satisfied become more valuable customers. First, delighted customers tend to pass along many more positive word-of-mouth messages than do customers who are just satisfied. Second, these highly satisfied customers are also more likely to purchase again and spend more in the future than are customers whose expectations were met but not exceeded. Finally, highly satisfied customers are unlikely to pay attention to competitor's advertising and promotional offers. Customers who are merely satisfied are more willing to try out a competitors' service to see if it might just be better than the service they have been using.[8]

So now that we have discussed how expectations about services are formed, how can this information be used to improve service and ensure that guests are delighted? Keep reading and you will discover the answers to this question.

Methods to Ensure High-Quality Service

Guest services almost always require active guest involvement. Other than situations in which self-service is preferred (for example, a salad bar where you want to load up without feeling self-conscious), services are rarely prepackaged, automated, or even predictable. In fact, the level of guest involvement can positively influence the perception of service quality, provide favorable memories, or create disappointments. Therefore, services must be managed and continuously measured and improved. To achieve these goals, successful service processes must rely on three principles: a guest-driven focus (understanding, anticipating, and complying with guests' needs and desires), employee involvement, and continuous improvements in quality.

Table 9.1 provides a quick list of the methods needed to ensure high-quality service. The first step in delivering high-quality service is to learn and fully understand what customers want in a particular tourism service. Tourism managers can uncover specific needs and expectations of customers in a number of ways. First, marketing research can be used to gather information from potential and existing customers. Many companies regularly survey members of their target market to better understand the changing needs and desires of segments they hope to serve. For example, when the PepsiCo company acquired Taco Bell, management conducted a study of fast-food customers (any fast-food customer, not simply customers who liked Mexican food). From this survey, they concluded that fast-food customers had expectations about four things, which can be remembered by the acronym FACT. Customers wanted their fast food really **F**ast; they expected their orders to be **A**ccurately delivered; they wanted the premises to be **C**lean; and they expected foods and beverages to be served at appropriate **T**emperatures. With this knowledge, top management redesigned the entire Taco Bell system to better deliver these expected qualities.[9]

Management can also learn about customer expectations and experiences by communicating frequently with customers and by welcoming suggestions from front-line employees who deal one-on-one with customers every day (see Table 9.1). At times customers may not know what they want, so efforts should also be made to uncover unknown customer needs. This flow of communication from customers to management is more likely to occur if there are fewer levels of bureaucracy through which the information must pass. After making the restaurant manager's job more customer- and employee-interactive, Taco Bell has been able to streamline its organization. In fact, since 1990, Taco Bell has eliminated two levels of bureaucracy so that all members of the organization are closer to the customer.

In addition to understanding the customer's needs and expectations, tourism managers must be able to hire the right people and train them well. To delight guests, tourism employees must have a positive service attitude; they must have the necessary abilities to learn and perform jobs well; and they must be flexible enough to meet different customers' needs and expectations. Management must decide on proper training for employees and set standards and policies that result in high quality and high satisfaction. However, management needs to remember that customer expectations will differ and quality perceptions will vary, so employees need to be able to make judgments and adaptations to best satisfy each guest. Remember, one of the key elements to service quality is empathy, and empathy means understanding and appreciating each customer's specific needs. Employees who are trained to follow policies strictly cannot empathize with customers and meet their needs. Managers are learning that delivering successful customer service requires allowing employees "to think while doing."

In addition to individual efforts, employees must also work together as a team. If you have worked in any tourism industry job, you already know that delivering good service is a team effort. Imagine two different restaurants. One features servers who have a "that is not my table" attitude. The other has servers who constantly help each other out by refilling water at any table needing it and by delivering meals to any table when the meals are ready to come out of the kitchen. The second restaurant is obviously the higher-quality one and demonstrates the benefits of teamwork.

Allowing employees to think as they serve and building teams are not easy managerial tasks, but the rewards are worth the effort. Recognizing individual efforts that lead to team success promotes employee involvement and commitment. When employees understand organizational goals and how to measure their performance in accomplishing these goals, the foundation for improving service delivery has been laid. Understanding

TABLE 9.1
Management Methods That Ensure High-Quality Service

Learn and Understand Customer Wants	Emphasize Team Goals	Select and Train the Right People
1. Regularly survey customers.	1. Actively participate, support, recognize, and reward teams in achieving goals.	1. Reinforce basic skills and abilities.
2. Frequently interact with customers.	2. Recognize, reward, and reinforce individual behaviors that support and further team progress.	2. Select employees with the following character traits: • Positive and willing service attitudes, and • Flexible and team-based behaviors
3. Actively seek and listen to front-line employee opinions.	3. Give teams the training, tools, and technology needed to achieve the organization's goals.	
4. Reduce the number of management levels.	4. Train and empower team members to make decisions, solve problems, and make process and service improvements.	

A well-trained team working in harmony.
Photo by A. Talg.

the importance of their individual and team efforts leads to organizational success. Promoting teamwork also serves as a powerful tool for overcoming problems created by cultural differences as well as generating shared understandings, building appreciation across functions and between individuals, and increasing skill and knowledge levels.

Teams can be developed and supported by management in a variety of ways. First, management can convey team spirit by being an active member of the team. Employees should be hired, trained, and supported so that all team members know their jobs and can carry their shares of the load to achieve the team's common goals. Team members also need to be supported with well-maintained and appropriate technology. Finally, team members should be able to make decisions without constantly having to check with a supervisor.

Some companies allow employees to make decisions using their own best judgment. Other firms train employees to handle a wide variety of customer scripts and problem situations. Management should take on the role of coach rather than boss so that the entire team can win.[10] After all, management is ultimately responsible for continually improving the service quality delivered to guests.

SERVICE MISTAKES

As illustrated in the chapter opener, although management and employees may want to delight guests in each and every service encounter, problems can occur. Fortunately, most consumers are willing to forgive "service mistakes" when appropriate responses to them occur. What constitutes a service mistake that can result in a guest being dissatisfied? In simple terms, a mistake occurs when the customer's expectations are not met—when a customer's "service script"[3] is broken. We have learned that customer's script expectations develop from word-of-mouth and marketing communications, from personal needs and from past experiences. When customers experience an unexpected change from their **expected script,** we call this a "break from the script."

A tourism-focused research study investigated these breaks from customers' scripts.[11] Interestingly, the researchers found that there were two categories of breaks from a script. The first type of break is a *positive* change from what the customer expects. For example, a particularly cheerful and efficient front desk clerk who provides a suggestion for a good, inexpensive place to dine that evening might be perceived as a pleasant change from the expected script—a "positive break" from the script. Positive breaks lead to highly memorable and highly satisfying service encounters that guests enjoy recounting to friends.

Unfortunately, the opposite type of break also can occur. When a change from the expected script is *negative*, the customer will be dissatisfied. If a front desk clerk doesn't look up from the TV program he is watching when a guest approaches the desk, the guest is likely to perceive this behavior as a negative break from her expected script and be more than a little annoyed at the lack of service!

Mistakes Happen

The researchers found that common negative breaks from the script occur from (1) failures in the core service (a broken-down mattress in a hotel room, an overdone, cold steak, or a bus that breaks down mid-tour); (2) unwillingness to accommodate a customer's special need or request (to locate an elderly guest on the ground floor of a hotel, to modify an entree to fit a patron's special dietary needs); and (3) unsolicited tourism employee actions (inattention, rudeness, or thievery on the part of an employee). What was the negative break from the script the Johnsons faced in the chapter opener?

Fortunately, the research team discovered that all is not lost when a negative break from a script occurs. Customers will often give tourism providers a chance to make things right. When a tourism encounter is less than satisfactory, the tourism employee can right the situation and "turn the guest's frown upside down." This reversal of a service problem is called **service recovery.**[12] However, if a mistake is made and the employee does not make a sincere effort to better the guest's situation, highly memorable dissatisfaction occurs.

So the bad news is that mistakes are inevitable in tourism businesses. The good news is that, with proper handling, a negative break from the guest's script can be reversed and turned into an extra satisfying, memorable service encounter. Keep in mind that satisfied guests represent potential future flows of revenues and profits while dissatisfied guests represent future losses because they fail to return and they pass negative word-of-mouth comments to their friends.

Be a Can-Do Problem Solver

Most service unreliability is rooted in poorly designed service processes, inattention to detail, and simple carelessness. The tourism service team members need to have a "do-it-right-the-first-time" spirit. All team members, managers and front-line employees, should constantly search for fail points—steps in the process that are vulnerable to failure. Attention to these details and suggestions on improvements should be paramount in the minds of all team members. But we know that sometimes service will fail. What can be done then to try to retain the customer? Thankfully, there are several ways.

When a customer complains or a service employee somehow senses that a service mistake has occurred, what happens next is critical to customer satisfaction. If the problem is ignored, the customer is likely to be furious and subsequently spread negative comments about the company. If the problem is handled but not to the customer's complete satisfaction, the customer is still likely to be dissatisfied and also speak ill of the experience. However, if the problem is solved, the guest is likely to be pleased and recount the story of the incident to friends. In this way, tourism service providers can take a bad situation and make it positive.

How can tourism managers ensure that problems are handled and their guests leave smiling? To solve problems, employees must know problems exist. Therefore, managers must encourage customers to voice their problems immediately so that employees can solve them. Because most guests are hesitant about voicing complaints, employees should also be trained to recognize problem situations so that they can fix the problem. And the problem solution needs to occur immediately. This quick response handling is most likely to occur when management gives employees the knowledge and authority to solve problems on their own, without having to check with supervisors.

"Making things right" for most customers simply involves doing a few simple things. Customers want acknowledgment that the problem exists. They also like to be told why the problem arose in the first place. Next, they want a sincere apology. Finally, customers want to be made "whole" again. In other words, they want some form of compensation that will lessen the cost of the problem to them. They need to be compensated for any bother or annoyance they perceived or experienced because of the problem. Which of these steps did Mike use in the chapter opener to make things right for the Johnsons?

LAUGH

Need help remembering the problem solution steps? Just LAUGH. Each letter of the word laugh stands for a step on the road to turning a dissatisfying encounter into a satisfying one. **L**isten. Let the guest relate the problem in detail and really listen to what is said. **A**cknowledge that the problem really is important. **U**nderstand. Indicate that you understand the situation by reviewing with the customer what has occurred. **G**ive solutions. Provide the guest with a variety of solutions to the problem and allow him or her to choose the preferred solution. **H**it home with a follow-up. When possible, contact the guest a short time after the problem is solved to make sure that the guest is now satisfied.

Think of a recent tourism service situation in which you were less than satisfied and voiced your dissatisfaction. What happened? Did the service employee respond appropriately as we have just outlined? Did you leave frowning or smiling?

Correcting the immediate mistake and satisfying the customer is a great start to creating a truly service-oriented organization, but there is still more to do. Steps should be taken to make sure that the problem does not recur. This requires figuring out why the mistake happened and making operational or training changes so that it does not happen again.

These changes could be very simple or creative. One example of a simple change would be to color code keys on the cash register to make it easier for employees to ring up correct amounts. A more creative example comes from a theme park in South Korea. Managers were having trouble with employees sticking their hands in their pockets during work. The solution: sew up the pockets until employees broke this annoying habit.

SERVICE GUARANTEES

One way to instill more confidence in guests regarding quality of service is by guaranteeing it. You are probably familiar with guarantees for hard goods. When a good you purchase, for example a portable CD player, proves to be unsatisfactory, producers frequently guarantee your satisfaction by offering you one or more options. In the case of dissatisfaction with a CD player, the manufacturer may replace it, repair it, or refund your money. In the tourism service environment, it is more difficult to use these options. How does one "replace" an unsatisfactory visit to a theme park? How does management "repair" an unpleasant stay at a motel? You could get your money back, but that may not fully satisfy you. In most tourism services, one other important difference exists. You must complain face-to-face to another human being to get your money back or have your problem solved. Many of us do not like the confrontational nature of such direct complaining. Our server may "complain" back or become overly embarrassed by our complaint.

So how can a tourism service provider guarantee service quality? By using a customer satisfaction guarantee that has five important features.[13]

1. The guarantee should be unconditional with regard to the elements that are under the control of the management and employees. Airlines and other transportation providers cannot control the weather but they can control most other aspects of your flight or ride experience.

2. The service guarantee should be easy to understand and communicate to guests. It should be brief and worded very simply. Fine print and legal language should not be used to confuse the customer.

3. The guarantee should be meaningful, guaranteeing an important quality aspect to guests. For example, if speed of service (responsiveness) is an important element of quality to lunch-time restaurant patrons, the restaurant might use the following guarantee: "Your meal in just 5 minutes or it's free!"

4. The guarantee should be easy to collect. The customer should not have to "jump through hoops" to collect, and no guilt should be heaped on the guest for asking for the guaranteed **restitution.**

5. Compensation should be appropriate. How does management decide what is appropriate compensation for a service failure? Management needs to consider the price of the service to the customer in money but also the seriousness of the failure in inconvenience or other bother. Finally, but probably most important, what does the customer think is fair given the problem?

Companies that are excellent at problem-solving give the customer a list of problem solution choices or ask the customer what would make him or her happy. In that way, the customer decides what the guarantee pay-out should be.

SERVICE GUARANTEES

Service guarantees come in many different forms. Some are in the form of a commitment. For example, management at the Best Rest Inn in Boise, Idaho, uses their welcome sign, "We delight every guest, every day, one guest at a time," as a statement of their service commitment. The Hampton Inn chain uses the slogan, "Get what you expect—guaranteed!

Others are more direct and detailed. For example, Holiday Inn calls its service guarantee their Hospitality Promise. The promise is prominently displayed in each guest room. It reads, "Making your stay a complete success is our goal. Just let our Manager on Duty or front desk staff know if any part of your stay isn't satisfactory. We promise to make it right or you won't pay for that part of your stay."

SUMMARY

Quality, hospitality, and satisfaction are all crucial concepts in tourism. To a large extent, quality is like beauty: It is "in the eye of the beholder." The marketing and management challenge lies in identifying how guests judge quality and then measuring these factors so service delivery can be continually improved. Guests judge the quality of a tourism service by five factors; the tangibles of the tourism service, the reliability of the service performance, the responsiveness of employees, the assurance they feel from the tourism provider, and the empathy they are shown during their tourism experience. These five factors combine and yield a guest's overall quality perception.

Guests have expectations of tourism services that they compare to the actual service they receive. This comparison determines the level of satisfaction they feel. Guests can be highly satisfied, just satisfied, or dissatisfied with a tourism service. Quality is more variable in tourism services than in manufactured goods because so many factors can change the quality of the service, from the weather to the mood of the service employee. When guests are dissatisfied with a service, problem-handling becomes paramount. Every effort should be made to fix the problem and satisfy the guest.

Tourism managers can ensure high-quality service and guest satisfaction by researching guest expectations, by acting on employee suggestions for improvements, by hiring and training employees well, and by emphasizing a team approach in service delivery. Providing guarantees for services is also an effective way to reassure customers and to focus employees' attention on the important aspects of service quality.

You Decide

Tourism service mistakes are becoming costly—and not just to tourism service providers. More and more travelers are suing their travel agents when things go wrong on a vacation. There has been a marked increase in claims against travel agents and tour operators in recent years. Why? First, lawsuits to "make things right again" are commonplace in all industries now. Second, travel agents and tour operators are far more accessible than distant service providers such as a resort in Belize. Finally, people are taking far more expensive once-in-a-lifetime trips, for which they have extremely high expectations. When things damage their dream vacation, they look for someone to blame.

People are dragging their travel agents into court for canceled flights, for inferior hotel rooms, even for injuries suffered during a trip. Most court-awarded compensation is small, about one to three thousand dollars, but the increased frequency of such awards has many travel agents purchasing liability insurance.

Prior to the 1980s, travel agents were rarely held accountable if their inadequate research or failure to disclose information caused their client to have a dissatisfying vacation. But in 1986, Regina Tuohey won $25,000 in damages from Trans National Travel Inc. Ms. Tuohey's Caribbean vacation was ruined when she arrived in St. Marten only to discover that the hotel her travel agent had booked for her was under construction and had no electricity. The judge in

the case wrote: "Loss of a year's vacation, long awaited and eagerly anticipated, is an irreplaceable loss." Estimates are that vacation-related lawsuits have doubled or even tripled since that court decision.

Travel agents and tour operators are being encouraged to purchase professional liability insurance to cover them against "errors and omissions." They have also begun asking clients to sign disclaimers; contracts in which clients agree not to hold the travel agent or tour operator responsible for problems outside of their control. For example, Carlson Wagonlit travel agencies print such a disclaimer on every "ticket jacket" they give to their clients.

Vacationers can also win damage awards from tourism service suppliers. For example, in 1990, the Semrod family of New Jersey won $3,000 from Mexicana Airlines because they were bumped off their flight, which resulted in a 24-hour delay. As travelers become more sophisticated and demanding, it may be more difficult—and expensive—to turn that frown upside down! Who do you think should be held responsible for tourism service mistakes?

Sources: Abbott, Je Anna, & Abbott, Steven (1997). Minimizing tour operators' exposure to lawsuits. *Cornell Hotel and Restaurant Administration Quarterly, 38*(2), 20–24; Kettner, Ronald, & Anolik, Alexander (1994). When vacations turn sour, travel agents need E & O insurance. *American Agent and Broker, 66*(10), 67–68; Miller, Lisa (1997, May 2). When vacations go wrong, more travelers sue. *Wall Street Journal*, pp. B1, B5.

Net Tour

To learn more about the concepts and organizations presented in this chapter access the homepage for *Tourism: The Business of Travel*. Select "Chapter 9: Putting Quality into Hospitality." From this location test your knowledge by taking the chapter quiz, read industry insights, and discover links to other useful sites. You may also want to visit electronically with other tourism students through the website.

Discussion Questions

1. Define quality using the many meanings the word can have.

2. Explain why the quality of tourism services is harder to define and manage than the quality of hard goods.

3. How are expectations of a tourism service formed?

4. What is a break from the service script? How do breaks from the script affect customer satisfaction?

5. What should a tourism service employee do to "turn a frown upside down"?

6. What can management do to ensure high-quality service?

APPLYING THE CONCEPTS

1. Use an airline flight to illustrate the variety of factors that can effect the tourism service encounter highlighted in Figure 9.2.

2. Choose a local tourism supplier and rate it on the five dimensions of quality. Why does it rate high, average, or low on each dimension? Be detailed in your answers.

3. Describe a recent tourism service encounter in which a service mistake was handled to your satisfaction or dissatisfaction. What was done, or could have been done, to turn your frown upside down?

4. Develop a service guarantee for a tourism service with which you are familiar. Critique your guarantee using the five important features of service guarantees.

GLOSSARY

Actual quality   The level of quality a consumer perceives following the consumption of a good or service.

Expected quality   The level of quality that a consumer predicts he/she will receive from a good or service.

Expected script   The set of steps and statements that a guest expects to occur during a service encounter.

Market share   The percent of the total market for a good or service that a single company has.

Marketing communications   Any communication between a marketer and a consumer.

Restitution   An amount of money or other item given to make up for some mistake or wrongdoing.

Service encounter   A single episode during which a customer and service personnel interact; often also called a "moment of truth."

Service expectations   The quality level of the five dimensions of service expected by a customer.

Service recovery   The process of reversing a service problem.

Service script   Learned patterns of behavior that guide interactions during a service encounter.

Specification   A detailed written description of a procedure or ingredient.

Standard   A predetermined procedure or amount of an ingredient.

REFERENCES

1. Lovelock, Christopher H. (1996). *Services marketing*. Upper Saddle River, NJ: Prentice-Hall.

2. Buzzell, Robert D., & Gale, Bradley T. (1987). *The PIMS principles: Linking strategy to performance*. New York: The Free Press.

3. Solomon, Michael R., Surprenant, Carol, Czepiel, John A., & Gutman, Evelyn G. (1985). A role theory perspective on dyadic interactions: The service encounter." *Journal of Marketing, 49*, 99–111.

4. Bateson, John E. G. (1995). *Managing services marketing: Text and readings* (3rd ed.). Fort Worth, TX: The Dryden Press/Harcourt Brace College Publishers.

5. Parasuraman, A., Zeithaml, Valarie, & Berry, Leonard (1985). A conceptual model of service quality and its implications for future research. *Journal of Marketing, 49*, 41–50.

6. Oliver, Richard L. (1980). A cognitive model of the antecedents and consequences of satisfaction decisions. *Journal of Marketing Research, 17*, 460–469.

7. Jones, Thomas O., & Sasser, W. Earl, Jr. (1995, November/December). Why satisfied customers defect. *Harvard Business Review*, pp. 88–99.

8. Zeithaml, Valarie, Parasuraman, A., & Berry, Leonard L. (1990). *Delivering quality service*. New York: The Free Press.

9. Schlesinger, Leonard (1991). *Taco Bell Corp*. Harvard Business School case. Cambridge, MA: Harvard Business School Publishing.

10. Berry, Leonard L., Zeithaml, Valarie A., & Parasuraman, A. (1990). Five imperatives for improving service quality. *Sloan Management Review, 31*, pp. 29–38.

11. Bitner, Mary Jo, Booms, Bernard H., & Tetreault, Mary Stanfield (1990). The service encounter: Diagnosing favorable and unfavorable incidents. *Journal of Marketing, 54*, 71–84.

12. Hart, Christopher W.L., Heskett, James L., & Sasser, W. Earl, (1990). The profitable art of service recovery. *Harvard Business Review, 68*, pp. 148–156.

13. Hart, Christopher W.L. (1988). The power of unconditional service guarantees. *Harvard Business Review, 66*, pp. 54–62.

CHAPTER 10

Economic and Political Impacts of Tourism

A frequent first stop for many motoring visitors.
Photo by D.A. Yale.

Nobody goes there anymore; it's too crowded.

—YOGI BERRA

CHAPTER OUTLINE

LEARNING OBJECTIVES

After you have read this chapter, you should be able to:

- Identify and explain the economic benefits of tourism.

- Identify and explain the potential economic problems that can be created by tourism.

- Explain why tourism revenues are considered an export.

- Explain what is meant by the tourism output multiplier effect.

- List the various organizations that help promote tourism.

- Explain how convention centers are used to generate tourism in a city and how these centers can be funded and managed.

- Explain the steps involved in tourism planning.

- Explain why tourism development can lead to political tugs of war.

Chamber Director Headache #1456

Maria Sandoval, Executive Director of the Ocotillo, Arizona, Chamber of Commerce, tossed two extra strength pain relievers into her mouth and washed them down with the lukewarm remains of her second cup of coffee. This was a day she had been dreading. Today, six advertising agencies were making presentations to the Board of Directors of the Chamber of Commerce in attempts to receive the $450,000 annual contract for promoting Ocotillo as a tourism destination.

The selection of which six agencies (out of the forty-five that had submitted written proposals) had been a political nightmare. Most citizens, businesspeople, and government officials agreed that tourism was an economic engine for the local economy, and that the Chamber of Commerce, in its role as development leader, had an obligation to coordinate tourism promotion. However, many locals, including the editor of the *Ocotillo Times*, believed the promotion contract should be granted to a local advertising agency. Maria had received dozens of calls from irate citizens when they learned that four of the six finalist firms were from outside the Ocotillo area.

Maria sympathized with these dissenters. If the agency selection goal were to generate additional jobs, revenue, and tax dollars within the community, it was easy to understand why folks felt that local companies should receive the marketing business. But still, if the primary goal were to bring an increasing number of tourists to the region, and get them to stay longer in the area, shouldn't the most capable firm receive the contract, no matter where that firm was located?

Maria sighed and gathered up the proposals from the six finalist advertising agencies, placing them in her briefcase. It was going to be a long day and a tough decision. But that's why they pay me the big bucks, she chuckled, as she hurried off to the meeting.

Introduction

How important is tourism to your area? What percent of the jobs available in your city or town are in tourism-related businesses? How much tax revenue is raised through taxes paid by tourists on goods and services they purchase during their visits to your region? Whatever the answers to these questions, the worldwide economic impact of tourism is massive (see Tables 10.1 and 10.2). The World Travel and Tourism Council estimated that the world's tourism-related businesses contributed $3.7 trillion dollars to the world's economies in 1995, providing over 200 million jobs around the globe. Incredibly, about 30% of all tourism expenditures are made during trips within the United States or Canada.[1]

TABLE 10.1

Top 10 in International Tourism Receipts, 1995 (excluding international transport)

Rank	Country	Millions in U.S. Dollars	% Share of World Total
1	United States	58,370	15.7
2	France	27,322	7.3
3	Italy	27,072	7.3
4	Spain	25,065	6.7
5	United Kingdom	17,468	4.7
6	Austria	12,500	3.4
7	Germany	11,922	3.2
8	Hong Kong	9,075	2.4
9	China	8,733	2.3
10	Thailand	7,556	2.0

Source: Waters, Somerset R. (1996–97) *Travel industry world yearbook: The big picture.* Rye, NY: Child and Waters, Inc. This information is based on statistics gathered by the World Tourism Organization (WTO).

TABLE 10.2
Top 10 International Tourism Payments, 1995 (excluding international transport)

Rank	Country	Millions in U.S. Dollars	% Share of World Total
1	Germany	47,304	14.7
2	United States	44,825	13.9
3	Japan	35,322	11.0
4	United Kingdom	24,625	7.6
5	France	16,038	5.0
6	Italy	12,366	3.8
7	Netherlands	11,050	3.4
8	Austria	9,500	2.9
9	Canada	9,484	2.9
10	Taiwan	8,595	2.7

Source: Waters, Somerset R. (1996–97). *Travel industry world yearbook: The big picture.* Rye, NY: Child and Waters, Inc. This information is based on statistics gathered by the World Tourism Organization (WTO.)

How do researchers arrive at these estimates of tourism activity? They typically take two steps. First, they estimate the number of "arrivals" at a destination (a city, a state/province, a country). Second, they estimate average expenditures per visitor by surveying samples of travelers or through estimates based on hotel and other tourism-related taxes. Then they multiply these two estimates together to arrive at a total amount of tourism spending in the specific destination. You will find that tourism activity estimates vary widely due to the differences in the methods used to approximate the number of travelers and their expenses as well as the different definitions used to determine just who is a tourist. Some agencies define tourists as individuals who travel more than 50 miles away from home while other agencies may use 100 or even 200 miles. Some require that the person stay overnight at his or her destination while others do not. So when you see statistics like those in the first paragraph of this chapter, realize that other numbers might be quoted from other sources of information, with the difference in the numbers depending on the different methods and definitions used.

NEW ORLEANS

City officials in New Orleans use an unusual measure to determine the success of the annual Mardi Gras festival. They look at the additional tons of garbage collected during the week-long festivities to estimate the number of visitors to the city!

LOOKING TO TOURISM FOR ECONOMIC GROWTH AND VITALITY

The people of every country around the world survive or thrive on the income-producing possibilities of the country's resources. Citizens all over the world need income to provide the necessities of life for themselves and their families. Income options may range from subsistence farming to investment banking. More and more countries are finding that the development of tourism offers an effective means of increasing economic well-being. Debate over appropriate tourism development for an area results in political action—by individuals, special interest groups, and governing officials and bodies. In this chapter, we will begin by discussing why and how tourism activities affect the economic vitality of a region. Then we will look at some of the many ways that politics comes into play to affect and shape the tourism industry.

Economics is the "social science that seeks to understand the choices people make in using their scarce resources to meet their wants" (p. 27).[2] For tourists, these scarce resources are money, available time, and the physical energy to travel. A small amount of any of these three resources will decrease tourists' ability to travel, while a large amount of these three resources will increase tourists' ability to travel. Scarce resources for promoters and suppliers of tourism businesses are human resources (the availability and quality of tourism service employees) and **financial resources** (the amount of money that the developer can raise by borrowing money or by selling stock). Scarce resources for communities or countries are the amount and variety of their natural resources and the pool of human resources available at differing skill levels. Scarce resources for governments are primarily tax revenues that can be used (1) to develop natural and human resources productively and (2) to pay for the many services that governments can provide their citizens.

Comparative Advantage

Many towns and cities, states/provinces, even entire nations, have determined that development of their visitor-inducing resources can add to the economic well-being of local residents. Economic decisions are often based on a concept called **comparative advantage.** Tourism can be said to have a comparative advantage over other industries if it yields a better return from the region's human and natural resource inputs than another industry would. Leaders of many communities believe this comparative advantage exists because of the many economic, social, and environmental benefits tourism offers. Let's take a closer look at how comparative advantage might favor tourism development.

Tourism may have a comparative advantage over other industries in two ways. First, the region may be especially appealing to tourists because

a) it has features that are highly attractive;

b) it may be easily accessible to many potential tourists; and

c) it has the necessary **infrastructure** and an abundant labor force to serve in the tourism industry.

In other words, the area may have the necessary ingredients for both the demand and supply of tourism.

Second, tourism may also be the best industry to develop if there are no other alternatives. For example, many island economies are based on tourism because these small nations have little else of economic value to offer the world. Its citizens, therefore, are best able to achieve a better standard of living through employment in tourism businesses. Due to very limited natural resources (other than beauty), the islanders have few, if any, industrial alternatives. So tourism has the comparative advantage because the island country is at a comparative disadvantage for all other industries.

Tourism and Foreign Exchange Rates

One of the most important factors influencing the level of international tourism to a country is the relative **exchange rate** of its currency for other currencies. When international travelers decide to visit a foreign land, they need to trade their currency for the currency of the nation they will visit. For example, if a U.S. citizen were to take a trip to Spain, he or she would need to trade U.S. dollars for Spanish currency, called "pesetas." A Spanish traveler would do just the reverse if he decided to visit the United States.

Most currency exchange rates vary daily depending on the supply and demand for each currency. The exchange rate of a nation's currency greatly affects the amount of international tourism that a country will experience. For example, in the mid-1980s, the U.S. dollar was one of the strongest currencies in the world; dollars "bought" lots of other currencies, and record numbers of U.S. citizens traveled abroad. However, the relative value of the dollar began to "sink" and the tables soon were turned: International travel by U.S. residents to other countries became quite expensive, but travel to the United States from

TABLE 10.3

Top 10 U.S. States Visited by Overseas Travelers, 1995 (excludes Mexico and Canada)

Rank	State	% of Overseas Market	Visitation (in Thousands)
1	Florida	25.9	5346
2	California	25.7	5304
3	New York	21.7	4479
4	Hawaii	14.1	2910
5	Nevada	9.0	1858
6	Illinois	5.4	1115
7	Massachusetts	5.1	1053
8	Arizona	4.3	887
9	Texas	4.2	867
10	Washington	2.9	599

Source: Waters, Somerset R. (1996–97) *Travel industry world yearbook: The big picture.* Rye, NY: Child and Waters, Inc. Based on information gathered by the U.S. Department of Commerce.

other countries became cheaper so international visitors flocked to the United States in record numbers (see Table 10.3).

To demonstrate how exchange rate changes can effect the cost of a trip, consider the cost of a trip for a Japanese businessman we will call Mr. Nagai. Suppose that the exchange rate is 250 yen to one U.S. dollar. A short business trip might cost Mr. Nagai about $1,000 (for hotel accommodations, meals, etc.). He would have to exchange 250,000 of his hard-earned yen to pay his bills. Suppose the exchange rates change and a few years later when Mr. Nagai makes a similar trip, 100 yen purchase one dollar. In this new case, Mr. Nagai would only have to exchange 100,000 yen. What a bargain compared to the 250,000 he paid before! Is this example impossible? Hardly. Over a 5- or 10-year time period, it is possible for currencies to fluctuate a great deal.

The example of Mr. Nagai shows just how big the difference in purchasing power can be when exchange rates change. During the 1990s, the United States became a very reasonably priced destination for international travelers. In fact, famed tourism economist Somerset Waters stated that visitors find the United States the least expensive rich country. "For visitors from most countries, America represents a shopper's continent-wide, bargain basement" (p. 55).[1]

THE MULTIPLIER EFFECT

Why are tourism expenditures important to an area? And just how big a benefit do they have? One of the most common measures of the economic impact of tourism is called the **output multiplier effect.** Money is added to an area when someone from outside its borders buys a good or service produced within the area. In addition, this new money to the area is respent, generating additional value. Tourism is usually a very good source of new money for an area because visitors travel to the area and "leave" their money behind as they buy goods and services during their visit.

Realizing Tourism's Export Potential

Let us first focus on the multiplier effect of tourism expenditures from an export point of view. An **export** is defined as a good or service manufactured or provided in one country that is purchased by a person or business from another country. Exports therefore "add" money to one economy and "deduct" money from another economy. Most countries desire international visitors because tourism services sold to foreign travelers are considered exports.

Faces from around the world become familiar through tourism.
Photo courtesy of VIA Rail Canada Inc.

For example, when an Irish businessman travels to Toronto and spends money on restaurant meals, taxicabs, and hotel rooms, some of the money and purchasing power he earned in Ireland becomes part of Canada's economy. In this way, the tourism receipts from his visit add to the Canadian economy the same way that selling a Canadian manufactured good in Dublin would. Likewise, his tourism expenses represent an **import** in Ireland, the same way that a manufactured good does because the traveler's money left Ireland and was gained by Canada.

Here is a more detailed example of a tourism export. Imagine that an Australian family decides to vacation in California, taking in all the entertainment attractions and recreational activities that it has to offer. They arrive at LAX airport and then spend seven fun-and-sun-filled days experiencing Southern California. Think of all the expenses they incur during their week-long visit: meals, rental car and gasoline, admissions, souvenirs, accommodations, and a host of other services. The family pays for all these services and goods by spending the money they brought with them from Australia to cover all these expenses. This money represents "new" money for the U.S. economy and for California in particular. This exchange is an export for the U.S. and represents an import for Australia because the family purchased foreign goods and services with their Australian money rather than spending their money at home.

What Goes Around Comes Around

The multiplier concept also applies to domestic travel. Imagine you have a friend, Sam, who goes to college and works in Bloomington, Indiana. Sam decides to spend spring break vacation in Fort Lauderdale, Florida. She takes her hard-earned money and "leaves" it in Florida as she pays for her travel needs there. In other words, the purchasing power Sam earned in the Bloomington economy is transferred to the economy of Fort Lauderdale, and the businesses and citizens there benefit from it (see Figure 10.1).

But how does this money "multiply"? The output multiplier effect occurs when some of this new money is respent within the local economy. For example, while in Fort Lauderdale, Sam had dinner at a local hot spot, dining, dancing, and having a wonderful evening. Her total bill for the evening of fun came to $45. The lion's share of the $45 she paid was then used to pay Joe, her server, as well as the bartender, the dishwasher, the

FIGURE 10.1
Output Multiplier Effect

1. Sam leaves her home in Bloomington, IN, with $500 dollars. She is going to Fort Lauderdale, FL, for spring break.

2. Sam pays way too much for a lobster tail at an expensive restaurant on the intercoastal waterway. But what the heck – she's on vacation. Sam's waiter Joe goes the extra mile for her, recommending a few great night spots and even draws Sam a walking map. Sam is so grateful she tips Joe $25.

3. Joe worked 7 days a week for the past 3 weeks. He hasn't had time to get a haircut, do his laundry, or even visit the bank. He decides to go see his hairdresser Sarah and get a haircut – $25 with tip.

4. "Good thing Joe came in today," Sarah thinks. "His $10 tip was the only tip of the day. I've got to start cutting a better class of hair." Sarah looks down as she is driving and notices she's almost out of gas. She pulls over and puts the $10 in her tank.

5. The owner of the gas station lets out a sigh of relief as Sarah pays him. He was just shy of $10 to cover his payroll deposit – he can go to the bank now and then go home and relax for the rest of the weekend.

And the continued to move through the economy increasing the multiplier effect.

city's local taxes (sales, property, and income), the manager's salary, the local bakery for that delicious bread—you get the idea. In this way, the purchasing power of Sam's $45 is multiplied because it then becomes Joe's purchasing power, which he can use to purchase goods and services he needs. When Joe spends "Sam's share" of his paycheck on a haircut, Sam's purchasing power multiplies again, and now becomes purchasing power to be used by the hairdresser. And so on.

However, all of that new purchasing power that has been added to the Fort Lauderdale economy does not stay in the local economy forever because of **leakage.** Just as Sam took some of her purchasing power from Bloomington to Fort Lauderdale, that purchasing power will eventually leak out of the Fort Lauderdale area. For example, Joe's hairdresser could purchase gasoline for his car. Relatively little of the money he pays for gasoline gets to stay in the local economy because the gas station owner needs to purchase gasoline made from oil from another country. By purchasing this import, the purchasing power has "leaked" out of the Fort Lauderdale economy so it is no longer available for locals to use within the area. The faster the leakage, the lower the output multiplier effect.

Tracking the Impact of Tourism Expenditures

How big or small can this multiplier effect be? Tourism researchers and economists have tried to estimate the tourism output multiplier effect for countries, regions and even cities. For example, Adrian Bull[3] reported that the tourism multiplier effect for Canada is approximately 2.5: For every new dollar injected into the Canadian economy from an international visitor, $2.50 of purchasing power is generated over time before that original dollar is leaked out through expenditures on imports coming into Canada.

Multipliers are an indicator of the economic independence of a country. The higher the multiplier, the more economically self-sufficient the country. Some countries such as Ireland, Turkey, the United Kingdom, and the United States have multiplier factors of approximately 2 or more. Other countries experience much lower multiplier effects, for example, 0.64 for Iceland and 0.39 for Western Samoa.[4] Although island countries tend to depend on tourism for economic growth, they also have very quick leakage and, therefore, very low output multipliers because almost all goods associated with tourism need to be imported to the area. These imports may be as simple as the food and beverages served to visitors or as complex and costly as the steel to build the hotels.

OTHER ECONOMIC IMPACTS

In addition to the output multiplier benefit, tourism offers other positive economic benefits. First, tourism can provide stability in an economy. Although recessions affect virtually all industries, tourism historically has seen relatively minor declines in revenue during recessionary times. As we mentioned in Chapter 2, business travel remains relatively constant during changes in economic cycles. And, even though people may cut back on the amount they spend on travel during harder economic times, citizens of most industrial nations have come to view vacationing as a necessity of life.

Second, tourism provides economic diversity. A stable economy is one that provides jobs and revenues from a variety of industries. Tourism can be added as another economic engine to the industry mix. Obviously, the addition of any industry to a community will increase the employment opportunities of that community. However, unlike many other industries, tourism provides a wide variety of job possibilities, such as

a) entry-level employment for relatively unskilled and semiskilled workers;
b) positions for highly skilled craftspersons, such as chefs and artists; and
c) many professional-level career opportunities for well-educated decision-makers.

Third, tourism often provides the economic incentive to improve infrastructure that can be enjoyed by residents as well as tourists. For example, state-of-the-art airports are built by communities primarily to increase accessibility, thereby enticing more visitors and increasing business activity. But the airport can also be used by locals to meet their travel needs.

Tourism offers a fourth additional positive impact that *you* may find particularly appealing. Unlike most manufacturing-based enterprises, a tourism business can be started in the form of a small business. In this way, the tourism industry can be used to encourage **entrepreneurial** activity. Have you ever considered developing your own business? Many people today like the idea and challenge of being their own boss. Tourism provides plenty of chances for creative, motivated individuals to start their own businesses. Small retail shops, restaurants, bed and breakfast homes, and guide and taxi services are just a few of the many tourism-related small business opportunities.

Tourism can offer the opportunity to make income from a personal interest or special skill. For example, two Columbia University graduate students developed a business based on their love of urban history. Seth Kamil and Ed O'Donnell started Big Onion Walking Tours in New York City to earn income to pay for school expenses. Seth's major in urban and ethnic history has really paid off. In 1996, the company had 10 guides and was conducting over 700 walking tours, 25% more tours than in 1995.

Source: Plotkin, Hal (1996, August). Student uprising. *Inc.*, pp. 30–38.

So tourism has many economic benefits. But, unfortunately, the development of tourism is not without drawbacks. Up to this point, we have been looking at the economics of tourism through rose-colored glasses. Next we will consider some of the not-so-positive economic effects tourism can yield.

Potential Problems in Tourism-Based Economies

Like all industries, tourism has the potential for negative as well as positive impacts. Overdependence on tourism can lead to a dangerous lack of economic diversity, so that a major event affecting tourism can threaten an area's economy. In the early 1990s, Hawaii was hit by a triple whammy. Its two prime market areas, California and Japan, both slipped into recessions and then the islands were bashed by Hurricane Hugo. The state struggled through several years of an economic slump before it regained the level of tourism activity (and economic prosperity) that it enjoyed in 1990.[5,6] Florida, Mexico, and many Caribbean island countries can suffer similar catastrophic declines in their economies due to the relatively frequent occurrence of hurricanes. In 1995, six hurricanes pounded the Caribbean region, inflicting billions of dollars of damage to hotels and other facilities. Hurricane Marilyn in September 1995 crippled the tourism industry of St. Thomas in the U.S. Virgin Islands. By Christmas of that year, only about 60% of the hotel room capacity was available to welcome arriving tourists (p. 14).[7]

The Caribbean islands are suffering now more than ever because of their tourism-only-based economies. When the cruise industry began to flourish, cruise ships brought thousands of eager spenders to the islands and boosted the economy. However, the trend in the cruise business now is to provide more on-board shopping and recreational opportunities. Although cruise passengers represent almost half of the international visitors to the Caribbean, they now generate only 10% of tourist revenue.[8] Many cruise lines, such as Holland America Cruise Line and the Disney Cruise Line, have even acquired their own private islands where their guests can play. Because these islands are owned by the cruise lines, no local island economy gains much benefit of tourism revenues generated on them.

Tourism can also highlight too much of a good thing and bring too many visitors to an area. By showcasing the beauty and other tourism resources of an area, tourism marketers can increase the popularity of the area and bring in many more people interested in playing and living there. This increase in demand frequently leads to increased prices for goods and services as well as higher housing and land values. Occasionally, this problem becomes so severe that workers can no longer afford to live near their work. Such an impact has occurred in the beautiful central California beach towns and many mountain towns of the Rocky Mountain states and provinces.

Large increases in the number of tourists to an area usually increases costs of providing services for both the increased numbers of tourists and the increased number of residents. Services such as police and fire protection can be strained by increases in the numbers of visitors, while school systems can be strained by increases in new residents who decide to move to their favorite travel destination. Utilities, and other infrastructure resources such as roads, can also feel the strain from increases in the numbers of visitors and residents and the development required to serve their needs.

Tourism in the Economic Balance

Determining whether the total economic impact of tourism will be positive or negative is not an easy task. Many decision-makers are turning to **cost–benefit analysis** for help. By using cost–benefit analysis, dollar values are assigned to the benefits of tourism (such as increased tax revenues and increased employment opportunities) as well as the costs associated with tourism (such as the increased need for utilities, schools, and police protection). If the value of the positive impacts (the benefits) is greater than the value of the negative impacts (the costs), the total economic impact of tourism is positive. If the costs are larger than the benefits, then tourism may not be the economic engine it is often believed to be. Recently, to be as thorough as possible, decision-makers have tried to quantify difficult-to-value plusses and minuses (such as increased entertainment options for residents and increased crowding and traffic jams) to include these benefits and costs in the equation.[2]

So, as you can see, tourism can have both positive and negative economic impacts. How, then, are tourism development decisions made and who is involved in the decision-making process? In the next section, we will look at how governments and citizens try to make choices concerning the development and growth of tourism.

TOURISM AND POLITICS

Remember, economics is all about decisions concerning scarce resources. Politics is about how decisions concerning the public are made. Therefore, in a democratic society, economic decisions that can affect large groups of people are likely to involve some political process. An easy way to define politics is "[P]olitics is about power, who gets what, where, how, and why."[9] So politics is about decision-making; how decisions are made, who is involved in the process and how decisions are implemented. The politics of tourism is usually about how decisions concerning use of scarce resources are made. In a way, economics is about the *quantity of life*, while politics involves debates over the *quality of life*.

Often, decision-making about promoting and developing tourism does not happen through a rational decision-making process in which all interested parties have a chance to voice their opinions or vote for their favorite alternatives. Frequently, the most influential "players" in tourism are outsiders—developers from other areas, even other countries, who see profit opportunities from developing tourism-related businesses. Development of tourism in an area frequently leads to heated political debates over the benefits and costs of tourism, creating political tugs of war among constituent groups (covered later in the chapter).

The Role of Government in Tourism

Governments, from the local to the national level, can and often do play an important role in tourism development. Why do governments devote scarce funds to the promotion and development of tourism? As we discussed in the first half of the chapter, tourism can provide many economic benefits. First, a wide variety of jobs are created through the development of the hotels, restaurants, retail shops, and other facilities and services needed to satisfy the needs of travelers. Second, additional jobs are generated to serve the needs of the employees of the tourism industry. These job-holders earn wages that, in turn, are re-spent in the local economy, creating the multiplier effect. Third, and maybe most important from a government perspective, tax revenues are boosted by taxing the goods and services that visitors buy. By taxing visitors, a portion of the tax burden is shifted from local residents to tourists (see Table 10.4).

For example, the small country of Monaco receives virtually all of its tax revenues from taxes paid by tourists, primarily through Monaco's famous gaming casinos.[3] Communities and other governmental units commonly tax hotel rooms, restaurant meals, and gasoline, and often add **passenger facility charges** on departing flights from the local

TABLE 10.4
Examples of Tourism-Related Taxes

City	Hotel/ Lodging Tax	Restaurant Tax	Gasoline Tax per Gallon	Auto Rental		
				Base Tax Rate	Dollar Surcharge	Off Airport Fees
Baltimore	12.00%	5.00%	$0.19	11.50%		
Chicago	14.90%	9.75%	$0.484	18.00%	$2.75/rental	
Houston	15.00%	8.25%	$0.384	10.00%		6%
San Francisco	14.00%	8.50%	$0.450	8.50%		7%
New York	13.25%	8.25%	$0.413	13.25%		
Miami	12.50%	8.50%	$0.476	6.50%	$2.05/day	
Seattle	15.20%	8.20%	$0.414	11.50%		4%
Washington, DC	13.00%	10.00%	$0.384	10.00%	$1.25/day	4%

Note: While many in the tourism industry believe these tax revenues should be used for travel/tourism programs, much of it goes directly to the general fund or to programs unrelated to travel. Airline taxes collected from travelers are significant revenue sources for the Federal Government. Consumers pay a 10% federal air ticket tax on each airline ticket sold in the United States. Additionally many airports impose a passenger facility charge (PFC).
Source: Travel Taxes in America's TOP Destinations (1996, January). Washington, DC: Travel Industry Association of America.

airport. These tax revenues can then be used to further develop and promote tourism or, as is common, to improve the quality of life by funding services for local citizens.

National and state/provincial governments can support tourism development by performing many activities. These actions can include collection of tourism information, regulation of tourism-related businesses such as airlines, international promotion of tourism, encouragement of development of tourist areas (especially by funding infrastructure or providing government-backed loans), and development of tourism policy. In some countries, the national government actually takes part in the tourism industry through government ownership of certain businesses such as hotel chains, tour companies, and airlines. In the United States and Canada, government agencies are an integral part of the management of a valuable tourism resource—the national park systems. However, more and more national governments are getting out of the tourism businesses through **privatization** and limiting their roles to tourism promotion and regulation.[10] For example, in the mid-1980s, the government of New Zealand owned hotels, tour companies, and the national airline. Since then, the New Zealand government has privatized virtually all of these tourism enterprises.[11]

GREEN BAY

Did you know that the citizens of Green Bay, Wisconsin, own the National Football League team the Green Bay Packers? Unlike so many other teams, we won't be seeing the Packers leaving their city for greener pastures!

Governments can also aid tourism development by financing necessary infrastructure such as roads and airports and by offering government-backed low-interest loans to private developers who develop **superstructure** facilities. Recently, many local governments, aided through state funds, have attempted to revitalize inner-city areas and turn them into leisure, entertainment, and shopping meccas.[10] Local governments can also sponsor "hallmark tourist events" like the Superbowl or a World's Fair to generate increased visits and gain publicity for the region that can pay off in the future. Think of the international awareness that will be generated for Salt Lake City by its hosting of the 2002 Winter Olympic Games!

TABLE 10.5
Top 10 U.S. State Tourism Office Budgets.

Rank	State	1996–97 Budget	% Change from Previous Year
1	Illinois	32,756,500	+4
2	Hawaii	25,319,907	+3
3	Texas	22,990,979	+11
4	Pennsylvania	18,490,000	+22
5	Virginia	17,436,922	+34
6	Florida	17,000,000	+1
7	Massachusetts	16,933,000	+17
8	South Carolina	16,173,870	+1
9	Louisiana	15,422,254	+13
10	New York	14,500,000	0

Source: Waters, Somerset R. (1996–97). *Travel industry world yearbook: The big picture.* Rye, NY: Child and Waters, Inc. Based on U.S. Travel Data Center statistics.

Tourism Promotion Agencies

Many governments have an agency that is charged with promoting tourism (see Table 10.5). At the national level, this agency is called a "national tourism organization/office" or the NTO. National and state/provincial governments fund such offices to fulfill two primary functions. First, the government agency collects visitor and industry information that can be used by tourism businesses to become more successful and grow, employing more citizens and generating more tax revenues. Visitor information is often gathered at welcome centers run by states, provinces, cities, and towns. Second, government agencies promote entire areas as destinations. Tourism businesspeople are usually unable or unwilling to fund advertising that does not expressly sell their individual businesses. But we know that tourists are first sold on a destination area and then look to buy specific services to fulfill particular travel needs, such as hotel accommodations, restaurant meals, guide services, etc. So national and state/provincial governments engage in destination marketing to generate sizable numbers of tourists. Individual tourism-related businesses are rarely able to afford ad campaigns large enough to create a distinctive destination image.

Many towns and cities also have agencies that are charged with attracting visitors. Sometimes counties have an organization to market the county as a tourism destination. There are even a few organizations that promote a set of states or provinces, such as Ski Country USA and the Blue Ridge Parkway Association. Regional tourism promotion organizations can even be cross-border. For example, the Council of Great Lakes Governors and the provincial governments of Ontario and Quebec joined efforts to establish the Great Lakes Circle Trail to encourage travel on both sides of the Great Lakes.[12]

PUBLIC/PRIVATE ORGANIZATIONS

Decisions concerning tourism promotion are complicated and raise many questions. Should more be spent on leisure travelers or should the bulk of funds be spent trying to attract conferences and other meetings to the area? Should a mass marketing strategy be used, trying to attract any and all comers to the area or should segmentation and targeting be used to attract a specific group? In addition, organizations need to determine how much money should be spent on attracting tourists from their own region, from outside their region, and from outside the country.

A common way for tourism promotion and development decisions to be made and funded is through **public/private organizations** or partnerships. A public/private partnership is an organization whose members include government officials as well as private citizens. A tourism-related public/private organization usually has a membership composed of local or state government officials, tourism business owners and managers, and

TOURISM IN ACTION

No longer does the United States have a government-funded national tourism organization (NTO). In 1961, the United States began a national tourism office within the Department of Commerce to promote international tourism to the United States, but the office was never well funded. For example, in 1985 when U.S. tourism promotion funding was at a relatively high level of $12 million, 23 nations (including Greece and Italy) outspent the United States on travel promotion. In 1996, Congress voted to suspend all funding of the office and, in effect, ended federal support of the U.S. tourism industry.

Canada has taken a different path. In 1994, the national government joined with private tourism members and formed the Canadian Tourism Commission (CTC) to coordinate the promotion of Canada's abundant tourism resources both internationally and domestically. The CTC also supports and oversees the development of Canada's tourism industry. In its first year, private tourism businesses contributed $40 million and the federal government funded

$50 million toward support of the new public/private partnership. Budgets in subsequent years have exceeded $150 million with the majority of funds now provided by the private industry partners instead of the Canadian government through its citizens' taxes. Since the beginning of this new joint venture, Canada has steadily risen in the ranking of the World Tourism Organization's travel destinations. In 1995, Canada moved from 12th to 11th position, and in 1996, Canada broke into the top 10.

The CTC has developed into a successful partnership among Canada's tourism private sector, the provincial and territorial governments, and the federal government. Many tourism industry members in the United States hope for the development of such a partnership to replace the United States Travel and Tourism Administration. But so far, no such organization has been created. Only time will tell if the United States can maintain its high rank as an international visitor destination against better-organized and better-funded competitors such as Canada.

Sources: Various Canadian *Tourism Commission Communique* issues; Frechtling, Douglas (1996, March). America's wake-up call. *Tourism management*, pp. 139–141; Lavery, Patrick, & Van Doren, Carlton (1990). *Travel and tourism*. Sussex, England: St. Edmundsbury Press.

local citizens. These partnerships are being used more and more to fund the promotion and development of tourism. Often, the government partner funds infrastructure improvements; the private enterprise partners fund the superstructure (often with the help of tax incentives); and then together the government and private business partners fund tourism promotion through contributions and the collection of special tourism related taxes, such as a room tax.[13]

Chambers of Commerce and Convention and Visitors Bureaus

Two common examples of local public/private tourism promotion organizations are chambers of commerce and convention and visitors bureaus. As suggested in the chapter opener, in smaller communities, chambers of commerce often perform the tourism promotion role (as well as many other economic and business developmental roles). Frequently, as communities grow, the tourism promotion role is conducted through a special organization called a **convention and visitors bureau.** In very large cities, Chicago for example, responsibility for attracting tourists is further divided. Promotion to leisure travelers rests with the Chicago Tourism Council while attracting professional travelers is the concern of the Chicago Convention and Visitors Bureau. A priority of all of these types of organizations is literally to put their area on the map by educating prospective visitors and meeting planners about the destination.

Convention Centers

Convention centers are also frequently public/private organizations. An increasing number of cities worldwide have been developing and renovating convention center facilities to attract the professional traveler segment of tourism. As you learned in Chapter 2, a major portion of the professional traveler segment involves meetings. This "meetings" market is composed of two subsegments, conventions and trade shows. Convention centers are designed to serve the special needs of conventions and trade shows and range from tiny facilities that are little more than a single large room to immense complexes that can hold tens of thousands of conventioneers (see Figure 10.2). For example, the

FIGURE 10.2
Example of a Trade Show Layout

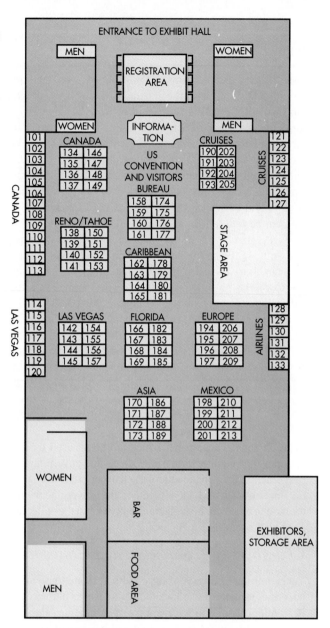

All booths are 10'x12' and all aisles are at least 10' wide
Booths = ▭

Dallas Convention Center in Texas now boasts a total size of over 2 million square feet—equivalent to 42 football fields.

In the 1990s, cities engaged in a "space race" with more and more cities expanding or building centers, trying to edge each other out to be the biggest and the newest. The reason for this convention center building frenzy? Lots of revenues. The average convention center in the United States generates tourism receipts of about $68 million per year.[14] Because of this potential economic payoff, virtually every large city (and many smaller ones, too) invested in convention center facilities during the 1990s.

Marketing to attract convention and trade show business is very different from efforts used to entice leisure travelers. Single decision-makers, or more commonly a small committee of decision-makers, decide where to locate their group's convention, meeting, or trade show. This decision process usually begins years before the event takes place, re-

Convention centers are magnets for business and professional travelers.
Photo courtesy of the Los Angeles Convention and Visitors Bureau.

quiring the coordination of many tourism-related businesses in developing a proposal presented to the site selection committee. Key determinants for these site decisions are price, size, and quality of facilities and a wide variety of amenities or add-ons that will likely encourage prospective attendees to sign up for the convention or trade show. Convention centers need a staff of knowledgeable and efficient people to sell the center and ensure that conventioneers/trade show participants are satisfied with their experience and will return in some future year.

Convention centers are funded and managed in a variety of ways. Some are funded and managed by local governments. Some are public/private **joint ventures** while others are completely financed and managed as nonprofit private associations of tourism-related businesses. Often the convention center facilities are built with public money, usually a combination of city and state funds. The annual marketing and operating costs are covered through tourism-related taxes, membership fees, and revenues generated directly from services provided at the center and sold to attendees. But most centers lose money. For example, the huge McCormick Place center in Chicago loses about $30 million dollars annually.[14] However, given what you now know about the economics of tourism and the multiplier effect, you can see that the state of Illinois and its citizens stand to gain incalculable revenues from the money spent by convention visitors on other tourist services during their stays. In a nutshell then, the primary purpose of most convention centers is to attract greater numbers of visitors—to put "heads-in-beds"—encouraging more tourism expenditures and generating additional tax revenues.

TOURISM PLANNING

Another major function of government and **nonprofit tourism associations** is **tourism planning.** Planning involves predicting the future, setting objectives to attain future outcomes, and then outlining and implementing the actions needed to attain these objectives. You now realize that tourism is a conglomeration of many industries and needs the coordination of a wide variety of enterprises and agencies to thrive. However, because so many organizations are involved in the industry, planning is not easy.

Tourism planning is a continuous process and involves many steps to develop and sustain tourism revenues. A wide variety of decisions must be made, including the timing of development, size of the infrastructure and the superstructure, targeting of promotional campaigns, and efforts to enhance and preserve attraction resources. In addition, plans must include studies of the increased burdens on resources such as water, roads, and police and fire protection, and how the strains on these resources can be met or minimized. Table 10.6 provides a list of the basic steps that must be included in a comprehensive tourism plan.[15]

Usually tourism planning rests with a government agency, typically at the state/provincial and local levels, although many countries have strong national organizations as well. Government agencies are often charged with conducting research and making predictions concerning likely tourism industry trends. Based on research results, plans can be drawn up to achieve the desired level of tourism activity to maximize benefits and minimize the costs that can occur.

Here is an example of tourism planning. In the 1980s, the state of New York conducted a study that indicated that the state's ski industry would soon decline due to changing demographics. The aging of the region's population and the change in its ethnic mix toward ethnic groups that did not traditionally ski, such as Hispanics, suggested a gloomy future for the state's winter tourism season. The state and ski industry members joined together in a cooperative campaign to bolster the skier segment through learn-to-ski discount packages and a promotion campaign to encourage skiers to ski more often.[12]

Through tourism planning, states and provinces can also encourage more widespread tourism development. In many cases, tourism is concentrated within a relatively small area. By conducting research, funding infrastructure, and providing direction and limited funding, a state or province can help develop attractions that entice the tourists from primary travel areas to other areas throughout the state or province. Agencies in Georgia took a variety of steps to encourage attendees of the Atlanta Olympic Games to venture out to other Georgia locales and spread tourism dollars throughout the state.

A tourism planning organization, whether at the national, state/provincial, or local level, needs to modify and refine its plan continually. First, research to learn the changing trends in market segments needs to be conducted regularly, along with studying emerging economic impacts of tourism (both positive and negative). Second, planners must constantly gain and enhance the cooperation of the industry sectors to ensure effective promotion and delivery of high-quality tourism services to visitors. Third, planners need to determine if changes in priorities for tourism marketing are needed. For example, research may show that the area has successfully developed the domestic tourism market and now should start developing international promotion campaigns. Or maybe the idea of hosting a hallmark event, such as a World's Fair or Olympic games, should be seriously considered. Last, but certainly not least, planners need to monitor and preserve the very resources that attracted visitors in the first place. Often these resources are fragile

TABLE 10.6
Steps in the Tourism Planning Process

1. Determination of tourism development **policies** and **objectives.**
2. Survey and inventory of existing situation.
3. Analysis of survey/inventory information.
4. Determination of scope of tourism development needed to achieve objectives.
5. Recommendations for specific projects in specific locations.
6. Implementation of the projects.
7. Monitoring of the plan to determine if objectives are being achieved.
8. Modifications made to the plan as the future unfolds and new objectives become important.

Adapted from Inskeep, Edward (1991). *Tourism planning: An integrated and sustainable development approach.* New York: Van Nostrand Reinhold.

natural or heritage sites so plans must include ways to protect them from erosion and harm so that they are preserved for future enjoyment.

POLITICAL "TUGS OF WAR" OVER TOURISM

Under "Tourism and Politics," we defined politics as power and about who gets what. Whenever a finite amount of resources, especially financial resources, needs to be allocated, there will always be tugs of war among providers and users of these resources. In politics, groups with common needs or wants are called **constituent groups.** In the world of tourism, these constituent groups include:

- tourism business owners,
- employees of tourism businesses,
- other business owners/managers/employees,
- government officials,
- government employees,
- taxpayers,
- local community/region citizens, and
- tourists.

Each of these constituent groups has its own set of priorities concerning how resources, especially tax dollars, should be used. In addition, these groups also have differences in opinion concerning issues such as the quality of life. For example, some people believe jobs and higher incomes (quantity of life) are the basis for attaining quality of life for citizens, while others believe environmental and cultural aspects are equally or even more important.

Tourism business owners want the number of tourists traveling to their area to increase so that their investments generate more income and profits. Employees of these businesses want secure employment with fair wages and safe working conditions. Business owners, managers and employees in other industries want the continued growth and success of their businesses. Government officials want strong economies and to be reelected, while government employees want job security and good wages. Taxpayers want a wide variety of government services and a bearable tax burden. Local residents want a clean, safe community with a high quality of life. Tourists want enjoyable and safe places to visit that offer a full range of services to meet their travel needs.

Unfortunately, with all of these differing objectives, it is difficult for decision-makers to please all constituents. Frequently, a decision for the benefit of one group is often seen as negative by another group. Local taxpayers may welcome the tax revenues generated by visitors to the area but then fight additional tourism development because it would change the landscape of the region and add to the industrialization of the community. Tourism business owners strongly support the promotion of their industry by governments, but owners of businesses in other industries often believe that their industry should receive equal government support. Rarely is there enough tax revenue to promote all industries so priorities must be established. Determining priorities is where the political tug of war among constituent groups occurs.

You may live now (or have lived) in an area that has experienced a tourism development political battle. We hope you now have a better understanding of the economic and political impacts of tourism development and promotion and how different perspectives can lead to debate. The words of tourism writer Uel Blank may give some food for thought concerning tourism development: "Citizens' rights to enjoy amenities of lakes, cities, and facilities away from home carry with them the responsibility to also share local amenities with travelers from elsewhere."[16]

HOW FRIENDLY IS YOUR TOWN?

1. Are the main routes into the area equipped with visitor information centers?
2. Does the airport have a full range of visitor information resources?
3. Do front-line visitor contact personnel, such as taxi and bus drivers, receive formal hospitality training?
4. Do hotels and motels offer in-house television channels with information about local sites, transportation, restaurants, and special events?
5. Is a single organization responsible for generating visitor business to the area?
6. Does that organization have a marketing profile of visitors, and is this profile used in developing marketing activities?
7. Does the area accommodate international visitor needs?
8. Is there a range of accommodations provided to match the range of visitors expected?
9. Are attractions and events easily available and affordable?
10. Do visitor service personnel and the local citizens welcome visitors and accommodate their needs with flexible hours, parking availability, etc.?

Adapted from Kotler, Philip, Haider, Donald H., & Rein, Irving (1993). *Marketing places*. New York: The Free Press, p. 228.

The international tourism arena is also effected by political tugs of war. One of the most noticeable deterrents to international tourism is the threat of terrorism. You may recall the terrorist attack on tourists in Egypt during November 1997. Tour operators and individuals alike shunned Egypt after this chilling incident. Even the threat of terrorist activities will cause tourists to rethink their travel plans. As you recall from Chapter 1, a feeling of safety is one of the necessary conditions for high levels of tourism activities.

SUMMARY

Economics and politics are forever linked, and the economics and politics of tourism are no exception to that rule. The use of scarce resources by the tourism industry can lead to a variety of positive economic impacts, as well as some not-so-positive effects. Virtually, everyone has an opinion about tourism, and the process of deciding the role tourism will play in the economic development of an area gives rise to a great deal of political debate.

As you learned in this chapter, the tourism industry is often used to bring added economic vitality to an area and frequently has a comparative advantage over other development alternatives. A primary reason for tourism's popularity as an industry is its ability to generate new money for a region, especially in the form of exports.

Tourism revenues enter an economy and then are respent, creating additional revenues until the added money finally leaves the economy through leakage—money spent on imports to the area. This increased economic activity is called the "multiplier effect," and its size depends on the amount of imports a region needs to utilize to provide goods and services for visitors and residents alike.

Even though tourism adds diversity and stability to an economy and provides a wide variety of employment, business opportunities, and increased tax revenues, it is not without its costs. Large numbers of visitors strain utilities, public services, and natural resources. Often, these tourists also put upward pressure on prices, which increases the cost of living for local citizens. Researchers use cost–benefit analysis to try to determine if, all things considered, tourism brings substantial economic gain to an area.

Given the importance of the tourism industry to most countries, states/provinces, and cities, governments often become involved in tourism development. The most common role for government is collection of data on tourist activity and promotion of the area

Old Faithful geyser in Yellowstone National Park——always true to its name! *Photo by D.A.Yale.*

London——renowned for its courtesy toward visitors.
Photo by C.E.Yale.

National parks preserve priceless tourism assets for future generations to enjoy.   *Photo by Dusk Edwards, courtesy of Fort Lewis College.*

Pilgrims to Jerusalem continue to arrive even in times
of political unrest.
Photo by C.E. Yale.

Spain's rich cultural traditions make it one of the world's most visited countries.   *Photo by C.E. Yale.*

A culture's unique beauty and art are showcased in its handicrafts.
Photo by C.E. Yale.

The next generation of supersonic travel.
Photo courtesy of The Boeing Company.

Tourism, like Australia's Ayers Rock, dominates the horizon of the
21st century.   *Photo by C.E. Yale.*

as a destination. A recent trend is for government and private tourism associations to join together to help sustain and increase the tourism industry. Building and promotion of convention centers are just one function of these public/private organizations.

A continuing challenge for government officials and tourism industry members will be to balance the special interests of constituent groups who have conflicting opinions concerning the development of tourism that lead to political tugs of war. Tourism, like any industry, has benefits and costs, and these impacts will always be viewed and prioritized differently by different members of communities.

YOU DECIDE

The following two letters to the editor appeared in a resort town's newspaper.

To the Editor:

Summer is approaching again and, as in every year, I am dreading it. By the middle of June, our town will be inundated with tourists. The price of gasoline will jump and all of the "local appreciation" specials at restaurants will disappear. The traffic jams will start and the number of car accidents will escalate. All of the stores and restaurants will be mobbed and service will suffer. And forget trying to park downtown. All the spaces will be filled by out-of-state cars. Our policemen will find it harder to protect us because they will have all of these "foreigners" to watch. And our fire departments will begin their annual campaign against forest fires started by careless transients. And now our chamber of commerce wants us to celebrate tourism and be extra nice to the "guests" to our area?

Frankly, I am sick and tired of some of my state tax dollars (and I bet some of my local taxes, too!) going to promote our state as a tourism destination! All these new people in the area just serve to increase my taxes in order to pay for the increased costs they lead to! Enough is enough

already. This area is losing its small town feel and its small town security. Why should we pay to decrease the quality of life of our community?

Signed, Jack Smith

To the Editor:

After reading the letter from Jack Smith who sees only the negatives of tourists to our community, I felt compelled to respond. Without these "foreigners" that he decries, he may not even be able to live here. Many of us, either directly or indirectly, owe our livelihood to the money that tourists spend here every year. And, contrary to Mr. Smith's opinion, the tourists to our town and state actually reduce our taxes by paying taxes on the goods and services they purchase here.

In addition, do the people of this town think we locals by ourselves could support the number of restaurants and shops we have, let alone the jet-capable airport we enjoy? Instead of cursing out tourists, we should smile, wave, and thank our lucky stars that we get to live where they can only visit.

Signed, Linda Jones

With which letter do you agree? Why?

NET TOUR

To learn more about the concepts and organizations presented in this chapter access the homepage for *Tourism: The Business of Travel.* Select "Chapter 10: Economic and Political Impacts of Tourism." From this location test your knowledge by taking the chapter quiz, read industry insights, and discover links to other useful sites. You may also want to visit electronically with other tourism students through the website.

DISCUSSION QUESTIONS

1. In what ways can tourism benefit the economy of an area?

2. Why are tourism receipts from international visitors considered exports?

3. How does the output multiplier effect work? Why do island countries have small tourism multipliers?

4. What are some of the negative effects that can come from tourism development?

5. What are the various roles that governments can play in supporting the tourism industry?

6. How do convention centers add to the economic activity of an area? How can they be funded and managed?

7. What steps are needed to develop a tourism plan?

8. Why can political tugs of war arise over decisions concerning tourism development?

APPLYING THE CONCEPTS

1. Look at Table 10.1. Why are these countries the top 10 in international tourism receipts? In other words, what is it about these countries that enables them to attract so much international tourism?

2. Look at Table 10.2. Why are these countries the top 10 in international tourism payments? In other words, what is it about these countries, and their citizens, that makes them so likely to travel internationally?

3. Visit a chamber of commerce, convention and visitors bureau, or a state welcome center in your area. Interview one of the managers about the visitor-friendliness of your city/town, using the FYI visitor-friendliness test as your discussion guide.

4. Research the taxes that are added to visitor services in your city/town and your state/province. How do they compare to the examples provided in Table 10.4?

GLOSSARY

Comparative advantage The benefits of one alternative relative to another.

Constituent groups Subgroups of citizens with a set of common needs or wants.

Convention and visitors bureau An organization whose mission is to develop tourism to an area by attracting both professional and leisure travelers.

Convention center A property developed to serve the special needs of groups, especially regarding meetings and trade shows.

Cost–benefit analysis A method used to determine the relative impact of a development, in which total costs and total benefits are estimated and then compared.

Economics The study of the choices people make in using scarce resources to meet needs.

Entrepreneurial Assuming the risks of a personally owned business.

Exchange rate The number of units of one currency necessary to be exchange to obtain a unit of another currency, for example, 121 Japanese yen for $1.00 U.S.

Export A good or service produced in one country and purchased by a resident of another country; the opposite of "import."

Financial resources The amount of money available for a given project through the use of debt and equity.

Import A good or service purchased in one country but produced in another country; the opposite of "export."

Infrastructure The foundation utilities and other systems necessary for an economy, such as roads, electricity, and water and sewerage systems.

Joint venture Combined efforts of two or more partners, usually organizations.

Leakage Purchasing power that is spent on imports to an area, resulting in a transfer of income out of the local economy.

Nonprofit tourism association An organization that exists to support the tourism industry of an area and often promotes the area as a destination.

Objective A specific target for which measurable results can be obtained.

Output multiplier effect The additional economic activity that results when money is spent and respent in a region from the purchase of local goods and services.

Passenger facility charges A charge added to airline tickets for enplanement. The monies collected are to be used for airport improvements.

Policy A general statement that provides direction for individuals within an organization.

Privatization The action of converting a government-owned business to private ownership.

Public/private organizations Organizations made up of private and public members, usually to coordinate efforts between government and private businesses.

Superstructure The facilities needed to serve the specific needs of tourists, such as hotels, restaurants, and attractions.

Tourism planning A continual process of research-and-development decisions to create and sustain tourism in a region.

REFERENCES

1. Waters, Somerset R. (1995–96), *Travel industry world yearbook: The big picture*. Rye, NY: Child and Waters, Inc.

2. Lundberg, Donald E., Stavengaand, Mink H., & Krishnamoorthy, M. (1995). *Tourism economics*. New York: John Wiley and Sons, Inc.

3. Bull, Adrian (1991). *The economics of tourism*. Melbourne, Australia: Pitman Publishing.

4. Fletcher, J. (1987). Input-output analysis and tourism impact studies. *Annals of Tourism Research, 16*(4), 514–529.

5. Carlton, Jim (1996, July 7). Hawaii's allure for tourists has faded, and some say state has itself to blame. *Wall Street Journal,* pp. B1, B8.

6. Rowe, Megan (1996, March). Hawaii: What went wrong? *Lodging Hospitality*, pp. 30–31.

7. Alonzo, Vincent (1995, November). Tourism slow to rebound after hurricanes. *Incentive*, p. 14.

8. Dahl, Jonathan (1995, August 11). Why go ashore when the ship's so nice? *Wall Street Journal*, pp. B1, B3.

9. Lasswell, H.D. (1936). *Politics: Who gets what, when, how?* New York: McGraw-Hill.

10. Hall, Colin Michael (1995). *Tourism and politics: Policy, power and place*. New York: John Wiley and Sons, Inc.

11. Pearce, D.G. (1992). *Tourism organization*. Harlow, UK: Longman Scientific and Technical.

12. Loyacono, Laura (1991). *Travel and tourism: A legislator's guide*. Denver: National Conference of State Legislators.

13. Kotler, Philip, Haider, Donald H., & Rein, Irving (1993). *Marketing places*. New York: The Free Press.

14. Fenich, George G. (1995). Convention center operations: Some questions answered. *International Journal of Hospitality Management, 14*(3/4), 311–324.

15. Inskeep, Edward (1991). *Tourism planning: An integrated and sustainable development approach*. New York: Van Nostrand Reinhold.

16. Blank, Uel (1989). *The community tourism industry imperative*. State College, PA: Venture Publishing, Inc.

CHAPTER 11

Environmental and Social/Cultural Impacts of Tourism

Jeep tours provide access to more travel vistas.
Photo by Tom Johnson, courtesy of Pink Jeep Tours, Sedona, Arizona.

[T]he long-term viability of the [tourism] industry in any location depends on maintaining its natural, cultural, and historical attraction.

—EDWARD MANNING/T. DAVID DOUGHERTY (1995)

CHAPTER OUTLINE

LEARNING OBJECTIVES

After you have read this chapter, you should be able to:

- Describe how tourism can aid as well as harm the preservation of nature.
- Describe how tourism can benefit as well as undermine a culture.
- Explain the factors that determine an area's carrying capacity.
- Explain the concepts of ecotourism and mass tourism and their differences.
- Explain ways to fulfill the five principles of ecotourism.
- Describe the benefits that may be achieved through use of ecotourism principles.

As the sun set slowly in the western sky, the tribal council paused in its discussion to take in the beauty of the moment. This was not the first day of their discussions and it surely would not be the last.

Some of the younger tribal members had brought up the idea of developing a golf, tennis, and ski resort in the heart of the reservation. The area would be perfect—great views, optimal weather conditions, and easy access from several large metropolitan areas. There was even talk of adding a casino to the mix and creating a series of activities and events with year-round appeal.

Development of any of these ideas sounded exciting to some members because of the variety of jobs that would be created, but there were other concerns. The tribal council was familiar with the economic benefits of tourism because the tribe already operated a motel and other small-scale attractions to encourage visitors to the reservation. However, extensive tourism development was a completely different story. Questions were raised about how many new visitors would be attracted and what effects these additional visitors would have on the natural environment and the cultural traditions that tribal members cherished. The lands of the reservation were fragile and untouched in an environmental sense. Some members of the council believed that an influx of tourists would forever damage the lands on which a hundred generations had lived. Other members expressed dismay about allowing tens of thousands of outsiders into the heart of the reservation. Would these outsiders show respect for the ways of the tribe? Could the tribe keep visitors out of the sacred areas, or would four-wheel drive vehicles be racing everywhere, ignoring any restrictions the tribe might impose?

As the council members settled back into their discussions, they reached one decision. Before a final conclusion was made on the matter, they would need a professional analysis of the potential environmental and social/cultural impacts of each alternative.

INTRODUCTION

In the previous chapter, you learned about tourism's many economic and political impacts. While reading Chapter 10, as well as many of the other chapters, you may have thought of other benefits and problems that tourism can bring. For example, in Chapter 8, we considered the range of commercialization that exists at different types of resort locations. But what impact does commercial development have on the environment? Can the natural attractiveness of an area be preserved when tourism development occurs? How are residents affected by the creation and growth of tourism in their area? As the chapter opener suggests, the economic impacts of tourism are not the only important impacts that must be considered when tourism development is proposed. Effects on nature, peoples, and cultures of a region are just as important to study and predict as the economic effects of tourism. In this chapter, we will discuss the environmental pluses and minuses of tourism as well as the benefits and costs of tourism to a society and its culture.

TOURISM AND THE ENVIRONMENT

How can tourism be used to preserve the environment? Education and appreciation are probably the two most important ways. When visitors see firsthand the wonders of nature and are educated about nature's fragile balance, they are more likely to understand the importance of preservation efforts. In addition to its educational role, tourism can be used to help finance the preservation of natural areas. Revenues generated from entrance fees and other guest services can be used to improve animal habitats and maintain wilderness areas. Think about the hundreds of thousands of acres of national parks and preserves that have been set aside all over the world primarily to preserve them for future generations to enjoy. North Americans and visitors from around the globe owe U.S. President Theodore Roosevelt a great deal of thanks for his foresight in instituting the U.S. National Park system. Similar systems, public and private, exist in countries on all continents, from Australia to Africa.

BRITAIN'S NATIONAL TRUST

The United Kingdom boasts a private organization whose mission is preservation—The National Trust for Places of Historic Interest or Natural Beauty. Started in 1895, it is the largest private landowner in Great Britain (Scotland also has a National Trust). Along with a huge portfolio of stately homes and gardens, the Trust owns or controls 550 miles of coastline. To further "save-the-coastline," plans are for the organization to acquire an additional 500 miles. The combined total of over 1000 miles would equal one third of the coasts of England, Wales, and Northern Ireland combined!

Source: Mairson, Alan (1995, October) Saving Britain's shore. *National Geographic, 188*(4), 38–57.

But how can tourism managers and planners determine just how much tourism a natural site can handle? What types of positive and negative impacts does tourism have on the environment? The first question can be answered by determining the **carrying capacity** of a location. After we discuss the concept of carrying capacity, we will then consider some of the particular environmental benefits and costs tourism yields.

Defining Carrying Capacity

Just how many visitors are too many? The answer is "It depends," and what it depends on is the carrying capacity of an area. Carrying capacity is a key concept in analysis of the potential environmental impacts of tourism. Different people mean different things when they use the term *carrying capacity*, but essentially there are three elements to the concept.

1. **Physical capacity**—the limit on the actual number of users that can be accommodated in a region. Such things as the number of roads, the size of parking lots, and the amount of water resources influence the physical carrying capacity of an area. Acadia National Park in Maine is frequently marred by bumper-to-bumper traffic during the height of tourist season.

2. **Environmental capacity**—the limit on the number of users that an area can accommodate before visitors perceive a decline in the desirability of the area. This capacity is more subjectively defined and varies depending on season, etc. The beaches of St. Tropez in France are uncomfortably crowded in August.

3. **Ecological capacity**—the maximum level of users that an area can accommodate before ecological damage is incurred. For example, the alpine flora of Waterton-Glacier Peace Park spanning the Canadian/U.S. border has suffered from the tens of thousands of hikers swarming the park. Ecological capacity will vary depending on the type of use made of the area. Backpackers will have less impact on a national park than campers who travel through the park on horseback or in four-wheel drive vehicles. In addition, different types of environments are affected more or less by use. Beaches and other dune-like areas tend to be even more fragile than mountainous areas.[1]

Determining Carrying Capacities

As you can see from these definitions, preserving the natural features that attract visitors requires managing the carrying capacity of a location. To determine the carrying capacity, planners must look at a variety of factors, including:

- the number of visitors,
- the amount of "use" by the average visitor (for example, just traveling through vs. extended stay RV camping),

- the quality of resource management and facility development/design,
- the number of area residents and their quality-of-life needs, and
- the number of other users of the area and its resources, for example, industrial users and farmers/ranchers.[2]

Wyoming's Grand Teton National Park provides a good example of all of these factors. About 3.5 million visitors arrive each year to play and marvel at the mountain majesty of the area. At the same time, the nearby town of Jackson Hole has exploded with new full- and part-time residents. The area also supports its traditional agriculture-based industries such as cattle ranching. And the amount of "use" by visitors has increased. In the past, use was primarily hiking and low-impact sports of nature (such as fishing), but visitors now bring all the comforts of home—and more—with them. Dan Burgette, chief of the Colter Bay subdivision of the park, states:

> The toys people bring to the park have changed. Twenty-five years ago they would have a car and a tent. Now they come with a motor home, a boat, trail bikes, and a car in tow. Parking lots built in the 1960s just aren't big enough. One of our biggest chores is getting people to turn off their TV sets and gas-powered electric generators at ten o'clock at night (p. 136).[3]

DENSITY

Take nothing but photographs, leave nothing but footprints. You probably have seen this statement on signs in many natural areas including North America's national parks. Surely these simple activities—looking and walking—are harmless? Unfortunately, they can be harmful.

1. At a density of 1 person per square kilometer, little of the natural environment is likely to be lost.

2. At 10 persons per square kilometer, the likelihood of being alone and of seeing wildlife are likely to be sacrificed.

3. At 100 persons per square kilometer, most wildlife will depart; in the absence of any management intervention, there will be visible pollution of the site and noticeable ecological degradation.

4. At 1000 persons per square kilometer, urban densities are reached, and the experience is no longer a natural one; human-created values are found; and intensive management is needed to maintain the site and to remove trash and human waste.

Source: Manning, Edward & Dougherty, T. David (1995). Sustainable tourism. *Cornell Hotel and Restaurant Administration Quarterly, 36,* 29–42.

This quote suggests that the carrying capacity of an area changes when any one or more of capacity's determining factors changes. For example, if a town begins to see an increase in permanent residents, it will not have as high a "visitor" carrying capacity as before because the additional residents "use up" some of the finite carrying capacity of the area. On the other hand, the carrying capacity of a site can be increased by reducing the amount of "use" by each visitor. Constructing visitor walkways allows more foot traffic in a fragile natural area; busing visitors from remote parking lots cuts down on air pollution within a park; and creating viewing platforms allows many more visitors to view the scenery without endangering the pristine site. Park managers at the Athabasca Falls site in British Columbia have used all of these means—walkways, buses, and view platforms—to decrease the erosion and vegetation trampling that had threatened its natural beauty.[4]

As you can see, identifying the carrying capacity of an area requires thorough research. The management of a natural attraction demands careful environmental planning

Environmental and cultural issues are not restricted to natural destinations. One of the world's most beautiful and historic cities—Venice, Italy—is suffering from tourism's success. This cradle of European civilization, 1500 years old, includes incredible riches in terms of art, architecture, and history. Ten million visitors each year travel to it and marvel at its beauty. So what's the problem?

The problem for Venice is its location and its size. Venice is an island city, constructed on pilings sunk into the sea and connected by causeway to the rest of Italy. The ancient city is a mere 3 square miles in size, with a permanent population of only 70,000 residents. And the streets were built hundreds of years ago, which virtually prevents the use of cars, buses, and trucks. Its famous canals and gondolas are a prime form of transit, but they, too, are small. Each day between 50,000 and 150,000 tourists descend on the city and crowd the streets to the point that simply walking across a town square becomes nearly impossible.

This overcrowding is taking its toll on more than just citizens' blood pressures. The amount of garbage and trash is massive and difficult to dispose of due to the city's size, location, and lack of transportation options. And the crowds of visitors are taking their toll on the ancient churches, palaces, and other historic places. Solutions that are being considered include selling tickets and limiting the number of guests who can visit the city each day, as well as allowing only tours that follow differing itineraries so that the crowds are more evenly spread through the streets and the city's monuments.

Unfortunately for Venice, tourism is becoming more important as other industries leave due to the high costs of doing business on the island. The government and citizens of Venice will need to become very creative in managing the physical and social carrying capacity of their tiny but beautiful city.

Source: Zwingle, Erla (1995). Venice. *National Geographic, 187*(2), 70–99.

and creative carrying capacity design to balance visitor enjoyment and education with the well-being of the flora and fauna of the location.

ENVIRONMENTAL IMPACTS OF TOURISM

To provide services to visitors, a region must first develop the necessary infrastructure to support these services. Infrastructure is the underlying foundation or basic framework for a system or organization. In the case of tourism, infrastructure includes roads, ports and airports, and utilities such as electricity and water and sewerage systems. In addition, superstructures will also be needed. The superstructures of tourism are the facilities directly associated with serving visitors' needs such as welcome centers, hotels, restaurants, car rental facilities, tour company offices, and retail establishments.

Obviously, the development of the infrastructure and superstructure necessary for tourism will have an impact on the environment of an area. However, the impact can be minimized with good design and planning. For example, the use of underground lines for utilities can retain the more natural look of vistas, while appropriate design of buildings, in terms of colors, height, signage, and landscaping, may even enhance the beauty of the region. Many resort communities have ordinances that require harmony in architecture, color, and signs so that manmade structures blend into the natural setting. For example, in Sedona, Arizona, architecture, color schemes, and signs must follow design restrictions so that the community fits into its awe-inspiring red-rock formation setting.

Unfortunately, such design foresight does not always occur. In the earlier days of tourism development of Hawaii, hotels were built along the beautiful beaches of Oahu with little regard to the "scenic impact" they would have. Today, these hotels completely block the view of the ocean. Developers of the other islands of Hawaii have learned from the mistakes made, and regional planners and developers are now more careful with their designs.[5]

A substantial increase in the number of people using an area's resources is likely to have a detrimental impact on the environment. This impact may simply be annoying, such as increased traffic or crowded parks. But the impact may be severe enough to cause harm to a fragile natural area. For example, the Grand Canyon and the Colorado River and its banks are deteriorating due to the ever-increasing numbers of visitors descending into the Canyon and the thousands each year who enjoy its river-rafting thrills. Likewise, Banff National Park, Canada's oldest national park, continues to suffer from the millions of visitors it receives annually. Many places in its tundra wilderness have been "trampled by so many hikers that in places the route resembles a boggy, 20-foot-wide cattle trail." (p. 50)[6]

Air pollution can become a problem with the increased level of vehicle traffic in an area, along with other activities that cause air-quality problems. For example, the congestion of cars through Yosemite Park causes the very air pollution that visitors try to escape by fleeing to national parks. Some communities have taken serious steps to try to reduce the other forms of air pollution that can be caused by tourism's success. In the mountain valleys of the Rockies, it is now common for towns to prohibit hearth fires on many winter days because wood smoke is so dense and dissipates so slowly. In addition to air pollution, noise pollution is becoming a new problem in many communities, especially with the relocation and/or expansion of airports. Noise pollution is even a problem with the Grand Canyon. Each year, about 80,000 scenic flights take tourists low over the canyon, creating an airplane buzz that disrupts the tranquility of its splendor.[7]

Possibly most damaging, however, is the impact that can occur to vegetation, wildlife, and precious historical attractions. Unplanned or poorly planned development can lead to the endangerment of flora and fauna species and to the slow erosion of the very sites that are the destination's "reason for being." For example, the government of Egypt is excavating more of the dozens of pharaoh burial sites in hopes that by providing more sites, they can reduce the amount of tourist traffic to the Great Pyramids in Giza. In 1995, 12 million visitors trooped through the most famous pyramids, worsening the water vapor problem that causes salt to leach from the stones and weaken the structures.[8]

Historic site deterioration can occur in more modern locations as well. Many historic towns in the United States have applied the brakes to tour buses rolling through their streets. For example, in 1996, New Orleans officials stopped all tour bus access to the French Quarter due to the damage inflicted on the delicate architecture by the vibration of hundreds of buses passing through the narrow streets. Other cities are considering similar restraints.[9]

Virtually every year, the National Park Service considers limiting the number of people into Yosemite National Park. In 1980, the National Park Service developed a master plan for Yosemite, but major changes in the park's infrastructure and superstructure are expensive to fund and take a long time to implement. However, in 1997, roads were expanded to allow better bus traffic through the park to try to encourage visitors to leave their cars outside. Mesa Verde, a world-famous archeological site of early Native American settlements, has begun to limit access to the more popular ruins by utilizing tickets. As the market for tourism grows, carrying capacity increases as a major issue of concern.

To try to preserve the environment and still gain the economic benefits of tourism, a new form of tourism called **ecotourism** has evolved. Although protection of the natural environment is the key component of ecotourism (sometimes called "green tourism"), protection and appreciation of the native peoples of an area is also one of its guiding principles. Therefore, we will save discussion of ecotourism until we have learned about tourism's potential effects on a culture.

SOCIAL AND CULTURAL IMPACTS OF TOURISM

The concepts of society and culture are closely linked. A **society** is a community, nation, or broad grouping of people who have common traditions, institutions, activities, and interests. **Culture** represents the practices of a society; its customary beliefs, social roles and material objects that are passed down from generation to generation. As we saw in the chapter opener, tourism's potential effects on the culture of a society are often major concerns when tourism development is being considered. Tourism's impacts on a society can be both positive and negative. Because tourism brings "outsiders" into a society, it has the possibility of influencing that society by changing its culture.

Host Community

Tourism, by its very definition, takes place at a location distant from one's hometown. The community a tourist is visiting is often termed the **host community.** Local residents of the host community share facilities and services with the guests to the area. In this way, the town and its inhabitants become "hosts" to the visitors.

A host community is composed of three resources. The most obvious resource is the local residents, the hosts themselves. They interact directly or indirectly with tourists on many levels; for example, serving tourists at restaurants or in retail stores, enjoying the local parks with them, or talking with visitors while waiting in line at the local amusement park. The community's economic system is also a resource of the host community. The economic health and wealth of the area is created and used by both residents and the community's guests. Finally, the infrastructure and basic government services are the third resource of the host community. The residents of the community literally share the roads, the sidewalks, the water system, and police and fire protection with the guests to their area.[2] This blending of local people and their resources with outsiders can have many social and cultural impacts, some positive and some not so positive.

Social and Cultural Benefits of Tourism

In addition to economic gains, tourism can provide many social and cultural benefits. By bringing people from a wide variety of places and cultures together, visitors and locals learn about each other, their differences and their similarities. They also become aware of new tastes and ways of thinking, which may lead to increased tolerance among the hosts and the visitors. In 1997, Iran began offering a limited number of tourist visas to U.S. citizens.[10] Only time will tell if the face-to-face interactions of Iranians and Americans will warm the relationships of members of these very different cultures.

Another important cultural benefit of tourism is the attainment of the "critical mass" of interest necessary to maintain the viability of a society's culture, especially the culture's art forms.[11] The opportunity to sell native crafts or to perform to an enthusiastic audience can entice local craftsmen and artists to continue traditional art forms that otherwise may no longer be seen as a viable means of income. For example, in Fiji, islanders have turned their crafts of palm mats and shell jewelry into lucrative tourist businesses. They also earn additional income by performing folk dances, including fire walking.[12]

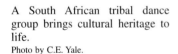

A South African tribal dance group brings cultural heritage to life.
Photo by C.E. Yale.

In many cases, the growth of tourism in developing countries has led to improved standards of living and greater educational opportunities, especially for women and young people who were formerly "enslaved" by tradition. In Spain, for example, growth in tourism led to the employment of many young women outside the home and gave them lifestyle choices other than the homemaker role that had been their only option in the past.[13]

At the same time, tourism provides the opportunity to preserve the region's historical and natural sites. Revenues from tourist fees and taxes afford the host area the ability to gain income and job creation from lands and historical sites that would otherwise have to be industrially developed to achieve a higher standard of living for the local people. It is the influx of tourist "piastres" (the currency of Egypt) that is providing Egypt with the funds necessary to uncover and preserve that culture's ancient past. Spain has similarly used tourism demand to aid in historic preservation. The Spanish government developed a system of inns—Paradores de Turismo—that utilizes the room capacity of many of Spain's historic castles, monasteries, and convents. By generating revenue from these classic buildings, Spain can afford to maintain them, preserving them for the future.

Using Culture to Attract Tourists

Remember that culture includes the practices of a society, including its material objects. These practices and objects, listed in Figure 11.1, can be grouped into three categories: material goods of culture; daily life activities of culture; and special expressions of culture (that is, special events or sites of special historical value). The material goods of a culture include its distinctive arts and crafts. Daily life activities of a culture include its food and dress forms, its language and its special ways of playing, living, and working. Special expressions of culture are found in a culture's unique history, architecture, and special traditions. One of the most well attended cultural expressions in the world is the daily changing of the guard at Buckingham Palace in London.

FIGURE 11.1
Elements of Culture That Attract Tourists.
Source: Ritchie, J.R., & Zins, M. (1978). Culture as a determinant of a tourist region. *Annals of Tourism Research, 5,* 252–270.

1. Handicrafts
2. Language
3. Traditions ✈
4. Gastronomy ✈
5. Art & Music
6. History & Visual Reminders ✈
7. Work & Technology
8. Architecture ✈
9. Religion & Its Manifestations
10. Educational Systems
11. Dress
12. Leisure Activities ✈

✈ Indicates the most common elements for attracting tourists

Look at Figure 11.1 again and think of the many destinations that attract visitors based on one or more of these elements of culture. Many destinations experience a substantial influx of tourists who are attracted by the local handicrafts and traditions of the area. The American Southwest, for example, is world renowned for its beautiful Native American crafts. The Bahamas are famous for the variety of straw goods produced by its people. Spain attracts tens of thousands of students each year who are studying Spanish. France attracts visitors eager to partake of its renowned cuisine and to view the wealth of art exhibited in its museums and galleries. Greece is a popular tourism destination because of its important historical role in the evolution of Western civilization. And the United States and Canada have turned into the world's playgrounds, attracting millions of international visitors who partake in the vast array of leisure activities available on the North American continent.

Need more examples of the importance of cultural elements in attracting visitors? The Middle East is the cradle of three of the world's most prominent religions, Christianity, Judaism, and Islam. Literally millions of people trek to various sites in the Middle East as a form of pilgrimage. Salt Lake City serves a similar role for members of the Church of Jesus Christ of Latter Day Saints. Italy, Mexico, and Peru provide unique opportunities for visitors to see the architectural marvels of past civilizations.

Even industry and education can attract visitors. You have probably toured "industrial attractions" yourself. How about the Hershey chocolate plant in Pennsylvania? How about wineries in California, New York, or Washington state? And many colleges and universities are popular sites; Oxford and Cambridge in England, Yale and Stanford in the United States, the Sorbonne in France, and many more.

The list of destinations and attractions that are based on culture is infinite. The cultural resources of a society provide many opportunities to generate tourism revenues. Often the society also gains by meeting and sharing with people from other cultures, each learning and appreciating the other. But sometimes tourism brings problems to a culture.

UNINTENDED CONSEQUENCES OF TOURISM ON CULTURE

Although we have provided a long list of benefits that tourism can offer, there can be some unintended negative effects of tourism on a society and culture.[11] The term **social carrying capacity** is sometimes used to label the amount of people that a society and its land area can bear without substantial damage to its culture. Newcomers or visitors to a society may cause problems due to overcrowding or by bringing unfamiliar behaviors.[14] Once tourism in an area becomes successful, it is common for local residents to resent sharing "their" resources and facilities with visitors. Frequently, the residents of the area forget that many of the facilities in the area (both infrastructure and superstructure) were developed to serve the tourist market and would not be available for locals' use if the tourists did not return year after year. As we saw in the "You Decide" of Chapter 10, communities can split apart from the debate over the effect of tourism on the area.

A more serious societal problem can occur in lower-income areas. In some locations, tourism has caused what is termed the "demonstration effect." Compared to their own lifestyles, the local residents often see the visitors as uniformly wealthy and in possession of all the "good things" in life. This display of material goods and affluence may lead to envy and resentment from the locals. This effect can happen in developing island countries, such as Jamaica, as well as industrialized countries. In Great Britain, many locals resent the large number of wealthy Arabs who visit that country each year.[15]

Tourism's effect on young people may have a detrimental effect on the culture of an area. The youth of a region are the most likely to seek the jobs created by the tourism industry, which are often higher-paying than the traditional work available, for example, farming. It is common for a young man or woman in a developing nation to be able to earn much more than his or her elders and to flaunt this disparity through the purchase of material goods. This apparent casting away of the society's traditional ways can cause rifts in families. The younger generation is also the most likely to copy behaviors of the tourists that may be considered improper in the region's culture.

> The advent of a substantial [tourism] industry in an area tends to diminish the traditional ways and inject the styles, tastes and behaviors of the tourists into the local people. Tourism tends to increase the standard of living of those involved in it but also transforms the very fiber of the community, frequently separating a formerly homogeneous group into classes and divergent generations (p. 143).[11]

Developing countries can experience a subtle change in their class system from tourism. It is common for ownership of the tourism businesses to rest with foreigners, who also frequently bring **expatriate** managers to fill the higher-skilled, higher-paying jobs created. In these instances, tourism can be viewed as a modern form of colonialism, in which the host country is "exploited" for its natural beauty but does not participate in the most lucrative return from the industry. This foreign ownership resentment also can occur in industrialized countries. Quite a furor arose when a Japanese company purchased the famous California golf course at Pebble Beach.[16]

Many areas find that tourism development is the only viable "export" industry and, therefore, change their political and economic structures to accommodate the needs of tourism developers and tourists. To encourage tourism, the local governments often waive taxes, import restrictions, and environmental safeguards on tourism investors and develop infrastructure that is mainly available to tourists and not the native population. In this way, the natives see the trappings of a better life but do not participate in it.

Crime also can become a serious societal problem when tourism succeeds. Researchers believe this phenomenon is due to both the increase in number of potential victims and the resentment and envy of the apparent wealth and carefree attitude of the tourists. Milman and Pizam[17] found a relationship between tourist season and crime season: Crime increased at the height of the tourist season, but was lower during the off season. Researchers suggest that the larger numbers of people in an area increases a criminal's potential gain from crime and decreases the chance of being caught. This increase in crime becomes a social and economic burden on the local area because it raises fear and necessitates funding of a larger police force.

Unfortunately, another social ill that sometimes occurs with the development of tourism is a decline in the moral conduct of the local people. This moral decay—promiscuity, prostitution, alcohol, and drug use—is particularly damaging to a society that had little of these behaviors due to a strong religious or cultural taboo against them. As you learned in Chapter 7, gaming has been used by many areas to attract tourism. In some cases, this plan has resulted in an unintended social toll—residents have been caught up in gaming and some have become compulsive gamblers.

> In Harrison County, Mississippi, . . . the number of divorces rose from 440 in 1992 to nearly 1,100 in 1993, the first full year after casinos were introduced. According to Judge William L. Stewart, gambling is the factor for about one third of the divorce cases he oversees (p. 5).[18]

Finally, some cultures have balked at the effect tourism has had on their language. Because so many tourists and business travelers use English as a common communication means, the native tongue loses its value and is replaced by English because of employment qualifications and the demonstration effect. The French seem especially sensitive to threats to the French language. One of the biggest fears concerning the development of Disneyland Paris was the effect that English usage in the park would have on the native language.

The examples just mentioned are only a few instances of the unintended consequences that tourism can have on a society and its culture. Most of tourism's negative impacts on the physical environment are also unintended. The influx of thousands of visitors to a region is often too many for the environment and the host community to withstand without stress. Tourism to an area in large numbers is called **mass tourism.**

MASS TOURISM VERSUS ECOTOURISM

The tourism industry has exploded in recent decades and the number of travelers grows year after year. Quicker, cheaper, and safer transportation to almost every corner of the globe is one reason for this growth. A second reason is the explosion in the number of the world's citizens who now have the leisure time and money to travel. The longer lives and better health of many of the world's peoples is a third reason. Finally, the global communications available everywhere make people more aware of the wondrous sites of the world and the endless activity options available to them.[19]

This boom in tourism has given rise to millions of new jobs and increased economic prosperity in countries across the world. But, as we began to see in Chapter 10, tourism can usher in problems along with economic benefits. The millions of additional tourists have strained the resources of many destinations, sometimes straining natural resources to the point where the initial appeal of an area is diminished and visitation to it declines. Figure 11.2 provides one tourism expert's idea of the stages that a destination may go through from beginning to decline.

When Is Tourism Too Much of a Good Thing?

The costs of tourism, especially its environmental and cultural costs, have led many destination residents and tourists alike to become disillusioned with mass tourism. Mass tourism to these critics of tourism's growth includes:

* the architectural pollution of tourist strips,
* the herding of tourists as if they were cattle,
* the disruption of traditional cultural events and occupations,
* the diminished natural environment and beauty of the area, and
* the low priority paid to local needs with funds used instead to increase tourism amenities to keep the community competitive in the marketplace.[19]

Many of the gains of tourism are economic and often short-term in nature. The costs, however, especially to the beauty and natural resources of an area, are more likely to be long-lived or even permanent. Too many times, nonlocal developers are the biggest winners and, when the area has become saturated and starts to decline, these developers move on to the next trendy destination with no backward glance at the damage that may have been done.

So far in this chapter, we have included quite a list of problems, both environmental and cultural, that can result from tourism. What can be done to try to minimize these problems? Many efforts can be taken that help safeguard the environment and the native people of a tourism destination. These efforts are encompassed in a type of tourism that has come to be called **ecotourism.**

Ecotourism

Ecotourism, sometimes called "green tourism" or "alternative tourism," has evolved in reaction to the problems of mass tourism. Ecotourism is a form or philosophy of tourism that emphasizes the need to develop tourism in a manner that minimizes environmental impact and ensures that host communities gain the greatest economic and cultural benefits possible. The goal is to "integrate tourism development into a broader range of values and social concerns. (p. 11)[19]

Mass tourism, as opposed to ecotourism, tends to strain the environment through the development of more and more superstructure and the increasing wear and tear from the presence and actions of more and more tourists.[20] It is probably obvious to you that building lots of hotels, restaurants, roads, and airports can cause serious problems for an area's environment. For example, the construction of ski resorts in the Alps has led to mudslides and landslides that are damaging the mountainsides. How do individual tourists

FIGURE 11.2

Stages of Tourism Development.

Source: Butler, R. W. (1980). The concept of a tourist area life cycle of evolution: Implications for management of resources. *Canadian Geographer, 24,* 5–12.

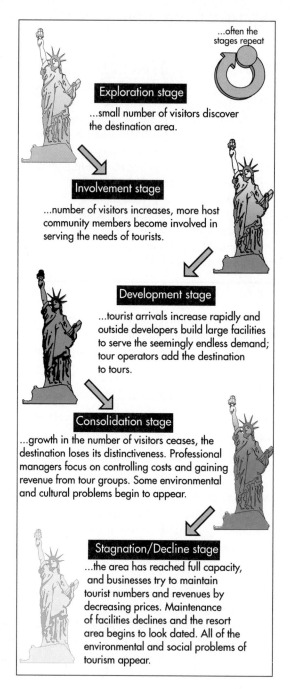

...often the stages repeat

Exploration stage
...small number of visitors discover the destination area.

Involvement stage
...number of visitors increases, more host community members become involved in serving the needs of tourists.

Development stage
...tourist arrivals increase rapidly and outside developers build large facilities to serve the seemingly endless demand; tour operators add the destination to tours.

Consolidation stage
...growth in the number of visitors ceases, the destination loses its distinctiveness. Professional managers focus on controlling costs and gaining revenue from tour groups. Some environmental and cultural problems begin to appear.

Stagnation/Decline stage
...the area has reached full capacity, and businesses try to maintain tourist numbers and revenues by decreasing prices. Maintenance of facilities declines and the resort area begins to look dated. All of the environmental and social problems of tourism appear.

threaten the environment? One way is simply by blazing trails while walking through nature. One person walking through a wilderness area may not have any significant impact on the area, but 10,000 people within a short period certainly will. The simple action of trampling grass multiplied by 10,000 can lead to erosion of land. For example, several of New York State's Adirondack Mountain peaks are now bare due to hiker traffic. And driving through a natural area causes more damage. The manufacture and promotion of "off-road" vehicles may be the biggest threat to nature. To view ever more remote areas, travelers and tour operators are venturing further into our national forests and parks, scaling fragile rock formations and converting dirt paths into rutted mud holes.

As opposed to mass tourism, ecotourism primarily involves travel to sensitive natural and cultural environments to observe and learn about a very different culture and environment and participate in low-impact (on nature) sports such as canoeing and hiking. In addition, **ecotravelers** generally desire to mingle with the local culture and have their travel needs filled by locals in their traditional ways (such as dining on the local gastro-nomical delights).

Compared to psychocentric travelers, **ecotourists** tend to be wealthier, college-educated, and willing to spend large amounts of money on extended trips.[21] They also tend to participate in active yet nature-focused sports such as climbing, canoeing, and kayaking.[22]

So how does ecotourism address the environmental and cultural problems that tourism can create (or at least aggravate)? What kind of development can yield the twin goal of nature preservation and host community benefit and cultural respect? In the next section, we will suggest ways that tourism can deliver its economic gains while sustaining the natural and human resources of a region.

Sustaining Tourism's Benefits

There are five basic principles to ecotourism development.[5] The central guiding principle is that tourism should be blended with, or assimilated with, the environment and the local culture of an area. The boundary between the tourism industry and the host community should not be startling: Tourism should fit into the community and share in its ways. This blurring can occur, for example, by matching architecture to the existing local structures and using the area's natural vegetation for grounds landscaping.

A second principle of ecotourism is that the tourist experience should focus on the host community's existing scenic and activity opportunities. In other words, tourism should evolve from the area's natural and historical/cultural attractions. Third, ecotourism is associated with local ownership and management of all or most services. Tourist needs should be filled by local businesspeople and local employees rather than foreign investors or managers. In this way, more of the economic benefits of tourism flow to the local citizens and their local governments.

To further benefit the host community economically, the fourth principle is that a high proportion of local materials should be used to fulfill tourists' needs, from construction materials to foodstuffs. For example, in Zambia, there is a unique resort called Tongabezi. The architecture of the "hotel" is a sight to behold. Most of it is built from native lumber and grasses, and many of the guestrooms are open air. One suite, called the Bird House, is built high in a huge tree and neither the bedroom nor its private bath need

Carefully blending tourism with the environment—accommodations in Africa.
Photo by C.E. Yale.

to have walls for modesty's sake. The height of the rooms alone provide all the privacy needed.

Finally, the fifth principle highlights the importance of conservation of resources. By using what are called "ecotechniques," local utilities such as water, heat, and electricity can be stretched to accommodate the needs of both the tourists and the local population. Ecotechniques include use of solar power, rain water collection, and bioclimatic design of structures to aid in heating and cooling.

From these five principles, host communities can gain many potential benefits that they may not gain from mass tourism, including:

- generating more income for more local community members,
- promoting understanding between locals and members of different cultures,
- educating local populations on matters of health, education, energy use, business, and environmental conservation, and
- providing a financial incentive to protect and conserve a globally significant natural/cultural resource.[23]

Many of the techniques just described can be used in already-developed tourism areas to improve or sustain the existing tourism industry. Although applying one or two techniques would not change an area from a mass tourism to an ecotourism destination, efforts like water conservation and sign codes (limiting their size, height, and lighting) can help alleviate problems that may have arisen.

Other means of managing the physical and social carrying capacity of developing and developed tourism areas have been attempted.[24] To try to eliminate crowds, policies of dispersion have been used. Rather than allowing one area of a destination to become the center of all tourism activity, the infrastructure and superstructure is spread throughout the region to force visitors to be more evenly distributed as well. Zoning can also be used to limit the amount of development that can occur in any one place.

To manage the carrying capacity of specific sites, restrictive entry is often used. Sometimes this limit to the number of visitors is accomplished through reservations or tickets. At other times the number can be limited by charging higher fees, thus limiting the number of visitors able and willing to pay the price of admission, and usually reducing the number of times any tourist chooses to visit the site. Limiting types of usage can also reduce the number of users of a site or the impact to the environment any user has on it. Some of the national lands of the United States are restricted to wilderness camping only, forbidding RVs, off-road vehicles, snowmobiles, and even horse transportation into certain areas. However, decisions to restrict access have been criticized by older travelers and those with disabilities who rely on vehicles for the opportunity to enjoy natural areas.

WILDERNESS ACT

In addition to national parks and national forests, the United States has wilderness areas. In 1964, realizing that the growing population would strain the natural resources of the country, U.S. Congress enacted the Wilderness Act, which set aside large pieces of land to be retained in their primeval state: "areas where man himself is a visitor who does not remain."

Use of these areas is highly restricted. Although there have been exceptions made, in general, the following are not allowed in federal wilderness areas:

- commercial enterprises,
- permanent or temporary roads,
- motorized or mechanical vehicles, including boats, snowmobiles, and bicycles,
- landing of aircraft, and
- structures or installations of any kind.

Ecotourism and ecotechniques can be used by newly developed and fully developed tourist destinations to try to minimize the negative impacts that large numbers of visitors can have on host communities and the environment. At the dawn of the 21st century, more and more nations and communities will need to apply the principles of ecotourism and conservation to ensure that the tourism industry of the area remains viable.

Ecotourism will not replace the every-growing demand for mass tourism, but it can teach us some valuable lessons. Unchecked and unplanned tourism growth can lead to the eventual destruction of the very assets that originally served to attract visitors. Taking steps to preserve and protect tourist attractions will create a legacy for future generations.

SUMMARY

In addition to economic impacts, the tourism industry has an impact on the environment and societies. Visitors to natural attractions often increase their awareness of nature's fragile condition and provide funds for its preservation through admission and user fees. They also provide societies with new markets for local arts, crafts, and folklore. Many of the world's precious historical and cultural sites have survived because of visitors willing to pay to view treasures of the past.

Carrying capacity is a key concept in determining the impact that tourists may have on an area. Both the physical and social carrying capacity of an area can be analyzed by considering factors such as number of visitors, type of use, and number of residents. The carrying capacity of an environment of host community will be increased or decreased by changes in the situation such as better planning or increased intensity of use by visitors. The increase in visitors to tourist destinations, whether natural or manmade, has heightened the need for managers to expand carrying capacity through creative facility designs.

For hundreds of years, communities have utilized natural and cultural resources to attract visitors. However, the development of mass tourism in this century has had a number of detrimental effects on the environment and often on the culture of host communities. Ecotourism has arisen to attempt to minimize many of the problems created by the influx of thousands of guests to an area.

The basic philosophy of ecotourism is that tourism needs to be developed in a manner that fits with the natural and cultural environment of a region. By paying special attention to the needs of nature and the local people of a region, tourism can fit into the local environment without creating many of the problems associated with mass development. Although ecotourism is not the answer to all of the problems that tourism can generate, it offers communities and nations solutions to some of concerns.

YOU DECIDE

In 1985, an organization called CAMPFIRE was begun in Southern Africa. The acronym stands for Communal Areas Management Program for Indigenous Resources, and seven nations belong to this environmental management association—Zimbabwe, Zambia, Malawi, Mozambique, Namibia, Botswana, and South Africa. The organization was founded to generate conservation funds and give rural villagers an economic benefit from preserving wildlife, especially elephants.

In general, villages and elephants don't mix. Elephants are not bothered by the fences subsistence farmers use to try to protect their crops from grazing animals. Elephants are also dangerous and many villagers have lost their lives to them. CAMPFIRE tries to compensate villagers for the costs of increased elephant populations by selling a limited number of (very expensive) hunting licenses for elephants and then passing on the revenues generated to wildlife conservation officials and small villages.

Revenues generated through CAMPFIRE can be substantial. For example, a single hunter may spend over $40,000, and half of these funds go to local communities. The Worldwide Fund for Nature estimates that CAMPFIRE has increased participating area household incomes by 15 to 25%. The villagers are free to decide how to use the funds, frequently using the money to pay for electrified fencing but also for funding pure water systems, schools, health clinics, and other human services that they could not otherwise afford.

The elephant population of Southern Africa, estimated to be 66,500 in the late 1990s, has been growing at 5% per year. At the same time the amount of animal habitat in Africa is shrinking, partly due to human encroachment but also due to drought and the animals themselves. Elephants are particularly resource-hungry. One elephant drinks 13 gallons of water per day and rips down 1500 trees per year. Herds of elephants can trample grasslands into dust. Smaller animals therefore have less water and habitat as the elephant population grows.

Western animal activists do not approve of CAMPFIRE's pro-hunting stance and have called for the United States to stop its aid to the organization. However, with the increasing elephant population and its associated problems, some form of control needs to occur. The villagers have come to rely on the precious currency that tourists bring and wildlife conservation is a luxury most developing countries cannot afford. How can all concerns be satisfied?

Sources: Butler, Victoria (1995, March/April). Is this any way to save Africa's wildlife? _International Wildlife_, pp. 38–43; Fisher, Jonathan (1997, May/June 5). To ban or not to ban? _International Wildlife_, pp. 36–37; Hess, Karl, Jr. (1997, June 5). Environmentalists vs. wildlife. _Wall Street Journal_, p. A22; Miniter, Richard (1997, July 17). Too many elephants. _Wall Street Journal_, p. A22.

NET TOUR

To learn more about the concepts and organizations presented in this chapter access the homepage for _Tourism: The Business of Travel_. Select "Chapter 11: Environmental and Social/Cultural Impacts Of Tourism." From this location test your knowledge by taking the chapter quiz, read industry insights, and discover links to other useful sites. You may also want to visit electronically with other tourism students through the website.

DISCUSSION QUESTIONS

1. How can tourism aid in the preservation of nature?
2. What are the major factors that determine an area's carrying capacity?
3. What negative effects has tourism had on the natural environment?
4. How can tourism be used to benefit a culture? What are some of the cultural problems that can result from large numbers of visitors?
5. How is ecotourism different from mass tourism?
6. What are the major principles of ecotourism?
7. What benefits may be achieved by a host community through use of ecotourism principles?

APPLYING THE CONCEPTS

1. Find an article in a recent magazine (for example, _National Geographic_) that discusses how some host community manages the demands of tourism. Be prepared to summarize the article for the class.
2. Using the World Wide Web, find an environmental impact study conducted on one of North America's national parks. What steps are suggested to alleviate any problems found?
3. Interview a travel agent about the ecotraveler market segment. How many of his/her clients would be part of this segment? What destinations does s/he consider ecotourism destinations? Collect information from one of these destinations to bring to class.

GLOSSARY

Carrying capacity   A key concept in environmental impact analysis that relates to the amount of use an environment is capable of sustaining under certain circumstances.

Culture   The practices of a society; its customary beliefs, social roles, and material objects.

Ecotourism   A form of tourism that focuses on environmental and cultural preservation.

Ecotourists   Leisure travelers who prefer to visit less popular, more primitive destinations.

Ecotravelers   see _Ecotourists._

Ecological capacity   The maximum level of users that an area can accommodate before ecological damage is incurred.

Environmental capacity The limit on the number of users that an area can accommodate before visitors perceive a decline in the desirability of the area.

Expatriate A citizen of one nation who lives in a nation of which s/he is not a citizen.

Host community The community that a tourist is visiting, including its economic, human, and government service resources that are all shared by residents with visitors.

Mass tourism Tourism targeted to all potential visitors with the goal of ever-increasing number of visitors to an area.

Physical carrying capacity The number of users than can be accommodated in an area.

Social carrying capacity The number of outsiders to an area that can be accepted without having damaging psychological effects on the locals of the area.

Society A community, nation, or broad grouping of people who have common traditions, institutions, activities, and interests.

REFERENCES

1. Lavery, Patrick, & Van Doren, Carlton (1990). *Travel and Tourism.* Suffex, England: St. Edmundsbury Press.

2. Blank, Uel (1989). *The community tourism industry alternative.* State College, PA: Venture Publishing, Inc.

3. Hodgson, Bryan (1995). Grand Teton. *National Geographic, 187*(2), 136.

4. Manning, Edward, & Dougherty, T. David (1995). Sustainable tourism. *Cornell Hotel and Restaurant Administration Quarterly, 36*, 29–42.

5. Ayala, Hana (1995). Ecoresort: A "green" masterplan for the international resort industry. *International Journal of Hospitality Management, 14*(3/4), 351–374.

6. Krakauer, Jon (1995). "Rocky times for Banff. *National Geographic, 188*(1), 50.

7. Noisy skies over the wilderness (1996). *National Geographic, 190*(2), 139.

8. Powell, Eileen Alt (1996, June 12). Forgotten pharaohs being remembered (Associated Press article). *Durango Herald,* p. 4B.

9. Coleman, Calmetta Y. (1996, July 12). Quaint towns apply brakes to tour buses. *Wall Street Journal,* pp. B1, B6.

10. Kinzer, Stephen (1997, June 8). Old animosities aside, Americans are touring Iran. *New York Times,* p. 18.

11. Mathieson, Alister, & Wall, Geoffrey (1982). *Tourism: Economic, physical and social impacts.* New York: Longman, Inc.

12. Vaughn, Roger (1995). The two worlds of Fiji. *National Geographic, 188*(4), 114–137.

13. Lever, A. (1987). Spanish tourist migrants—The case of Lloret de Mar. *Annals of Tourism Research, 14*(4), 449–470.

14. Catton, William R., Jr. (1980). *Overshoot: The ecological basis of revolutionary change.* Urbana, IL: University of Illinois Press.

15. Kotler, Philip, Haider, Donald H., and Rein, Irving (1993). *Marketing places.* New York: The Free Press.

16. Pollack, Andrew (1990, September 8). Anxiety under that fabled cyprus. *New York Times,* pp. 29, 31.

17. Milman, A., & Pizam, Abraham (1988). Social impacts of tourism on Central Florida. *Annals of Tourism Research, 15*(2), 191–205.

18. Agrusa, Jerome (1997). Casino development: Is it the economic solution? *News and Views* (International Society of Travel and Tourism Educators newsletter), *13*(2), 5.

19. Smith, Valene L., & Eadington, William R. (1992). *Tourism alternatives: Potentials and problems in the development of tourism.* Philadelphia: The University of Pennsylvania Press.

20. May, Vincent (1991). Tourism, environment and development. *Tourism Management, 12*(2), 112–118.

21. Chipkin, Harvey (1994). Tracking the green traveler. *Travel Weekly, 53*(73), 8.

22. Wight, Pamela (1996). North American ecotourists: Market profile and trip characteristics. *Journal of Travel Research, 35*, 2–10.

23. Gurung, Chandra, & De Coursey, Maureen (1994). The Annapurna Conservation Area Project: A pioneering example of sustainable tourism? In: Cater, Erlet, & Lowman, Gwen (Eds.). *Ecotourism: A Sustainable Option?* Chichester, England: John Wiley and Sons.

24. Ryan, Chris (1991). *Recreational tourism: A social science perspective.* London: Routledge, Chapman and Hall, Inc.

CHAPTER 12

Exploring the Future of Tourism

Tomorrow's travelers will look for new extremes.
Photo courtesy of Southwest Adventures.

The more things change, the more they stay the same.

—ALPHONSE KARL

CHAPTER OUTLINE

ON THE ROAD AGAIN

Look into the future with us to this imaginary setting. The scenario facing Myra was a familiar one. She had completed all of her sales reports and was ready to head out "on the road again." Once a month, she follows up on her video telephone calls with a personal visit to each of her accounts. Video-calling had improved customer service and made it easier to handle some of the day-to-day details of her job, but the personal touch of regular meetings with her clients was what kept them coming back. Although a routine trip, it would be hectic. Seventeen sales calls in three cities on Tuesday, Wednesday, and Thursday, followed by some well-deserved rest and relaxation over a long weekend.

Setting the itinerary for the business portion of her trip would be easy as she had called on these clients many times in the past. Although she could use the information and booking capabilities of numerous web sites to plan and book reservations for her trip, she left the details up to one of the agents at the company-managed travel agency.

The professional knowledge, convenience, cost savings, and superior service provided through the in-house company agency made business travel a hassle-free experience. A computer database containing client profiles on employees' travel needs and desires took the guesswork out of scheduling business travel. Everything from the preferred color and style of rental cars to the room types and locations of favorite hotels were stored in the database and used to schedule and meet travel needs. Computer technology also mapped out the most efficient routing along with approximate travel times for each sales call or business meeting.

Although she could have used the services of the company travel agency for help in planning the weekend getaway, she decided to have some fun and do a little exploring. Once again, the technology to plan and dream about a fun-filled weekend was as close as her fingertips. After giving her computer a voice command, she was taken on a virtual tour of San Francisco. She was instantly transported to the sights, sounds, and smells of the city on a virtual reality site maintained by the city's convention and visitors bureau.

There were so many things to do and see that the choices would be difficult. However, the opportunity to sample before selecting made the decisions a little bit easier. Fisherman's Wharf and a cable car ride were definitely on her list of things to do, along with a visit to the virtual reality museum of past civilizations. After a quick tour through the videos of boutique hotels in the heart of Old San Francisco, she selected the perfect spot to unwind.

Only one more decision to make and then she could pack her bags. The final stop on her business trip would be Phoenix, and she still had to get to San Francisco and back to Phoenix for her flight home. Which would be more fun: the peace and quiet of a train ride with speeds of over 300 miles per hour or a shuttle flight in one of the new wide body jets with 500 other weekend travelers? Technology was definitely changing, but the planning, adventure, and fun of traveling were still the same.

INTRODUCTION

Peering into the future of travel and tourism is similar to looking into a cloudy crystal ball. We may not be able to bring the future into a clearly focused picture for you, but the bright light of a growing industry is glowing from the center of our crystal ball. The knowledge you have gained through studying the information in this textbook has given you a sound foundation for thinking about the future. Based on this knowledge you can begin to see some of the challenges and opportunities the tourism industry will face. As you look to the future, can you see yourself becoming a professional member of this industry?

In this chapter, we will gaze into the next century by considering some of the emerging trends in the tourism industry. These trends may shift and new ones may emerge, but thinking about the future allows you to plan for it. As you read about each of the trends, think about the changes you see happening around you and imagine what the world of tourism might be like 5, 10, or even 20 years from now. No matter how much uncertainty the future holds, there is good news. There will always be the need for talented professionals to tackle the management, marketing, and financial challenges of tourism.

The Shape of Coming Tourism Markets

You read about many of the important tourism market segments of today in Chapter 2. Will these segments still be as important in the future? There is no question that tourism markets will change, but what will these markets look like? Two possible scenarios are beginning to unfold. One scenario points to mass markets and a "one size fits all" approach to delivering tourism services; the other points to highly focused services that are targeted toward meeting the needs of specific market niches.

In developing countries such as Poland, Hungary, China, Vietnam, and Brazil, many tourism services will be developed to meet the needs of mass markets. We will see this type of development as levels of disposable income, leisure time, and infrastructure improvements in these countries encourage tourism growth.

Increased economic activity will lead to increased levels of leisure travel both domestically and internationally. As more citizens of the world discover the enjoyment that comes from tourism activities, increasing participation in travel will drive the development of new facilities and services. Many of these new offerings will be provided at **price points** that can meet the needs of larger numbers of these less-affluent new participants. Expanded air and rail services and increased lodging capacity as well as new and expanded attractions and entertainment opportunities will be developed.

Tourism markets will probably take a very different path in developed countries like Canada, Germany, Japan, the United Kingdom, and the United States. In these countries, economic, social, and cultural conditions have already created a large and growing demand for tourism services. We will continue to see mass market tourism, but marketers in these countries will also refine their service offerings to meet the needs of increasingly sophisticated travelers.

Demographic Shifts

One of the biggest changes that will occur in the tourism market in the 21st century will be the increasing size of the mature traveler segment. The Baby Boom generation, those tens of millions of post–World War II babies born between 1945 and 1964, will retire. As you learned in Chapter 2, mature travelers are a very important tourism segment because of their affluence and ability to travel at any time of the year. By 2010, over 80 million members of the U.S. population will be 55 or older, nearly a 40% increase over the number of seniors in 1996.[1] In Canada, almost one quarter of the population will be over 65 by the year 2040, about double the number in that age group today.[2] This explosion in the number of senior citizens is happening in virtually all of the industrialized countries of the world. Consider the potential long-term impacts of the demographics shifts shown in Table 12.1.

Baby-boomer retirees will be even more likely to travel than their parents and grandparents were, and they will be somewhat different in their tourism interests. Senior baby boomers will be healthier, better educated, and wealthier than seniors of previous generations. Many will have already traveled throughout their country and in foreign lands, often as students or businesspeople. Therefore, they will be seeking new adventures in their future travels.

So what can we predict about baby boomers' travel needs once they achieve senior citizen status? First, they will use computers as a source of travel information. Although they may not be as computer-wise as their children and grandchildren, many of them will have owned and used computers for decades. Second, they are likely to be interested in vacations that include a big dose of healthy food, exercise, and the great outdoors. Because

TABLE 12.1
U.S. Population to 2050*

	1996	2010	2030	2050	Percent change 1996–2010	Percent change 2010–30	Percent change 2030–50
All Ages	265,253	297,716	346,899	393,931	12.2%	16.5%	13.6%
Under Age 5	19,403	20,012	23,066	27,106	3.1	15.3	17.5
5 to 13	34,809	35,605	41,588	47,805	2.3	16.8	14.9
14 to 17	15,167	16,894	18,788	21,207	11.4	11.2	12.9
18 to 24	24,616	30,138	31,826	36,333	22.4	5.6	14.2
25 to 34	40,374	38,292	42,744	49,366	5.2	11.6	15.5
35 to 44	43,311	38,521	44,263	47,393	−11.1	14.9	7.1
45 to 54	32,341	43,564	38,897	43,494	34.7	10.7	11.8
55 to 64	21,360	35,283	36,348	42,368	65.2	3.0	16.6
65 and older	33,872	39,408	69,379	78,859	16.3	76.1	13.7
85 and older	3,747	5,671	8,455	18,223	51.3	49.1	115.5

*The U.S. Census Bureau revised its fertility assumptions, and one result is rapid projected growth in the number of U.S. children. (Projected U.S. population by age, 1996–2050; and percent change, 1996–2010, 2010–30, and 2030–50; numbers in thousands)
Source: U.S. Census Bureau.

they have been more health-conscious all their lives, the baby-boom generation will be a very physically active group of senior travelers. They will probably place more importance on *doing* rather than simply seeing attractions. Many will have already "been there and done that" during trips when they were younger, so baby-boomer seniors will want to go to new destinations that offer different things to experience and learn.

WALKABOUT TOURS

The preferred guided tour of the future may not be conducted via motorcoach but instead via the oldest form of transportation: on foot. Recently there has been a boom in the number of tourists taking walking tours. Butterfield & Robinson, a Toronto-based walking tour packager, reports that its business has doubled in the past few years. A U.S. counterpart, Country Walkers of Waterbury, Vermont, saw business nearly double in a single year.

What is driving this phenomenal growth? One reason is that walking is now the most popular form of exercise among adults. Another is that walking tours can run the gamut from extreme tourism for serious trekkers to "soft-adventure" tourism for families or mature travelers. Distances covered per day range from a mere 3 miles to a heart-pumping 12 miles. Walking tour packagers also offer a variety of accommodations and meal plans: rustic for the ecotourist segment through luxurious for the walker who wants to be pampered at the end of the trail.

Source: Flanagan, William G. (1996). Walkabout. *Forbes, 157*, pp. 182–184.

Many baby boomers will want to travel with their children and grandchildren. Because so many families live far away from relatives and have so little common leisure time, vacations have already become family reunion time, and this trend should pick up steam as the baby boomers enter the ranks of grandparents.

More baby boomers will be single in their golden years because, as a generation, they have been less likely to marry and more likely to divorce. Baby boomers will continue to use travel to meet other single people and to fulfill social needs. Savvy tour companies and travel agents will set up travel companion matchmaking services so that boomers do not forgo travel for lack of a travel buddy or due to expensive **single supplement** prices for cruises and tours. Grand Circle Travel, a tour operator, has already taken steps to aid the single traveler by offering shoulder season tours that have no single supplements.

Don't think that the traditional family vacation will disappear. Members of the baby boomlet, those born between 1977 and 1994, will begin their own families as 2000 arrives. Just like the generations of travelers before them, they will want to enjoy the mountains, the seashore, and theme parks with their children. The early years of the 21st century should see another boom of babies, whose unborn members are already being called the echo boomers.

Another demographic shift, which will have an impact on international travel especially, has been the shift in the ethnic mix of North America. During the 19th and first half of the 20th century, most immigrants to the United States and Canada were Europeans by birth. These ethnic groups enjoyed traveling back to their mother countries and fueled transatlantic tourism in the 20th century. But the majority of immigrants during recent decades have come from Latin and Central America, Asia, and former Soviet Union nations (see Figure 12.1). These individuals, as they become more affluent, will also want to visit the lands of their heritage, generating a substantial increase in travel to their homelands.

Changes in Business and Professional Travel

What will happen to the ever-important business and professional travel segment of the tourism market? That is where our crystal ball becomes particularly cloudy: Current trends support the possibility of a decrease or an increase in business and professional travel. Trends in communications, such as computer networking and satellite video image transmission, seem to indicate that business travel will become less necessary. Technological advances will allow businesspeople to see each other and share information as if they were in the same room.

For example, technological improvements in **video conferencing** could slow the rate of growth in business and professional travel. Improvements will allow video conferencing to be conducted with the same convenience and ease of today's telephone conference call. It will be possible to link participants at multiple sites without loss of picture quality, creating the sensation that you are there. These advances will reduce some travel needs, but they may create other needs.

Think about the potential for a publishing company like Prentice Hall. Sales representatives from each of its regions could gather at a designated video conferencing center within their region. They could then share ideas and participate in training programs

FIGURE 12.1
Countries of Origin 1991–1994 (percent distribution of naturalizing citizens in the United States by region of birth).
Source: U.S. Immigration and Naturalization Service.

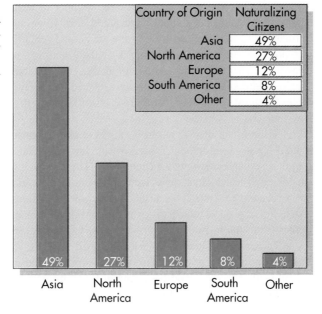

Country of Origin	Naturalizing Citizens
Asia	49%
North America	27%
Europe	12%
South America	8%
Other	4%

with others throughout North America or even the world. Travel would still be involved, but by gathering its sales force at regional sites, Prentice Hall could increase efficiency by saving on both travel expenses and time. Where will these video conferencing centers be located? The logical locations are those properties—conference centers, hotels, and resorts—that can afford to build and equip quality video conferencing facilities.

Even though video conferencing may help to control travel expenses, more and more companies will be doing business with firms across the world. Representatives of these organizations may feel the need for face-to-face meetings to build trusting relationships that can come only from sharing time together. North American businesspeople in particular are being forced by economic necessity to work with other businesspeople from Asia, the **Pacific Rim,** Central and South America, and former Soviet Union nations. In all these locations, trust is the primary foundation for business transactions.[3] These relationships can be developed only by spending time together, sharing meals, and getting to know one another. Because this type of relationship-building requires time and face-to-face interactions it is unlikely that technology will override these cultural factors.

Our best guess is that travel for business and professional reasons will continue to increase in spite of further advances in communication technology. Doing business in the future will involve more, not less, collaboration with others. Some of this increased need for interaction among businesses will be satisfied with telecommunications. However, as Myra noted in our chapter opener, there is no substitute for the personal contact that requires physical travel and meeting with others face to face.

The Future of Ecotourism

As you learned in Chapter 11, the ecotourism segment has evolved in response to the problems brought on by mass tourism. Will ecotourism destinations be able to cope with this growing demand and sustain their natural and cultural preservation goals? One problem facing ecotourism is the large number of travelers who are expressing interest in taking an ecotourism vacation. A recent survey of travelers reveals that 34 million Americans took a nature-based trip during their last vacation or plan to on an upcoming vacation.[4] With environmentalism becoming more important to more people, especially to North Americans and Europeans, the size of the ecotourist segment should increase dramatically in the 21st century. However, large numbers of tourists are contradictory to the goals of ecotourism.

To handle more visitors to fragile natural and cultural sites, tourism planners could limit tourist facilities such as hotels to small areas of the site, but concentrated development would need to be high-rise and high-density and would not blend with the landscape of the area. However, dispersing a large number of lodging properties throughout a natural region would necessitate widespread development of both infrastructure and superstructure and would mean little of the area could remain entirely undeveloped. Adding to the potential problem of crowding is the fact that most ecotourism destinations will be at least somewhat seasonal. Although the area may be able to satisfy off-season and shoulder season demand, peak season demand would surely strain limited resources and services facilities. Therefore, ecotourism itself is likely to be threatened in the future by its own success.

Ecotourism also may not be the best choice for many of the nations that are well suited for its development. Third World countries tend to have many of the natural and cultural resources that attract ecotourists. These same countries are also the most in need of jobs and **hard currencies** from industrialized nations. Ecotourism tends to result in slow revenue generation because "in the wilderness there is nothing to spend money on."[5] Areas relying on ecotourism for economic development will need to be patient as revenues from this form of tourism take time to accumulate.

In addition, citizens in less-developed countries are often most vulnerable to the demonstration effects of affluent tourists. Finally, the native people of these areas have traditionally used the land for farming, foresting, and hunting activities. These activities would have to be curtailed if ecotourism were expanded.

Preserving the past becomes more challenging as the number of visitors increases.
Photo by L.J. Yale.

Unless the emerging ranks of ecotourists are willing to go without the most basic standards of comfort and convenience, most ecotourism destinations will need to cater to Western tastes to be able to attract a substantial number of visitors. Therefore, ecotourism may be the double-edged sword of the 21st century. It may represent one of the fastest-growing segments of tourism, but it may also lead to the development and exploitation of the last natural regions and primitive cultures on Earth. Our future actions will answer a very difficult question: Can we enjoy nature yet keep from loving it to death?

IDENTIFYING AND MEETING FUTURE TOURISTS' NEEDS

In the 21st century, two forms of market segmentation will become more common. **Microsegmentation** and **mass customization** began to be used in the 1990s, but these two concepts will gain further use once 2000 dawns. Subsegments, also called "microsegments," are market segments that represent a relatively small group of consumers such as Californian young professional Asian-Americans or Manitoban back-country fishing enthusiasts. As companies attempted to lure customers from competitors, they began developing product offerings to meet the needs of smaller and smaller market segments.

Mass customization is the extreme of microsegmentation.[6] A company mass customizes when it produces a good or service to fulfill the unique needs of an individual buyer. For example, during the 1990s, several computer manufacturers built personal computers to individual customer specifications. All the components, including the size of the hard drive, the number of floppy drives, and the amount of RAM, could be chosen by the consumer from a menu of options and then the manufacturer assembled the pieces to deliver exactly what the buyer needed. Tourism businesses in the future will use both microsegmentation and mass customization to attract guests.

Tourism service suppliers and intermediaries will increasingly design and sell services to meet the needs of more specifically defined target segments. Cruise lines have already started offering special cruises to appeal to microsegments. The Carnival Line, for example, offers "Soaps Afloat" cruises for fans of major network TV daytime dramas.

Cruise lines must attract more targeted microsegments to fill the ever-increasing number of berths on even larger future ships.[7]

Mass customization will allow travelers to customize their service packages and travel itineraries. Hotels specializing in the business and professional segments are building rooms that can be **configured** to suit individual guest's needs for multimedia presentations, conference calling, telecommunications links, etc.[8] Tour companies will use mass customization to allow more flexibility in touring. As the tourism market becomes more competitive, the empathy component of service quality you learned about in Chapter 9 will become more and more important. Both microsegmentation and mass customization can add the personal touch of empathy to a tourism service.

Mass Customization = Personalization

The Ritz-Carlton luxury hotel chain is taking the concept of mass customization seriously. Guest preferences are entered into the hotel database so that service during return visits can be more personalized. For example, if a guest requests a hypo-allergenic pillow, for her next stay, housekeeping will make up her bed with that type of pillow without waiting for a request. And if a guest eats only the complimentary peanut butter cookies (forgoing the chocolate chip and sugar cookies), he will receive more peanut butter cookies during subsequent stays. Talk about making you feel at home!

Source: Brown, Tom (1996). Efficiently serving customers uniquely. *American Management Association, 85,* pp. 60–61.

Database marketing, also called **data mining,** will aid tourism suppliers in targeting microsegments and customizing marketing mixes to fulfill the needs of specific travelers. Because computers can store and rapidly sift through vast amounts of information, marketers can build immense databases to provide them with extremely detailed profiles of prospective consumers.

For example, American Express Travel Related Services Co. partners with hundreds of tourism suppliers to target very specific direct mail promotions. Here is a hypothetical example to show you how a tourism business might use this database marketing partnership. Through American Express credit card company records of client purchasers, the sales director of a resort property could request a mailing list of active golfers residing in the northwest region of North America. These golfers could then be sent information about a special golfers' holiday package.

Privacy concerns have been raised about the sharing of consumer information, so database marketing may be limited in some way through government regulation. However, given its power and targeting potential, companies of the future will become more sophisticated in their acquisition and use of information.[9]

Moving into an Era of Competitive Cooperation

The tourism industry has historically been fragmented, with many different suppliers serving an ever-growing market. This fragmentation has resulted in varying levels of service, quality, availability, and pricing. At the same time, the traveling public has become more knowledgeable and demanding about tourism services, forcing managers to search for new ways to control costs and improve quality. As organizations respond to the converging demands of improving quality and controlling costs we will witness an era marked by an increasing number of mergers, acquisitions, alliances, and cooperative agreements.

Manufacturing and other services have led the way by consolidating to gain market share and increase operating efficiencies and profitability. In the early 1900s, there were hundreds of automobile manufacturers in the United States alone. Now there are only a handful. Smaller, less-efficient manufacturers were overtaken by larger, more-efficient, and better-capitalized companies that could respond to changing consumer demands. The same type of trend is beginning to emerge in the tourism industry as suppliers begin to consolidate. Several airlines have been acquired by larger rivals, and cruise lines are merging as well. Similar combinations will continue and become more common in other segments of the industry as organizations seek economies of scale and broader name recognition across national and international markets.

Airlines have pioneered the development of cooperative alliances to gain greater brand recognition and operating synergies. For example, the alliance between British Airways and American Airlines that signaled dominance in the north Atlantic marketplace gave rise to the competing Star Alliance. The Star Alliance created a global airline network consisting of United, Lufthansa, Air Canada, SAS, Thai Airways, and Varig, which together serve almost 600 cities in over 100 countries. This alliance "plans to create 'the airline of the earth,' with the goal of serving every major city on the planet. . ." (p. 1).[10]

Airline alliances meet customer needs by delivering " 'seamless service'—simplified ticketing, better connections, through baggage checking and frequent flyer reciprocity." (p. 73).[10] They also provide another important economic benefit by allowing airlines to gain access to landing slots and gates at already crowded international airports. Stay tuned to industry publications for more changes as the number of major participants in the airline industry continues to shrink and the remaining organizations increase their levels of cooperation.

As we discussed in Chapter 6, the move toward industry partnering is also accelerating in the food-service segment of the tourism industry. Every link in the supply chain, from manufacturers and distributors to operators and customers, is being brought closer together to improve service and reduce operating costs. These efforts have been dubbed **efficient food-service response,** or EFR. The partnership agreements that are evolving through EFR are providing lower food costs, fewer inventory errors, and higher levels of customer satisfaction and value.[11]

There will also be an increase in **subcontracting** of many functions needed to support guest services. Operations such as cleaning, laundry, and food service will be performed by outside contractors. In some situations the operating company will own the facilities and equipment and rely on the expertise of outside contractors to provide and manage labor. In other situations space will be leased to subcontractors, who in turn will make the investments in equipment as well as manage the entire operation. This trend is already becoming evident in the number of fast-food outlets that are appearing in hotels, airports, theme parks, service stations and food courts in malls.

ACCELERATING TECHNOLOGICAL ADVANCES

One thing about the future of technological advances is for sure. The rate of change will continue to increase. To get some idea of future technological changes, think back to the computers you used at home, work, or school just 5 years ago. How fast could they operate? What software did they run? How were they linked to information sources around the world? What you thought was fast and efficient back then is slow and cumbersome by today's standards. And computer technology is just one facet of the technological changes that will shape the future of the tourism industry. Advances in new and lighter materials will produce opportunities for more efficient forms of transportation as well as new recreational opportunities.

Maximizing Operating Efficiencies

Technology will become more important to service providers as rising wages force cuts in staff size, creating the need for increased productivity. For example, the use of central kitchens will allow large operations to provide a variety of menu items to several satellite dining locations with fewer preparation and production employees and less equipment.

Communication technologies will make internal ordering and inventory stocking more efficient by allowing employees to communicate through remote devices. Dining room and housekeeping employees will transmit orders and inventory needs through wireless headsets and hand-held order-entry equipment. Successfully responding to customer requests and coordinating service response in a timely manner among multiple departments will become the norm rather than the exception.

Internet access is also being used to improve the efficiencies of yield-management programs. American Airlines alerts users who have signed up on the company's website about weekly specials, which helps to fill otherwise empty seats.[12] When a large group unexpectedly canceled their reservations at the Ritz Carlton in Aspen, Colorado, management offered the rooms at a special rate to travel agents and Internet users. The first 50 takers of the special rate were able to save over $250 per night, and the hotel was able to fill up on short notice. This turned out to be a win-win situation.[13]

Amplifying Guests' Experiences

Not all technological advancements will be used to enhance business efficiencies. Some of these advances will be designed for education and entertainment. Virtual reality (VR) technology is already showing usefulness in the tourism industry. At Zoo Atlanta, a VR exhibit is being developed that will allow visitors to enter a virtual jungle playing the role of a young gorilla who interacts with his environment and other gorillas.[14] In England, VR technology is being used to help preserve the fragile Stonehenge archeological site. Stonehenge Millenium Park will provide visitors with a three-dimensional view of the massive stone circle, incorporating the local terrain, the night sky, and with sunrise special effects.[15] British Airways used VR to promote its new first-class flying bed. Curious travelers can sample the new seat free of charge by connecting to its virtual reality version offered through its website.[16]

Restaurants will be able to use the Internet's marketing muscle to provide detailed information to prospective diners. Helpful information such as unit locations (with detailed directions), menu information, and reservation e-mail could all be provided via the Web.[17] Accommodations suppliers could use websites to provide similar information along with virtual reality tours of different room types, meeting rooms, and other facilities. Making reservations hassle-free for Internet users would be a real money-maker for ho-

TOURISM IN ACTION

Have a spare hour or two this Friday night? How about taking a tour of the Grand Canyon? Niagara Falls? Or would you prefer Yellowstone National Park? Motion picture and virtual reality technology advances have given birth to a new form of entertainment: the synthetic destination. Some of you may have already experienced a synthetic destination by attending one of the growing number of IMAX theaters. These big-screen projections, along with motion simulators and computerized rides, can recreate scenery, history, and culture. Synthetic destinations are sometimes offered far from the real thing, such as via the IMAX theaters in various cities, but often they are close to the attractions they simulate.

Visitors to London can now experience its past by taking a ride called the Tower Hill Pageant, located just minutes from the city's famous Tower fortress. In New York City, the second floor of the Empire State Building now houses the New York Skyride, a simulated flight above the city. When visiting Niagara Falls, you can "Ride Niagara," a 30-minute journey "over the falls" for the price of a $7 ticket.

Children particularly seem to enjoy combining the (often boring) actual attraction with its more exciting simulated twin. After all, the Grand Canyon and the New York skyline are just panoramic views. Movies and rides are where the action is! Richard Crane, an attractions designer from Orlando, says tourists today "want to be interactive. . . . Why they can't Zen out and look at the view, I don't know. But they want more" (Carey, 1996, B6).

Emerging entertainment technologies are also being used to protect fragile historic/cultural sites. In the United Kingdom, visitors are no longer allowed near the prehistoric Stonehenge monument. To replace this opportunity, a virtual reality tour will soon open that allows guests to view a three-dimensional model and "touch" the stone monoliths with special tactile gloves. In the United States, the National Park Service is developing a new visitors center at the Gettysburg Civil War battle site that will include interactive media and a Sony IMAX theater.

Sources: Carey, Susan (1996, May 3). Unnatural wonders: Simulated tours beat real thing. *Wall Street Journal*, pp. B1, B6; Kiley, David (1997). Gettysburg addressed," *Brandweek, 38*(35), pp. 42–44; Yamada, Ken (1996, September 2). VR's virtual visit to Stonehenge. *Computer Reseller News*, p. 61.

tels. Holiday Inn management estimates that it saves 25% on website reservations over those made over the phone or through travel agents or other reservation systems.[18]

The Green Frontier

One technology that is being embraced by the tourism industry is recycling. For example, the National Restaurant Association has reported that more than 7 of 10 operators purchased products made from recycled materials and roughly 3 of 4 operate recycling programs.[19] Recycling is being adopted as an operational responsibility, and many organizations such as Northwest Airlines are discovering the resulting benefits of employee pride, care, and motivation.

Have you stayed at a **green hotel** yet? If you haven't, chances are that you will in the future. As you learned in Chapter 5, environmental issues are becoming more important for lodging properties. Therefore, more green hotels are appearing. In a green hotel, guests place a card on their pillow that indicates whether or not they would like their sheets changed and only the towels left on the floor replaced. These simple practices save millions of gallons of water and prevent the release of tons of detergents into the environment. From an operations standpoint, it saves on the cost of linen, labor, and equipment. Most employees and guests are embracing green hotel practices with enthusiasm. Recycling holds the future promise of additional operating efficiencies and environmental benefits.

Transportation Transformations

Future transportation needs will be met with expanded air and rail service. As the world's major airports continue to become more congested, airline executives and airport managers are pushing aircraft manufacturers to develop larger, quieter, and more-efficient aircraft. Several prototype aircraft that could carry anywhere from 530 to 840 passengers (see Figure 12.2), depending on the manufacturer and the seating configuration, are moving from the drawing boards to reality. In addition to looking at aircraft with more room, several alternatives are being considered to replace the aging supersonic Concorde, which will be retired in 2005. All these alternatives would rely on using variable-cycle engines

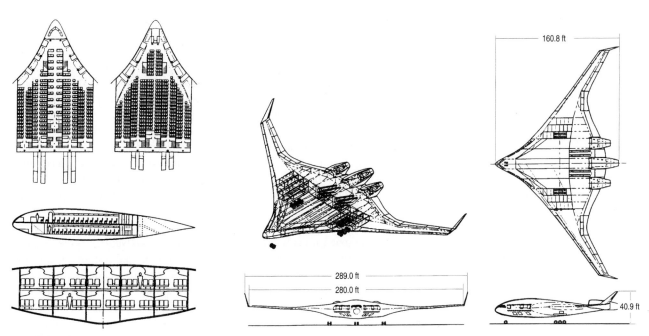

FIGURE 12.2
Prototype design of 21st-century passenger airplane.
Design plans courtesy of the Boeing Company.

to overcome noise and efficiency concerns by allowing flight at both subsonic and supersonic speeds.[20]

Expanded passenger rail service will also provide additional relief to crowded transportation corridors. Before the turn of the century, train service with speeds of 250 mph and faster will be the accepted norm in Europe,[21] and similar advances will also be seen in Japan. Speeds in excess of 500 mph are not far behind. These advances may be slower in coming to the United States and Canada because of greater distances between large population centers and the poor quality of existing tracks and roadbeds. However, trains will perform a different function in the form of **light-rail** service. This new service will be introduced or expanded between major airports located in more remote areas such as the Denver International Airport and downtown business areas. In fact, new airport construction will be focused on remote locations to alleviate noise and air-space congestion concerns. When remote locations are combined with efficient light-rail service the benefits of hub-and-spoke operations will be enhanced.

Light-rail transportation systems are the key component of pilot projects designed to reduce traffic in several of the most crowded U.S. National Parks. Soon parking lots and many roads in Grand Canyon, Zion, and Yosemite National Parks will be torn up and returned to nature. Most visitors will be transported to park interiors via mass transit such as light rail. Only visitors with overnight accommodations will be allowed to drive vehicles into the parks to reach their lodge or campground. Once there, even these vehicles would have to remain parked.

TRAVEL AGENTS' CHANGING ROLES

There is nothing like a little uncertainty about the future to create concern and cause a good debate. One of these hotly debated areas in the tourism industry is the future role of the travel agent. As we discussed in Chapter 3, travel agents have been important intermediaries in the industry, performing a valuable service by bringing together tourism service suppliers and the traveling public. Will the role of the travel agent remain the same in a world that appears to be turning in ever-increasing numbers to new information sources such as the Internet?

You be the judge in this debate. Some experts say that the role of the travel agent will become unimportant in a world where everyone has access to travel-related information and reservation sources through personal computers. Other experts say that the role of the travel agent will become more important and specialized as people have access to more data and less time to sort through this sea of information. "The most vulnerable travel agents are, at one end of the spectrum, the neighbourhood stores whose owners are in it for the perks rather than the profit and, at the other end, the big firms that serve corporate clients. Such clients are not after romance, just efficiency" (p. 9).[22]

Some people may use the information and reservation capacities provided through the Internet to book simple travel arrangements such as traveling from point A to point B, but, as travel needs become more complex, the services of travel professionals may prove to be invaluable. Rapid technological changes and the need to possess detailed knowledge may force more and more travel agents to focus on one particular part of the industry, such as cruises or ecotourism destinations.[13]

The technology provided through the Internet has the power to make travel planning more exciting. Computer users will become more informed consumers as they explore travel and other leisure-time options ranging from transportation and accommodations to attractions and entertainment. As networking capabilities continue to increase in availability and speed, computer terminals, serving as electronic smart agents that utilize **artificial intelligence,** will develop to meet travelers' specific needs. Booking a preferred flight time, reserving accommodations that meet specific criteria such as price range, level of service, or driving distance from the airport, and reserving tickets for the evening play are all future possibilities. For other people, the personal service and professional expertise provided by a travel agent will continue to be the travel department store of choice.[13]

Scanning the Horizon for Future Tourist Activities

How will the activities and attractions presented in Chapter 7 and the recreational opportunities presented in Chapter 8 change in the 21st century? **Adventure tourism,** sometimes called **extreme tourism,** is likely to grow in popularity. Adventure attractions involve activities with an above-average element of physical risk. Bungee jumping, parachuting, rock climbing, and cliff skiing/snowboarding are all examples of adventure or extreme activities. Growth in participation in these sports has been escalating in recent years. For example, the U.S. Parachute Association reports that its membership has increased by 10% in each of the past 2 years. Although young men are most likely to seek out extreme thrills, nontraditional groups such as women and those over 40 years old are the fastest-growing **subsegments.**[23]

Why are these more dangerous activities gaining in popularity? One reason offered by industry leaders is that these sports have been spotlighted and glamorized in the media, including motion pictures. (Did you see *Cliffhanger* with Sylvester Stallone?) Another reason suggested is that our everyday world is so secure—from tamper-resistant packaging to automobile air bags—that people want to feel that physical rush of danger, even if the rush comes more from the appearance of living on the edge than from actual terror. Growing demand for extreme activities is also driven by increasing affluence and the increased safety and better equipment of many of the sports.[23] To some extent, tried-and-true activities and attractions have become boring because they are so familiar to so many.

The worldwide consumer research firm, SRI International, estimates that 12% of all adults could be labeled thrill seekers, and, in Generation X, the percentage is even higher—33%. The high percentage of Xers who are present—or future—adventure tourists comes from that generation's desire to be different from their baby-boomer parents.

Extreme sports are typically outdoor or wilderness sports and go hand-in-hand with ecotourism. A sea kayaking trip off the coast of Costa Rica qualifies as both ecotourism and adventure tourism. Tourism suppliers, especially tour operators, will create at least two different ecotourism packages. One ecotour type will be more educational and observational while the other will be more physically challenging, including one or more extreme sports.

Theme parks will also continue to "push the envelope" by adding rides or activities that allow visitors to be more active and to at least think they are in a potentially dangerous situation. For example, roller coaster speeds will be pushed to the level of human endurance. Virtual reality technology will be especially useful in adding a realistic rush to the rides of the future. Virtual Kourier, at Funset Boulevard in Appleton, Wisconsin, is a virtual reality ride that allows the guest to play big-city bicycle courier, dodging traffic and all.[24]

As you learned in Chapter 7, casino gaming spread throughout North America at an amazing rate in the past decades. Will it continue to grow? Increasingly, casinos will position themselves as mainstream good clean fun, blending gaming with a theme park/shopping mall environment. Large-scale casino resorts will add entertainment and interaction to their gaming locations, both to attract younger gamers with children and to add to revenues. Slot machines of the future will be more similar to arcade and video games so that those new to gaming will feel comfortable trying their hands at wagering. Casino Data Systems is developing Gold Fever, a slot machine for the 21st century. The machine features an 18-minute movie, and the company is working on computer-animated slots as well.[25]

Keeping the Human Touch?

To help reduce labor costs, many tourism-related businesses are automating services that until recently were provided by people. More and more businesses within the tourism industry are making greater use of computer terminals and interactive screens to allow travelers to "do-it-yourself." Although this step depersonalizes service, a growing number of travelers prefer speed and efficiency to the more personal interaction with hospitality service employees.

Will technology replace the need for human service in the tourism industry? If you look at the technological enhancements to service delivery that have already been introduced to the tourism industry, the answer may be yes. For years, many hotels have allowed guests to check out without stopping by the front desk. Now, some properties have added "electronic concierges" that give information about hotel services, directions to places within the area, etc. At other properties, self-service kiosks similar to automated teller machines (ATMs) are being used to speed up the delivery of guest services.

Cyber Suites

Los Angeles's Century Plaza Hotel is working on the hotel room of the future. The Cyber Suite has been constructed as a prototype 21st-century hotel room. Features of the Cyber Suite include:

- video conferencing and desktop broadcasting capability,
- in-room virtual reality interactive game possibilities,
- the "Butler in a Box," which uses voice recognition to operate lights, heating and air-conditioning, draperies, television, and other appliances, and
- a cellular phone, allowing guests to receive calls made to their room even when they are out of the hotel.

Source: "World Trends & Forecasts: Technology, Hotel Room of the Future (1997). *The Futurist, 31*(2), p. 59.

In certain motels in Europe, guests use an ATM-type machine to communicate their room needs. If a suitable room is available, the machine dispenses a plastic keycard for the room. It is predicted that "self-service check-in/check-out kiosks will become the norm

Cookies—a sweet touch of hospitality.
Photo by A. Talg.

in the hotel industry in the years to come" (p. B1).[26] Rental car agencies are also using self-service kiosks at many airport locations.

These technological advances may make life simpler and more convenient for tourism service providers and tourists. However, many (possibly the majority of travelers), still seem to value the personal touch of dealing with another human being. Most people, especially older travelers, do not see doing-it-themselves as a savings in time, but as an unnecessary added effort.[27] Extending heart-felt hospitality will always be the centerpiece of the tourism industry.

CONCLUSION

It seems that the more things change, the more they stay the same. We may not stick a fresh pineapple on the front fence like the old New England ship captains as a symbol of hospitality, but the welcoming touch provided by service employees will remain a key factor to service success in this growing industry. This bold prediction is good news for both future tourists and employees in the industry: "Despite advances such as virtual reality, new technologies will more likely become marketing tools for travel agencies, rather than replacing real vacations" (p. 49).[28] Real vacationers need real people to meet their needs and expectations. As we stated in Chapter 1, the number of jobs created by tourism organizations is projected to continue increasing in the years to come.

You have made a great start in developing a sound foundation for becoming a professional member of the tourism industry or an informed consumer of tourism services. There will always be new things to do and learn in our rapidly changing world. We hope you decide to become a part of this excitement. You can build a bright professional future by dedicating yourself to lifelong learning and a never-ending desire to continually improve your knowledge, skills, and abilities. If you would like to become a part of the growing cadre of tourism professionals, take a look at Appendix C and learn more about how to conduct a successful job search.

 ## YOU DECIDE

Microsegmentation, grouping consumers into smaller market segments than those more commonly used in the past, has been employed by more and more companies as markets have become saturated. Many companies have found sales growth difficult to come by: To gain increased sales, consumers must be won away from competitors. The best way to win a customer is to satisfy the customer's unique needs better than a competitor does.

By grouping customers into more-specific groups, firms can better fulfill customer needs. As the tourism industry becomes more competitive, tourism suppliers have begun focusing on the needs of less-traditional segments of potential travelers. For example, instead of targeting the business segment, a hotel company might target the young, technologically savvy, traveling saleswoman subsegment of the business and professional market.

A subsegment that is being targeted more and more is the less-affluent counterpart of other segments, such as the low-income mature traveler or the low-income young-family subsegment. Lower-income travelers represent potential growth for travel providers because they have not been able to afford many of the travel services that other more-affluent travelers have been purchasing. To appeal to these lower-

income segments, some tourism suppliers are offering special financing services.

The Princess Cruise Line is now offering its own "Love Boat Loan Cruise Financing" plan. Their slogan for the plan is "Bringing Your Dream Vacation within Reach." Prospective passengers unable to afford a cruise due to a lack of savings are encouraged to "spread the cost over two, three or four years, into very manageable monthly payments." Clients can even include on-board spending for drinks, shore excursions, and shopping as part of the loan. Interested customers simply call an 800 number to apply: "There is absolutely no paperwork to fill out and you will communicate by phone directly with the bank." Interest rates vary from 15 to 27% depending on the individual's credit history and desired payment schedule.

For decades, travelers have been able to play before they pay. Banks have long offered vacation loans and credit card companies encourage purchasing travel services on credit. Tourism company–based financing is just one more means that customers can use to gratify their vacation desires now and pay later. Should tourism service suppliers encourage customers to "travel now and pay later"?

NET TOUR

To learn more about the concepts and organizations presented in this chapter access the homepage for *Tourism: The Business of Travel*. Select "Chapter 12: Exploring the Future of Tourism." From this location test your knowledge by taking the chapter quiz, read industry insights, and discover links to other useful sites. You may also want to visit electronically other tourism students through the website.

DISCUSSION QUESTIONS

1. Based on your knowledge of the tourism industry, do you think services will be developed to serve mass markets or specific market niches?

2. How could data mining be used by an airline or other tourism service provider to meet current and future customer needs?

3. Based on your knowledge of the tourism industry, which of the following groups holds the most promise for future growth—mature travelers, international travelers or business and professional travelers?

4. How will technology affect the future of the tourism industry?

5. If the ecotourism segment of the tourism industry continues its current rate of growth, what problems will be encountered?

6. Why will the number of suppliers in the tourism industry decrease, and how will this consolidation of suppliers take place?

7. Will advances in technology replace the need for the human touch in the tourism industry?

APPLYING THE CONCEPTS

1. Using the resources of your local library or the Internet, access either the United States Statistical Abstract or Statistics Canada. What recent trends have occurred in tourism-related activities? Do you think these trends will continue? Why or why not?

2. Arrange an interview with an experienced travel agent. Ask what changes s/he has observed in the tourism industry in the past 5 years. Some areas you might ask questions about include changes in business and professional travel, ecotourism, international travel, and technology.

3. Choose any one of the tourism service suppliers that has been discussed in this course. With two or more students brainstorm ways that mass customization and

microsegmentation could be used to improve customer service and revenues.

4. Interview a friend or relative whom you think is a member of the adventure tourism segment. Ask about his or her most recent vacation. Also ask why s/he participates in extreme activities and what benefits are derived from these activities.

5. Interview a manager of a tourism business to determine what s/he thinks are some of the major challenges facing his/her sector of the industry in the 21st century. Are any changes being made to meet these challenges, such as EFR, greater automation, subcontracting, etc?

GLOSSARY

Adventure tourism Tourism that involves activities with an above-average element of physical risk; also called "extreme tourism."

Artificial intelligence A segment of computer sciences devoted to the development of computer hardware and software that is designed to imitate the human mind.

Configured (rooms) Rooms with a well-planned design developed to meet user needs for efficiency and effectiveness.

Cooperative alliances Creating long-term relationships that enhance operating efficiencies, profitability and market share for all parties.

Data mining Analyzing information stored in computer databases with the help of statistical techniques to uncover hidden relationships and patterns.

Efficient food-service response (EFR) Partnership agreements created among manufacturers, distributors, and food-service operators to lower food costs and improve the quality of service.

Extreme tourism see *Adventure tourism*.

Green hotel A lodging property where guests and employees are actively involved in resource conservation and pollution reduction.

Hard currencies A currency, such as Canadian dollars and Japanese yen, that is valued in all countries and is easily exchangeable into other currencies.

Light rail A form of passenger rail transportation designed for use over short distances in metropolitan areas.

Mass customization The production of a good or service to fulfill the unique needs of an individual buyer.

Microsegmentation The process of identifying and serving small subsegments of the market.

Pacific Rim The land masses that have Pacific Ocean coastline.

Price points Different levels of prices designed to appeal to varying market segments.

Single supplement The additional charge added to the price of a tour or cruise when a traveler does not share

accommodations with another traveler; often 50% to 100% of the double occupancy rate is added to arrive at a single occupancy rate.

Subsegments A group within a larger market segment, sometimes called a "microsegment."

Subcontracting Hiring another organization to perform one or more operational functions or services.

Video conferencing Meetings among geographically dispersed individuals using video, sound, and data transmission technologies so participants can see and interact with each other.

REFERENCES

1. Dortch, Shannon (1996a). Rise and fall of generations. *American Demographics, 18*(7), 6–7, 43.

2. Statistics Canada (1997). *A portrait of seniors in Canada.* Catalogue 89-503-XPB, Ottawa.

3. Harris, Philip R., & Moran, Robert T. (1996). *Managing cultural differences* (4th ed.). Houston: Gulf Publishing Company.

4. Rennicks, Jennifer Stucker (1997, January/March). Nature-based tourism. *B & E Review*, pp. 8–11.

5. Cater, Erlet (1994). Ecotourism in the Third World—Problems and prospects for sustainability. In: Cater, Erlet & Lowman, Gwen (Eds.) *Ecotourism: A sustainable option?* Chichester: John Wiley & Sons, pp. 69–86.

6. Pine, B. Joseph II (1993). *Mass customization: The new frontier in business competition.* Boston: Harvard Business School Press.

7. Dortch, Shannon (1996). Kaleidoscope: A swiftly changing scene. *American Demographics, 18*(11), pp. 22–27.

8. Bigness, Jon, & Dahl, Jonathan (1996, February 2). Soon, hotels only a boss could love. *Wall Street Journal*, p. B5.

9. Berry, Jonathan, Verity, John, Kerwin, Kathleen F., & DeGeorge, Gail (1994, September 5). Database marketing: Potent new tool for selling. *Business Week*, pp. 56–62.

10. McDonald, Michelle (1997, May 19). Six carriers create global "Star Alliance." *Travel Weekly*, pp. 1, 73.

11. Malchoff, Kevin R. (1996). The future is spelled E-F-R. *Restaurant Business, 95*(16), p. 229.

12. Gunther, Marc (1996, September 9). Travel Planning in cyberspace. *Fortune*, pp. 187–188.

13. Wolff, Carlo (1997, February). Is the travel agent headed for extinction. *Lodging Hospitality*, pp. 18–22.

14. Zoo goes ape over VR (1997). *R & D Magazine, 39*(2), p. 34.

15. Yamada, Ken (1996). VR's virtual visit to Stonehenge. *Computer Reseller News, 699*, p. 61.

16. BA offers first class cyberspace (1996). *Air Transport World, 33*(4), p. 71.

17. Grimes, Rob (1997). Foodservice's success on the Internet seems a virtual reality. *Nation's Restaurant News, 31*(5), p. 28.

18. Buchanan, Leigh (1996, March/April). Rooms with a view. *CIO, WebMaster Supplement*, pp. 34–42.

19. National Restaurant Association website, <http://www.restaurant.org>.

20. Will size overtake speed? (1995, April 13). *The European*, p. 26.

21. "New TGV Could Be Built in the UK," (1995, April 30). *The London Sunday Times*, business p. 2.

22. Travel and tourism: Home and away (1998, January). *The Economist*, p. 9.

23. Heath, Rebecca Piirto (1997). Extreme thrills. *American Demographics, 19*(6), pp. 47–51.

24. Minton, Eric (1997). Going to extremes. *Fun World, 13*(6), pp. 28–34.

25. Heubusch, Kevin (1997). Taking chances on casinos. *American Demographics, 19*(5), pp. 35–40.

26. Bigness, Jon (1996, June 18). Impersonal touch: More hotels automate front desk. *Wall Street Journal*, pp. B1, B7.

27. Bateson, John, E. G. (1983). The self-service consumer: Empirical findings. In: Berry, Leonard, Shostack, Lynn, & Upah, Greg (Eds.), *Marketing of services.* Chicago: American Marketing Association, pp. 50–53.

28. Gaede, Diane (1994). Lifestyles: Tourism tomorrow. *Futurist, 28*(1), pp. 49–50.

Readings

Satisfaction Guaranteed

■

SOME CALL IT A MARKETING GIMMICK, OTHERS SAY IT CAN
REVOLUTIONIZE SERVICE. WHY ARE MORE AND MORE HOTEL
COMPANIES HOPPING ON THE GUARANTEE BANDWAGON?

BY GRACE WAGNER, ASSOCIATE EDITOR

Nordstrom, L.L. Bean and Wal-Mart have built solid reputations around them. Saturn, Lands End and Sears have successfully implemented programs of their own. By backing their products with unconditional, 100-percent satisfaction guarantees, these companies have attracted new customers and kept loyal ones for years.

In the 1993 book, *Extraordinary Guarantees*, quality guru and author Christopher Hart explains that, for a guarantee to be effective, it can't be anything short of extraordinary.

"An ordinary guarantee," Hart writes, "is designed to alleviate the customer's loss in the case of a product or service failure—within certain limits. An *extraordinary* guarantee is more ambitious: In its strongest form, it promises exceptional, uncompromising quality and customer satisfaction, and it backs that promise with a payout intended to fully recapture the customer's goodwill, with few strings attached."

For retailers like Bean, Nordstrom and Wal-Mart, the concept is simple: They have a product, they have a customer. If the customer isn't satisfied with the product, they offer to exchange or return it for a full refund. No hassles. No questions asked.

For hoteliers, whose product is the ever-intangible "hospitality"—the concept isn't as cut and dried. Unhappy guests can't ship a lousy lodging experience back to a hotel via UPS. Often, they can't even identify what angered or alienated them in the first place.

Despite such obstacles, Hart claims that an extraordinary guarantee is equally appropriate for the lodging industry. In fact, he says, a well-communicated, well-executed guarantee can turn the hospitality experience into something tangible.

"An extraordinary guarantee tells you up front exactly what you should get, and promises to give it or else," Hart says. "That concept is applicable not only to hotel room accommodations but to banquet and meeting services as well."

In recent years, several hotel companies have embraced the guarantee concept; Hampton Inn is the acknowl-edged leader. In 1989, the relatively young chain rolled out its 100-Percent Satisfaction Guarantee, pledging "high-quality accommodations, friendly and efficient service, and clean, comfortable surroundings." The campaign hit newsstands with full-page ads in *USA Today, Sports Illustrated* and *U.S. News & World Report*.

In his book, Hart praises every aspect of Hampton's program: "Not only were they the first," he says, "but they were the first to do it right." He credits then Hampton President Ray Schultz (now president of the Promus Hotel Group) and marketing V.P. Mark Wells for having "pushed the guarantee concept further, by implementing it in a situation many would have considered untenable: a multi-site franchise organization."

Schultz recognized that while a complaint isn't exactly a positive thing, it presents the ultimate opportunity to increase customer retention. Thus, it becomes a positive. Giving unhappy guests a refund may have a short-term cost, but the long-term economic benefits of such a practice are immeasurable.

Wells, now senior vice president of marketing for all Promus brands (including Hampton Inn), says the guarantee has helped Hampton improve its image of product consistency. "We've kept customers in the fold. It's that simple," he says.

"A hotel isn't like a car," Wells notes. "We don't offer test drives or trials. In fact, we take the money up front," he laughs. "So having a guarantee equalizes the process. We still take their money, but we ensure that our guests will be satisfied once they touch, feel and experience the product. That's the most we can do to show confidence in what we have to offer and a commitment to pleasing the end user, no matter what the cost."

A company's ability to create the infrastructure necessary to make a guarantee operate smoothly separates those that will be successful from those that will eventually fade away, says Hart.

"Satisfaction guarantees require a full-time network of support on the interior side of an organization," he says. "They can be a tremendous quality improvement catalyst, provided every department asks itself, 'What changes do we need to make in order for this to work?' Departments must also work well together, sometimes even pinch-hitting for each other."

In Hampton's case, the personal commitment of top management to ensure understanding of its guarantee at the property level sets it apart to this day, Hart claims. "In addition to giving his GMs and owners the proper introduction and education that allowed them to see the benefits of having a guarantee, Ray Schultz followed the program all the way down the line." Apparently, he phoned every general manager following regional rollout meetings to inquire about employee acceptance of the program.

At Choice Hotels, which just introduced a satisfaction guarantee at all its Sleep Inn brand properties, field education has been the program's cornerstone, says Steve Mullinger, senior vice president of Choice's franchise system division.

His department conducted seminars for managers from every Sleep property, each of whom returned to their hotels with training videos and instructions to indoctrinate all employees. "We've concentrated heavily on empowerment," Mullinger says. "I know it's an overused term, but it's the key ingredient to making this program work."

If Sleep Inn employees become aware of an unhappy guest, it's their responsibility to address the situation and attempt to fix it, regardless of job description, he claims. "If they can't satisfy the guest, then they're empowered to offer the refund," Mullinger says.

Mullinger's comment brings up a point of contention among guarantee advocates: If a hotel promotes a "100-percent satisfaction guarantee or your money back," should a guest have to give the property a chance to correct whatever it was that made them unhappy? If damage is done, can it be undone, and should a hotel get a second chance before paying up?

Hart thinks not. "If you're advertising an unconditional guarantee, you'd better be good. But if something happens that exposes a pothole in your product, make the payout *and* fix the hole," he says.

Ironically, Hart adds, hotels with lukewarm reputations are those most in need of the marketing muscle a guarantee can provide. However, they're also least equipped to provide the right components necessary to make it work. Should they initiate a guarantee yet not clean up their act, they'll be gouged with payouts and will further alienate customers.

What are the limits? Should guarantee pledges include disclaimers? Last year, Howard Johnson Franchise Systems announced "Sleep Tight or It's a Free Night," a guest satisfaction guarantee promising "a clean, comfortable room and prompt, courteous service, or guests get a free night's stay." Although it doesn't make such assertions in marketing collateral or in ads, chain President Eric Pfeffer maintains such promises don't come without exceptions: We can't guarantee there won't be a citywide blackout during a hurricane or that we won't lose power because of a storm," he says.

Statistical data drove Pfeffer and members of his chain's International Operators' Council to consider a guarantee: "It has been proven that a guest with a complaint that is satisfactorily resolved is 92-percent likely to return, whereas a guest whose problem goes unsolved is less than 50-percent likely to return," he says.

An extraordinary guarantee, claims Hart, is broken down into three parts. A "meaningful, powerful payout is the most important," he asserts. Prior to payout is a clearly communicated up-front pledge, which tells customers exactly what they can expect and exactly what they'll get should their experience fall short of their expectations.

Part and parcel with the actual monetary payout, although of separate importance, is the process a customer must go through to collect. Was it a hassle? Was it condescending? Did it take five hours to find the five managers who needed to approve it?

Bargaining and negotiating have no place in the exceptional guarantee realm, Hart adds. He cites a personal experience to make his point: "I was staying at a hotel in New Orleans, where I was called in to do some consulting work. My magnetic door lock had malfunctioned, so the manager suggested I wait in the lounge while it was repaired. They offered me free drinks, which was very nice. After two hours had passed and I still couldn't get into my room, I went on to dinner in the restaurant. As my partner and I were enjoying our meal, the manager approached and asked if the drinks were sufficient compensation for the inconvenience. Not to be rude, but I didn't think so. I proposed complimentary dinner for two, to which she replied, 'How 'bout for one?'"

Such bargaining does more harm than good, Hart says. The following day, when he was looking over the property's training manual, he found an entire section on how to *negotiate* a payout with a dissatisfied customer. "That's a mistake," he asserts. "Either you have a guarantee or you don't."

Resorts Go Up . . . and Down

■

BY ANDREW NEMETHY

*A FREELANCE WRITER/AUTHOR LIVING IN THE HILLS NEAR MONTPELIER, VERMONT, ANDREW NEMETHY HAS WITNESSED
20 YEARS OF CHANGES IN GREEN MOUNTAIN RESORT TOWNS.*

Destruction is usually associated with unexpected natural disasters. But, according to futurist August St. John, "destruction" is perfectly natural—indeed, inevitable—for resort and tourist towns.

St. John is a professor of marketing and future studies at Long Island University in New York. He has developed a comprehensive theory on the life and death of tourist towns, which he says go through a cycle of five stages: Welcome, Development, Resentment, Confrontation, and, finally, Destruction.

It's the last stage, not surprisingly, that has raised eyebrows. By "destruction," St. John doesn't mean a physical catastrophe, but the ruin or disappearance, as growth overwhelms a resort area, of the things that were the original attractions: neighborliness and sense of community, a rural landscape, small-town atmosphere, friendliness, low traffic and low taxes.

As this occurs, he says, communities break into hostile camps over development. Growth moratoriums, lawsuits and contentious hearings often ensue. Many residents find they can no longer afford to live and shop in their town. Faced with constant irritants to remind them of their situation—traffic jams, soaring rents—locals wear resentment on their sleeves.

And on their bumpers. In the resort community of Manchester, Vermont, where St. John has had a home since 1962, cars sport stickers saying, "Welcome to Manchester. Now Go Home."

This is obviously no way for a resort to greet tourists, but St. John says Manchester is in the Destruction Stage and this kind of animosity is typical. Not surprisingly, local powers-that-be vehemently disagree. They call him names, such as "Professor Gloom-and-Doom." St. John has been branded everything from pro-development to anti-development, and accused of having a "hidden agenda" by the president of nearby Bromley and Magic Mountain ski areas.

He takes it all in stride, insisting he isn't taking sides, just telling it like it is.

"Everything has patterns," St. John says. "Everything changes if you wait long enough. If something is hot you wait long enough, it's cold. That's all I'm saying. It's not better or worse. It's just different."

Though his tourism cycle is based on five years of studying Manchester, he says it applies to resort communities everywhere. Manchester has been an ideal guinea pig, St. John says, because it has virtually every facet of a tourism-based economy. The town has a business sector dependent on tourists, imported workers who service the resort trade, old-wealth summer residents, affluent newcomers, developers, assorted professionals, and long-time natives.

It has a historic, 150-year-old resort village dominated by the sprawling, restored Equinox Hotel. It's also home to a booming commercial center with the upscale fishing and clothing company Orvis, all manner of outlet stores and boutiques, and grand development schemes.

And three ski resorts are nearby—Stratton, Bromley and Magic Mountain.

Most of the flak St. John faces comes from his use of the word "destruction," but he says this stage isn't all negative. It can also be "creative" and a "rebirth," once a community realizes its original draw has disappeared and "something else has to be put in its place." But if negative attitudes toward tourists do not change and conflicts remain, "there's no guarantee once you hit bottom that you can come back."

St. John, 62, a tanned, animated man with a neat salt-and-pepper moustache and a vague resemblance to Sean Connery, is an unlikely lightning rod. He has spent most of his career teaching or consulting quietly behind the scenes, using his background in economics, sociology, psychology and marketing.

Cycles fascinate St. John, much as statistics thrill a baseball fanatic. He points out that as far back as 500 B.C., his favorite Greek philosopher, Heraclitus "The Obscure," said everything is always in "flux," and that "one cannot step twice into the same river."

Tourism communities must realize their business is in a state of flux and not immune to cycles, says St. John. Sitting underneath the dark, exposed beams of an old, restored carriage barn that is his home, he predicts many changes for ski and resort areas:

- "There are only going to be two types of ski resort: The very expensive and the very cheap." Ski resorts in the middle face difficulty and some will go bankrupt.

- "People today want their money's worth." Ski areas have to deliver value to survive, whether it's a decent hamburger or coupons that give a discount at local restaurants.

- Fancy resorts that cater to the cream of the market have to "savor the customer" and concentrate less on capital investment and more on service. "They've got the apple: They better start shining it."

 280 *Readings*

He points out that 20 years ago no one ever imagined going to a ski resort and "never putting on skis." But a long list of activities and amenities now provide plenty of diversions to attract non-skiers.

"The concept is wider. It's not just skiing," he says.

Some communities fail to recognize that as growth occurs, the local economy becomes driven less by tourism than by development and a phalanx of architects, lawyers, planners, contractors and engineers. When development runs out of steam, the community is forced to confront how to maintain its economy.

While he insists that going from the "welcome" to "destruction" stage is inevitable, St. John says active planning can prolong and control the progression by helping preserve a resort town's appeal and character.

"It's like the difference between two people. One of them stays fit and takes care of himself, the other drinks and gets dissipated," he says.

St. John has developed a way to rate local attitudes so communities can find out where they fit in his five-stage cycle (*see accompanying box*). Using the information, a community can look ahead and plan.

"The future of the future," he says, sounding like a modern-day Heraelitus, "is in the present."

From Nemethy, Andrew (1990, November). Resorts go up . . . and down. Snow Country, pp. 149–150.

FIGURING A RESORT'S STAGE

Professor August St. John devised a survey, excerpted below, to pinpoint the development phase of a resort town. Respondents rate the accuracy of the following statements on a scale of 0 (never happens) to 5 (always happens) for any small resort town. The total points categorize the town in one of the five stages.

1. **Name-verbing.** Residents of other areas turn the town's name into a verb (as in Freeport, Maine). *Example: "Don't 'Freeport' our town."*

2. **Teflon officials.** Difficult or confusing to place responsibility for a town's growth pattern on elected or appointed officials. *Example: "Who's in charge around here?"*

3. **Growth backlash.** Growth reaches a point where a town's development no longer pulls people in, but pushes people out. *Example: The rural simplicity, historic character, charm or mystique is eroded by pockets of glitzy adornment and clutter.*

4. **Character flip-flop.** The character of a town no longer affects growth decisions, rather growth decisions affect the character of the town. *Example: Commercial projects such as malls, shopping centers, strip development, subdivisions, etc., dominate the townscape (overall visual impression), not the other way around.*

5. **The "window effect."** New arrivals view the town as it is, not what it was or should be. *Example: As historic architectural heritage is consumed by a contemporary motif, the new arrivals see the present townscape and adapt accordingly. As this process of "dwindling architectural heritage" continues, changing profiles of the town unfold.*

6. **From feverish to sick.** The "have nots" will "never have." *Example: Land values soar and/or affordable housing becomes prohibitive.*

7. **Departure of posh.** Quality market replaced by a quantity market. *Example: Clutter, retail glitz and fast-food restaurants dominate the town; "upscale" shoppers depart and "middle/low-end" arrive.*

8. **A new template.** A general consensus that the town has changed. *Example: The town's new look is better to some, worse to others, different to all.*

9. **A bitter pill.** Present "high" prices of real estate make past "lower" prices, to most previous sellers, a resentful memory.

10. **Wishful thinking.** Traffic activity does not equal business activity. *Example: Roads choked with day-trippers bound for other destinations.*

Total: 0–10 = Welcome stage; 11–21 = Development stage; 22–32 = Resentment stage; 33–43 = Confrontation stage; 44–50 = Destruction stage.

The Impact of Indian Gaming on a Tribal Economy and Economic Development Strategy: The White Mountain Apache Experience

■

BY CHARLES P. O'HARA, MPA

MR. O'HARA IS DIRECTOR OF PLANNING AND DEVELOPMENT, WHITE MOUNTAIN APACHE TRIBE, WHITERIVER, ARIZONA.
HIS PREVIOUS POSITIONS INCLUDE THE GOVERNOR'S OFFICE OF MANPOWER AND ECONOMIC DEVELOPMENT (ARIZONA),
COUNTY HEALTH PLANNER, COCHISE COUNTY, ARIZONA, AND ECONOMIC AND COMMUNITY DEVELOPMENT PLANNER,
PASCUA YAQUI TRIBE OF ARIZONA. HE RECEIVED A MASTER OF PUBLIC ADMINISTRATION FROM THE KENNEDY SCHOOL
OF GOVERNMENT, HARVARD UNIVERSITY IN 1988 AND A BACHELOR OF ARTS DEGREE FROM BOSTON COLLEGE IN 1962.
HE CAN BE CONTACTED AT 602/338-4346, EXTENSION 213 OR 309 (VOICE) OR 602/338-1514 (FAX).

ABSTRACT

The economic development efforts of the White Mountain Apache are described, including the development of casino gaming. The direct and indirect benefits of gaming for the tribe are also presented. Conclusions about the role of casino gaming in the economic and human development of the reservation are drawn.

INTRODUCTION

With the advent of casino gaming on Indian reservations, a new industry has spawned a variety of development strategies and economic activity in Indian Country. This article attempts to trace the experience of one tribe, the White Mountain Apaches of Arizona, in the development of casino gaming on their reservation, the role that gaming plays in the Tribe's overall economy, and its influence on current economic development strategy. Further, the article will explore some of the direct and indirect benefits that are being ascribed to the development of casino gaming on the reservation.

BACKGROUND AND DESCRIPTION OF THE WHITE MOUNTAIN APACHE TRIBE

The Fort Apache Indian Reservation, located in east central Arizona about 190 miles northeast of Phoenix, is the homeland of the White Mountain Apache Tribe. Encompassing more than 1.6 million acres, the reservation is 75 miles long and 45 miles wide, or roughly twice the size of the State of Rhode Island, and has a wide range of topography and climate. The southwestern desert foothills area, with an elevation of 2,700 feet contrast sharply with the mountainous, forested northeastern portions of the reservation, where elevations approach 11,500 feet.

The population of the Tribe numbers approximately 14,000 people with the vast majority residing on the reservation, primarily in the community of Whiteriver. The White Mountain Apache Tribe has a young population with approximately 50% of the people 18 years old or younger and a median age of 21.3 years as compared to a median age of 32.2 years for the State of Arizona. The median family income on the reservation according to the 1990 Census was $13,020 compared to $27,540 for the State. With an unemployment rate estimated at 25% and a population growth rate of approximately 3.3%, the young growing population exerts extraordinary pressures on the tribal government. Unlike state or local governments, the Tribal Council plays a more direct role in the creation of jobs, creation of affordable housing, expansion of schools and provision of additional governmental services to meet the increasing demands of the tribal population.

THE PRE-1992 TRIBAL ECONOMY

Historically, the economy of the White Mountain Apache Tribe has been resource-based and included livestock grazing, recreation, and forest industries. Initially, business operations in these economic sectors were conducted by non-Indian lease holders who often exploited the resources to the detriment of the Tribe. Beginning with livestock grazing in the 1940's, the Tribe began to take exclusive control of its economic activities. Non-Indian grazing leases were terminated and tribal cattle herding, including community livestock associations, was expanded. In the 1950's the Tribe began to develop a number of recreation lakes and licensing of fishing and hunting on the reservation, an activity which had previously been conducted under the purview of the State of Arizona. In 1965, the Fort Apache Timber Company (FATCO) was established and the Tribe began milling its own timber. Eventually the Tribe restricted the sale of all reservation timber to FATCO and FATCO has since developed into one of the most successful inland sawmills in the United States. In the 1970's the Tribe began seriously to develop its outdoor recreation with the development of Sunrise Ski Resort, the largest ski area in Arizona. Sunrise has become one of the premier ski areas in the Southwest offering challenging terrain and excellent facilities for more than 250,000 skiers each winter.

In nearly every case where the Tribe began to exercise its sovereignty and take control over its economic activities, it met resistance from the Bureau of Indian Affairs (BIA), the State of Arizona or some other non-Indian interest. For example, the development of FATCO was opposed by the BIA, ostensibly because they feared the Tribe would fail, but undoubtedly their long term dealings with non-Indian sawmill operators also influenced their position. The State of Arizona fought the construction of recreation lakes on the reservation because of the implications on water rights and opposition to the Tribe's hunting and fishing license program led to court battles which were ultimately decided in the Tribe's favor at the Supreme Court level. Quantification of the Tribe's water rights continues to be a hotly contested legal issue.

In spite of this opposition or perhaps in part because of it, the White Mountain Apache Tribe has been relatively successful in the development, management and operation of its tribal business enterprises. Cornell and Kalt, in their article, "Reloading the Dice: Improving the Chances of Economic Development on American Indian Reservations," argue that it is just such an exercise of tribal sovereignty that increase a Tribe's chances of experiencing successful economic development. According to the authors, the reasons why tribal sovereignty is so crucial to successful development is because it links decision making to the results of the decisions, thus increasing accountability and because sovereign status offers distinct legal and economic opportunities which often go unrecognized if sovereignty is not exercised. Simply stated, the development and expansion of the White Mountain Apache Tribe's economy has gone hand-in-hand with the exercise of its tribal sovereignty, often to the consternation of the federal government, state government, and non-Indian business developers that either harbor a desire to maintain a paternalistic relationship to the Tribe or covet access to the Tribe's abundant resources.

FATCO, which grew to become the major industry of the Tribe employing about 350 workers in the two sawmills on the reservation, generated sufficient revenues to allow the Tribe to establish other businesses, generally intended to capture retail dollars. The Whiteriver Commercial Center, a retail shopping center, was established in the late 1970's which includes a supermarket, variety store, movie theater, post office and several other retail businesses. Apache Enterprises expanded to include an automotive repair shop, tire sales, and several gas station/mini-mart stores located in various communities on the reservation. Additionally, the Tribe established a 900 acre farm to complement the livestock industry. Fort Apache Materials utilizes the abundant high quality sand and gravel deposits on the reservation and Apache Aerospace, an industrial "cut and sew" operation, supplies sewn insulation parts for McDonnell Douglas' Apache helicopter.

INDIAN GAMING APPROACHES THE RESERVATION

In 1991, the real possibility that the White Mountain Apache Tribe could establish casino gaming on the reservation began to impact the Tribe's economic development strategy. Following the Supreme Court's "Cabazon Decision" and the subsequent passage of the Indian Gaming Regulatory Act (IGRA) in 1988, high stakes Indian Bingo began popping up on a number of Indian reservations, primarily on reservations in close proximity to urban areas. High stakes Indian bingo was not economically attractive to the White Mountain Apache Tribe due to the Tribe's rural setting and the high population densities usually required for a successful bingo operation.

However, by 1991, with the federal court success of the Pequot Tribe in Connecticut and the Lac du Flambeau Chippewa Tribe in Wisconsin to extend the interpretation of IGRA to include Las Vegas style casino gaming where the public policy of the state allows such gaming "by any person for any purpose," the attention of the Tribe began to focus on the advantages and disadvantages of casino gaming on the reservation. Legal and business research was initiated to explore the parameters of this industry which was totally new to the Tribe, which had not been involved with bingo. The Tribal Chairman and tribal staff made a number of site visits to Indian casinos in California, Washington, Minnesota and Wisconsin, consulting with tribal leaders and staff regarding their experiences with this new industry. Las Vegas casino management staff was also consulted. Tribal legal staff consulted with attorneys specializing in Indian law and, specifically, Indian gaming law, to determine the most appropriate legal course of action to effect a favorable Tribal/State Gaming Compact within the provisions of the IGRA in the State of Arizona.

Based on the experience learned on site visits and other consultations, the Tribal Chairman Ronnie Lupe felt strongly that casino gaming would be beneficial to the Tribe by broadening the economic foundation of the Tribe and by reducing the pressures on the Tribe's forest resources upon which the Tribe's economy had depended. Since the mid-1980's, it had become apparent that, despite assurances to the contrary from the BIA, the Tribe's timber had been over cut and that reductions in the annual allowable cut were required to maintain the sustainability of the forests. Reductions in the cut had been initiated, but not without negative impacts on revenues and employment levels. Indian gaming could render those harvest reductions much less painful by providing new jobs and a new revenue stream with virtually little environmental impact. The combination of a growing population, timber harvest reductions, and the lack of any other economic expansion were creating significant socio-economic and political pressures on the Tribal Council.

In the spring of 1992, the White Mountain Apache Tribe initiated a request to the Governor of Arizona to enter into a Tribal/State Compact for Class III gaming. Negotiations were conducted, but were stalemated almost from the outset by the State's refusal to discuss any type of casino gaming other than a limited number of slot machines. It is interesting to note that at the same time, in the state of Washington, state negotiators agreed to virtually any type of casino gaming except slot machines. These types of contradictions and non-rational positions permeated Tribal/State compact negotiations and continue to cloud discussions regarding the costs and benefits of Indian gaming.

Failing to achieve any measure of progress after six months of negotiations, the White Mountain Apache Tribe, in conjunction with the Tohono O'Odham Nation and the Pascua Yaqui Tribe sued the Governor and the State of Arizona in federal court for "failure to negotiate in good faith." In accordance with the provisions of IGRA, the federal court judge appointed a mediator who was required to select either the Tribe's compact proposal or the State's. The mediator, a former Arizona Supreme Court Chief Justice, conducted fact finding visits to the reservation as well as briefings by state agencies and officials. In the spring of 1993, the mediator selected the proposals of the three tribes which were virtually identical and permitted a full range of casino gaming, including: slot machines, blackjack, roulette, and keno. However, the implementation of the Tribal/State Compact reflecting the mediator's decision required the approval of the Secretary of Interior. Because of his concerns about the political ramifications of approving a compact that was vehemently opposed by the Governor, he initiated another round of "unofficial negotiations." These discussions resulted in a compromise compact which excluded "banking games" such as blackjack and craps, but permitted live keno and many more slot machines than previously offered by the state.

DEVELOPMENT OF THE TRIBE'S HON DAH CASINO

Throughout the extended compact negotiation process which took nearly 18 months to conclude, the Tribe continued to explore the various available options for the development of an Indian casino on the reservation. Under IGRA, Indian casinos are permitted to be either one of two basic business organization forms. The Indian casino can be either tribally owned and operated or can be operated by an outside manager under a management agreement. The Tribe was pursued by a wide range of aspiring managers anxious to develop a management agreement with the Tribe. The experience level and financial backing of these potential managers varied from large Las Vegas casino corporations to ex-pit bosses looking for a lucky break to attorneys and business promoters convinced that they had the packaging skills necessary to develop a successful casino.

After a number of meetings with hopeful managers, it became obvious to the Tribe that there were only two reasons why a tribe would enter into a management agreement and share the profits of their casino. The first was that the outside manager could bring financing to the casino venture and the second reason was that they could bring a level of casino management expertise lacking to the Tribe. Too often, the prospective managers interviewed by the White Mountain Apache Tribe brought neither financing nor expertise and intended to "shop" for both following the conclusion of an initial agreement with the Tribe.

At some point about halfway through the development process, the Tribal leadership decided that the casino would be tribally owned and operated. The decision was based on the fact that because the Tribe would be able to leverage its own financing it did not require the financial assistance of a manager and because of the operational complexities and requirements of FATCO and the Sunrise Ski Resort, the Tribe had experience in hiring management expertise as tribal employees whenever needed. At this point, the Tribe focused on locating and hiring an experienced casino manager to develop the Tribe's casino. This proved to be a more lengthy process since the demand for such managers was quickly outstripping the available supply.

The other major decision guiding the development of the casino was the selection of its location. Sunrise Ski Resort Hotel had been considered but its remoteness in the mountains was cause for its rejection. One consistent recommendation from various casino industry personnel was that the casino should be located as close to the nearest population center as possible. The Hon Dah (which means "Be my Guest" in Apache) motel and restaurant site close to the reservation boundary and close to the non-Indian community of Pinetop-Lakeside was selected. The motel and restaurant had been marginal operations but the facilities provided a relatively low cost start-up opportunity for the Tribe and any expansions could be funded out of cash flow.

THE HON DAH CASINO

Tribal Chairman Ronnie Lupe personally led the search for the type of experienced casino manager that could meet the high standards of the Tribe. The old saying that "luck comes to those that are prepared" seemed to apply to the selection of the casino manager for the Hon Dah casino. The Tribe was rather fortuitously able to hire a former casino owner that had operated casinos in rural Nevada and brought a rural perspective to the strategy for the development of the Tribe's casino. This strategy focused on developing a casino that would cater to the local communities, provide a high quality experience, and establish rigid standards of integrity and accountability.

To oversee the operations of the Hon Dah Casino and insure that the operations comply with the Tribal/State Compact and Tribal gaming regulations, the Tribal Council established a five member Tribal Gaming Commission. The Commissioners included three tribal members and two non-members. One of the tribal members is a private businessman, another is the Tribal Personnel Director and the other is a Tribal Livestock Manager. The two non-members include a certified public accountant who is also the mayor of a nearby community and the other is a retired FBI agent. The executive director of the Commission is a retired police chief from a metropolitan community near Phoenix.

The Hon Dah Casino opened on December 29, 1994, offering live keno and 148 slot machines and employed 125 persons, 85% of whom were tribal members. By July of 1995, the size of the Casino was doubled, the number of slot machines increased to 278, a new gas station and mini-mart were added to the casino complex and employment increased to 170 employees, with 80% tribal members. Revenues have exceeded initial projections and the Hon Dah Casino has earned a reputation as the best managed Indian casino in the state. The internal controls of the casino, which have withstood the testing of external auditors and reviews by the Tribal Gaming Commission, have served as a model for other Indian casinos.

The success of the Hon Dah Casino has spurred the continued expansion of the casino complex and fueled the overall economic development strategy of the Tribe. By July of this year, a new RV Park adjoining the casino will be opened offering 75 RV spaces in a forest park setting. By fall, the casino will complete the addition of a restaurant and lounge, and increase the total number of slot machines to 350. At that point, employment is expected to reach 250. Future plans for the casino include the development of a 100 room hotel and the feasibility of a public golf course is being explored.

Direct and Indirect Benefits of Casino Gaming for the White Mountain Apache Tribe

Some of the direct benefits of the Tribe's casino are obvious. Over the past 18 months, the Hon Dah casino has created over 170 permanent positions and a number of temporary positions associated with the construction projects at the casino. Additionally, the Tribe has been able to pledge casino revenues as collateral for a capital improvement bond issue that will provide funding for the construction of several needed projects that would have been indefinitely delayed or impossible without the availability of casino profits. These projects include a twenty-five bed alcohol/substance abuse treatment facility, a Tribal museum and cultural learning center, a youth center, and an elderly day care center. "Additionally, the tribe donated $1 million dollars toward the construction of the public school gymnasium in the community of Whiteriver on the reservation".

One of the less direct benefits associated with the success of the Tribe's casino has been the re-focusing of the Tribe's development strategies and project implementation on the expansion of the Tribe's tourism industry. This re-focusing has occurred because of two factors. The first is that the Tribe recognized that Indian casino gaming may be a short lived economic opportunity. Indian tribes, perhaps more than any other political group in the country, are aware of the uncertainties of Congress. It is commonly understood in Indian Country that "what Congress giveth, Congress can take away" and American Indian history is awash with such political swings and changing legislation. Against this backdrop of such uncertainty, the White Mountain Apache Tribe has decided to build on its historic and recreational tourism attractions, while casino gaming is available to provide the development capital.

The second reason is that the Tribe has recognized that tourism is a three trillion dollar a year business and that the Tribe is uniquely positioned to attract an increasing number of visitors searching for different scenery, a new historic attraction or a new outdoor adventure, and with them, an increasing share of the revenues of that huge industry. Over the past twenty years, tourism has become an integral component of the Tribe's economy. In 1993, Tribal businesses grossed over $12 million dollars in tourism related revenues and employed more than 500 people in full or part-time positions. But the development of the Hon Dah Casino has added a high demand tourist activity to the existing array of recreation based tourist attractions on the reservation that range from camping and fishing to related projects such as the previously mentioned Tribal Museum and Cultural Learning Center, the Hon Dah RV Park and the renovation of buildings at historic Fort Apache. Tribal leadership and staff are convinced that increasing tourist traffic will be reflected in increased revenues, at least at the Hon Dah Casino.

Perhaps one of the more intangible indirect benefits stemming from casino gaming, not only for the White Mountain Apaches but for many Indian tribes that have established casinos, is that a measure of guarded optimism is beginning to replace the hopelessness and depression that are all too prevalent on many reservations. This new hope is critical in capitalizing on the economic development opportunities provided by Indian casino gaming because without hope that first leap from strategy to reality cannot be realized.

Conclusion

This article has focused exclusively on the positive benefits that have been experienced by the development of casino gaming by the White Mountain Apache Tribe. Obviously there are negative impacts associated with such development. There are strains on the infrastructure, parking, traffic. Undoubtedly, some people, including tribal members, will become addicted to gambling. But problems associated with addictions are no stranger to reservations, including the White Mountain Apache's, and the experience to date strongly indicates that the benefits of jobs, income, and an increased self-esteem of casino employees far outweigh any gaming related problems that have been experienced by the Tribe.

Perhaps the most fitting conclusion to this article is found in the statement of Ronnie Lupe, Tribal Chairman of the White Mountain Apache Tribe, made to the House Committee on Interior Affairs. Chairman Lupe said, "Mr. Chairman, I've watched the development of Indian gaming enterprises closely and with care and personally visited other reservations around the country studying gaming enterprises that have developed in Indian Country. I spoke with tribal leaders and learned firsthand the benefits that improve these tribes as a direct result of these operations. Jobs were created where there were no jobs, income generated where there had been no income. I saw small tribes that had little hope of any kind of self-sustaining existence above the poverty level transformed into communities bustling with economic activity, vitality, pride and a sense of accomplishment. That opportunity is there for all of us."

Note

Cornell, Stephen & Kalt, Joseph (1992). Reloading the dice: Improving the chances for economic development on American Indian reservations," pp. 1–59. In Cornell, Stephen & Kalt, Joseph (Eds.) *What can tribes do? Strategies and institutions in American Indian economic development*. Los Angeles: American Indian Studies Center, University of California.

From O'Hara, Charles P. (1995, fall). The impact of Indian gaming on a tribal economy and economic development strategy: The White Mountain Apache experience. Economic Development Review, *pp. 12–15. Reproduced with permission of copyright owner. Further reproduction prohibited.*

Appendices

APPENDIX A

Problem-Solving and Decision-Making

PROBLEM-SOLVING

Managers and service employees in the tourism industry are constantly faced with a variety of problems, some small and some large. The ability to recognize and solve these problems is an important skill for anyone working in the tourism industry. The problem-solving process shown in Figure A.1 can be used for making either personal or business decisions.

Some personal decisions such as choosing an entree in the cafeteria are present every day and are seldom thought of as problems. Problems that we face on a regular basis are called "routine." Other decisions, such as selecting which college to attend are unique and may only happen once in a lifetime. These types of problems and the decisions we make on an infrequent basis are called "nonroutine." Regardless of how simple or complex the problem, the problem-solving process can be used in either situation to develop effective solutions (Figure A.1).

The exercises found at the end of each chapter and cases presented in this book will provide several opportunities to develop problem-solving and decision-making skills. The following example illustrates how a simple problem-solving and decision-making process works.

College students must decide each year what to do on spring break. If there were no choices, there would not be a problem. But like most situations in life, choices must be made. Identifying the problem (choices) is the first step in the process.

FIGURE A.1
Problem-Solving and Decision-Making

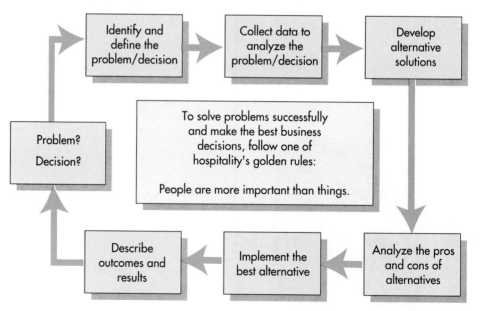

The second step is collecting data. This data may include finding out what friends will be doing, looking at brochures about spring break trips, figuring out a budget, and/or seeing if time off from a job can be arranged. Once the data have been collected, they must be analyzed before decisions can be made.

After collecting and analyzing the data, the third step is to develop alternative solutions. The first solution considered should always be to do nothing. However, a good problem-solver will develop several alternative courses of action. Having only one or two choices available may mean that unforeseen circumstances (e.g., the car breaks down, the flight is delayed/canceled, the weather changes, or your instructor assigns a last-minute project) determine the decision.

The fourth step requires an analysis of each proposed alternative. This is accomplished by ranking each choice, beginning with the most desirable and ending with the least desirable. After this, move on to step 5 in which you select the best alternative and implement it.

The final step in the process is evaluation. If everything went as planned and the chosen alternative was a success, this process could then become routine. However, if the alternative was not a success, the process would be nonroutine, and the entire decision-making process would need to be repeated next year.

This example is fairly straightforward. However, many problems facing managers and service employees in the tourism industry are not so easily recognizable. The ability to identify potential problems (issues management) and develop effective solutions will help you to succeed in meeting employee and guest needs. As a tourism professional, you will most likely face several of the following managerial decisions:

1. Setting objectives,

2. Planning activities,

3. Allocating resources and equipment to support and empower employees to meet guest needs and desires,

4. Creating an environment and supplying the support that employees need to provide high-quality service, and

5. Establishing performance and customer satisfaction measures to ensure that performance standards are being met to achieve efficient and effective operations. Performance measures must also be designed to recognize and appreciate the individual and cooperative contributions made by the members of support and service teams.

Although a problem may be classified as routine, it probably will not present itself in a prepackaged, ready-to-answer form. Each time a problem is faced and solved, problem-solving skills are developed. Think about the issues presented at the beginning of each chapter and use the exercises at the end of each chapter to develop and hone your problem-solving and decision-making skills. Each time you make a decision, ask yourself one very important question: Is my decision ethical?

Ethics: An Important Part of Problem-Solving

Long before you stepped into a classroom, your basis for ethical decision-making had begun to form. You began to form opinions that allowed you to decide right from wrong, good from bad, and just from unjust. Lessons learned from family members, friends, relatives, teachers, religious leaders, and others have helped shape your views on ethical behavior. Whether you knew it or not, as you learned these lessons, you were studying the basics of ethical behavior. Ethics are concerned with the moral principles and values that govern how people and organizations conduct their daily lives and activities.

Although most people can easily distinguish between right and wrong based on their own personal experiences, they are often faced with decisions in which it is difficult to make these clear distinctions. In an effort to promote ethical behavior, organizations often

FIGURE A.2
Code of Ethics: Hospitality
Service and Tourism Industry.
Source: Code of ethics: hospitality service
and tourism industry (1992). In Hall,
Stephen S.J. (Ed.). *Ethics in hospitality
management*. Education Institute of the
American Hotel and Motel Association.

1. We acknowledge ethics and morality as inseparable elements of doing business and will test every decision against the highest standards of honesty, legality, fairness, impunity, and conscience.

2. We will conduct ourselves personally and collectively at all times so as to bring credit to the service and tourism industry at large.

3. We will concentrate our time, energy, and resources on the improvement of our own product and services and we will not denigrate our competition in the pursuit of our own success.

4. We will treat all guests equally regardless of race, religion, nationality, creed, or sex.

5. We will deliver standards of service and product with total consistency to every guest.

6. We will provide a totally safe and sanitary environment at all times for every guest and every employee.

7. We will strive constantly in words, actions, and deeds to develop and maintain the highest level of trust, honesty, and understanding among guests, clients, employees, employers, and the public at large.

8. We will provide every employee at every level all the knowledge, training, equipment, and motivation required to perform his or her task according to our published standards.

9. We will guarantee that every employee at every level will have the same opportunity to perform, advance, and be evaluated against the same standard as all employees engaged in the same or similar tasks.

10. We will actively and consciously work to protect and preserve our environment and natural resources in all that we do.

11. We will seek a fair and honest profit, no more, no less.

Seven tests for ethics

1. Is it legal?
2. Does it hurt anyone?
3. Is it fair?
4. Am I being honest?
5. Can I live with myself?
6. Would I publicize my decision?
7. What if everyone did it?

---

publish codes of ethics (see Figure A.2) to help guide individuals in their daily activities and decisions.

Even without the help of a code of ethics, there are some very simple questions you can ask yourself about any situation or problem to identify ethical and unethical behavior.

- Will someone be hurt in this situation?
- Is anyone being coerced, manipulated, or deceived?
- Is there anything illegal about the situation?
- Does the situation feel wrong to you?
- Is someone else telling you that there is an ethical problem?
- Would you be ashamed to tell your best friend, your spouse, or your parents about your contemplated actions or your involvement?
- Do the outcomes, on balance, appear to be positive or negative?
- Do you or others have the right or duty to act in this situation?
- Is there a chance that you are denying or avoiding some serious aspect of the situation?[1]

Finally and possibly the simplest, yet most thorough, ethical guideline is the Golden Rule: Do unto others as you would have them do unto you.

REFERENCES

1. Wood, Donna J. (1990). *Business and society*, Glenview, IL: Scott, Foresman/Little, Brown Higher Education.

Manners Matter

No matter which profession you enter, manners will matter. Whether you become a tourism professional, choose another career, or simply travel for pleasure, you will frequently meet new people and dine in formal restaurants or at banquets. Making introductions, being introduced, and practicing proper table manners will all come into play in these common settings.

In today's business world, manners are relatively simple to learn and abide by. They indicate that a person is intelligent, confident, and considerate of fellow human beings. There are manners for almost every situation, from making apologies to stifling a yawn. Most libraries and bookstores offer books that are veritable encyclopedias of proper manners or etiquette. This appendix is provided to give you a few of the most basic rules of business etiquette for the situations you will encounter most frequently.

INTRODUCTIONS

A good introduction makes everyone present feel comfortable, flatters the person being introduced and communicates important information about the person to the group.

—Letitia Baldridge, former White House Chief of Protocol

The rules of introductions are quite simple and you can show yourself to be a poised person if you follow them. Use the following example as a model. If you know Mary but she has never met Joe, you would say the following: "Mary, this is Joe a friend from my Tourism class. Joe, this is Mary, my roommate since our freshman year." Notice that you should always include a brief comment about each person so they have some basic knowledge of each other.

Introductions of persons you know from a business context or for whom you would like to show special respect (a professor, your grandmother, etc.) have a special twist. The rule is to introduce the person of lesser authority, rank or age to the person of higher authority, rank or age, and then followup, doing the reverse. Clients should be granted the "most respected" position. Here are a few examples to show how this introduction hierarchy works:

- "Mr. Senior Executive, let me present Ms. Junior Executive. Ms. Junior Executive, this is Mr. Senior Executive."
- "Dr. Cummings, this is my roommate Mary Welch. Mary, this is my tourism professor, Dr. Cummings."
- "Mrs. Gonzales, I would like to introduce Jim Smith, who will help you with your airline reservations. Jim, this is Mrs. Gonzales."
- Often you will need to introduce yourself. Simply approach the person you do not know, extend your hand, smile, and say, "I am [your full name]" and then say something appropriate given the circumstances such as "I am the host's cousin" or "I am here representing the Town Center Hotel."

When you are introduced, you are expected to respond in some way. It is a good idea to add the name of the person you just met to whatever pleasantry you use. This helps you remember the person's name. So after being introduced, you might say, "How do you do, Mrs. Gonzales?" or maybe, "I am pleased to meet you, Mrs. Gonzales."

Today, it is common for both men and women to stand when they are being introduced to another person no matter whether the other person is a man or a woman. In a business situation, it is especially respectful to stand when a client enters one's office. Well-mannered businessmen and women often come around their desk and shake hands with a client before getting down to business.

HANDSHAKES

In most countries with a European heritage, individuals usually shake hands when they are introduced. Here are the do's and don'ts of hand shakes.

1. Be firm but considerate. Gauge your hand shake to the strength of the person whose hand you are shaking.
2. Pump the other person's hand once or twice.
3. Break from the handshake quickly: Don't continue to hold the other person's hand during the entire introduction.
4. Make eye contact with the person but don't stare.

In general, the shaking of hands is the proper response when you are:

1. meeting someone for the first time.
2. meeting someone you haven't seen in a long time.
3. greeting your host or hostess.
4. greeting your guests.
5. saying good-bye and want to show extra respect.

You should shake hands with someone when that person extends his or her hand to you, no matter what the situation. It is rude to refuse to shake hands when someone extends a hand to you first.

TABLE MANNERS

Having lunch as part of a job interview is your opportunity to demonstrate your social skills: that your manners are good, that you're bright and energetic and respectful, and that you know how to handle your knife and fork.

Linda Phillips, The Executive Etiquette Co.

In today's hurried world of fast food and eating on the run, it is not uncommon for people to be unfamiliar with the etiquette of sit-down dining. The rules of table etiquette were developed primarily to avoid chaos (such as whose coffee cup is whose at a banquet). Table manners are especially important to follow when you are making a first impression, such as when you are interviewing for a job or when you are dining with a client or other business associate.

Although there may be hundreds of rules for proper table etiquette, for example, how to eat snails properly, there are a few that make all the difference. We will discuss table manners in their chronological order of appearance in a four-course business lunch— soup, salad, entree, and dessert/coffee.

Sit down with your back straight and your hands in your lap. Look at the table setting to determine which china and flatware is for your use. Figure B.1 shows a typical place setting that you would find for a four-course meal.

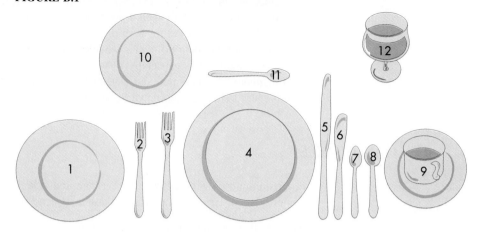

PLACE SETTING.

1 = Salad plate (optional);
2 = Salad fork;
3 = Dinner fork;
4 = Dinner plate;
5 = Knife;
6 = Butter knife;
7 = Teaspoon;
8 = Soup spoon;
9 = Coffee cup and saucer;
10 = Bread plate;
11 = Dessert spoon;
12 = Water glass.

It is important that you know the placement of china and flatware so that you will reach for those that belong to you. Notice especially that your coffee cup is to the right of the dinner plate and that your water glass is above your knife and spoon. Your bread plate will be either to the left of your forks or slightly above them. At banquets with close seating, these logistics can prove very important.

After you sit down, pick up your napkin, unfold it, and place it on your lap. If you stand up and leave the table during the meal, be sure to place your napkin on your chair, not on the table. This is considerate of those dining with you and also signals the wait staff that you are not through eating.

The first course in our hypothetical business lunch is soup. Wait until everyone at your table is served before you begin eating. Your soup spoon should be located to the right of your plate. It is the largest of the spoons in the place setting. Dip your spoon into the soup, retrieve a small amount, and sip it. Do not blow on the soup to cool it and try not to slurp. Bread or rolls are often served with the soup or salad course. If the basket of bread or rolls is near you, you should pick it up, retrieve a roll or piece of bread, and then pass the basket to the person to your left. If the basket is not near you, you may ask someone to pass it to you (likewise with the butter). Place your bread selection onto your bread plate, which is to the left of your place setting. Break off a bite-sized piece of roll or bread, pick up your butter knife or regular knife, and butter that piece only. Pop the entire piece into your mouth and chew with your mouth closed. Place the knife you used to butter your bread onto the bread plate, not back onto the table surface. After you have finished your soup, place your soup spoon onto the saucer underneath the soup bowl. Never place the spoon in the bowl or soup cup.

The next course served to you will be the salad. Your salad fork will be to your left. It is smaller and to the outside of the dinner fork. Salads are sometimes served with your choice of dressing already applied but, at many banquets, two or more dressings are available in bowls or cruets on the table. In this case, when you are passed your choice, ladle a modest amount of dressing onto your salad and then pass the dressing on or set it in the center of the table. Eating salad can be tricky: Sometimes ingredients are not cut into bite-sized pieces. Therefore, be sure to cut any large pieces so that they will fit into your mouth easily. Be particularly cautious with cherry tomatoes. They should be cut in half so that they do not explode juice when you bite into them.

The main course follows the salad course. There are too many different entrees and side dishes with their own set of manners to include here, but some general rules will help no matter what you are served.

1. Always cut food into small pieces so that you can chew them quickly. You should never talk with your mouth full. You may need to respond to a question and should not have to chew for several minutes before you can answer. Cut off one small piece at a time: never cut your entire entree into pieces right away.

2. Lean forward slightly each time you take a piece of food from your plate so that if it should drop from your fork it will fall back onto your plate.

3. Don't push food onto your fork with your knife or a piece of bread.

4. Don't place your elbows on the table.

5. Don't gesture when you have silverware or food in your hands.

6. Feel free to pick up foods that are almost always eaten with the fingers such as french fries, but, when in doubt, for example with fried chicken, cut up the food and use your fork.

7. Frequently dab your mouth with your napkin to remove any crumbs, etc.

8. When you are finished eating your main course, place your knife and fork on the dinner plate side by side with their tips in the center of the plate and their handles setting on the right edge of the plate.

To conclude the meal, your server will bring dessert and offer you coffee. Your dessert utensil, a fork or spoon depending on what the particular dessert requires, will sometimes be brought when dessert is served but often it will be part of the original place setting. It is sometimes placed in line with the rest of your silverware but frequently it is located above your dinner plate area, lying crosswise. Refer back to Figure B.1 for an example. When you are through with your dessert, place the dessert utensil on the dessert plate or saucer.

Your hot beverage cup is to the right of your knives and spoons. After the server pours your coffee, customize it to your taste, stir it with the teaspoon, and then place the spoon on the saucer beneath your cup. If you used a product that came in a packet, such as artificial sweetener or creamer, place the empty packet out of sight under the saucer. When everyone is through eating, fold your napkin and place it on the table beside your plate. Do not put a linen napkin onto your used plateware.

After reading these pages devoted to table manners you may think it impossible to remember all of the little rules. All you need is practice. Proper table manners can be used and practiced everywhere. Soon they will become second nature to you.

PHONE MANNERS

Another sign of poise and professionalism is communicated by phone manners. Telephone etiquette is not complicated. How you handle yourself on the phone says a lot about you and the company for which you work. When you answer the phone, say a greeting and then identify yourself. For instance, you might say, "Good Morning. John Smith speaking" or "Good day. Thank you for calling the Town Center Hotel. This is John. How may I help you?"

When speaking on the telephone be sure to speak clearly, enunciating carefully. It is also a good practice to speak just a bit slower than if you were talking with someone face to face. If you need to find some information for a caller while he or she is on the line, put the caller on hold. Offer to phone the caller back if you need to place him/her on hold for more than a minute.

When leaving a message on an answering machine or voice mail, be brief but to the point. Give your name, telephone number and a brief explanation of why you called. State what time would be best to return your call. It is also helpful to give your phone number a second time as a conclusion to your message. A final telephone etiquette point—when you tell someone you will call back right away or by a certain time, be sure to fulfill your promise.

INTERNATIONAL ETIQUETTE

Manners or etiquette are the rules of a society. Therefore, it should come as no surprise that different societies will have different manners. For example, in Great Britain, parts of Canada, and several European countries, it is customary to hold the knife in the right hand and use it to push food around the plate and onto the fork. This is called the "Continental style," while the table manners described above are considered "American style." In general, European-based cultures have similar rules of etiquette. Asian and Arab manners tend to be very different from Western manners.

Because different countries will have different manners, you need to be sensitive to the rules of other cultures when you travel abroad or when you are in the company of citizens of other countries. No matter where you are or with whom, politeness will go a long way in making a favorable impression and showing respect for others. Saying please and thank you in the language of the other culture is often considered especially respectful and polite.

In general, North Americans tend to be less formal than people from other parts of the globe. Therefore, when you are in another country or with people from another area of the world, a good rule of thumb is to be more formal in your behavior with them than you usually would be. For example, address people by their titles and last names until you are told to use their first names.

The custom of handshakes also varies from one country to another. In several Asian cultures, it is more common to bow than to shake hands when you meet someone. Arabs also do not tend to shake hands. In Arab cultures, it is inappropriate for men and women to shake hands or touch. Due to religious teachings, Arabs also refrain from drinking alcohol, do not eat pork or shellfish, and eat with their right hands only. Many people of the Jewish faith also avoid these foods.

Differences in good manners between cultures are endless. The saying "When in Rome, do as the Romans do" may help you remember to look for and be sensitive to cultural differences. Overall, being considerate and respectful to people is proper etiquette the world over.

SOURCES

Baldridge, Letitia (1996). *The executive advantage*. Washington, DC: Georgetown Publishing House.

Dunckel, Jaqueline (1992). *Business etiquette*. North Vancouver, BC: Self-Counsel Press.

Lord, Ken (1996). The ins and outs of international etiquette. *Hosteur*, 5(2), 29–31.

APPENDIX C

Choosing a Career and Finding a Job

Choosing a career and finding that first full-time job after graduation is no easy task. In fact, most college graduates change jobs several times after they obtain their degrees. It seems as if the grass is always greener on the other side of the fence. As a student studying in the fields of hospitality, travel, and tourism, you have the chance to beat those odds and find a career and job that will fit your needs prior to graduation. Look at Table C.1 for the host of job opportunities that await you and strategies you can use to achieve your career goals.

The tourism industry offers many opportunities to gain career-related experiences through part-time jobs and experiential learning activities such as cooperative education programs and internships. Some of you may already be working in the industry and pursuing a college degree for professional growth and development. Taking advantage of any of these options while still in school will allow you to sample a variety of career options and provide you with important workplace experience.

Many large organizations are using cooperative education and internship programs to select future employees. These programs serve as a realistic job preview for the student and a long-term interview for the employer. These efforts have proven to be an effective approach to screening and selecting employees for entry-level supervisory or management trainee positions.[1] These programs help develop professionalism as well as industry- and company-specific knowledge demanded in today's competitive environment.

Whether you are considering a part-time job, an experiential learning activity, or a full-time job, you should not jump at the first opportunity that comes along. Before committing yourself, take some time to find out more about the job and the organization. What will you learn on the job? How will that prepare you for the future? In your first job, your goal may have been to earn some spending money, but later jobs should help prepare you for increased responsibilities in your chosen career field. Therefore, investigate the learning opportunities before you invest your time.

You can start your investigation by visiting your school's career planning and placement center, participating in on-campus interviews, attending job fairs, visiting with alumni and speakers who come to campus, reading trade publications, and talking with friends, family, and professors. Once you have discovered the types of organizations for which you would like to work and the knowledge skills and abilities they are seeking in potential employees, you can prepare for the job search process.

PREPARING YOUR RESUME

You should start thinking about and preparing your resume early in the job-search process. You will need to send it along with every job-hunting letter you write and take it with you on interviews. You should also share your resume with references, friends, relatives, and other associates to let them know about your career goals and qualifications.

Your resume is like a photograph, highlighting your qualifications on one sheet of paper. It is not your life story, but a promotional piece that serves as an attention-getter

TABLE C.1
Tourism, Hospitality and Hotel and Restaurant Administration (What can I do with this degree?)

Areas	Employers	Strategies
Retail/site management Property management Facility management Rooms management Beverage management Kitchen management Production supervision	Historical, cultural, and natural attractions Lodging: hotel/motel, bed and breakfast, time-shares, and campgrounds Destination areas: amusement centers, theme parks, and resorts Special event and festival organizations Entertainment industry: casinos, theaters, and stadiums Food service: catering, schools, hospitals, military, concessions, and institutions Restaurants, dining clubs, taverns, and fast-food operators Leisure organizations: sporting clubs, recreation centers, fitness facilities, private and/or country clubs Self-employment	Develop a strong foundation in food-service, administration, and customer service. Courses in communications, marketing, management, law, accounting, and food and beverage controls are a must. Gain an ability to make quick and independent decisions. Check the placement office, faculty members, and professional organizations for employment leads. Create a network in the industry to establish contracts for advancement. Take leadership roles in student organizations. Gain experience working with budgets.
General Services Office operations Reservations Purchasing Customer services Travel planning	Tour operators Historical, cultural, and natural attractions Lodging: hotel/motel, bed and breakfast, time-shares, and campgrounds Reservations companies Destination areas: amusement centers, theme parks, and resorts Special event and festival organizations Entertainment industry: casinos, theaters, and stadiums Food service: catering, schools, hospitals, military, concessions, and institutions Restaurants, dining clubs, taverns and fast-food operators Transportation/travel industry: airlines, cruise companies, care rental agencies, travel agencies, airports, motor coach/tour carriers, and rapid transit, e.g., AMTRAK and VIA Rail Canada Leisure organizations: sporting clubs, recreation centers, fitness facilities, private and/or country clubs State, provincial, federal, and local government: tourism offices, visitor bureaus, convention centers, and park systems Self-employment	A high interest in working with the public and problem-solving is a must. Start in reservations or telephone sales. Master the product line, learn to give excellent service. Understand and use office machines and office systems in your area of expertise. Serve as treasurer or financial officer of an organization. Gain experience working with budgets. Acquire supervisory skills and experience. An orientation toward service and detail is necessary to succeed. Learn state, provincial, federal and local government job application process

Career area	Where they work	How to prepare
Special events Convention/trade show planning Entertainment/event planning Activities planning Recreation manager Convention services management	Lodging: hotel/motel, bed and breakfast, time-shares, and campgrounds Destination areas: amusement centers, theme parks, and resorts Special event and festival organizations Entertainment industry: casinos, theaters, and stadiums Cruise companies Leisure organizations: sporting clubs, recreation centers, fitness facilities, private and/or country clubs State, provincial, federal, and local government: tourism offices, visits bureaus, convention centers, and park systems Trade and professional associations Public or private corporations and businesses	Gain an ability to make quick and independent decisions. Prepare interpersonal and public speaking skills. Be creative, have good planning and organizational skills. Gain experience through planning activities/events for civic/community organizations. Attend conferences for student organizations and professional associations. Include classes in marketing, promotions, commercial recreation, activity planning, resort management, advertising, public relations, and business. Learn how to do fund-raising. Gain experience working with budgets. Learn state, provincial, federal, and local government job application process.
Marketing Product research Communications General sales Meeting and convention sales Incentive travel sales	Tour operators Historical, cultural, and natural attractions Lodging: hotel/motel, bed and breakfast, time-shares, and campgrounds Reservation companies Restaurants, dining clubs, taverns, and fast-food operators Equipment suppliers and manufacturers Transportation/travel industry: airlines, cruise companies, car rental agencies, travel agencies, airports, motor coach/tour carriers, and rapid transit, e.g., AMTRAK and VIA Rail Canada Leisure organizations: sporting clubs, recreation centers, fitness facilities, private and/or country clubs State, provincial, federal, and local government: tourism offices, visitor bureaus, convention centers, and park systems	Gain competency in a variety of computer programs. Gain experience in customer service and communications skills. Learn about geography and international travel regulations. Take a part-time job in any area and move up. Strive for excellent interpersonal and public speaking skills. Consider a foreign language or business minor. Take classes in marketing, promotions, advertising, public relations and business. Start in reservations or telephone sales. Learn the product line, deal with travel agents and the customer. Work in a major port city like Los Angeles, Miami, New York, or Vancouver. Learn state, provincial, federal, and local government job application process.

TABLE C.1
Continued.

Areas	Employers	Strategies
Advertising Product design/illustration Media planning and development Public relations Publicity/promotion	Lodging: hotel/motel, bed and breakfast, time-shares, and campgrounds Destination areas: amusement centers, theme parks, and resorts Special event and festival organizations Entertainment industry: casinos, theaters, and stadiums Leisure organizations: sporting clubs, recreation centers, fitness facilities, private and/or country clubs State, provincial, federal, and local government: tourism offices, visitor bureaus, convention centers, and park systems Trade and professional associations Public or private corporations and businesses Restaurants, dining clubs, taverns, and fast-food operators Product and equipment supplies and manufacturer Transportation/travel industry: airlines, cruise companies, car rental agencies, travel agencies, airports, motor coach/tour carriers and rapid transit, e.g., AMTRAK and VIA Rail Canada	Gain competency in a variety of computer graphics programs. Strive for excellent interpersonal and public speaking skills. Consider a public relations or marketing minor. Take a part-time job in any area and move up. Volunteer to advertise/promote events for parties, outings, and organizations. Learn state, provincial, federal, and local government job application process. Attend conferences and trade shows, join student clubs and professional associations, attend field trips. Include classes in marketing, promotions, advertising, public relations, and business. Join student organizations in your field of study and join the publicity committee.
Human Resources Personnel management Training Employment support services Recruitment Labor relations Compensation and benefits	Lodging: hotel/motel, bed and breakfast, time-shares, and campgrounds Destination areas: amusement centers, theme parks, and resorts Entertainment industry: casinos, theaters, and stadiums Food service: catering, schools, hospitals, military, concessions, and institutions Restaurants, dining clubs, taverns, and fast-food operators	Take courses in labor relations, industrial psychology, personnel management, public speaking, organizational behavior, business, communications, management, and law. Foreign language or human resources are good minors. Gain experience in decision-making, planning, budgeting, and personnel issues through an internship or co-op. Be a leader in student organizations and professional associations. Plan to be flexible geographically.
Corporate administration Property acquisition and development Legal areas Research/market areas Financial relations	Lodging: hotel/motel, bed and breakfast, time-shares, and campgrounds Destination areas: amusement centers, theme parks, and resorts Entertainment industry: casinos, theaters, and stadiums Food service: catering, schools, hospitals, military, concessions, and institutions Restaurants, dining clubs, taverns, and fast-food operators	Take classes in human relations, food-service production, marketing, law, accounting, food/beverage controls, and resort management. Obtain a graduate degree in business or law. Be prepared to work "up from the bottom" to gain industry experience. Attend conferences and professional association meetings. Study the industry leaders and trends by reading trade journals.

Career Area	Employers	Skills/Preparation
	Transportation/travel industry: airlines, cruise companies, care rental agencies, travel agencies, airports, motor coach/tour carriers, and rapid transit, e.g., AMTRAK and VIA Rail Canada Leisure organizations: sporting clubs, recreation centers, fitness facilities, private and/or country clubs	Be willing to work long or unusual hours and on holidays. Gain an ability to make independent decisions. Strive for excellent interpersonal and public speaking skills. Be flexible geographically. Create a network of contacts for advancement. Gain experience working with budgets, details, meeting deadlines, and supervising others.
Publishing Guides Journals Books News writing/editing	Self-employment Newspapers, magazines and trade journals Tour operators State, provincial, federal, and local governments: tourism offices and visitor bureaus	Experience living abroad. Gain an understanding of world history, geography and international travel regulations. Study and gain an in-depth knowledge of the industry trends. Consider a journalism major. Learn writing skills. Emphasize research methods and computer skills. Learn to be objective. Work for your student newspaper; write for student organization newsletters; or work in publications areas at your college. Practice giving attention to detail and meeting deadlines. Learn about etiquette and social customs.
Government Community relations Travel information Tourism bureaus	State, provincial, federal, and local governments: tourism offices, visitor bureaus, convention centers, special event and festival planning offices, historical, cultural, and natural parks/attractions. Food service: catering, schools, hospitals, military, concessions, and institutions	Take classes in political science, government, social research methods, public polity, marketing, promotions, advertising, public relations, and business. Learn state, provincial, federal and local government job application process. Seek experience in customer service and planning. Increase skills in public speaking. Learn about etiquette and social customs. Gain sales skills. Learn grant-writing skills. Understand and use office machines, systems, and computers. Serve as treasurer or financial officer of an organization or secure experience with budgets.
Education Teaching/training Research	Lodging: hotel/motel, bed and breakfast, time-shares, and campgrounds Destination areas: amusement centers, theme parks, and resorts Entertainment industry: casinos, theaters, and stadiums Food service: catering, schools, hospitals, military, concessions, and institutions Restaurants, dining clubs, taverns, and fast-food operators State, provincial, federal, and local governments: tourism offices, visitor bureaus, convention centers, and park systems. Trade and professional associations Self-employment Colleges and universities	Possess objectivity, an inquiring mind, and an interest in working with both data and people. Determine an area of expertise. Gain an in-depth knowledge of that industry, its leaders, and trends by reading recent books, journals, and annual reports. Obtain a degree in the subject you plan to teach or research. Learn writing and research skills. Consider a graduate degree in research methods or a specialty of the trade. Gain professional industry experience. Attend and speak at conferences, trade shows, and professional associations. Network in the industry for professional contacts.

TABLE C.1
Continued.

Areas	Employers	Strategies
General information		
Obtain volunteer, part-time, summer, internship, and/or co-op experience.		
Bachelor's degree qualifies for entry-level government and industry positions.		
Master's degree qualifies for community college teaching and advancement in industry and government.		
Ph.D. is required for advanced research or teaching positions in colleges and universities and senior positions in government.		
Join professional organizations such as The National Tour Association, The American Hotel and Motel Association, or the National Restaurant Association.		
It may be necessary to move around geographically to get promotions.		
Obtain computer experience.		
Develop strong communications and customer service skills.		
Be prepared to "work your way up from the bottom."		
Be willing to work on weekends, holidays, evenings and long or unusual hours.		

Source: Career Planning Staff (1994). Knoxville: Career Services, University of Tennessee.

that can be read in 30 seconds or less. Your resume should show what you have to offer a prospective employer and create enough interest so that they will want to learn more about you. One word of caution, do not exaggerate, since most organizations will verify the accuracy of the information you provide.

The format and content of your resume should be factual and to the point. There are several formats you can use that allow you to highlight or focus on specific information. The chronological resume focuses on when and what, the functional resume focuses on skills and accomplishments, and a targeted resume allows you to do both when and what and skills and accomplishments.[2] Use the following outline to organize your thoughts.

1. Contact information: Put your name, address and a telephone number where you can always be reached. (*Note*: Make sure you have a professional message on your answering machine and tell anyone who will answer the phone while you are away to answer professionally and take detailed messages.)

2. Career objective: Give the reader some idea of where you want to go with your career. If you are too vague, employers may not know if you will fit in their organization. However, if you are too specific, you might disqualify yourself from related jobs. General statements such as, "seeking an entry level or supervisory position in ____" (fill in the blank with your desired position such as restaurant operations, passenger services, or hospitality services) are probably best as you enter the full-time workforce. More directed statements can be made in your cover letter. As you gain more experience, it will be appropriate to express more specific career goals.

3. Education and training: List your college degree(s) and major. Highlight your grade point average if it is good. Include any special training or certifications you have received. If your work experience is limited, expand this section by including an explanation of special skills you have acquired.

4. Work experience: List all employers for whom you have worked. Do not forget summer and part-time jobs, internships, and cooperative education placements. Include the name and location of the organization, dates of employment, positions held, and a brief description of your skills and accomplishments. You can present this information in a chronological format (the most recent job first) or in a functional format (highlighting specific skills and accomplishments).

5. Activities and honors: Show what you do when you are not in school or working. List such things as professional, social, and civic organizations to which you belong as well as honors, awards, and scholarships you have received. Describe your accomplishments and responsibilities with these organizations such as officer positions, committee assignments, and completed projects.

Use action words, phrases, and quantifiable accomplishments to show that you are a dependable, can-do, take charge problem-solver.

Once your resume is complete, have several people critique it for you. Your career services office can assist you throughout this process. This will help you find mistakes as well as test whether it is painting the picture you want the reader to see. After it has been checked and double-checked for clarity and correctness, you are ready to have it printed. Use either a laser-quality printer or have your resume professionally printed on high-quality cotton bond paper. Be sure to save some of the paper so you can send your cover letter on the same type of stationery.

WRITING YOUR COVER LETTER

Your resume is only one step in the job-search process. You will also need to prospect for jobs by writing cover letters and including your resume with this correspondence. Cover letters are written in response to advertisements or job announcements, as follow-up to a telephone inquiry, or when inquiring about possible job openings.

Your cover letter serves as an introduction to prospective employers and entices them to read your resume and invite you to interview. Since it is an introduction, personalize it. Do not send a cover letter to "whom it may concern" or "human resource director." Call and ask for the name, title, and correct spelling of the person to whom the letter should be addressed.

There are two basic types of cover letters that you will write. One is a letter of inquiry, seeking to find out if the organization is looking for employees. The other is a letter of application, which is written in response to a known job opening. In either case, since there may be many people corresponding with the organization, be sure to follow up with a phone call after you have sent the letter and ask for an interview.

PREPARING FOR THE INTERVIEW

Finding a job may be one of the most difficult challenges you will ever face, but it is also one of the most rewarding. Do not get discouraged. You may send out hundreds of letters of inquiries and resumes and make many calls before you land your first interview.

Before you land your first interview appointment, take advantage of any on-campus recruiting opportunities and attend career fairs to practice your interviewing skills and learn more about what employers are expecting from job applicants. Once you have been invited to interview, prepare yourself for success by using the following outline.

1. Research the company: Find out everything you can about your prospective employer. What services do they provide? Who are their primary competitors? How big are they? Where are their offices/properties/outlets located? Do they have a formal training program? What is a typical career path? Your librarian or career planning professional can help you with this task. Be prepared to relate your skills and accomplishments to the organization's needs.

2. Prepare yourself: Arrive at the interview at least 15 minutes before the scheduled time. Be sure that you are neat, clean, rested, well-groomed, and dressed appropriately. Be sure to know all the information in the materials that have been sent to you before the interview.

3. Sell yourself: Stress your achievements and be prepared to answer some typical interview questions in a positive manner.

4. Do not rely on your resume to answer any of the following questions:

    *   How do you plan to achieve your career goals?
    *   Why did you choose the career for which you are planning?
    *   How has your education prepared you for a career?
    *   What were your favorite subjects in school?
    *   What subjects did you like the least?
    *   What motivates you to put forth your greatest effort?
    *   Why should we hire you?
    *   What have you learned from participation in extracurricular activities?
    *   What do you know about our company?
    *   What have you learned from your mistakes?

5. Stay professionally engaged: Watch for cues that indicate when an interview wants more information or wants you to shorten your answers. Maintain eye contact; don't slouch in your chair; do not wander from answering the question. Watch for signs that the interview is over. If you are not offered a job on the spot, ask if it would be okay to call back in about 10 days and check on the status of the search.

6. Follow up after the interview: Write a thank-you note to everyone with whom you interviewed. Thank them for their time and indicate whether you are interested in being considered further. Respond quickly to any requests for additional information.

One final reminder: Before you go on that all important career interview, review the key points on business etiquette that are presented in Appendix B. The final choice a recruiter will make between you and another equally qualified candidate may come down to your attention to detail and professionalism.

REFERENCES

1. Farnham, Alan. (1993, July). Out of college: What's next?, *Fortune*, pp. 58–64.

2. Parker, Yana. (1993). *Resume pro: The professional's guide*. Berkeley, CA: Ten Speed Press.

Integrative Cases

Integrated Cases

BREWSTER TOURS

What began as a small family business has grown into one of the largest travel suppliers in Canada. Jim and Bill Brewster began transporting visitors from the Canadian Pacific Banff Railway Station to the Banff Springs Hotel in 1892. A typical visitor would stay at the hotel for 3 to 4 weeks, and the Brewster brothers would guide these guests on horseback, fishing, and hiking tours of the area.

The business grew and, during the 1920s, the brothers upgraded their horse-drawn carriages to touring cars and purchased the hotel. In the late 1920s, they acquired a Gray Line sightseeing franchise.[1]

During the 1960s Brewster began marketing tours to international clients in Australia, the United Kingdom, and Europe. A new division, Royal Glacier Tours, was added to accommodate the independent-tour-package clients from the international market.

Brewster now provides tourism services to more than 600,000 visitors annually. A marketing budget of almost two million dollars supports the activities of the company including Gray Line Sightseeing, Charter Coach Division, Brewster Group Tours, Great Canadian Train Vacations, Royal Glacier Independent Package Tours, The Columbia Icefield Snocoach Tours, The Mount Royal Hotel, and Mount Norquay ski area.

As operations grew, so did Brewster's marketing efforts. Staff members now attend more than 70 travel trade shows throughout the world each year, and the company distributes 1.2 million brochures annually. A customized computer system manages reservations, product inventories, itineraries, dispatching and data reporting for all operations. Continuing efforts to grow has led the company to focus a great deal of attention on the Japanese market.[1]

JAPANESE TRAVEL TO CANADA

Japanese tourists are attracted to Canada in increasing numbers because of its positive image, which can be attributed to the following factors:

- The spectacular natural beauty which is a major drawing card. Japanese tourists refer to this as "big nature." The primary areas of interest are the Canadian Rockies, Niagara Falls, and all lakes, forests, and other natural resources.

- The perception that Canada is a very safe destination. The Japanese are extremely security-conscious and do not go where they feel unsafe.

- The importance of cleanliness in a destination choice. Canada offers clean uncrowded cities with a slower pace of life, leisurely walks, picture-taking opportunities, and a chance to enjoy other sightseeing activities in a pleasant atmosphere.

- The perceived friendliness of Canada. The Japanese do not go where they feel unwelcome.[2]

Visiting the Canadian Rockies is a critical component of Japanese tours to Canada. Even Eastern Canadian tours will usually feature a two-day stopover in Banff en route. Every major Japanese tour operator includes the Columbia Icefields snow-coach tour in their itinerary. These tours have proven to be so popular that regularly scheduled Brewster motorcoaches destined for the Icefields in September and October often have up to 70% Japanese visitors on board.

Canada has the greatest Japanese visitor return rate of any foreign destination. Canada is, however, the seventh destination choice overall in numbers of Japanese visitors. The Japanese are annoyed by the goods and services tax (GST), although their price/value perceptions of Canada are favorable, except for cigarette prices.

Australia is seen as one of Canada's leading competitors in the Japanese market. While the product is different, Australia competes with Canada for certain segments, especially young women and honeymooners. Australia is targeting 1.8 million Japanese annually by the year 2000. Although seen as long-haul travel, Australia (Sydney) has only a 2-hour time difference and is served by Japan Airlines, All Nippon Airways, and Northwest Airlines. In addition, Malaysia, Great Britain, and several American states are spending more on marketing to the Japanese. Apart from the usual states such as California and Hawaii, states such as Florida and regions like the U.S. Rocky Mountains are aggressively seeking Japanese visitors.

CHARACTERISTICS OF JAPANESE TRAVELERS

A survey by the Japan Travel Bureau Foundation (JBF), produced some important findings (see Table IC.1) about Japanese consumer patterns and preferences regarding travel decisions. First, the number of holidays taken by individuals has a very important effect on overseas travel. While most workers receive 2 weeks of paid vacation each year, they feel obligated to actually take less or to break it up into small chunks of time around long weekends.

TABLE IC.1
Purpose of Travel Abroad

Purpose	All Market Segments	Single Women	Single Men
To enjoy nature and scenery	75	71	73
To see famous historical sites and works	56	60	49
To taste food I like or try delicacies of the country	5	52	47
To enjoy shopping	47	77	46
To relax and rest	45	39	40
To experience a different culture	38	50	48
To visit museums	29	36	28
To stay in a famous hotel	24	31	26
To enjoy marine sports (windsurfing, scuba diving)	13	29	33
To enjoy sports (tennis, golf, etc.)	12	13	23
To experience the latest fashions and trends	12	34	9
To travel abroad with my own money	10	9	16
Dislike group travel	4	4	6

Source: JTB Report (1990). Tokyo: Japan Travel Bureau Foundation.

Second, Japanese travelers like to spend a brief period of time at each stop on the itinerary and then move on. They are keen to fill their limited vacation time to the brim with as many sights and experiences as possible.

Third, when asked to describe the qualities that were most desirable, half (50%) preferred a location abundant in nature (e.g., lakes and mountains, etc.); over a third (38%) desired a destination with plenty of sun, white sand, and blue ocean; and the third most desirable place was one that had a variety of cities with an abundance of modern culture and tourist attractions (36%).

Fourth, when asked what they expected to do on their overseas trip, most Japanese surveyed (74%) replied that they intended to "enjoy nature and scenery." The second-most-mentioned activity (55%) was "to see famous historical sites and works of architecture," while 50% desired to sample the local cuisine.[3]

A well-known characteristic of Japanese travelers is their preference for group travel. Approximately 80% of Japanese pleasure tourists travel in affinity groups of one kind or another (for example, single women, honeymooners, family and friends, schoolteachers, etc.) This pattern reflects the group ethic that dominates Japanese culture and provides a safe environment for them to explore new countries and situations where their knowledge of language and local culture may be limited.

The types of groups taking tours varies from honeymoon tours, in which 20 newly married couples all go away together, to the incentive tour, sightseeing/pleasure tour, and industrial tour. Because the Japanese tour business is managed to a great extent by a number of large Japanese wholesalers and travel agencies, they can strongly influence where Japanese travelers will go.

The Japanese visitor traveling in a tour group will expect:

* ease of passage through Canadian customs,
* transfers from airports to be carried out smoothly and on time,
* to be greeted appropriately (preferably in Japanese),
* a competent and experienced Japanese-speaking guide,
* guides who are smartly uniformed,
* to be counted when back on board,
* interesting commentary, sights and routes,
* written communications in Japanese/English,
* comfortable, luxury coaches or railcars with amenities,
* first-class hotels,
* early wake-up calls at the hotel,
* food/beverage service (both Japanese and Western foods),
* personal service for personal needs,
* politeness and helpfulness from everyone in the company,
* assistance on and off the coach/train if required,
* sufficient time for shopping,
* time for social activities.

Although the majority (80%) of Japanese travelers prefer to travel with a tour group, Japanese wholesalers believe that the independent traveler will grow in importance. The result will be that more Canadian tourism businesses seeking to succeed with Japanese customers will have to adapt their resources to meet this market's high service expectations.

The Japanese service industry is highly labor-intensive, and Japanese customers are accustomed to the highest quality of service standards at home. They expect the same when they travel abroad, especially to some of the world's more prestigious destinations. Because they can be in a hurry, it is vital that service be quick, efficient, and punctual.

SEGMENTATION OF JAPANESE TRAVEL MARKET

Japanese travelers tend to fall into four major groups: single, working people between the ages of 18 and 30; honeymooners; retired couples over 55; and students. Constraints of time and money restrict the number of Japanese families taking long-haul, overseas trips to a very small portion of the total. The growing wealth and independence of Japan's new post-war generation has not only freed the older generation for more travel, but has also created a large youth market. As the Japanese become more accepting of, and curious about, other cultures, the youth become eager to explore and the seniors to tour.

The female segment is one of the most important for Canada. While Japanese women account for one third of overseas travel, they account for one half of Japanese travel to Canada.

While the average income of the female office worker is less than that earned by managers, their disposable income is far higher because they live at home. Furthermore, the female office workers use 100% of their annual leave entitlement while the average Japanese worker uses less than half of his or her entitlement of 15 days or more. The typical tour profile for an "office lady" would be a package tour with friends from college or the office, most likely focusing on shopping or, more frequently in recent years, sports.

A growing male bachelor market has been fueled by the rise of well-educated, well-paid single men looking for adventure. Most Japanese men choose the more familiar but exotic locations of Asia. However, because of a growing interest in active holidays, more Japanese males are turning their attention to Canada and are showing interest in recreational activities and less-well-known destinations. In one survey, 36% of the single men surveyed named Canada as their preferred destination, which places Canada in second place behind Australia for this market.[4]

The largest single market for package tours to Canada is couples on honeymoon. Seventy to eighty percent of all wholesale tour sales during the heavy spring and autumn bridal seasons are honeymoon couples. Over 700,000 marriages take place each year in Japan, and as many as 96% of these newlyweds planned to travel overseas on a honeymoon.

The average honeymooners travel for almost 8 days and they prefer destinations not yet visited by the majority of their friends and colleagues. They are "trend-setters" because of their powerful word-of-mouth effect on other market segments. While Hawaii dominated the honeymoon market in the late 1970s, it was surpassed by Australia in the 1980s. Canada continues to gain market share for Japanese honeymoon travel.

Japan is rapidly becoming an elderly society. In 1955, 5% of the population were aged over 65; in 1983, this percentage was 9.8%; and, by 2000, will surpass 15%. Whereas the younger generation is attracted to sports and other outdoor activities, the older generation travels at a more leisurely pace. Not only does the opportunity exist for longer tours, but this segment of the market has also demonstrated a greater propensity to make return visits to the same destination.

While still a rather small group, student travelers constitute the fastest-growing market segment. The majority of trips taken by teenagers are either home stays or "study tours." Numbers are estimated to be as high as 100,000 and take place mostly on the west coast of North America and Europe. There have also been noticeable increases in the number of overseas trips organized by the schools as part of the curriculum. The Ministry of Education is lifting restrictions on overseas trips.

Another small but growing segment includes special interest tours. Tours offering the most potential include skiing, golf, cycling, and fishing. While special-interest tours have tended to be run by smaller, specialized companies, the large tour operators are showing increasing interest. JTB International, for example, has a division that concentrates on technical visits and has established a databank in Tokyo of tours relating to such subjects as urban revitalization, ski resort development, waterfront development, status of women, park management, and services for the disabled.

Brewster's Japanese Travel Business

Brewster entered the Japanese travel market through a partnership with Canadian Pacific Airlines (CP). CP sold airline seats and hotel rooms while Brewster sold motorcoach charters, sightseeing tours, and snowmobile tours at the Columbia Icefields. Brewster has owned and operated the Mount Royal Hotel in Banff since 1912. The company did not, however, regard the hotel as a first-class property suitable for selling to Japanese group tours.

Brewster's business volume from the Japanese market grew steadily. In 1984, an agreement was made with Greyhound International to retail Brewster products at Greyhound International's foreign-based tour offices, including Tokyo. When Dial Corporation, the parent company of Greyhound International, sold Greyhound Bus U.S. in 1990, a decision was made to close the Tokyo office of Greyhound International. Several former employees of Greyhound International's Tokyo office joined Universal Express Company Ltd., which Brewster chose as their nonexclusive representative in Japan.

Having a Japanese office solved several problems: language barriers, long-distance communications costs, explaining products in detail face to face with clients, and greater exposure to the market. The Japanese agent also reduced selling expenses by selling more products to the demanding Japanese clientele. Rapid communication from Canada is very important for conducting business in Japan.

Brewster found Japanese clients were more willing to work with companies that had an office in Japan. It usually requires many years to gain the trust of Japanese tour wholesalers. When this trust level has been established, companies like Brewster are allowed to include their products in the wholesaler's travel brochures.

Brewster hosts an intern from Universal Express for 3 months each summer in Banff. The intern assists Brewster's Japanese clients in Canada with language, cultural, or tour-related issues. Cross training occurs when the intern returns to Japan and educates Universal Express office staff on Brewster's operations.

Brewster initiated an education/familiarization tour to Japan for employees in 1986. Each year, 10 Brewster line-level employees are awarded this experience. Participants include drivers, ticket agents, hotel service staff, icefields staff, and others. Selection is based on merit and interest rather than seniority. So far, 70 Brewster employees have gained firsthand knowledge of the Japanese market through this tour.

A video, "Japan Outbound," was produced for Brewster staff training by Bob Sandford. The video provides an overview of the history of Japanese culture, development of Japanese travel habits, consumer likes and dislikes, and service techniques. Comparisons are made to Western-style service. For example, Japanese taxi drivers wear white gloves while working.

Copies of the video were eventually acquired by Brewster's Japanese clients. The existence of the video, plus educational employee tours to Japan and other training commitments, earned Brewster additional respect with their Japanese clients.

Future Trends in Japanese Travel

The Japanese travel industry expects outbound travel to reach 19.8 million by the year 2001. The fastest-growing segment of the inbound Japanese market is currently the well-educated 20-plus age group. This group as well as many other Japanese travelers are beginning to purchase foreign independent travel (FIT) products rather than group tours. The use of rental cars is increasing at the expense of motorcoach travel. Group tour departures are decreasing in the number of participants per tour.

Brewster has responded by modifying several products to accommodate these changing needs. Brewster's Canada Tours (formerly known as Royal Glacier Tours) operates in eastern and western Canada. The tours are FIT, unguided, and unescorted. Tour products have been enhanced by focusing on shorter itineraries of 2, 3, 4, and 5 days. Examples of tour formats include a two-day Vancouver to Banff and a four-day David Thompson tour from Calgary, Banff, Icefields to Vancouver. The average Japan-to-Japan holiday is 6.9 days in length.

According to the Japan Travel Bureau Foundation, foreign travel trends are marked by a diversification of destination, a shrinkage of the package-group size, and a new matter-of-fact attitude to travel that takes the overseas trip for granted and sees travel as part of an ordinary lifestyle.

More and more Japanese are repeat travelers and, as a result, are more confident, adventurous, and willing to try new activities and destinations. Many travelers are now challenging tour operators by negotiating lower rates through various channels such as the redemption of frequent-flyer miles.

The Japan Travel Bureau Foundation has predicted that there will be a shift in emphasis in future travel requirements from a mere expansion of quantity to an upgrading of quality due to an increase in travel by the older market segments, who value high comfort standards, and increased travel by individuals, not groups, mostly among repeat travelers.

Japanese travel to Canada specifically is expected to follow the following trends:

1. increasing shoulder and off-season travel as tour operators find ways of combating air and ground capacity restrictions during the peak periods,

2. a growing number of "stay-put" packages, in which Japanese tourists stay several days in a resort or city and make more activity-oriented trips from the same base, and

3. a growing number of independent travelers—Japanese tourists who will want to explore less-well-known places and will need more information and promotional brochures to be produced in the Japanese language.

Ski traffic to the Canadian Rockies from Japan is increasing. Western Canada is the preferred global destination for Japanese skiers. Skiing is a price-sensitive market due to the younger age group involved, Air fares determine a destination's success, European air carriers have recently expanded marketing efforts to Japan by offering low price fares to European ski destinations.

The long-term prospects for outbound travel by the Japanese are good for a number of reasons. Despite the substantial growth in outbound travel, the market is far from saturated. The Japanese government is committed to increasing outbound travel in order to rectify trade imbalances.

SERVING JAPANESE TRAVELERS

Many Japanese appear to be favorably disposed toward Canada. However, a large portion of Japanese travelers still hold some negative perceptions about Canada. For example, many perceive Canada as too big to travel in one trip and too far from Japan. Canada also has a poor image with some Japanese as a place to eat, visit historical and cultural sights, shop, or enjoy nightlife. On a positive note, Japanese people do like to buy "Canadian," but prefer quality handicrafts and "brand name" products associated with the destination.

Ground-handling is always done by Japanese companies from their Vancouver offices, for language reasons. In addition, Japanese staff are believed to be superior at meeting the needs of Japanese travelers.

Travel products and services are not always changed to suit Japanese tastes. Dietary concerns were not addressed initially. For example, menu offerings featured beef and salmon and Japanese travelers would often visit the local supermarket to obtain desired food items. Japanese travelers prefer sleeping rooms with separate beds, even for occupancy by husbands and wives. Japanese bathrooms all have floor drains, therefore, some travelers do not use shower curtains. Several Canadian hotels have incurred substantial multi-floor water damage from this practice.

Japanese travelers do not like surprises or unintended consequences such as last-minute schedule changes. Japanese-language copy is important for all written communications, including menus and brochures. Full travel days with comprehensive and extensive itinerary are important. Leisurely paced vacation packages are perceived as poor value by the Japanese. A maximum of 3 days is preferred at any destination. Japanese people are very punctual and expect the same from others.

Extended-time dining functions do not appeal to Japanese travelers. They do not want a 2.5-hour dinner, preferring instead to dine promptly and spend the remainder of the evening shopping. Lighter food portions are appreciated. Seating arrangements should integrate Japanese guests with other diners. Japanese groups do not want to sit in a segregated section of the dining facility.

Gifts and photographs are essential components of Japanese travel culture. Photo stops should be frequent. Local participation in photo posing is appreciated. Gifts are usually purchased for all close friends and family in Japan. Brewster 100th-anniversary T-shirts (1992) were very popular gifts for tour-operator clients when Brewster staff visited Japan.

WORKING WITH JAPANESE TOUR COMPANIES

All major Japanese tour companies have Vancouver offices. Major policy and strategy decisions are made at home offices in Japan. Brewster presently uses co-op visits with Tourism Canada and Travel Alberta to reach their major tour company sources in Japan. The co-op trips are followed by separate one-on-one visits from Brewster staff for heightened impact with Japanese clients.

Establishing working relationships with Japanese tour operators can be difficult. Personal chemistry and "fit" are important to establish trust and business discussion. Social skills and actions are critical. Business suitors must enjoy the Japanese business lifestyle. This usually involves an extensive commitment to social networking, including evening entertaining. Aggressive behavior is not appreciated. Suitors should be natural and normal, avoiding loud behavior such as back-slapping and hand gestures.

There are no deliberate tariff or duty barriers for Canadian tour operators entering the Japanese market. The major constraints are the high cost of conducting business in Japan and language and cultural differences. Decisions are made by consensus, followed by immediate action. Honor and honesty are virtues. The honor code of "a deal is a deal" is assured. Patience is very important, as extensive time may be required to consummate a sale. Emphasis is always focused on long-term relationships rather than a "quick deal." Respect for culture is imperative.

LOOKING TO THE FUTURE

Terry Gainer, Vice President of Sales of Brewster Tours, was contemplating future inbound travel market trends. As Canada's largest inbound (foreign visitors traveling to Canada) travel supplier to the Japanese market, Brewster had a significant stake in the future of the global tourism industry. Terry knew that previous sales and marketing strategies that had brought a century of successes for Brewster would require continued change and refinement to maintain the company's future competitive position. Since Japanese travelers generate significant shoulder and off-season revenues, Mr. Gainer must decide how to attract and serve this crucial market segment.

Source: This case was prepared by Donald J. MacLaurin of University of Guelph as a basis for classroom instruction rather than to illustrate either effective or ineffective handling of an administrative situation. This case was edited by Roy A. Cook and Laura J. Yale for inclusion in *Tourism: The Business of Travel*, copyright © 1998.

REFERENCES

1. Brewster, 100 years (1992, March 30). Special Supplement to the *Banff Crag and Canyon.*

2. Meeting Japanese Service Expectations (1992). Ottawa, Ont.: Canadian Tourism Commission.

3. JTB Report (1992). Tokyo: Japan Travel Bureau Foundation.

4. JTB Report (1991). Tokyo: Japan Travel Bureau Foundation.

Integrated Cases

THE COTTAGES RESORT AND CONFERENCE CENTER

Bud Briggs, Director of Marketing and Sales for The Cottages Resort and Conference Center, was preparing the annual marketing plan. He was having difficulty deciding what recommendations he should make regarding advertising, sales, and additions to property facilities. As he pushed himself away from the stack of papers in front of him and looked out the window, another foursome approached the green located just a few yards from the offices. The weather was perfect: bright, sunny and warm—typical for an August morning on Hilton Head Island, South Carolina.

Bud, an avid golfer, thought enviously that he would much rather be on the course than drafting next year's marketing plan. In the 8 weeks he had been Sales and Marketing Manager, Briggs had developed a thorough understanding of the operations of the property, but putting it all down on paper was difficult.

It was clear that the occupancy rates for The Cottages, approximately half of the Hilton Head Island average, would have to be improved during the coming year. Briggs was confident that the executives of Benchmark Management Company, which operated the property on a day-to-day basis, would support his recommendations with the necessary funding if he presented his case well.

Briggs had been reviewing the sales records to draw some conclusions regarding The Cottages' current customer base. The Cottages catered both to businesses as a meeting facility and to individual recreational travelers as a resort. On the business side, the largest number of groups came from Georgia and North Carolina, although many came from Texas, Illinois, and Massachusetts. The topics of their meetings were as diverse as the points of origin. On the recreational side, there were few patterns that Briggs could discern.

Briggs was convinced that the property had only scratched the surface of the market. Everyone who had actually seen the property had quickly fallen in love with the quiet surroundings and the concept of individual villas. The key appeared to be attracting more visitors, but how? The current sales team was doing all that could be expected. Would an additional salesperson add enough short-term business to cover the expenses of the new position? The advertising and promotional program certainly needed improvement. Even the operation of the property could benefit from more attention.

As he gazed out the window, one of the golfers sank a 50-foot putt. Bud shook his head and returned to his work, only to be interrupted by his secretary: "Bud, it's the

Consolidated Southeastern group. They want to talk to you about the lack of a restaurant here on the property." As he reached for the phone, Briggs made a mental note to highlight the prospect of adding a restaurant when writing the marketing plan. It seemed to be a major stumbling block in negotiating with some meeting planners.

THE COTTAGES PROPERTY

The Cottages Resort and Conference Center opened in 1985 to serve the needs of businesses and associations for convention and meeting facilities in a relaxing atmosphere and vacationers for a recreational resort. The actual facilities include 72 individual townhome villas, providing a maximum of 160 available rooms. The villas, within easy walking distance of the conference facility, are situated among southern oaks, palmettoes, and jack pines shrouded with Spanish moss. Villas are configured in one-, two-, or three-bedroom designs. Included in each are bedroom(s) with attached bath(s), a living room, a completely equipped kitchen, a dining room, and front and back porches. The layout of the villas typically provide a view of the adjacent golf course, a small pond or waterway (frequently under "management" of an alligator or two), or a wooded "wild" area. The entire property gives the impression of a well-cared for, quiet residential area rather than a fast-paced resort.

The conference center itself provides over 10,000 square feet of meeting space. The facilities were designed with the meeting planner's needs in mind, offering broad room designs for both small and large groups. The board room can seat up to 20 people in luxuriously appointed leather chairs around a large mahogany table. The ballroom can accommodate a meeting of 300 people or be divided into three smaller rooms.

The latest "meeting technology" was employed in the design of the conference center. The most advanced audiovisual equipment is available and most rooms are equipped with electronically operated drop-down screens for both front and rear projection, variable lighting controls, and complete sound systems. To provide the best meeting atmosphere, the rooms were designed with a maximum ceiling height of 17 feet; recessed lighting, including fluorescent, incandescent, and natural sources; and ergonomically designed "18-hour" chairs. Outside each meeting room, large decks and screened porches provide activity areas and a view of the golf course and its environs.

On-site, The Cottages offers a variety of recreational activities in addition to lodging and meeting facilities. The conference center houses a weight room, saunas, locker room facilities with showers, two racquetball courts, and an indoor/outdoor heated pool. A fleet of bicycles are available for guest use. A "general store" provides amenities and travel necessities and a lounge with full beverage service and casual seating adjoins the check-in area.

Off-site, The Cottages maintains a relationship with Shipyard Golf Course, Shipyard Racquet Club, Oyster Reef Golf Course, and Hilton Head Country Club. Guests are able to play at reduced prices and receive preferential treatment in scheduling and support. While The Cottages property is not actually on the beach, it is within comfortable walking distance. Guests have access to a private beach and the use of a beach house for private functions. In addition to the recreational activities provided directly by the resort, there are numerous opportunities, from fishing to paragliding, available in the surrounding Hilton Head Island area. The Cottages maintains a fleet of chauffeured vans to provide ground transport for guests. Even with all of these nearby amenities, Briggs commented that

> One of our major problems is our location. We aren't on the beach. It's about a fifteen-minute walk to get there. When people hear we aren't on the beach, it becomes a real obstacle to the sale. You just can't convince them that a few minutes walk or a bike ride or stepping into one of our vans is an acceptable alternative.

Hilton Head Island

In 1663, Captain William Hilton, an English ship captain, recorded a high bluff on his nautical charts. Over the years, Captain Hilton's headland became known as Hilton Head Island. The island is actually a small, foot-shaped barrier island just off the coast of South Carolina. In 1956, the first bridge to the mainland was completed, beginning the modern development of the island. It is divided into "plantations" (planned communities).

Hilton Head Island is approximately 30 miles north of Savannah, Georgia, and roughly 90 miles south of Charleston, South Carolina. The island is 12 miles long and 5 miles wide, encompassing 42 square miles of semitropical marshlands and woods with 12 miles of white sand beaches. The average annual temperature is 65°F. During the spring and fall, the temperature is in the mid-70s to 80s during the day and about 60° at night. In the summer, the high temperatures are in the 90s and the lows in the 70s. In winter months, the days are generally in the high 50s to 60s and the nights in the 40s.

While the island is considerably developed, it still offers sanctuary to many species of wildlife. Over 140 species of birds have been seen on the island. Alligators are common, as are porpoises. Fishing and shelling are excellent.

Market and Competition

Economic conditions for Hilton Head Island had been consistently favorable for many years. The meeting and convention business had grown over the past several years. Briggs believed that the competition for The Cottages Resort had to be divided into two basic classifications—business/group competition and resort vacation competition. The markets for each were considerably different, and the key factors on which properties competed differed from one classification to the other as well. Liz Kiley, Sales Manager for The Cottages, described the decision-making process in selecting a meeting site:

> When a company is looking at Hilton Head, they usually look for the best location, and chain hotels. They have all of the amenities and the beach. Whenever we speak with a potential group, we know that they are talking to at least one of the other properties in addition to The Cottages. Economics play a part in the decision making, but it really comes down to the "personality" of the property. The big hotels are all the same: elevators, long hallways, lots of hustle and bustle. The Cottages quiet "home away from home" atmosphere is a big difference.

The process of planning a meeting is complex and varies widely from company to company. While the trade press suggests that there is a trend toward companies employing professional meeting planners, many simply give the responsibility of planning a meeting to a secretary. Frequently, the secretary is told to "make a few calls and get some information together about a few places on Hilton Head" and nothing else. The secretary often decides which places to call and what information is needed. Larger groups tend to be managed by well-informed meeting planners while smaller meetings are generally planned by secretaries.

Many business travelers also rely on travel agents to book reservations and make recommendations for meeting needs. Because travel agents can be so influential in the decision-making process, they are heavily targeted by tourism industry marketers. Travel agents are commonly inundated by direct mail advertising pieces, free trips, and a variety of travel magazines and directories.

On the tourist/vacation side of The Cottages trade, the competition was even more fragmented. In addition to the major hotels on the island, there were also many villas available. Some of them were configured as a resort (The Cottages) while others were rented privately. Competition for the vacationers was, therefore, more difficult to pinpoint. As Kiley explained,

Our vacationers come to us in different ways. Some are return visitors. They have been here for a meeting or convention and enjoyed it, so they came back with families or friends. A second group heard about us from friends and relations . . . word of mouth. We do a fair amount of promotion with travel agencies and they recommend us to their clients. Occasionally, one of the other hotels has overbooked and sends us some business. They usually stay with us after that. The other Benchmark properties work with us to refer clients back and forth as well. We don't get much walk-in trade due to our location and the regulations here about signs.

THE COTTAGES ORGANIZATION

The ownership and management of The Cottages consists of a complex set of relationships. The overall property belonged to the American Service Corporation of Greenville, South Carolina. American Service Corporation, a banking and investment company, had originally developed the property, and the Benchmark Management Company reported to them. Benchmark was responsible for the management of the property on a day-to-day basis and received a management fee based on the profitability of the property. The normal activities of the property (sales and marketing, engineering, housekeeping, reservations, conferences services, catering, front desk, and accounting) were their responsibility. Benchmark also operated several other resorts: The Woodlands Inn (Houston, Texas), Seabrook Island Resort (Charleston, South Carolina), Chaminade (Santa Cruz, California) and Cheyenne Mountain Inn (Colorado Springs, Colorado).

Most of the 72 villas at The Cottages were owned by approximately 25 to 30 investors. Benchmark paid the individual owners a percentage of the room revenues generated by the rentals of the villas. In addition, the owners could reserve the use of the villas at their discretion, making the inventory of available rooms variable. In some instances, the private use of the villas had come in conflict with the efforts of the sales group to schedule large meetings.

While there was no restaurant on the premises, Benchmark maintained a contract with a local caterer to provide meals for Cottages guests. The caterer offered a complete selection of gourmet meals, wines, and beverages. The meals, snacks, and special events were determined by the meeting planner from The Cottages menus and delivered to a staging area in the conference center for set-up and service. The actual serving was done at tables set in the meeting rooms. While the atmosphere was pleasant, the ambience a restaurant could provide was missing. The Cottages was also willing to arrange group or individual dining at island restaurants if requested. Hilton Head Island was home to a wide variety of restaurants of all types, from fast-food chains to regional gourmet specialties. The nearest restaurants were within walking distance or a short ride in one of The Cottages' complimentary vans.

The Cottages' Meetings and Packages

Benchmark's philosophy was to combine "Living, Learning, and Leisure" in each of their properties. Thus, they provided the highest-quality accommodations, the best-engineered meeting facilities, and the broadest range of recreation possible at each of their resorts. The typical business meeting held at The Cottages generated roughly 200 room-nights. The average group consisted of about 60 people, mostly male, between the ages of 35 and 60. Meetings generally lasted 3.5 days, with one entire day spent in business sessions, one afternoon of golf sponsored by the organization, and the remainder split between business and individual leisure activities.

For the vacationer, The Cottages also offered a number of package plans. For example, the "Island Golf Package" included accommodations, maid service, 18 holes of golf each day (including golf cart), one bucket of practice balls per day, activities for children, and use of the fitness center, swimming pool, etc. The typical vacationers were a couple, aged 35 to 60 years, who stayed for 3 to 5 nights on one of the package plans.

Customers were generally impressed with what they experienced during their stay at The Cottages. According to Kiley,

> Whenever a meeting is held here, the participants leave raving about the quality of their experiences. They like the accommodations, the recreation, the personal service and the villa concept particularly. Having a small home all to oneself lets people "get away from it all," even in a big meeting setting. People really appreciate that.
>
> The villa concept is hard to conceptualize though. I don't really think that most of the meeting planners understand what it looks like and the advantages that it provides. We keep hearing that meeting planners want to have all their participants in the same building. But, once they have seen our property, that all changes. Somehow, we've got to do a better job of conveying the villa concept.

Pricing and Promotion

For transients, the prices varied according to a complex formula that took into consideration the number of people per room or villa, the type of villa, the season of the year, and the recreational "package." Comparisons with competing resorts on Hilton Head had convinced Briggs that The Cottages pricing was about average. The pricing for groups depended on the size of the group, the amenities requested, and the season of the year. More importantly, as was the common practice in the industry, the sales staff were free to offer a lower than standard rate if it became necessary to attract a group's business.

The Cottages' promotional efforts had taken a variety of forms. Regionally, major feeder cities such as Atlanta, Georgia, Columbia, South Carolina, and Charlotte, North Carolina, had been targeted with newspaper advertisements and billboards promoting golf and beach packages. The travel sections of *Southern Living Magazine* had been used monthly to promote the overall services of the resort and conference center. The travel agent market had been targeted throughout the year through advertisements in *HIT, Travel Agents Market Place*, and the *Official Airline Guide Travel Planner*. The Cottages had also participated in the placement of a cooperative advertisement with the other resorts represented by Benchmark. In addition, collateral materials including some 75,000 award-winning brochures had been distributed. Promotional activities included attendance at local, regional, and national trade shows for specific industries; delivery of promotional pamphlets and collateral materials; presentation of specialty advertising merchandise such as chocolate alligators; and invitations to special "FAM" trips.

The Cottages Sales Organization

The sales organization for The Cottages consisted of three segments: the on-site sales team, the sales representatives organizations, and the national sales organization at Benchmark. The on-site team consisted of Bud Briggs, Tina Burdette, and Liz Kiley. The three of them accounted for roughly 90% of the group business and virtually all of the vacation business for the year. The two sales representative operations, one in Atlanta and one in New York contributed roughly 10% of the group business in the past year, while the national sales organization had succeeded in booking only one group over that period. The sales representative organizations were paid on a retainer-plus-commission basis.

On-site sales people were paid salary plus bonuses. Tina Burdette had been with The Cottages from its inception, had worked for the previous management company and had stayed on with Benchmark. Burdette had extensive contacts in the industry and was well connected to the "grapevine" on the Island. Whenever a group was planning to come to Hilton Head, it seemed that Burdette knew immediately. Liz Kiley had been with The Cottages for about a year. She had started in conference services but had quickly moved into sales as well. Nearly all of The Cottages employees "pitched in" to help in areas other than their primary job responsibilities. Aside from the formal sales positions, everyone was a salesperson. According to Kiley,

Our people are our biggest asset. We really knock people out with our service. Everybody in the organization participates when a group is here—the sales people, the secretaries, everybody. We do whatever it takes to make our visitors' stays the best experiences they've ever had.

THE COTTAGES' RECENT PERFORMANCE

The Cottages had not been performing up to the expectations of Benchmark. Briggs had been installed as Director of Marketing and Sales specifically to improve The Cottages' financial condition. The latest figures available indicated that occupancy at the Cottages was only about half that of their major competitors. Briggs commented on the recent performance of The Cottages:

> At the current activity level, we are just about breaking even or perhaps generating a small profit. It seems that we are having to give deeper concessions to the groups than we ought to. The major task facing us, though, is simply to increase occupancy. I see no reason that we can't increase to 30,000 room nights this year. Our current mix is about 60-40 business to social, but I'd like to see it shift to about 70-30 business to social. I think Benchmark and American Services would be happy with those numbers.

PLANNING FOR THE FUTURE

Briggs was considering the option of adding another on-site salesperson. Both Kiley and Burdette were at their limits in terms of the number of group clients they could handle. The time spent servicing current groups and dealing with inquiries left too little time for prospecting. There was no question that coverage of potential accounts would improve and the goal of increasing the meetings side of The Cottages' business would be supported by the addition of a new salesperson. Further, Briggs believed that the nature of the sale almost required a personal contact to handle objections and to negotiate for the property. The cost involved in such a move concerned Briggs. The salary and benefits package would add a large amount to overall expenses.

Beyond the costs, Briggs was concerned over his ability to justify the need for an additional person. Adding a person was a long-term commitment, not a one-time expenditure. He was also wary of applying a long-term solution to a short-term problem. It would take time to recruit, select, and train a new salesperson. The time investment would put a real drain on the current sales force and take time away from the important task of gaining new business. Because of the complexity of the sale and the complex interactions with the rest of the organization, it could be months before the new salesperson could make a positive contribution. Given that American Services Corporation was thinking of selling The Cottages, Briggs was fearful that he would not be able to offer the security that the position would be there after a few months.

A second option was to increase the promotional budget by a sizable margin. The budget for last year had been approximately $500,000. Media advertising, direct mail, collateral materials, and merchandising were all included in that figure. Briggs commented,

> Awareness is the key. We simply have to make people aware that The Cottages exists, and that it is the premier resort and conference center in the southeast. When the sales people call on a potential client, if that meeting planner hasn't even heard of The Cottages, the sale is almost impossible. But, when people have seen the property, they are hooked. If we can increase the number of people that we can bring here on "FAM" trips, we can increase the business.

The difficulty with raising the promotional budget was the uncertainty and difficulty of measuring results. Briggs was at a loss as to how to prove the worth of advertising versus direct sales contacts. He also knew that the meeting planners and travel agents received many of the travel industry magazines, all of them full of enticing pictures and exotic resorts. At what level of expenditure did an advertisement "break through" into meaningful awareness?

A third option was to build an on-premise restaurant. Briggs was convinced that the lack of a restaurant on-site was a major drawback:

> The meeting planners are very concerned over the lack of a restaurant. They simply can't believe that we can serve quality meals in a quality fashion without a facility on-site. The caterer that we deal with is really excellent. The food is well-prepared and they offer us a good selection. Still, we have had some problems. Occasionally, we have the problem of having too few or too many meals or someone wanting to change from one selection to another. We can't do repair jobs. We also cannot provide traditional room service, although the kitchens in the villas alleviate that problem somewhat. Sometimes it just doesn't seem that the caterer is really giving us his complete attention. He runs two restaurants on the Island and does a lot of other catering.

Estimates for the cost of an addition to the conference center ranged from $490,000 for complete kitchen facilities to $700,000 for a "turnkey" operation. These figures did not include the costs of dining rooms, furnishings or other expenses normally associated with a restaurant. Briggs intended to use existing facilities for dining areas. If remodeling and furnishings were to be included, an additional $490,000 would be required. In the past year, Briggs estimated that The Cottages had sold approximately $420,000 in food and received a 10% commission. If the restaurant operated according to industry norms, Briggs could expect to receive the same 10% of gross food revenues as contribution.

Briggs was concerned about how the restaurant would fit in given the legal environment on the Island. The necessary zoning and permits were often difficult and sometimes impossible to obtain for any sort of building or improvement. A new restaurant could require several months of legal maneuvering, with no guarantee that the necessary permits would be forthcoming. Briggs recalled the difficulty that The Cottages had run into in placing a sign at the entrance to the property. After months of argument, they were still prohibited from displaying a sign. With no guarantee of permits, Briggs feared that Benchmark and American Services would deny any request for capital expenditures for the coming year. Further, once the caterer learned of the restaurant project, what would be the effect on the quality of food and service until the opening?

All of the options were complicated by the breadth of the market that The Cottages had been serving. Analysis of the past customers had yielded no consistent patterns. It seemed logical to focus their efforts because they could apply only limited resources toward gaining new business. Kiley had argued for targeting specific cities and concentrating promotional efforts there. Burdette favored more local efforts: "Once someone has decided to come to Hilton Head, it's a lot easier to convince them that The Cottages is the best place than to try to argue someone into coming to Hilton Head at all."

Briggs rose to his feet, stretched and watched as another foursome prepared to hit their approach shots to the green. As he observed, the first of the group hit an errant shot that rattled into the palm tree to the right of the green and dropped with a splash into the pond between the golf course and the conference center. As he went back to his work, Briggs thought, "Maybe working on the marketing plan isn't so bad after all."

Source: This case was developed and written by David W. Rosenthal, Miami University, Oxford, Ohio, as a basis for classroom discussion rather than to illustrate either effective or ineffective handling of an administrative situation. This case was edited for *Tourism: The Business of Travel* by Roy A. Cook and Laura J. Yale. Copyright © 1998.

Integrated Cases

Gateway Durango, Inc.

"Once we've served your group, we've gotcha," says Bob Morris, owner and president of Gateway Durango, Inc., a small tour operator located in Durango, Colorado. His firm packages, sells, and delivers travel experiences that take advantage of the unique character of Colorado.

Bob was born and raised in New York City. After graduating from high school, he immediately began working in the garment business in New York City and later moved to Dallas, Texas. As a successful independent salesperson of fabrics to manufacturers of women's garments, he found himself working long hours, traveling extensively, earning large commissions, and having previous little time to enjoy his monetary successes.

Ten years ago, Bob left the hectic lifestyle and a six-figure salary behind and moved to Durango to enjoy the beautiful mountain scenery and the active and "laid back" outdoor lifestyle for which the area is noted. To keep himself occupied and engaged in some type of business activity that would fit in with the community and the lifestyle he was seeking, Bob decided to enter the packaged tour business by providing preplanned travel experiences.

His first venture into this industry, Club Discovery, was on a partnership basis. He and his partners had grandiose expectations for their business and began selling tours to all areas around of the world. Their sales activities were so diverse that it can literally be said that they attempted to be all things to all people. For instance, they were selling travel packages to locations in the Colorado Rockies as well as to such distant places as Greece and South Africa. In addition, they followed a suicidal strategy of pricing their packages too low. The eventual outcome of this strategy was that they went broke.

Although business failure may have scared other people away, Bob was determined to be a success in the tour operating business. He began his new venture, Gateway Durango, Inc., after paying off all of the old partnership obligations. Bob decided to start small and focus on one specific market niche. Success in serving this initial market niche provided him with the expertise and capital to expand into other markets.

INDUSTRY AND COMPETITION

One call does it all! In the tourism and travel industry, group leaders or travel agents place this call directly to package tour operators. Tour operators engage to varying degrees in the planning, preparing, marketing, and operating of planned travel experiences. Tour operators play a vital and unique role in the travel industry. Although they neither create nor provide the end products and services purchased by the traveling public, they do facilitate the efficient delivery of two or more of the following: transportation, lodging, meals, entertainment, events, and extra services such as tour guides, transfers, and baggage handling. The configuration of these components depends on the marketing decisions of the tour operator as well as the desires of the package purchaser.

Successful tour operators must be able to identify appropriate components from various suppliers and then market these products and services to a sufficient number of customers at an attractive price. Tour operators pride themselves on their ability to deliver the packaged goods and services at a competitive price below the composite cost of the individually purchased components. Competition among tour operators is fierce since the two primary means of differentiating their offerings are either price or service. However, the tour operator does have a strong ally in the travel agent, who often views tour operators as a convenient source of one-stop shopping.

The large majority of today's tour operators can be characterized as small businesses, generating less than $100,000 in annual revenue, operating out of a single office, and having four employees or less. Yet, the industry is dominated by large firms, with the 20 largest firms accounting for 89% of total revenue. See Table 1 for a listing of some of the industry leaders. Tour operators market through intermediaries such as retail travel agents and associations, clubs, or tour organizers. However, tour operators may also market directly to the public since they also plan and operate tours. As intermediaries representing many providers and industries, tour operators are not subject to governmental regulations. While travel is one of the fastest-growing segments of the U.S. economy, the success of tour operators is far from guaranteed. This is due in large part to the competitive environment in which they must operate. They face competition from operators who package the same destination, special event, activity, or interest as well as primary providers such as airlines and hotels. The 15% annual failure rate of tour operators underscores the fiercely competitive nature of the business.

Developing a Client Base

Bob Morris began building the client base for Gateway Durango with a single focus. He targeted church groups through direct mail pieces and only offered packaged tours to the Purgatory Ski Resort in Southwest Colorado. These packages, for the most part, did not include air transportation since most church groups coming into the area arrived in their own buses. He further segmented this market and initially targeted only Baptist churches located in what has traditionally been referred to as part of the "Bible Belt" (Texas, Oklahoma, Louisiana, and Mississippi) and New Mexico because of their close geographic locations.

Over the years, Bob continued to follow his strategy of utilizing direct mail to reach his target market. Mailings focused on price and emphasized the ability of his company to serve the client better than anyone else. Extensive use of previous client references, combined with the exhortation to contact these individuals, helped to solidify Bob's view that "Once we've served your group, we've gotcha."

This approach could be exemplified by the First Baptist Church of Midland, Texas, which booked 5 groups with a minimum of 30 skiers per group, providing at least 150 packages to Purgatory each season. Repeat business with church groups comprised 60 to 80% of the bookings in this segment. In fact, one year the church arranged for a wedding at the top of a chair lift, complete with 75 members of the choir. The services provided by Bob Morris and his staff not only ensured the repeat business of the group, but also created powerful advocates, whose positive word of mouth comments have proven to be a successful marketing tool.

The strategy of building a client base by focusing almost exclusively on church groups appeared to be sound until the most recent ski season, when Purgatory experienced a disastrous snow year. Publicity about the lack of quality snow caused a significant drop in skier days. During this season, church group bookings dropped by 50%.

Prior to this weather-related downturn in business, Bob had already begun to question the wisdom of a singular focus on a narrow target market and one destination. From a skier's perspective, while Purgatory is a good 3- to four-day resort, it is not attractive to the 7-day skier. In addition, with its far Southwest location and limited snow-making abilities, Purgatory had experienced marginal snow conditions in previous years.

Bob addressed these deficiencies in two ways. First, a ski package was developed using shuttle bus service to the Purgatory ski area from Albuquerque, New Mexico. A complete 2-day ski package, including round trip bus transportation from Albuquerque, lift tickets, and skis, was offered for only $15 more than it would cost for lift tickets and ski rental. Therefore, the cost of the convenience and the round trip bus service amounted to only $15. The ski package was offered every weekend during the ski season and, after only 3 years, this package attracted over 2000 customers annually. Because of the volume generated in the Albuquerque market, Gateway Durango was able to have a sales representative in this market.

Second, a deal was negotiated with the Telluride and Purgatory Ski Resorts. This package allowed the purchaser to spend 4 nights in Telluride and 3 nights in Durango and ski each resort's slopes for 3 days.

As a tour operator, Gateway Durango was in a position in the distribution channel that requires a close affiliation with retail travel agencies. Although travel agencies were not the initial target market for the company, they became more important for current business; they provided 25% of current bookings and an opportunity for continued future growth.

Close affiliation with travel agencies proved to be a lifesaver during the most recent season. Although the church business was down dramatically during that year due to the poor snow conditions, travel agency business from the Southern California and Arizona markets helped to offset this downturn since the snow conditions at the California resorts were even worse. The company endeavored to build credibility and solidify travel agency ties. For example, Gateway Durango paid commissions to travel agencies for clients who previously booked through that agency and subsequently booked directly through Gateway Durango.

During the most recent ski season, Gateway Durango offered ski packages to the Monarch and Crested Butte ski areas in Colorado. As a receptive operator, Bob hired part-time representatives to meet the tour groups when they arrived to help the group leaders with check-ins at both locations. The representatives gave their home phone numbers to the group leaders and personally contacted the leaders every other night to check on their stays. However, after analyzing the results of these offerings, the package for these areas were dropped when Bob determined that his representatives at these remote locations were unable to provide the consistent high level of service his customers had come to expect.

Although packaging through America West to the Purgatory area was successful, not all of the company's ventures with the airline fared as well. Vail Associates approached Gateway Durango with the opportunity to package tours through America West to the Vail Ski Resort. Although no significant costs were incurred, since the tour package information was printed in shells provided by the airline and ski resort, the venture was deemed a failure since only 30 packages were sold during the entire season. Bob suspects that the package was priced too high, but has no evidence actually pointing to any specific cause.

BECOMING MORE THAN JUST A SKI TOUR OPERATOR

As lucrative and enjoyable as the ski package business became, it generated revenue only during part of the year, and the company was forced to operate on these seasonal revenues. In his search for expansion and diversification to stabilize the company's cash flow, Bob decided to explore opportunities to serve the summer tourist in the Durango area. The summer market appeared to offer many opportunities, since nearby Mesa Verde National Park attracts over 600,000 visitors during the warm weather season and the fa-

mous Durango-Silverton Narrow Gauge Railroad carries over 200,000 passengers during the same season. This extreme seasonal variation is shown in Table 2.

Although Durango is a fly-in market in the winter, it is a drive-in market in the summer. This dramatic difference in destination access required a complete reassessment of the market. The first packages offered by Gateway Durango into the summer market were fly–drive combinations through Continental Airlines. This program proved to be unsuccessful since vacationers from the California, Texas, and Arizona markets preferred to drive, and the company did not have enough capital to commit to a strong marketing program in the important but more distant fly-in markets of Florida and Southeast. Further, Bob found he had better cooperation from the airlines serving the California, Texas, and Arizona markets than he did from carriers serving more distant locations where the passengers would have to change carriers. The difficulty of Bob being personally present to sell in the more distant markets also contributed to the higher cost of serving those markets. In addition, Bob quickly discovered that summer tourists wanted to engage in many diverse activities.

Based on an analysis of the disappointing results of this offering and the company's strengths, Bob decided to try to develop a package for the golf market. This market was appealing because golf is the fastest-growing sport in the United States, and golfers are noted for being less price-sensitive than skiers. In addition, Bob felt that a package covering several days with similar activities (e.g., golf, rafting, jeep trips) could be effectively marketed to these enthusiasts. The outcome of these developmental efforts was the "Golf the Rockies"™ package. He felt the $1,000 expended to trademark this name would provide a distinctive competitive advantage to the golf package offering.

TABLE 2
Durango Area Tourism-Related Activities

| | Two Years Ago | | | |
Month	Airport Passenger Activity	Train Ridership	Skier Days	Mesa Verde Visitors
January	16,153	0	39,572	3,926
February	17,609	0	51,566	4,232
March	17,283	0	56,435	12,856
April	9,502	0	657	25,531
May	12,297	15,045	0	56,647
June	16,063	37,093	0	111,215
July	20,867	52,840	0	142,952
August	22,504	47,676	0	136,687
September	18,651	30,074	0	69,788
October	14,754	15,263	0	33,157
November	12,117	0	300	9,583
December	15,921	0	47,539	4,801

| | Last Year | | | |
Month	Airport Passenger Activity	Train Ridership	Skier Days	Mesa Verde Visitors
January	17,024	0	60,561	3,885
February	17,154	0	62,818	6,001
March	16,468	0	69,439	13,186
April	9,705	0	3,715	24,388
May	12,829	14,288	0	56,647
June	16,873	37,195	0	111,215
July	20,469	58,560	0	172,774
August	20,721	50,068	0	158,191
September	16,426	32,198	0	105,016
October	14,830	18,095	0	45,855
November	11,053	0	10,720	11,434
December	17,140	0	61,761	5,227

In the "Golf the Rockies" package, the customer could fly into Durango on either America West or Continental Airlines and then be provided with a rental car, accommodations, and tee times at some of Colorado's finest golf courses. The package included such courses as Tamarron near Durango, two courses at Vail, the Snowmass Club & Golf Resort at Aspen, Skyland at Crested Butte, and The Broadmoor in Colorado Springs. Customers could play up to 6 days of golf with guaranteed tee times and never have to backtrack as they enjoyed the scenic Colorado Rockies. At the end of the tour, the rental car was dropped off at Denver and the client returned by air from that location. The package could also originate in Denver and terminate in Durango, so clients could take advantage of outdoor activities offered in the Durango area at the end of the tour such as horseback-riding and whitewater-rafting.

Although this package had a promising future, it met an untimely death with the change in advance purchase air fares and the elimination of small-group pricing discounts by the airline industry. When small-group pricing discounts were eliminated and individual advance purchase discounts became more liberal, the margin available to the tour operator evaporated. Without the discounts, Gateway Durango was not able to compete price-wise with the individuals who found that "self-constructed" tours were less expensive.

Key Marketing Decisions

One very simple service concept drove the company—take care of the client. Unlike many operators, who are located in large population centers that serve as focal points for packaging and offering the product, Gateway Durango was located at the point of consumption. Therefore, company representatives could be on hand to greet clients when they arrived. In fact, any time a group of 10 or more arrived at the airport, a company representative was on hand to greet them.

This commitment to service was not simply relegated to pulling together the pieces of a package at an attractive price. It also included such policies as returning all phone calls within 2 hours and meeting the customers' needs at the location by greeting them when they arrive and calling them at least two or three times during their stay to make sure things were going as planned and promised. In addition, company representatives actually met beginning skiers on their first day on the slopes and took them to the ski school to make sure they were matched up with their instructors.

As previously mentioned, the cornerstone of the company's marketing efforts was direct mail. In addition to lists of church groups, active mailing lists of travel agents, country clubs, and meeting planners were maintained. Brochures promoting the skiing packages were purchased in quantities of 50,000 each year at a cost of approximately $10,000. This cost was, for the most part, offset by the suppliers who were included in the packages and purchased advertising space. By generating these co-op advertising revenues, the firm was able to enlarge its marketing reach.

Ski packages were advertised through a broad range of select media. Magazine ads were concentrated in both *Ski* and *Powder*. Small ads measuring one inch by two inches were placed in the classified section under the heading "Ski Packages." The same style of classified advertisement measuring four inches by four inches was run for 14 weeks during the height of the ski season in the *Albuquerque Journal*.

In addition, during the previous ski season, a local (Albuquerque) rock radio deejay, T. J. Trout, did a special series of 16 spots over a 3-week period. This program was repeated again during the current ski season, resulting in two full busloads of skiers (the break-even point for running the promotion). However, the benefits of the promotion may come more from getting the company name out to the public than from generating direct package bookings.

The "Golf the Rockies" package was initially advertised in *Golf Digest* (reaching over 3 million golfers), using a one-inch advertisement with a reader card inquiry (bingo card), which cost only $1,200 per issue. Over 3000 reader inquiry cards were returned after the advertisement had run for three consecutive months. These returned reader inquiry cards formed the basis for an initial mailing list. Although the *Golf Digest* campaign was considered a success, a similar ad costing $1,000 in America West's in-flight magazine resulted in zero inquiries. In addition, a direct mail piece was sent to over 10,000 travel agents to "tee off the program." Judging from the response, Bob also considered this to be a failure. By measuring the responses to these and other programs, Bob was able to focus his advertising efforts better.

Both advertising and direct mail were supplemented with information booths at ski shows in May and June. It cost approximately $550 to attend and exhibit at these shows, so the break-even point for this marketing effort was fairly low. It should be noted that the expenses of attending these shows are minimal since travel-related services such as airfare and accommodations can be obtained at low or no cost by tour operators.

The key to making money appeared to be fairly simple on the surface—buy right and price appropriately. For example, by purchasing on a bulk basis, Gateway Durango obtained 1-day lift tickets at the Purgatory Ski Resort for $8 less than their retail value. The price to the package client was marked up between 20 and 25%, depending on market conditions. By following this markup procedure, the company was able to compensate travel agents and sales representatives on a 10% commission basis. In addition, high-volume travel agencies and sales representatives could earn up to an additional 2% in overrides.

Phoenix customers had the alternative of driving to the Durango area (about a 10-hour trip), and the intensity of competition in the Phoenix market was higher. Consequently, that market was much more price-sensitive than any of the other markets served; packages could be marked up by only 10% and two free packages had to be provided to group leaders. Therefore, a sales representative was not feasible in this market if the company were to maintain its low-cost strategy. Bob was reluctant to make the transfer himself because it would also have a major drawback for him—leaving the Durango lifestyle.

Operations

After the failure of his initial partnership venture, Bob began operating his new business from a bedroom in his house. The company was set up as a Subchapter S corporation with Bob as President and sole stockholder. The offices for Gateway Durango were subsequently moved to rented space on the second floor above a sporting goods store in Durango, Colorado. Since maintaining a low-cost strategy had always been important to Bob, he took every opportunity to practice what he preached. For example, he paid only $10 for his office desk. As he was quick to point out, his type of business did not attract any walk-in clients and he did not need a palatial office to soothe his ego. As he said, "I can write just as much business on a $10 desk as I can on a $500 desk."

The staff in the Durango office consisted of Bob and two full-time employees, Renee and Nancy. Sales representatives were hired on a straight 10% commission basis and worked in the Albuquerque and Dallas markets. During the busy winter months, the staff was supplemented with a part-time employee.

Bob prided himself on having an unstructured office with an informal environment that allowed his employees to function as a team. All members of the staff, including Bob, equally divided service responsibilities and handled reservations whenever they were not busy with other tasks. A visitor to the office might have found Bob cleaning the restroom or taking a reservation. In addition, part-time employees were hired during peak booking periods to perform customer service work with groups as they arrived and stayed in the area.

Finances

Conservatism and low costs also influenced company policies in the area of finances. For example, the company maintained no debt and there was always enough cash on hand to finance a minimum of 6 months of operations. Beginning with the start of the current fiscal year, the goal was raised to have enough money on hand to operate for a full year. Historically, Bob had only taken out $2,000 a month in salary and the only perks he en-

TABLE 3
Gateway Durango, Inc.,

	Balance Sheets Three Years Ago	Two Years Ago	Last Year
Assets			
Cash	$81,589	$43,227	$26,378
Accounts receivable	43,001	60,740	40,211
Advance reservations	53,080	35,453	84,348
Depreciable assets	19,040	17,688	13,896
Total	$196,710	$157,108	$164,833
Liabilities & stockholders' equity			
Accounts payable	$13,883	$13,478	$8,110
Advance deposits	136,924	101,225	91,659
Payroll taxes payable	1,572	1,629	2,800
Notes payable*	6,771	3,012	0
Capital stock	4,000	4,000	4,000
Retained earnings	33,560	33,764	58,264
Total	$196,710	$157,108	$164,883

*Current Portion of Notes Payable three years ago: $3,759

joyed were a company car and insurance on that car. However, beginning this year, the salary figure was increased to $3,000 a month.

Basically, the company operated without any significant inventory costs. The only things that would have been considered inventory were the brochures explaining the packages. However, these brochures were developed so that advertising from the resorts or transportation providers paid for the cost of production. The balance sheets and income statements for the three previous years are presented in Tables 3 and 4.

LOOKING TO THE FUTURE

Bob realizes that by creating Gateway Durango, he "bought a job that will allow him to live and work in Durango." Although one of the keys to success that he continually emphasizes is work, work, and more work, Bob is quick to note that he has the unique opportunity of living in paradise and enjoying the type of work he does. It should be noted

TABLE 4
Gateway Durango, Inc., Income Statements

	Three Years Ago	Two Years Ago	Last Year
Sales	$1,089,268	$872,480	$993,044
Cost of goods sold	943,266	736,028	818,500
Gross profit	$146,002	$136,452	$174,544
Expenses			
Salaries and wages	$61,882	$60,700	$61,755
Rent	4,020	4,020	4,020
Taxes	5,662	5,283	5,972
Interest	635	1,060	511
Depreciation	5,126	4,667	3,298
Advertising	11,137	14,075	26,582
Commissions	9,834	9,025	12,079
Travels means and entertainment	9,002	10,221	9,602
Insurance	851	851	851
Telephone and utilities	14,557	15,572	14,174
Postage and supplies	6,653	7,188	6,216
Miscellaneous	2,699	3,586	4,984
Total expenses	$132,058	$136,248	$150,044
Net income	$13,944	$204	$24,500

that business has grown to the point where Bob can no longer personally meet all of the groups. Part-time company employees now meet many of the groups. However, Bob still meets as many of the group leaders as his schedule will allow, no matter what time of day or night they arrive. Bob remains excited about the future, but like most entrepreneurs, he questions how he should position his business for future survival and success.

Source: This case was prepared as a basis for class discussion rather than to illustrate either effective or ineffective handling of an administrative situation. Copyright © 1998, Roy A. Cook and Jeremy J. Coleman, both of Fort Lewis College.

Integrated Cases

LE PETIT GOURMET CATERING

Jim O'Connor, President and Owner of Le Petit Gourmet, an upscale catering firm in Glendale, Colorado, faced a crisis in December. While on vacation in California, he received a telephone call and was notified that a food poisoning incident of potentially epidemic proportion (hepatitis A) had been traced to his organization. The health department was shutting his business down indefinitely. O'Connor's reactions progressed from shock to defensive retreat to acknowledgment and, ultimately, to managing the crisis.

CATERING COMPETITION

The food service industry in general and the catering industry in particular are keenly competitive. More and more catering businesses are entering the market, and hotels that already have the physical infrastructure and client base are beginning to position themselves in the catering market. Free-standing restaurants are also expanding their take-out and delivery capacities to compete better with independent caterers. Jim O'Connor recognized that as the Denver economy grew, so could his competitors and the potential of his own catering business.

LE PETIT GOURMET

Le Petit Gourmet was a family catering business that had been operating in the Denver metro area for more than 30 years. The business was located in a 15,000-square-foot facility in Glendale, Colorado. Le Petit employed between 150 and 200 people, 75 of whom were full time. O'Connor also operated the Sweet Soiree, a sweets and bakery shop, in the same facility. Le Petit Gourmet had handled a wide variety of catering jobs, ranging from cocktail parties to weddings, receptions, and dinners. Le Petit Gourmet had historically been known for serving the cream of society and was perceived as the most expensive and upscale caterer in Denver. O'Connor, however, wanted his business to be known for good food on all levels, from cookies to lobsters, and said that Le Petit had to learn how to hustle to attract a wider market. Le Petit Gourmet's business as well as the whole catering business in Denver had been on the upswing in recent years.

THE INCIDENT

Tri-County Health Department officials notified O'Connor that they had traced a hepatitis A outbreak to a Le Petit Gourmet kitchen manager who had apparently served at least two holiday parties on November 22. Representatives of the Tri-County Health Department, the public health agency for the Glendale suburb where Le Petit is headquartered, said a case was first reported on November 30 after a doctor, treating a Le Petit catering employee on November 22, had laboratory confirmation that the patient had hepatitis A.

At the time, Tri-County Health Department officials judged the risk of transmission of the disease to be very low. Health department officials investigated the incident, assessed public health risk and recommended that all of the Le Petit Gourmet employees be given a gamma-globulin shot as a preventive measure. O'Connor, eager to work with the Health Department, informed all employees of this recommendation and urged employees to comply immediately. However, by early December, only 50 employees had received their immunizations. On December 17, Health Department officials confirmed that hepatitis A had developed in four additional Le Petit Gourmet employees. It was not until December 30 that all Petit Gourmet employees had been inoculated.

Tri-County Health Department officials still had made no public announcement of an outbreak. O'Connor, who at this time believed the incident had been contained, left for vacation in California. He received a telephone call on December 30 informing him of a further outbreak of hepatitis A and that his business was being shut down by Tri-County Health Department officials.

On December 31, state and other health department agencies ordered food-service workers in approximately 7000 food-service establishments in metro Denver to use gloves or utensils when handling food. This order was to remain in effect until February 2, the estimated end of the incubation period of the disease.

By January 4, there were 24 reported cases of hepatitis A, and estimates for future cases by health officials ranged from 50 to 100. It was calculated that 15,000 area residents might have eaten food from Le Petit Gourmet and the Sweet Soiree between November 21 and Christmas. Thousands of guests who attended parties catered by Le Petit and patrons of the Sweet Soiree that were exposed to the disease lined up at area hospitals for gamma-globulin shots. Le Petit Gourmet employees were forbidden to work as food-handlers anywhere else until January 31.

Managing the Crisis

When he returned from San Francisco, Jim O'Connor found that his business and family were under siege. Media representatives had swarmed over his Glendale facility and actually cornered his 75-year-old father in the Le Petit Gourmet offices. "I remember being extremely angry and struggling with my feelings to strike back at those I saw striking at me," said O'Connor. The media, his insurance agents, lawyers, and health department inspectors as well as Le Petit employees and customers were demanding answers.

Initially, O'Connor hired a public relations firm to assist him, at a cost of approximately $15,000, but decided that he needed to take a more active role to save his business. He made the decision that he personally needed to be the public relations spokesperson for Le Petit Gourmet, knowing that he could not be afraid to speak up when discussing crisis issues with attorneys, insurance agents, and media representatives.

His first priority would be the victims of the outbreak and his employees. He personally called the victims of hepatitis (those diagnosed with the disease) and apologized for what had happened. Jim felt that much of the success of his business was based on his and his family's personal reputation and, therefore, personal contact with victims of the disease was necessary. He also met with his employees to calm their fears.

O'Connor then prioritized other issues he needed to face. The first issue was cash flow. He knew that there would be no income for an undetermined amount of time and that many of the clients might not pay their bills. He also realized that many of the vendors with whom he did business would also expect to be paid. He asked for, and in some cases was offered, a delayed payment schedule from his vendors. O'Connor who until now had run a close to debt-free business, negotiated a larger mortgage, made an assessment of the amount of cash on hand, and cut overhead by approximately $300,000 within the first few days of the crisis.

O'Connor realized that public perception was more important than reality: Therefore, on January 1, he and his staff dumped $45,000 of food products into the trash. Many of these items were unopened and frozen products, not part of the infected food, but he felt that as a good faith measure he needed to discard all products.

In addition, Jim made a decision concerning potential new business. He had received several inquiries from prospective business clients asking for significant discounts if they gave their business to Le Petit Gourmet. O'Connor decided not to become a discount caterer.

Employees

The key concern for Le Petit employees during the crisis was whether they would be paid. Jim realized that taking care of employee concerns needed to be a priority in all his efforts. He met with his staff and honestly told them that pay cuts were imminent in the immediate future and their long-term status at Le Petit Gourmet was cloudy. He realized, however, that he needed to stand by the staff. If he could make the commitment to help them, then maybe they would also stand by him. O'Connor did not terminate anyone's employment because of the outbreak. He was able to ease employees' fears by telling them that the individual to whom the initial outbreak had been traced (what is referred to as the "index case") had already left Le Petit Gourmet.

Some employees were very wary of the situation and questioned the handling of the incident. O'Connor presented all available information honestly and quickly, which helped to relieve any lingering fears. This openness proved to be very powerful, since several employees initially believed that details about the outbreak were being kept quiet. This suspicion was probably natural since the holidays are a busy season for catering and silence about the issue would prevent any loss of business.

Tri-County Health

When Tri-County health officials learned on November 30 that a Le Petit Gourmet worker had hepatitis A, they weighed the potential risks in the incident according to the Centers for Disease Control's standards and decided that chances of an outbreak were too minimal to warrant a public announcement. Since a public announcement would not be made Jim decided to notify individuals who might be at immediate risk.

Historically, Le Petit Gourmet had always passed its health inspections, being cited only for inaccessible hand-washing sinks. Over the past several years, Le Petit had averaged a score of 74 of 100 points on their health inspections. Health department officials indicated that Le Petit's relationship with the Health Department was considered very cooperative, and the scores achieved by Le Petit Gourmet were comparable with other catering businesses in the area. A Tri-County health official stated that Le Petit had maintained a good record with health officials and had "run a good operation."

Media

Although the media had initially been ignored, O'Connor knew he would have to face them eventually. When he collected the information he needed and collected himself personally, he held a news conference at the Le Petit Gourmet facility and explained what had happened and what he and Le Petit Gourmet as a company were prepared to do about the crisis.

O'Connor stated that he and his associates were working diligently with health officials to get through the crisis. Media coverage of the event had reached a national level in both print and broadcast media. O'Connor was quoted in a local newspaper as saying "I thought I was on trial for murder." Christine Mendosa, a reporter for KUSA, Channel 9 in Denver, indicated that the coverage of the Le Petit Gourmet story was tremendous because so many people were affected.

Lawsuits

Several lawsuits were filed against O'Connor and Le Petit Gourmet, claiming negligence by Le Petit employees and pointing to O'Connor for managerial responsibility. A class action suit was filed covering all people (perhaps 20,000) who may have attended parties catered by Le Petit, in addition to three individual lawsuits. Victims complained that they had heard about the outbreak through the newspapers and were outraged that they were not personally contacted. In the press, there was also debate among victims and experts in the field of possible claims against Tri-County Health officials for the way that they handled the incident.

Competitors

In conjunction with the crisis at Le Petit, business boomed for competing caterers. Catering companies such as Three Tomatoes, Panache, Epicurean, and others all geared up for additional business. Business was so good for New Year's parties that many prospective clients were turned away because they could not be serviced. Each competitor reacted somewhat differently to the crisis affecting Le Petit Gourmet.

One competitor wondered, "if a crisis like this could happen to Le Petit, the biggest and best caterer in Denver, how would a smaller operation survive in a similar situation?" Another competitor charged that there was no reason for this to have happened. The potential problems which could be created from hepatitis A outbreaks had been known in the industry for years, and responsible business managers had dealt with it appropriately. Some competitors grasped the opportunity to secure more business by mailing letters to their clients as well as those of Le Petit Gourmet explaining that this incident was about one company and alluded to the fact that it would not happen to them.

THE REOPENING

Jim O'Connor and his staff worked diligently to meet the Health Department criteria to reopen Le Petit Gourmet and the Sweet Soiree. Health Department criteria for reopening included: (1) obtaining health certification for all employees; (2) installing approved hand-washing sinks; (3) ensuring that all employees wore gloves; and (4) removing all contaminated food.

After meeting all these requirements and receiving approval from the health department Le Petit Gourmet reopened on January 11. Thirty-five employees were cleared by the Health Department to return to work, including the executive chef.

Reopening was accompanied by an invitation from O'Connor to the press to visit the facility. O'Connor and his sales staff contacted all clients, past and present, by mail and telephone to notify them of the reopening. The first catering job after the hepatitis A outbreak was January 14. The Sweet Soiree reopened the following day, January 15. Jim O'Connor finally felt that he could stop apologizing for what happened and put the incident behind him.

PONDERING THE FUTURE

Jim O'Connor wondered if he should close for good or try to make a go of it. He had received a lot of personal support from friends and some of his long-time clients. Based on this support he believed he could hold on to a core of customers. He reviewed his financial situation, compared his previous profit-and-loss statements with his current one, and asked himself if it was worth it.

In the midst of this questioning and self doubt, Jim tried to remain optimistic about the future of Le Petit Gourmet. The crisis had created an opportunity to rethink his life and the future of his business. He felt that his business and personal credibility were at stake. Would people ever trust him again? Even with this self-doubt, he accepted a number of speaking engagements and interviews to discuss the crisis. Yet, he still wondered if he had handled the crisis correctly.

Source: This case was developed and written by Robert M. O'Halloran, Ph.D., Associate Professor in the School of Hotel, Restaurant, & Tourism Management at the University of Denver, Denver, Colorado, as a basis for class discussion rather than to illustrate either effective or ineffective handling of an administrative situation. This case was edited for *Tourism: The Business of Travel* by Roy A. Cook and Laura J. Yale. Copyright © 1998.

Integrated Cases

Resistance to Change?

Forest Park Hotels had been started as an outgrowth of a strategic planning process initiated by the board of directors of Golden Horizons, Inc. A desire to diversify out of a singular focus on intermediate-care nursing home facilities resulted in an initial decision to explore the opportunities in hotel operations. Based on extensive research, the development of a small chain of high-quality hotels appeared to provide a natural strategy for continued growth through diversification.

In just 5 years from the purchase of the first hotel, the chain had grown to six and was meeting both sales and profitability goals. The initial strategic plan adopted by the board had targeted the acquisition or construction of one hotel every 12 to 18 months. According to Paul Halsey, CEO of Golden Horizons, "The growth of the Forest Park Hotel Division had happened at a faster rate than any of us had anticipated. Our positive cash flow allowed us to take advantage of some unique opportunities, both for construction and acquisition. If current operation continue at the present pace and attractive acquisitions become available, I would anticipate the continued rapid expansion of this division."

Centralization

Rapid growth of the hotel division with properties located in Atlanta, Dallas, Orlando, Minneapolis, New Orleans, and St. Louis brought with it the need for many changes. A corporate office was formed for the hotel division, and professionals were hired from outside the organization to fill several key positions, providing the experience necessary to continue with the present plans for expansion. As operating plans for the new division were established, the division vice-president, with the input and consensus of the hotel general managers, decided to centralize the accounting, marketing, and purchasing functions. These decisions were well received, and immediate cost savings and operational improvements were noted.

However, a later decision implementing a centralized human resources program to achieve equity in the hiring, training, development, and compensation of the managerial and professional (exempt) employees had been difficult. Although the general managers has enjoyed the autonomy of making their own human resources decisions, they grudgingly realized, for both legal reasons and for the planned growth of the division to be successful, change was necessary. The unanticipated rapid growth of the hotel division had created the need to prepare employees for promotions and transfers to meet future human resource needs.

Centralized Human Resource Program Implemented

Under the recently accepted human resource program, minimum qualification of each position classified as being exempt from wage and hour regulations (including overtime provisions) were established through standardized job specifications. Training and development programs had also been outlined to prepare employees for promotions and transfers. A list of promotable employees was developed at each hotel and then forwarded to the division office to be compiled and shared with all the general managers. In addition, minimum and maximum salary levels had been established for all exempt positions based on competitive salary and benefit surveys.

All these guidelines has been developed by Cara Reynolds, division vice-president of human resources, and then sent to all general managers for possible changes before being officially adopted. When the proposed guidelines were sent to the hotels, the general managers had been instructed to work with the local human resource directors and other key members of their management teams in identifying any potential problems the guidelines could pose. After both formal and informal discussions between the vice-president of human resources, general managers, and local personnel directors, several modifications were made to the guidelines, and the division vice-president endorsed the implementation of the following policy and procedures:

> To provide for the future human resource needs of the hotel division while ensuring equity in the hiring, transferring, promoting, and compensating of all exempt employees, the following procedures will be followed to maintain our status as an equal opportunity employer:

1. The corporate human resource office will assist the human resources manager and management staff in each hotel in maintaining the proper levels of staffing.

2. Initial exempt employee staffing requirements and subsequent changes can only be made with the prior approval of the division vice-president, the vice-president of human resources, and the general manager of the hotel making the request.

3. All job candidates must meet the minimum specifications set forth in the job description for each exempt position.

4. When qualified local candidates are not available, the costs of reasonable interviewing expenses, including transportation, will be reimbursed through the corporate human resource office.

5. Final approval must be obtained from the vice-president of human resources before any job offers are extended, and all personnel records, including payroll or exempt employees will be maintained in the corporate office.

Everyone appeared to understand and accept the new procedures as they were implemented. Some minor problems were encountered, but these had been quickly resolved to everyone's satisfaction. However, the first serious challenge to the new program came just 6 months after the program had been implemented.

Request for an Exception

The challenge came from the management team of the Atlanta hotel that had been acquired first and formed the foundation for the present chain. Not only was it the first hotel, but it was also managed by Jim Evans, the general manager with the longest tenure. Jim has earned an enviable record of success by managing the most profitable operation in the division. Jim knew he was facing a problem and had made several calls to Cara seeking an exception to the newly adopted guidelines.

The problem was in the culinary department, which was under the supervision of the hotel's food and beverage director, Joseph Langemier. Jim's personnel staff had been unable to fill a key position, evening sous chef, in the hotel's gourmet dining room.

As Cara read the following memo from Joseph, she sensed the frustration of the local hotel's management staff.

TO: Cara Reynolds
FROM: Joseph Langemier
RE: Human Resource Policies and Procedures

This is to follow up on our conversation in which it seems we have differences of understanding as to the needs in the culinary department. After the resignation of George Deal, evening sous chef, the executive chef (Aaron Murphy) and I agreed to readjust our organizational structure with regard to the outstanding requisition to fill the sous chef position. We agreed to have the evening sous chef position currently held by George to be filled with a sous chef of perhaps not the same caliber in terms of years of experience, but rather by an individual with an excellent culinary background.

Because of my association with very good professionals in the past, I am in the position of recommending candidates from time to time. This has been the case with Walter Steiner. He may not have the years of supervisory experience you seem to feel necessary, but he definitely has the culinary background to qualify for the position of sous chef. With this in mind, I have asked Executive Chef Murphy to talk to Walter and determine his interest in being considered for the sous chef position. It was only after the executive chef talked to Walter that we recommended that he be flown from Baltimore to Atlanta to see the hotel and dining room and interview for the position.

He has indicated that he will not take less than the maximum amount specified in the salary range for the position since he is currently making just four thousand dollars less that this amount between wages and overtime. In addition, he has chosen not to be promoted in the past because he wanted to gain the experience of working for a first-class operation similar to the one he has been working for during the last two years.

By adhering to your human resource policies, we are punishing Walter by insisting on hiring a person with supervisory experience. Would he have been considered to be qualified for the current position if he had been a supervisor in a steak and potatoes-type restaurant? That would qualify him to meet your supervisory qualifications but not our culinary requirements. Your refusal to consider Walter for the job indicates that you do not understand the differences between a culinarian and a supervisor.

Cara realized the anger coming through in the memo because Joseph was aware that Cara had been a hotel food and beverage manager before moving into the human resource function and, as such, was very knowledgeable of culinary duties. After reading the memo, Cara decided to review the job description and gather more information before making any decisions.

Job Title: Sous Chef

General Description:
Assume full responsibility for the preparation, production, and presentation of quality food products for the dining room.

Duties and Responsibilities:
Supervise and coordinate all personnel under direct supervision.
Observe and train all food preparation worker in the preparation, portion control, and presentation of food items based on prescribed standards.
Requisition and maintain necessary supplies.
Consult with executive chef on menu changes, work schedules, payroll, and personnel matters.

Ensure adequate sanitation standards.
Other duties as assigned by the executive chef or executive sous chef.

Job Relationships:
Work under the direction of the executive chef and the executive sous chef.
Supervise all preparation personnel in assigned location.

Job Specifications:
High school education: advanced training in food preparation, kitchen supervision, and sanitation preferred.
Minimum two years' supervisory experience of food preparation in a full-service restaurant.
Must be knowledgeable of all basic cooking techniques, meats, and sauces.
Must be able to maintain rapport with superiors and subordinates.

Cara realized that Atlanta was experiencing a boom in new hotel construction that was resulting in an abnormally high turnover of skilled employees and upward pressure on salaries. In addition, the individual who had previously held the now-vacant position had been "lured" away by a new hotel as the executive sous chef (both a promotion in responsibility and title with a significant increase in pay). However, surveys completed by the Atlanta human resource staff within the past 3 months indicated that the hotel had remained competitive in salaries and benefits. In fact, salaries and benefits paid for the sous chef position in question were slightly above average for comparable hotels.

A review of the personnel files showed that the three sous chefs currently on staff met all minimum criteria set forth in the new human resource guidelines, and the open personnel requisition was for a person who would be in a comparable position. The fact that the position in question had now been vacant for 1 month and the hotel was entering its busiest season was puzzling since discussions with the local personnel manager indicated that two individuals meeting the guidelines had been screened and referred for interviews, but no interview comment forms had been returned. The personnel manager had also mentioned that Joseph and Walter has previously worked together and, based on some of Joseph's comments, they may have been "drinking buddies."

Source: The names of the parties, as well as all place names, in the case have been disguised. This case was prepared by Roy A. Cook of Fort Lewis College and Jeryl L. Nelson of Wayne State College as a basis for class discussion rather than to illustrate either effective or ineffective handling of an administrative situation. All rights reserved to the authors. Copyright 1998, Roy A. Cook and Jeryl L. Nelson.

Index